# Social Media, Work and Organisations

Social media use is a confounding aspect of organisations, aiding interconnection, communication, and productivity. Its use has undoubtedly impacted on human resource management and the establishment of harmonious contemporary employment relationships. Its use challenges the traditional boundaries which existed between work and privacy and, in doing so, seemingly increases organisational power and management control. This book discusses the impact social media has on work; how it is used to stage the organisation, self-identity, power, and control using four conceptual themes: adoption, shaping, and staging of social media in organisations; digitised regimes of power, control, and surveillance; evolving identity, employee voice, and dramaturgical performance online; and employee forms of resistance, sousveillance, and social media misbehaviours. These themes are brought to life through the lived experiences and narratives of workers who hold roles in human resources, management, and frontline operations. This approach highlights a unique multi-perspective on social media use by giving voice to these workers. The book uses these individual narratives to reposition the ways employees utilise social media for sousveillance, dissent, and resistance purposes. In doing so, the book encourages wider debate, critical reflection, and self-reflexivity on rarely discussed management approaches or (mis)behaviours associated with social media use and their profound implications for power dynamics in organisations.

**Claire Taylor** is a principal lecturer in human resource management at Nottingham Trent University. Her research interests and recent publications have focused on employment relations, social media use, identity, emerging surveillance and sousveillance practices, organisational (mis)behaviour, and the impact these have on freedom of expression, employee voice, management approaches, and power dynamics at work.

# Routledge Studies in Management, Organizations and Society

This series presents innovative work grounded in new realities, addressing issues crucial to an understanding of the contemporary world. This is the world of organized societies, where boundaries between formal and informal, public and private, local and global organizations have been displaced or have vanished, along with other nineteenth century dichotomies and oppositions. Management, apart from becoming a specialized profession for a growing number of people, is an everyday activity for most members of modern societies.

Similarly, at the level of enquiry, culture and technology, and literature and economics, can no longer be conceived as isolated intellectual fields; conventional canons and established mainstreams are contested. *Management, Organizations and Society* addresses these contemporary dynamics of transformation in a manner that transcends disciplinary boundaries, with books that will appeal to researchers, students and practitioners alike.

**Recent titles in this series include:**

**Ending Slavery in the Corporate Supply Chain**
Storytelling, Leadership, and the Coalition of Immokalee Workers
*Richard Herder*

**Organisational Ambidexterity and Strategy**
Design, Structure and Implementation
*Imo Enang and John M. Rudd*

**Social Media, Work and Organisations**
Narratives of Identity, Power and Control
*Claire Taylor*

# Social Media, Work and Organisations

## Narratives of Identity, Power and Control

**Claire Taylor**

Routledge
Taylor & Francis Group
NEW YORK AND LONDON

First published 2025
by Routledge
605 Third Avenue, New York, NY 10158

and by Routledge
4 Park Square, Milton Park, Abingdon, Oxon, OX14 4RN

*Routledge is an imprint of the Taylor & Francis Group, an informa business*



*Library of Congress Cataloging-in-Publication Data*
Names: Taylor, Claire (Lecturer in human resources), author.
Title: Social media, work and organisations : narratives of identity, power and control / Claire Taylor.
Description: New York, NY : Routledge, 2025. |
Series: Routledge studies in management, organizations and society |
Includes bibliographical references and index.
Identifiers: LCCN 2024029338 | ISBN 9780367683764 (hardback) |
ISBN 9780367683818 (paperback) | ISBN 9781003137269 (ebook)
Subjects: LCSH: Organizational behavior. | Social media. | Public relations. |
Industrial relations. | Personal internet use in the workplace.
Classification: LCC HD58.7 .T39 2025 | DDC 302.5/5–dc23/eng/20240816
LC record available at https://lccn.loc.gov/2024029338

ISBN: 978-0-367-68376-4 (hbk)
ISBN: 978-0-367-68381-8 (pbk)
ISBN: 978-1-003-13726-9 (ebk)

DOI: 10.4324/9781003137269

Typeset in Times New Roman
by Newgen Publishing UK

**For Dad, the brightest star and our much missed cheer-leader**

# Contents

# Figures

# Tables

# Abbreviations

| *Term* | *Abbreviation* |
|---|---|
| Chartered Institute of Personnel and Development | CIPD |
| Employer branding | EB |
| Employee voice | EV |
| Human resource management | HRM |
| Information and communication technology | ICT |
| Interpretative phenomenological analysis | IPA |
| The Office of Communications | OFCOM |
| Reflective practice | RP |
| Social media | SM |
| Social networking sites | SNS |

# Acknowledgements

This book has been a labour of love. The passion behind it started when I first started work in both commercial entities and human resource management. I recognised how technology and social media were massively changing how we work and communicate in and beyond work. I also felt that these devices were very much misunderstood and the root cause of many workplace conflict. At this juncture, I should thank my former colleagues, Alan Dainty, Jo Daley, and Sarah Swales, for contributing to my knowledge and practical experience in employment relations and HR development and for forcing me to begin a programme of study which fundamentally changed me and set me on a path towards an academic career.

My curiosity about people and my experiences of investigating their issues, coordinating, and facilitating interventions to support them, and addressing workplace conflict and misbehaviours through training and mediation have shaped and furthered my interest. This informed my doctoral and ongoing research. I could not have developed the outcomes and this book without the consent of some amazing participants. Their accounts and experiences helped contribute to my wider knowledge and understanding of this phenomenon.

On my journey, I have had much support and encouragement to develop my work from a rough draft thesis to a final book from an inspiring community of academic colleagues, chief among these are Rory Ridley Duff, Suzanne Tietze, Peter Prowse, Tracey Coule, Tony Dobbins, and Tony Bennett. I thank you for your friendship, insightful comments, and worthwhile discussions. A special mention to Mel Bull, one of my closest friends and all-round inspiration We have come a long way! We keep each other going in and out of work! Thank you for being a kindred force of nature.

I have used my empiricism to inform, inspire, and engage students of business, management, and HR to reflect and think differently about workplace policy, HR and management practices, disciplinary processes, or interventions in this context which is more illusory, boundary spanning, and complex. The many discussions we have had have helped me reflect on why this book is much needed.

Special mention to my wonderful friends – I am not naming any of you for fear of forgetting someone. You know who you are. Thanks for keeping me going with your love, support, dog walks, gym and swimming trips, banter, much-needed kitchen discos, and general life chaos. We are all amazing working mums with worries and concerns about our kids, our jobs, and use of social media too. I have kept this in mind as I wrote.

Eternal thanks and gratitude to my chief flag-wavers, my wonderful family.

My mum, Anne, my sister Kate, my bro-in-law John, and niece Rosie. All of you have continually teased, pushed, and inspired me to keep going in quite tough circumstances. You are my rocks.

This book is also dedicated to my own wonderful family, Team perfectly imperfect Taylor. My husband Carl and kids, Laurie and Honor. You mean the world to me. Love you to the moon and back. Now cry! I can only apologise for being annoying, taking up space in every part of the house to write this book! Thank you for keeping everything afloat when I had crises of confidence. All of which was annoying. Sorry! Not sorry! Finally, special thanks to the teams at Taylor Francis and Newgen especially Jessica Rech and Anitha AL for all your help and support.

# Introduction

## About this book

**Learning outcome**

- By the end of this section, you will understand the unique premise and breadth of this book.

*Social Media, Work and Organisations: Narratives of Identity, Power and Control* is intended to provide a unique exploration of our increasing use and reliance on social media, a phenomenon which has grown and morphed exponentially. From a business perspective, these devices are used to promote corporations, brands, goods, services, and experts. Significantly, from a sociological perspective these are not simply benign business tools. We use them to stage ourselves and our innermost thoughts to vast audiences. We are witnessing a major change in how we behave online. Whilst we interconnect and network in a business setting, we show every detail of our lives, speak more openly, and impact freedom of expression and privacy. These differing uses have, therefore, blurred traditional boundaries previously existed between our work and social lives. This has collided causing a spike in differing forms of organisational (mis)behaviour, which is rarely discussed and often not fully understood. These devices, therefore, are hugely fascinating from an employment relations perspective, where their use has led to a greater corporate need to control their use more.

Contextually, a raft of legislature is additionally being introduced in the UK and across the globe to develop measures which seek to more closely control forms of misbehaviour on social media to protect the most vulnerable in society. We have seen a rise in online hate crimes and speech. This paradigm shift creates a sense of intrigue, requiring greater understanding and exploration. For those studying people management, there is a greater need to understand the implications of the social media phenomenon more deeply and how human resource management (HRM) approaches are established in corporations. This text allows a deeper critical reflection on how we observe and control workforces

DOI: 10.4324/9781003137269-1

in this domain. The aim is to provide a wider discussion and debate on range of themes, including how we use social media and emerging veillance practices, shaping online identity, expression, employment, and online (mis)behaviours, which are rarely discussed.

## Characteristics of the book

Throughout this text I have used the metaphor of theatre, acting, and drama which is used purposefully. The term *staging* used in the title highlights the resonance social media has with more theatrical endeavours. This premise draws attention to how we use these devices to portray differing characterisations to stage the self online. This includes how we develop multiple self-identities across a variety of diverse social media platforms. These may jar with corporate expectations of the archetypal professional worker and create a Petri dish for different forms of (mis)behaviour to appear in both workers and management alike.

It is my view that social media are theatre-like, sharing many similarities. They operate using unique stage-like auditoriums where we engage in developing scripts with other social actors as users. This allows us to use thespianism as a way to act. We play out everyday dramas of the self or of corporate affairs. We create theatrical scenes for different audiences. We co-direct, co-design, and co-choreograph content on a variety of plots, performances, and subplots, like plays within plays, each of which serves our self-interest in viewing and observing each other.

Like theatrical productions, social networking technologies incorporate properties that allow us to alter how we look and perceive ourselves. We can make ourselves over as an avatar or emoji. We can airbrush out any perceived personal imperfections or create other-worldly or anti- and ulterior identities. Thus, our identity is less fixed and is not always as it may seem. Yet being online is less contained. This creates tension where our different *performances* and identity fluidity may bleed into one another. Our digital activity, therefore, begins to seep from within our cloaked social worlds in and into work. Here, our biographic, creatively imagined content, creates interesting subplots.

In terms of labour effort, we invest more time portraying our professional self online. We aesthetically arrange *sets*, *costumes, and properties* to promote both corporations, our self, and our personal achievements in an endeavour to showcase our talent and skills. This allows us to be more greatly commodified as workers. We manipulate our digital content and the historicity of our lives to great effect and to depict codes of meaning, glossy images which we use to ensnare or captivate future employers, friends, or followers. These activities influence HRM approaches for the attraction, recruitment, and selection of talent, performance management techniques, and the disciplinary nature of work.

We appear to be much braver online, expressing our thoughts and concerns more viscerally. This has led to a rise in abhorrent and harmful content such as misogyny, racism, and far-right politicking. A prominent feature is how social media is mobilised for differing forms of ideological expression which may collide with our work roles. These have ethical consequences and ramifications for corporations and society alike. To address the impact of such issues, in 2024, the major corporate social media organisations were called to face a USA senate judiciary committee which sought to review how major platforms address and control the publication of exploitative and offensive content reaching the eyes of children, which requires greater censorship.

Significantly, because of how we share content, we are more acutely aware of greater workplace conflicts and have greater visibility of the contested terrains of work. From a corporate perspective, this has led to greater forms of regulation, control measures, investigations, disciplinary action, and litigation. The text therefore explores and reflects on these themes to focus on workplace practices, policy, and procedures which challenge the assumption that we can say whatever we like online, particularly when employed.

The social media paradox therefore has changed the concept of *audience*. Users do not mutely, passively, or politely communicate with each other. Therefore, we need understand the terrain, the unpredictability, and murkiness of social media use.

There is a dearth of discussion in HR and management literature around forms of (mis)behaviour in general, with the exception of a few key writers who were an inspiration when writing this text, such as Ackroyd, McDonald, and Thompson, to name a few. The book therefore seeks to build on their work.

The key aim was to move away from oversimplifying social media use, a thesis which fails to fully connect with full range of agency and power in this context. Moreover, to challenge the myth that social media are thing-like objects which are easily controlled. I have sought to develop holistic review of how these devices are used by corporations, key workers, and the issues associated with methods of controls, power dynamics, emerging *veillance* practices, expression, identity, and a range of emerging (mis)behaviours, so that future leaders, managers, and HR practitioners may more deeply understand the impact these devices have had on workplace communications.

The book therefore focuses on integrating differing perspectives from HR, management, and workers to encourage readers to reflect more radically about how these devices are equally used by employees to resist and challenge management power in this domain. This type of social media use has significantly impacted employee voice and emancipatory workplace practices, drawing attention to how workers use social media to film, voice, or air work concerns, capturing real-time evidence of corporate leadership or societal wrongdoings.

## Dramaturgical approaches

The text is brought to life in a novel way to help readers connect more deeply with the issues presented in the book. William Shakespeare, an historic English playwright, wrote plays and poetry about love, angst, power, human existence, and the stages of life. His plays have longevity and capture the fragility of human-ness. Shakespeare is linked to the concept of dramaturgy which focuses on how social actors, individually or collectively, often play differing roles both transparently or covertly.

Shakespeare understood how we compete and vie with each other for power and control. He expertly captured character manipulation, politicking, and the effects this has on society and delicate interrelationships, which are intertwined throughout his plays. He understood our existential crises and depicted characters such as the fool, hero, leader, villain, underachiever, jester, and lover to make sense of human infidelities, unfairness, viciousness, and madness. These themes are prevalent on social media and span societal, political, and regal power structures.

Furthermore, Shakespeare captured the fluidity of self-identity where people are not as they seem in gender, personality trait, or role. Using an array of theatrical tricks he cloaked, masked, or disguised his central characters, techniques which have many parallels with both social media and the workplace. Therefore, dramaturgy is used throughout the book to explore how we stage ourselves on social media. To do so, I have developed case studies and characterisations to provide insights into this phenomenon more easily.

## Empiricism in the text

The text is developed from a programme of empirical research and powered by several research questions:

> How are social media used in work? How do social media change corporate power? How are social media used to exert control over workforces in much deeper ways? How are the rules for social media use developed? Do workforces understand these rules? What are the punitive actions for breaking social media rules? Is discipline and punishment applied fairly to workers across every level of the organisation? How do management use social media to observe and surveil workers? How do managers make sense of and judge differing fluid identities online? How do employees use social media to observe management? How do employees use social media to gain justice and voice workplace concerns? What types of social media

(mis)behaviours exist online? Do managers and HR practitioners misbehave online too? What happens in this instance?

These questions speak to how we use social media and the empirical findings are used to emphasise issues at work, a need for greater critical reflection and adaptation to how we stage and use social media.

## Setting the scene: Central themes and structure of the book

The text is set out in four *acts*. Each act uses two *scenes* and a cast of *dramatis personae* or social actors to bring several case studies to life. This purposefully enables the reader to connect with real human protagonists, their role perspectives, and ongoing challenges and issues in these contexts.

The book uses six sections creating a scaffold to contextualise and develop greater understanding. Combined these sections provide insights into *how we act* on and use social media in key work roles and in different corporate contexts. Each section is supported with wider literature and empiricism to develop applied learning, allowing readers the opportunity to reflect and think about approaches to integrate social media use in and beyond work more comprehensively.

## Act summaries

### *Section 1: The opening: Concepts, corporate environments, and central characters*

This section presents the main conceptual and theoretical perspectives used to underpin the text. These are a central frame of reference and referred to throughout the text:

1. Power, control, and the employment relationship.
2. Employee voice and (mis)behaviour.
3. Social media use.
4. Surveillance of social networking sites.
5. Resistance and the emergence of sousveillance.
6. Sense-Making, social media, and identity exploration
7. Dramaturgy and the digital self.
8. Critical reflection.

Additionally, this section presents the methodology, corporate environments, and social actors who participated in the empirical study, setting the stage for wider exploration, ethical discussions, and critical reflection to emerge.

## Section 2

***Act 1: Adopting, shaping, and staging social media use in organisations***

This section uses two scenes focusing on how corporations initialise social media use at work.

***Scene 1: Hegemonic forces: How organisations adopt, stage, and use social media in work***

This scene examines how differing organisations adopt and use social media. Discussion centres on the corporate strategies and expectations for social media use in the workplace.

***Scene 2: Players and voices: How differing organisational actors adopt, stage, and use a variety of social media in work***

This scene compares how individual workers use social media. Each social actor holds a unique organisational role located in human resources, operational management, or frontline work. These form the basis of contemporary employment relationships and how these are played out in organisational life. The scene explores how these workers use social media differently to the corporation, highlighting how antagonisms begin to surface.

## Section 3

***Act 2: Digitised regimes of power: How control and surveillance are established at work***

This section focuses on the act of controlling worker use of social media, highlighting the regulatory nature and performance management of this phenomenon. How management act illustrates how these approaches are often unclear, causing workplace conflict and forms of (mis)behaviour to manifest.

***Scene 1: Discipling discourses: Social media rules and regulation***

This section examines corporate rules, policy, and practices, exploring management approaches, mechanisms, and techniques used by HR and managers to control social media use in work. The scene provides ethical debate regarding corporate use of Firewalls, GPS tracking, analytics, and phone amnesties, allowing readers to critically reflect on the ethical repercussions of power and discipline in this terrain.

***Scene 2: Digital panopticons: Towers of surveillance in social media use***

This scene examines how key players incorporate social media as a form of surveillance to observe workers. The scene illuminates on how management extend the boundaries of work and highlights the invasive managerial regimes being used in this domain. The scene provides discussion on corporate failure to train and develop management in responsible methods of social media monitoring and the impact this has on employees.

## Section 4

***Act 3: Evolving identities and dramaturgical performance online***

This act focuses on how being on social media has morphed to highlight how individual identities are much more liminal and fluid.

***Scene 1: The multidimensional self: Identity and new ways of being online***

Social media allow us to shape multiples self-identities and unique behavioural performances. This scene focuses on the contradictory and unexpected nature of online identity work. The scene further examines how this deepens antagonisms and workplace conflict.

***Scene 2: Keeping up appearances: Aesthetic labour in digitised working contexts***

This scene examines the concept of aesthetic labour, the increasing use of how corporations use social media to observe and judge how we look, sound, and appear online. The scene discusses the rise of pre-profiling employees, an activity which moves beyond the curriculum vitae, which may flaunt labour law. The discussion calls for greater ethical HR management interventions and critically reflects the serious impact this has on self-identity, behaviour, and mental health at work.

## Section 5

***Act 4: Conflict, resistance, and social media (mis)behaviours***

This section focuses on the thornier issues of workplace conflict, employee resistance, and emerging online (mis)behaviours which future leaders in HR and management must be more aware of.

### *Scene 1: Can you hear me? Stories of resistance, employee voice, and sousveillance in online contexts*

This scene focuses on how employees use social media to observe, challenge, and resist the management and hegemonic power in organisations, which is rarely discussed in extant literature. The scene explores how social media allows workers capacity to voice concerns regarding workplace inequalities, precarious work, low pay, or poor conditions of work. The scene critically reflects on how social media enables new dimensions for worker freedom of expression and widens capacity for worker democratisation, particularly for those from diverse communities. The scene focuses on how *sousveillance* is used as a counter-approach by workers to redress the power imbalance, expanding conceptions of the panoptic device and challenging notions of surveillance in this context.

### *Scene 2: People do dumb stuff on social media: Novel crimes and contradictory social media (mis)behaviours*

This scene focuses on emerging forms of digital (mis)behaviour by both workers and management; the latter is rarely discussed. The scene examines how social media are used by leaders for increasingly ulterior portrayals of self-identity and a raft of corporate misbehaviour, such as profiteering, theft, absenteeism, online harassment, predatory behaviours, duplicity, countercultures, and radicalism. This provides readers the capacity to reflect more deeply on challenging behaviours of the elite and powerful. Future HR practitioners and managers need to be more aware and vigilant about online behaviours across all stratifications of the organisations.

## Finale: Illusory social butterflies: Conclusions, future reading, and research

The final act summarises the main points of discussion and learning from the text and concludes on the complex nature of social media and recommends future research and direction for further reading.

## Summary

In sum, the book offers readers:

- A uniquely personal, in-depth, multi-perspective on managing and using social media.
- Insights into the lived experiences of employees and management working within technologically mediated employment relationships.

- A broadened understanding of the complexity of metaphysical and fictional dimensions of digital work.
- Wider discussion on management (mis)behaviour, emerging veillance practices and employee resistance online.
- A self-reflexive space to explore our individual relationships with social media.

The book offers a broader discussion on the ethical debates these themes present.

Act 1 will present the core conceptual and theoretical framework used to develop this text.

# Section 1

# The opening

## Concepts, corporate environments, and central characters

**Learning outcomes**

- To provides an overview of the conceptual framework and develops greater awareness of the main bodies of theorisation used to underpin the text.
- To be cognizant of the empiricism used in the development of the text.
- To identify issues with human resources and people management which seek to control and performance manage aspects of social media use in and beyond work.
- To evaluate the links between dramaturgy, identity, misbehaviour, power, and employment relations practices in this domain.

This section introduces the reader to the key areas of theorisation which are used to underpin the main line of enquiry in this book. A conceptual framework is provided to visually illustrate the interlinking bodies of conceptualisation and a brief explanation of how these fit with managing social media in and beyond work.

This text relies on an empirical study which was used to develop greater understanding of social media use in different corporate environments by social actors who hold interlinking professional roles at work. The empiricism creates a multi-perspectival lens from which to explore social media use and the impact this has on employment relationships at work.

The social actor narratives and characterisations used in the text provide a range of case studies and vignettes which offer a sense-making of personal life-worlds, differing multiple identities and professional experiences of using or management of social media at work. The aim is to enable students of management and HR to critically reflect on the regulatory methods and practices observed in these major corporations. Using these, readers may critically reflect on approaches and use these to encourage adaptations and responsible human resource management (HRM) approaches in the future.

DOI: 10.4324/9781003137269-2

## The conceptual framework

The conceptual framework consists of six key theoretical bodies of literature (see Figure 1.1). The framework can be used as a central map for readers and moves beyond oversimplifying and describing social media as a thing-like, commodified device (Bell, 2005).

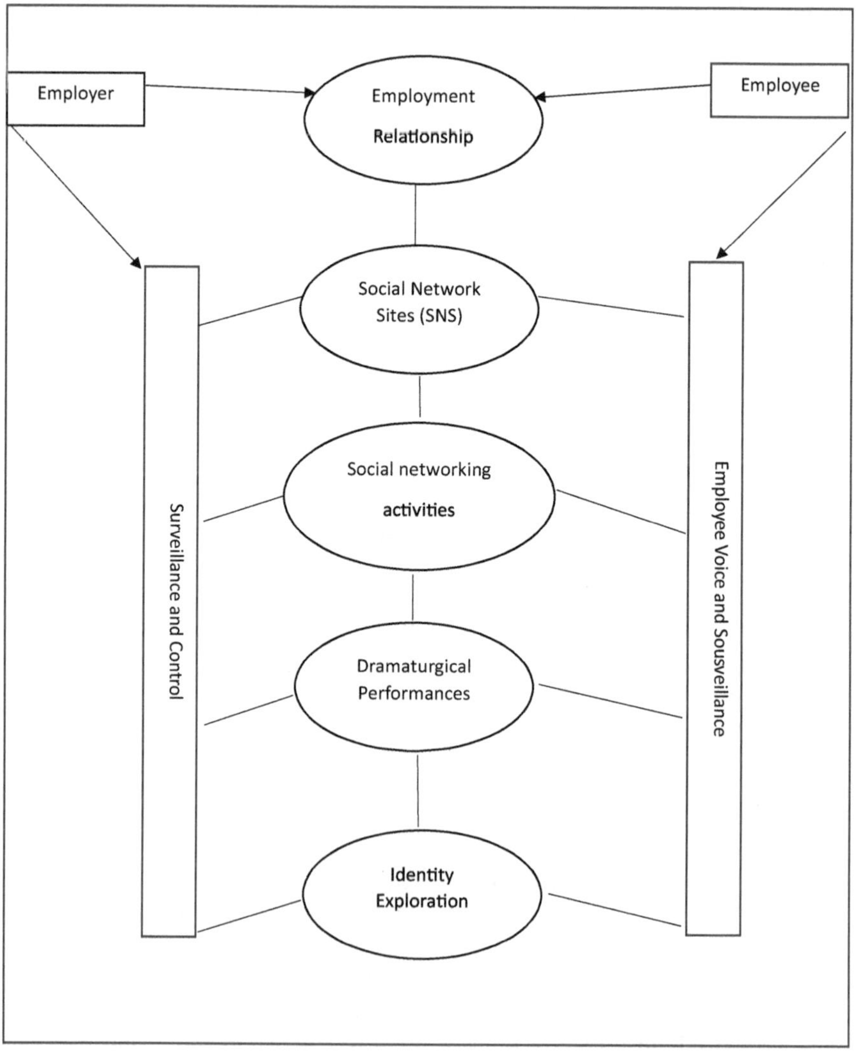


*Figure 1.1* The conceptual framework.

The interlinking areas of literature are:

1 The employment relationship.
2 Social networking platforms and activities.
3 Surveillance and control.
4 Employee voice (EV), resistance, and sousveillance.
5 Dramaturgical performances.
6 Identity exploration.

Each theoretical area is now briefly outlined.

The *employment relationship* is fundamental in anchoring the main debate on how social media impacts on workplace interrelationships. The discussion centres on corporate power dynamics and regulatory approaches used to govern and control social media use at work. This highlights emerging trends in observation, monitoring, and *surveillance* of employees using social media. This premise is used to reflect on the ethicality of these practices. This debate is vital in moving discussion beyond an oversimplification of social media which are all too often portrayed as benign business tools, enabling workers to network, market corporate brands, and sell goods or services.

This conceptualisation draws attention to emerging veillance practices where social media devices are used by workers to observe management using *sousveillance*. This element conceptually demonstrates a growing reality where workers use social media to observe corporate leaders to capture management (mis)behaviours or misdemeanours, which is rarely debated in management literature. The discussion provides readers with greater insight into the complexity, competing interests, struggles, ambiguities, and dilemmas associated with social media use in work and the impact this has on our self-identity. Each theoretical area is now discussed.

## The central importance of the employment relationship

Employment relationships are an enduring concept of employment relations study, which is a theoretical derivative of HRM. HRM is a collection of practices associated with people management approaches in work. Employment relations are principally designed to direct corporate labour processes and are strongly associated with controlling employees in work (Cappelli and Neumark, 2001; Dessler, 2015; Dundon and Rollinson, 2011; Guest et al, 2003; Martin et al, 2009; Milkman, 1997; Townley, 1994). Yet social media now goes beyond work. So we are witnessing management techniques, policies, and practices which control us beyond the working day.

Employment relations practices, therefore, inform and drive the employment relationships we have with our employers. These aim to leverage productivity and high performance, a perspective which infers workers need tight management control in order to achieve strategic corporate goals successfully. This suggests controlling workers requires the ongoing development of corporate rules and regulations to drive worker performance.

Work rules and regulations are said to be "formal and informal, structured or unstructured" (Bain and Clegg, 1974: 95). These are achieved through the development of professional behaviours, skills, and competency characteristics (Boxall et al, 2014; Boxall, 2013). Employment relationships are, therefore, an economic exchange which aims to secure the basis of agreement between employees in their capacity for work with the corporation (Blyton and Turnbull, 2004). Employment relationships are not cosily social or psychological; they are fiscal and political (Lewis et al, 2003: 6).

Extant management and HR literature reemphasises a need for corporate practices which create a stable, ordered workforce (Godard, 2014). Employment relationships, therefore, merge conflicting principles where employers seek to direct and control work, and where workers simply adhere, comply, and submit to management control. The employment relationship therefore infers there is a "...power to command and a duty to obey" (Kahn-Freund, 1972: 9). Yet, these common interests or "agreements" between employers and their workforces cannot naively be assumed or easily coordinated into existence (Blyton and Turnbull, 2004). This conception has its roots in the Master and Servant Act 1823, where the employer had (hegemonic) power to control workers and still does to this day.

Employment relations practices are considered a neoliberal ideology which encompasses three identifiable agendas: the individual, organisation, and society (Boxall, 2013). Social media and their use are located at this intersection and uniquely straddle all three agendas using them personally and in work contexts. Yet these conceptions underestimate the impact of social media which have created a fragility and extra layer of complexity due to their boundary spanning use which segues between both the public and private domains of life (Moussa, 2015).

This creates space to more deeply explore and understand management actions which seek to control and monitor the use of social media and the impacts this has on HR, management, and workforces (Biro, 2011; CIPD, 2013b; McDonald et al, 2016; Thompson et al, 2020; Taylor and Dobbins, 2021). This text aims to do just that.

A growing body of literature has focused on HRM and employment relations strategies in this context. Particular emphasis is placed on how organisations seek to legally protect their assets online. Much of this work is around quantitative studies which seek to understand social media policy development and practices. A growing body of work centres on forms of surveillance and observation of workers. This text builds on these developments.

A further area of discussion in this text will be to focus on the disciplinary and punitive nature of social media use in work. Predominantly, how organisations disseminate policies which aim to ensure greater employee awareness of information and communication technology (ICT) regulations and legislation. Essentially, how employees require training and development to be more knowledgeable and competent in their online and social media activities (Ulrich, 2010).

Yet, this area of work is increasingly murkier and more nebulous. There are many ethical challenges for HRM and management practices, including the growing use of observation and surveillance of employees through their digital activity which is more invasive (Edwards and Wright, 2001; Huselid, 1995; Kalleburg and Moody, 1994; McDonald et al, 2016; Taylor and Dobbins, 2021). An exploration of such practices are provided further in this text.

**Discussion box 1**

1. What do you think are the major implications for the employment relationship when we use social media in general?
2. Why do you think employers need to be clearer about performance management approaches for social media use?

**Social media rules, policy, and guidance**

Factually, employers have a right to direct and control employees and their social media activity in work. This is supported by a range of corporate regulations and practices, often captured in formal employment contracts. These legally binding documents provide employers with the power to strategically place a value on employees as a resource (Townley, 1994). Employment contracts outline how employees are expected to perform and behave and may include how we are to be controlled or managed by corporations (Spooner and Haidar, 2006).

Social media policy and regulatory protocols are uniquely developed and differ in each corporate environment. The approach of embedding policy with practice is often cascaded via induction processes and reinforced through employee handbooks or intranet sites which articulate or provide additional guidance on appropriate online behaviours and practices. These approaches set the parameters of social media use such as which SNS are accessible and wider protocols for internet, email, and other wider technology use.

In this text, I suggest these regulatory frameworks are often obscured and unclear for workers. Further, the success of appropriate professional behaviour is dependent on the robustness of management, HR development, and mandatory training, which is often overlooked in this area. Extant literature has enlivened the debate on social media policy and guidance (Broughton et al, 2010; CIPD, 2013b, 2013c). Quantitative studies have long sought to understand whether corporations have adequate policies in place or whether employees are aware of ICT or specific social media policies (Broughton et al, 2010; CIPD, 2013b; Deloitte, 2009). Common findings suggest employees are often unacquainted with such regulations. Moreover, few organisations can distinguish or articulate what a reasonable employee or management effort on social media looks like (Emmott, 2015). This suggests following regulations require employees to be highly self-disciplined. The discussion throughout this text calls for employers to provide clearer, coherent regulations and practices in this area of work. Particularly, as we are increasingly working in evermore hybrid contexts. How corporations regulate or provide development for skills in this unique area of work is therefore critical.

Empiricism has focused on developing greater understanding of how corporations use social media to extend the boundaries of control. Indeed, there are increasing concerns regarding the depth of power organisations have to direct, coordinate, organise, and control digitised work (Briken et al, 2017; Jacobson and Howle-Tufts, 2012; McDonald et al, 2016).

Yet social media use appears to have blindsided traditional management and HR practices, which are mostly based on calculability, rationality, hierarchy, and employee adherence or compliance of formal rules. A fundamental flaw with such notions of control is how corporate management perceive social media use can be easily contained (Taylor, 2018). A rising plethora of case law and social media misuse illustrates this growing conundrum and begs the question how do organisations and management seek to *fairly* control this rapidly developing technology?

Growing digitalisation and use of social media, therefore, must be counterbalanced with a corporate duty to protect individual human rights. The right to privacy and the right to freedom of expression are increasingly problematical. Growing management surveillance and societal and worker discontent illustrate how we symbiotically exploit social media to draw attention to workplace issues and contestations.

Further tensions illustrate how corporations and political and societal elite invasively access and harvest online personal data to manipulate opinion and silence workers. This includes censoring collective and individual online material and manipulating algorithms to court or change societal beliefs. These complexities have led to wider debate about the duty for social media corporations to address inappropriate online behaviours, particularly those which may incite hate, vitriol, or cause harm to individuals.

We need to be more informed as citizens and workers about how corporations gain greater access to our digital footprints. In the current context, it is relatively easy for organisations and powerful elite to interrogate our online activity. They use our profiles and online commentary to make value judgements about personal appearance, identity, and personas (Taylor, 2018). Thus, our privacy in digital environs is diminished, and these "decisions" may impact our career progression and longevity.

Of course, one can argue online digital activity is in the public domain. Therefore, it is in the corporation's interest to mitigate and address any damage caused to members of society, the workforce, or the corporation, particularly where any such activity brings an employer brand into disrepute. Moreover, these competing views highlight how the once boundaried nature of work is further eroded and challenged. Simply put, we cannot easily segregate work and our private lives. Moreover, these contexts are vastly visible to huge audiences. This contributes to the widening struggles which exist between management and workers (Keenoy and Kelly, 1998; Taylor and Dobbins, 2021).

This is not all bad news. Such contestations raise societal awareness of workplace inequalities and allow greater understanding of issues such as sexual harassment, abuse, coercive or predatory behaviours, racism, misogyny, EV, precarity, and low wages, which may be individual or collective in nature (McDonald et al, 2016). In some cases, these views have drawn greater attention to management (mis)behaviours which were previously easy to cover up and hide. Therefore, social media allow for greater worker democracy, transparency, and equity to a degree. This context, therefore, illustrates how social media use impacts on power dynamics, employee resistance, and forms of conflict to manifest in work.

**Discussion box 2**

- Do a quick search and list any legislative or regulatory areas which relate to controlling social media use in the UK.
- Individually or in groups reflect on how aware you were of such legislation.
- Individually or in groups discuss what associated policy, rules, and regulations you are aware of which seek to control social media use in your place of work or study?
- Does your workplace have a policy on monitoring social media use? If so, is it clear this may span into your private use of social media?

## Power, conflict, and resistance in work

Emerging digital technology and online contexts demonstrate how device such as social media contribute to the hidden vestiges of power in organisations (Foucault, 1980; Lukes, 2005; Thompson, 2011; Townley, 1994). Foucault prophetically suggested power is ever-present apparent everywhere and used to control, observe, and discipline workers (Foucault, 1991: 10 as cited in Rasmussen and Bernauer, 1988). None more so than the use of social media contributes to this argument.

Corporations and societal elite use these devices to increase their range to monitor, observe, and widen power to control workers. As employees, we are now more easily and deeply surveilled. Sadly, forms of surveillance are not always observable to employees (Lukes, 2005; Taylor, 2018).

Conceptions of power, conflict, and resistance are linked to three dominant employment relations frames of reference: unitary, pluralist, and radical HRM. These conceptualisations are explained to aid reader understanding of how power is filtrated in organisations and how differing corporate beliefs shape approaches which seek to harmonise and control workers through their employment relationships (Cradden, 2011; Fox, 1966; Lukes, 2005). The different empirical case studies presented in this text use these typologies.

### *Unitary*

A unitary perspective portrays corporations as a singular, harmonious entity. This view unifies the interests between the employer and their employees (Fox, 1966). The unitary perspective emphasises a shared corporate common purpose which is reliant on the mutual cooperation and loyalty of employees (Bingham, 2016; Cradden, 2011). Management have the legitimate power and authority to lead decision-making in this perspective (Edwards, 2003). A clear distinction with a unitary frame of reference is the perception that workplace conflict is irrational, pathological, or mischievous (Dundon and Rollinson, 2011). A clear criticism of unitary perspectives is the presumption that employee interests coincide with those of management. A unitary style organisation develops corporate mechanisms, therefore, to address any manifestations of employee conflict or resistance which may be punitively dealt with. This may engender worker discontent and mistrust of corporate leaders (Bingham, 2016).

### *Pluralism*

A pluralist perspective focuses on the collective nature of corporations. This view recognises workforces are made up of divergent subgroups and stakeholders who equally have legitimate aims and leaders (Dundon and Rollinson, 2011; Edwards, 2003). The regulation of workplace concerns, conflict, or resistance in this typology is both expected and inevitable and is contained in wider organisational discourse (Cradden, 2011). Management approaches in pluralist perspectives, therefore, accommodate and may seek to resolve the differing viewpoints of key stakeholders such as trade unions.

Trade unions are legitimately included in labour processes to support with the effective management of employee workplace concerns or issues. Collective bargaining is often the main method used for reducing tensions in the employment relationship. These processes are often orchestrated by corporate management through practices such as negotiation, consultation, and shared decision-making to resolve workplace tensions (Cradden, 2011; Bingham, 2016).

A common criticism of the pluralist approach is that management may not relinquish their authority on every aspect governing the employment relationship, particularly on issues such as key strategic financial decisions (Bingham, 2016; Edwards, 2003). Similarly, employees legitimately use their association with key trade unions in their respective role of sector to rail against their employers. Forms of activism undertaken by trade unions may protract workplace issues if common ground cannot be reached or agreed upon with management. At the time of writing, we are witnessing an upsurge in worker activism. Social media are widely incorporated to garner support for the differing sides in these arrangements. Thus, workplace malcontent is more visible to us all and is something which management and unions alike need to navigate, so any online commentary does not go incendiary.

### *Radical HRM*

A radical HRM perspective is a derivative of Marxian philosophy (1894/1974). This perspective focuses more closely on the corporate need to control means of production (Dundon and Rollinson, 2011). Radical HRM perspectives illustrate the discord which exists and occurs between the divergent worker subgroups and hierarchical stratifications in work and society. Forms of resistance are used creatively to reconfigure approaches or resolve workplace issues (Cradden, 2011; Edwards, 2003). These are expressed in workplace conflicts which affect the status quo of employment relationships (Bingham, 2016). Ongoing workplace inequalities highlight the uneven distribution of power which exists between the buyers and sellers of labour. In this perspective, employers use discretion to harness the talents of employees whilst simultaneously controlling workers to maximise outputs, which is considered a structural antagonism (Edwards, 2003), which highlights how conflict in work is both inescapable and contradictory.

These key perspectives illustrate how differing frames of reference are adopted in organisations to maintain control of workforces and ensure that corporate power and authority are maintained. The differing approaches are perceived to integrate five differing management styles to further enhance cooperation as follows: *traditional, sophisticated paternalist, standard modern, sophisticated consultative*, and *sophisticated constitutionalist* (Purcell and Sisson, 1983). These are briefly explained.

## Employment relations management styles

A *traditional* management style echoes a unitary perspective where management typically holds a legitimate right to manage without hindrance from other parties. There is little or no room for trade union presence. Therefore, management in this typology would view trade unionism with a sense of distrust (Bingham, 2016). S*ophisticated paternalist* style adopts a soft human resource approach which incorporates a strong desire to support effective employee performance. Trade unions in this perspective may be viewed as an obstacle. Therefore, management may allow employees limited involvement within wider labour processes, treating the workforce with a degree of tolerance to engender trust and productivity (Purcell and Sisson, 1983).

*Standard modern, sophisticated consultative*, and *constitutionalist* management styles engender a pluralist frame of reference. These typologies integrate trade union working approaches to accommodate employee views and their divergent interests in work. A s*tandard modern* managerial style may be more adversarial in nature. Management may focus on addressing a narrow range of recognised issues as they arise and potentially utilise wider legislation to secure compliance. A *constitutional* managerial style may seek to mitigate against perceived conflict to contain employment relations with trade union stakeholders, using processes, rules, and regulations to secure situations. Conversely, *consultative* managerial styles focus on developing joint-partnership arrangements with trade unions, typically encouraging employees and management to work together to resolve workplace issues.

The employment frames of reference and managerial styles illustrate variances in corporate contexts and differing approaches to influence power dynamics within contemporary employment relationships (Lukes, 2005; Townley, 1994). These will either work in favour of the employee or the employers and demonstrate whether there is an incentive to protect workers in this context. These approaches are used within the case studies throughout the text.

**Discussion box 3**

**Group exercise:**

Analyse the employment relations frame of reference (unitary, pluralist, and radical HR) and the six management styles for your current employer or place of study.

Discuss whether these approaches influence the rule-setting agendas for controlling social media use in workplaces.

## Social media networking, platforms, and activities

This section outlines what is meant by social media and social networking sites. Social media are web 2.0 services which are used across organisational and personal environments. These devices allow people to interconnect, share, and exchange ideas (Boyd and Ellison, 2007; Reid and Reid, 2004). Social media technologies are increasingly relied upon for social communications and networking purposes (Cammaerts, 2015).

SNS are different platform sites used to interconnect and engage with different online audiences where we interconnect with other users to stimulate interest, observe one another, or to increase collective intelligence. Additionally, these sites can be incorporated in work and contribute to business effectiveness (Bradley and McDonald, 2011). Significantly, we use a plethora of different platforms for social purposes. Thus, there is a crossover between the different elements of our private identity, persona, and behaviours which may diverge from our corporate, professional persona, all of which is observed online.

Social media increase the speed and expediency of work due to their multifunctionality. They offer huge opportunities to trade, market, collate data, and recruit or attract talent to corporate brands (Headworth, 2015; Uldam, 2017). In the UK statistics from the recent *Adult Social Media Report* (OFCOM, 2023) show YouTube is highly popular with 80% of adults commonly using the platform. This is closely followed by WhatsApp (79%), Facebook (77%), and Instagram (57%). All these sites have had a significant growth in their base usage year on year (see Figure 1.2 Adult social media users UK). In Figure 1.2a, we can see which platforms were accessed regularly by adults (Source Mintel).

For the purposes of this text, I am focusing solely on the use of these devices and not the technology itself. The technologies I refer to in this text are the internet, SNS, emails, internal corporate intranet sites, staff portals, individual online blogs, and vlogs. These technologies are widely incorporated for business and personal use, often interchangeably.

In the UK, nine in ten (92%) UK adults use the internet at home or elsewhere, which includes work. Findings from Ofcom (2023: 5) suggest we access internet sites to gather information on topics such as education, entertainment, and to build our social connections, which, they state, reflect the blurring nature of "life" and "life online". Whilst internet use is almost certainly universal, the way we use these devices shows little homogeneity. Each app or social media site we use differs markedly by age.

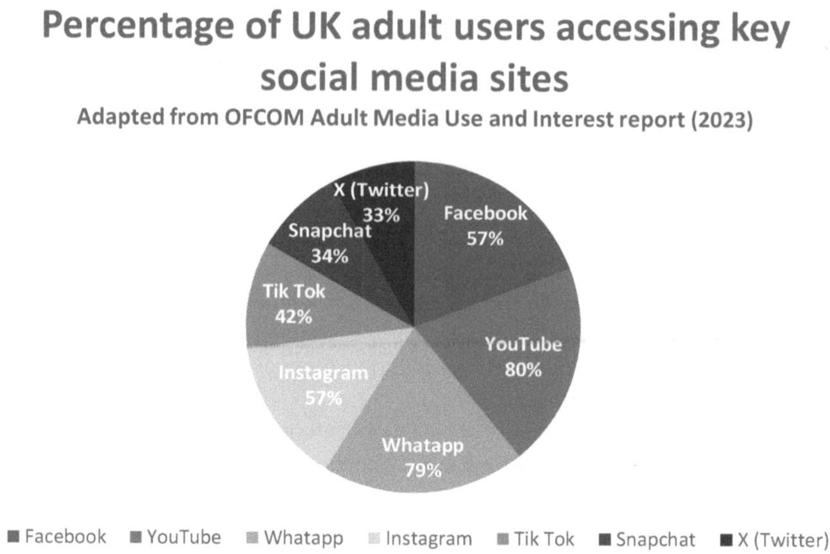


*Figure 1.2* Adult social media use UK.

Source: OFCOM (2023).

What can be gleaned from this information is the popularity of social media sites has exploded (see Figure 1.2a, Mintel, 2023). Currently, Facebook has billions of users; YouTube and Instagram have grown exceeding the use of X, formally known as Twitter, which exceeds over 140 million users worldwide. These sites are used and lauded in business (Jacobson and Howle-Tufts,2013). Facebook originally had a high penetration of users across all age groups; however, this has shifted with the site recently being favoured by the over 65-year age group.

Facebook users are saccharinely called "friends". The notion of friend in this context to me is spurious, ambiguous, and intriguing. This dynamic includes persons who are unknown to us as social actors (Ellison et al, 2007). So not a true "friend" in the traditional sense, which I think alters how we perceive what we think we can say and do online.

Whilst there is a sense Snapchat and TikTok have lower usage rates, these are expected to grow. Snapchat and TikTok have overtaken Instagram as the main social media platform used by 16–24 year olds, and few younger social media users (23%) cite Instagram as their favoured social media platform (–30%) (OFCOM, 2023). A number of new social media sites are growing in popularity, such as BeReal and Threads; these will naturally gain greater market share as audiences grow.

What is most apparent is we are increasingly using a wider selection of sites. One in five (22%) internet users has more than one profile on the same

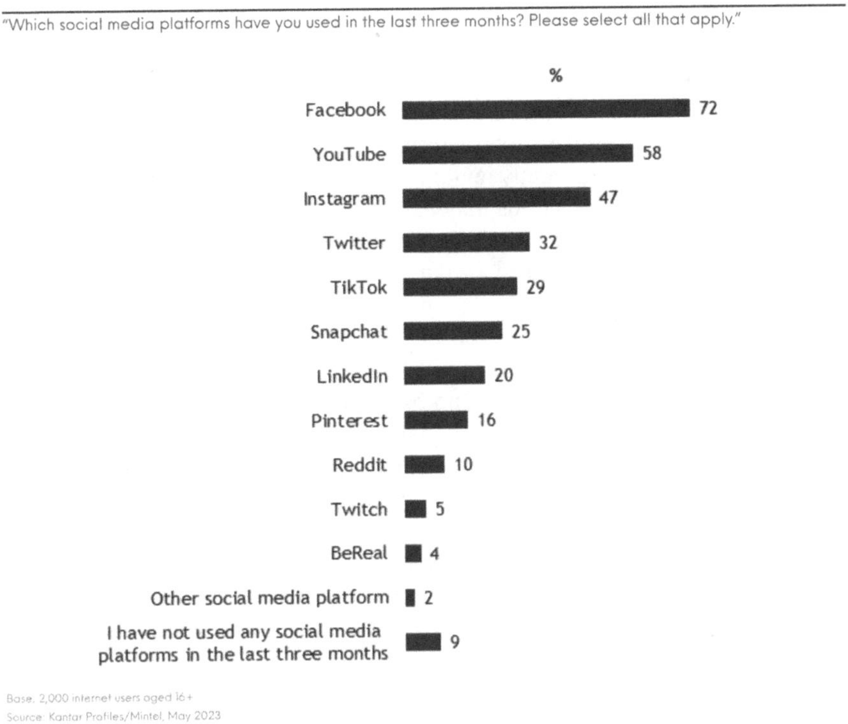


*Figure 1.2a* Adult social media use in last 3 months UK.

Source: Mintel (2023).

social media platform. This is a growing feature of use. This rises to more than half of internet users in the 16–24-year-old market (53%) (OFCOM, 2023) and illustrates how immersed social media are within younger generations. Instagram is the preferred platform for users with more than one profile (OFCOM, 2023). The reason for creating a number of profiles on the same sites is to garner interest and to connect with kindred spirits who may share in our pursuits and interests such as make-up, cooking, sports, and entrepreneurial endeavours.

Another changing factor regarding multiple site use is we are getting fed up of juggling more than one site. Ofcom suggests that this has reduced since the COVID-19 pandemic. This is thought to be because we now have less on-screen time availability to dedicate to the upkeep of these sites. This shows how much more complicated this endeavour is.

There are growing concerns regarding the amount of time spent online. Psychologists have long documented the increase in screen-time younger users devote to technology and social media. There is a perception that online behaviours and interactions have reached addictive proportions with many individuals reportedly spending increased amounts of time online (Rosen et al, 2010). Little has changed since this research was published and will remain a growing feature of life.

My point here is to urge parents, educators, future HR practitioners, and managers to see the need in constantly reviewing the implications of being more digitally immersed, and the effect this may have on multi-intergenerational workers. These statistics will grow, and, therefore, the rules and practices we use to supposedly control workers will need to adapt in line with how we evolve over time.

Combined, our social media activities now truly supplement our social and work routines. We routinely follow friends, companies, brands, celebrities, influencers, and people with similar interests (OfCOM, 2023). Moreover, the methods deployed by these technologies encourage us, algorithmically, to engage in a constant daily feed of personal discourse and narratives. This ultimately increases a psychological need to increase the visibility of our various personal identities. When we do this, we get personal high from the interactions. Dr Anna Lembke, author of *Dopamine Nation*, has raised concerns about our relationship with our personal devices and the effect this has on our neurological states. Each time we swipe or like something, we receive a dopamine hit which keeps us hooked and locked into using these technologies.

**Discussion box 4**

**Personal reflection:**

What social media sites do you use?

Do you have different profiles on the same site such as Instagram?

Do these profiles differ from your work identity or how your employer expects you to behave?

Calculate honestly how much time you spend online each day on these platforms? Does this surprise you?

**In pairs or groups:**

Discuss whether you differ across the use of these social media sites.

Discuss whether this could cause misperceptions about who you are to arise in a work context.

Discuss the ethical implications for HR practitioners and management observing us on our social media platforms.

Conceptually, social networking is conceived as *homophily*. This is defined as a conscious or unconscious tendency to associate with people who resemble us (Christakis and Fowler, 2011). Let's face it, social media corporations capitalise on this need and our want to be liked and loved. They have set up their devices to constantly hook us to interconnect across a plethora of platforms. This allows co-workers, consumers, and service users to interact together online. Such approaches establish new modes for workplace communications. Employee Voice (EV) is a common mechanism where workers and management engage in forms of communication and expression to inform business decision-making or air workplace concerns (Holland et al, 2016; Kaufman, 2015; Taylor and Dobbins, 2021).

## Social media discipline and case law

Clearly, we use social media to engage with workers; this includes allowing employees to have a voice. This suggests workers have a legitimacy to share their opinions, ideas, personal or organisational interests through formal or informal mechanisms via internal intranet or external SNS sites (Mowbray et al, 2015; Wilkinson et al, 2020). This must be balanced against the issues of associating with each other in any online fora. This clearly adds to wider corporate concerns and risks.

Online content and freedom of expression, therefore, may incite conflict between organisational expectations of being "professional" and what is considered an outward appearance of rebellion against the corporation (Ackroyd and Thompson, 1999; Ezzamel et al, 2001). Social media are simultaneously used to share concerns about the workplace. In doing so, we have further reduced and blurred the traditional boundaries which previously existed between employment and personal privacy (Archer-Brown et al, 2018; Jacobson and Howle-Tufts, 2013; Lam, 2016; Siegert and Löwstedt, 2019). The different employment frames of reference will determine whether sharing concerns are considered part of the employment deal or irrational employee (mis)behaviour.

Hence, management practices now incorporate more observation and monitoring of social media use. These devices attractively give management capability to synoptically observe differing individual identities or viewpoints (Fernback, 2013). There is a growing virtual sense of individual and corporate "every-where-ness". Interconnected users are observed as four-dimensional beings who are omnipresent (Scott, 2015). Therefore, our digital corporeality means that as individuals we are less containable, which has ramifications for the ordering of subjects at work (Barrett, 2002).

This has increased fears that our online activities and ever-changing self-identities, which are prone to constant renegotiation, may damage corporate reputation (boyd and Ellison, 2007; Richardson and Hessey, 2009; Webb, 2006). Undoubtedly, there has been a rise in online misbehaviours which, in turn, has caused a spike in case law. The main emphasis of these are now discussed to ensure management and HR practitioners are comprehensively aware how freedom of expression in online fora are subject to wider formalities, restrictions, or penalties in law. The Equality and Human Rights Commission in the UK states

> The Human Rights Act (1998) outlines the fundamental freedoms for individuals in the UK and incorporates rights which are set out in the European Convention on Human Rights (ECHR) and enshrines these within domestic British law. The Human Rights Act came into force in the UK in October 2000.
>
> EHRC (2024)

A litany of UK legal cases in the last decade demonstrates the problematical nature of social media use. Primarily, in the workplace (but not limited to), individuals have engaged on different platforms to voice radical ideologies, post obscenities, share abusive materials, air workplace discontent with organisational conditions, or make abhorrent comments about their peers or managers.

Examples of these have become mainstream news. Some of which really centred on employees voicing their concerns in work. These include the Bullied Blogger column (Times Higher Education Supplement Online) and the seminal workplace dismissal case in the UK *Gordon v Waterstones* (2005) (The Guardian UK). In both examples, digital platforms were used to publicly voice feelings about the workplace and work colleagues. Both share contradictory views of working life, management styles, and practices.

It is my view that more research is required to probe behind the veil of these cases. Hence, I focused my study on worker assumptions and experiences of using social media at work. Whilst on the face of it, these blogs certainly bring the corporation into disrepute. However, using social media, the creators effectively lifted the stone on corporate practices, and how these are enacted in different institutions by managers or powerful elite (Macky and Boxall, 2008).

Extant literature rarely focuses on ethical concerns about corporate management practices or behaviours. My aim here is to set an agenda to more broadly discuss issues in work and methods which seek to monitor, observe, and control employees through the use of social media and technology (Moussa, 2015). My view is these cases are not the sole fault of the employee. Underneath that stone, there are some shady management practices which need eradication. We never seem to focus on these issues because in corporations, we are too busy trying to shift the blame.

I have included discussion on UK case law, as this further highlights and problematises how we use platforms in work such as LinkedIn. Primarily, literature focuses on an oversimplification of how we use this site for business and professional use. LinkedIn is widely used in business for customer relationship marketing, career progression, and the recruitment of the self and others. Yet this perception underestimates the extent LinkedIn significantly blurs business boundaries or approaches. Case law in this area is of particular interest. Particularly, how LinkedIn is blended with the ownership of the means of production.

A key contestation is who owns LinkedIn contacts? This has proved to be a confounding area of employment legislation which principally centres on the commercial threat individuals pose to businesses. In *Whitmar Publications v Gamage [2013] EWHC 1881 (Ch)*, LinkedIn contacts were used by an employee to create a new business venture. This was perceived as a clear conflict of interest. The employer terminated the employment contract due to the perceived threat the venture posed to their business. However, for most workers, rules on how to engage on LinkedIn will prove nebulous.

LinkedIn is culpable in this area, as it encourages us to visibly develop our professional identities with the sole ideation that this will somehow advance both our employment and careers. As an educator, we encourage young graduates to regularly stage and display their skills or attributes to advertise their labour potential. This suggests we are open to wider career opportunities. For this reason, LinkedIn creates additional tensions between employers and employees who tout themselves as looking for work or wider. In *Flexman v BG Group plc ET/2701998/11*, this form of self-advertisement led to the constructive dismissal of the employee. Table 1.1 highlights a range of early UK case law: worker social media (mis)behaviour and misuse. The rise in case law illustrated in Table 1.1 shows how a lack of coherence in guidance, management practices, and policy exists in this context. This demonstrates, overtime, we need to adapt, amend, and strengthen regulatory and management practices in this area of work (Broughton et al, 2010; Van Gramberg et al, 2014).

I wish to be clear employers have a legitimate right to regulate, monitor, and punitively act upon perceived misconduct. The case law illustrates the power dynamics at play and how this is unequally weighted in favour of the corporation and rarely favours the employee in this domain (Biro, 2011).

Interestingly, case law demonstrates how the human rights law fails employees defending their social media actions, which in the current context is an important area of debate. The case examples highlight a right to freely express oneself is unlikely to succeed. This demonstrates the far-reaching power corporations have to challenge freedom of speech.

The issue of a right to privacy is equally challenged by the mere fact much of what we post is highly visible, even within closed groups. This forms part of a wider moral debate about censoring social media content. Curbing freedom of speech is unlikely to halt harmful forms of expression or misbehaviour. Additionally, those seeking wider regulation to censor content are also subject to censorship treatment and poses the question of whether this could lead to more regulation and even forms of tyranny (Steel and Petley, 2024).

*Table 1.1* Early UK social media case law

| *Case name/date* | *Category* | *Law* | *Outcome* |
|---|---|---|---|
| Chambers v DPP Neutral Citation Number: [2012] EWHC 2157Case No: CO/ 2350/2011 | Prosecution for menacing and grossly offensive material. | Communications Act 2003 S.127 | Fair |
| Gill V SAS Ground Services UK ltd Case No 2705021/09 | Unfair dismissal. Sickness absence. | Employment Rights Act 1996 S.98 | Fair |
| Young v Argos Ltd ET case No 1200382/11 | Gross misconduct. Derogatory comments. | As above | Unfair |
| Teggart v Teletech UK ltd Case no 704/11 | Unfair dismissal. Derogatory comments. | As above | Fair |
| Zavier V Dorchester ET case No 2201485/06 | Unfair dismissal. Disclosure of confidential material. | As above | Fair |
| Dixon v GB Eye Ltd ET Case 283642/10 | Grievance. Highly offensive comments. | As above | Fair |
| Taylor v Somerfield Stores ET case no 107487/07 | Reputational damage. | As above | Unfair |
| Gosden V Lifeline Project Ltd ET Case no 2802731/09 | Reputational damage. | As above | Fair (band of reasonable response |
| Jones v Tower Boot Co Ltd 1997 ICR 254 | Employers liable for acts of harassment and abusive comments | Equality Act 2010 s.26 | Upheld in favour of Jones |

Source: Case Law IDS Law Brief 957 & 958 (2012).

Currently, in the UK, The Regulation of Investigatory Powers Act (2000) and the much-awaited Online Safety Act (2023) illustrate political and legal attempts to address perceived online (mis)behaviours legally. The latter legislation thinly outlines the extent to which public organisations use covert surveillance. Yet such governance is not explicitly shaped for all commercial organisations to ensure harmful content is minimised.

What of an employee right to maintain privacy though? This discretion is rarely cited in corporate social media policy. Moreover, employers are rarely explicit about detailing when and how they access or use our data generally, let alone how they use and observe our social media data or profiles (Rifkin, 1994; Smith, 1993).

My point is monitoring and observation activities are becoming abstract terms which are "remote from everyday concerns" and hidden behind a veil of corporate practices (Cornelius and Radlund, 2011: 3). I wanted to illustrate how this occurs which you will observe in the later *Acts*.

You probably don't even give being observed through social media a second thought. We all do it, don't we? Therefore, this activity has easily slipped into everyday social activity and has enabled corporate management to capitalise on our social media endeavours. This allows them to integrate these devices to more deeply observe workers beyond work, judging and comparing us. Thus, we have taken our own privacy for granted.

Worryingly, it is not just corporations who are using social media to observe workers on social media. Governments are using social media, often potentially breaching equality and human rights legislation. They undertake hidden checks and monitor the online activity of potential critics of their governmentality, compiling secret dossiers on individuals with the sole aim of stopping them from speaking out at public events (*The Observer* 18/11/23). So if the people who decide legislative measure to control social media use it for unlawful surveillance purposes, what hopes do we workers have? My aim here is to highlight that there are major implications for all of us regarding how freedom of expression impacts on privacy and to show how very little we understand the daily inspection of our online activity.

**Discussion**

**In groups**

Look at past news articles on the Bullied Blogger or *Gordon V Waterstones* (2005) /case. Discuss the implications for yourself as an employee.

Do you think employees should parody and make comment about work issues?

Do you think employers should take this more lightly?

**Activity**

Draw up a list of things employers could do to control employee concerns and disgruntlement about treatment and performance management in work so that these issues do not get posted in blogs or on social media.

## Social media surveillance and control

Clearly, as the case law shows, corporations will take great exception to anything we may say online about the conditions of work or colleagues. This is dicey stuff and therefore warrants surveillance, monitoring, and observation "in work" which they claim are used to counteract supposed forms of employee misbehaviours. But it is how this is achieved which needs more scrutiny.

Surveillance and monitoring are not new per se; however, the rapid increase in digitalisation means corporations can get away with more sneakily monitoring employee online endeavours which may or may not be associated with work-related conduct. The growing range of surveillance activities in my view illustrates a deeper schism in the asymmetry of power relations at work and society in this domain (Dundon and Rollinson, 2011; McDonald et al, 2016).

Surveillance has a deeper connotation and derives from the French "*sur*" meaning above or over and "*veiller*" meaning to watch or observe (Foucault, 1975: 201; Mann and Ferenbok, 2013; Townley, 1994). Foucauldian disciplinary discourse emphasises how employees are subjects of work and rendered in a permanent state of visibility (Lukes, 2005). None more so than in social media contexts.

Foucauldian theory associates conceptions of surveillance with an architectural feature, the *panopticon*. The panopticon is a tower, platform, or mechanism which creates a lofty position from which to observe employees or inmates (Bain and Taylor, 2000; Foucault, 1975/1977; Sewell and Wilkinson, 1992; Townley, 1994). Watchtowers are concretely built into corporate entities such as call centres or factories. From these fortress-like entities, management elites have a wider capacity to gaze down and observe employees for the purposes of driving organisational effectiveness or for disciplinary approaches in work. An example of this is when I worked in a sales call centre management sat on raised platforms so they could view the sales floor. As technology advanced, systems were integrated which informed management of our individual activity; they knew how many calls were being taken, by whom, and the type of call, whether incoming or outbound, as well as how many minutes an individual had been inactive. This dictated how they viewed our productivity. This also dictated the behaviour they displayed towards us. With inactivity, this prompted a lot of shouting and eyeballing to shame workers into production.

Technology and digital networks, therefore, widen the concept of the panopticon. They enable corporations to observe individuals or groups more deeply via use of platforms and networks, signifying a *digital panopticon*. Such ethereal corporeality creates a sinister sense of the employer possessing an all-seeing-eye which is Orwellian and big-brother-esque in nature (Briken et al, 2017; Foucault, 1975; Scott, 2015; Thompson, 2003).

Digital technologies are so sophisticatedly incorporated to reimagine control methods within contemporary employment deals that we often don't give these much thought either. Yet such technologies allow corporations to track employees (Moussa, 2015, often acting as an "electronic leash" (Towns and Cobb, 2012: 205). Increasing forms of control include filtering software to inhibit access to social media platforms or websites (Riedy and Wen, 2010). More sinister surveillance practices include invasively microchipping employees to track our whereabouts, and using our PCs so we can be monitored at home through cookies and data usage.

When working from home, management distrust grows exponentially, probably since the COVID-19 pandemic (2020). Hybrid working meant there was a reduction in *eyeball* management where management can see and watch us visibly in the workspace. Working from home, our lack of physical presence and productivity are viewed sceptically by management. Indeed the media reported an expected rise in employment tribunal cases where organisations are seeking to reduce working from home (Source: The Guardian 2024b).

Our esteemed leaders may therefore may access our social media profiles to cross-compare them with our work activities. They may be surprised! Or more likely they will come to a negative conclusion that we are somehow less productive. Thus, we need to debate widening management philosophies regarding the attempts to observe and monitor workers, which have greater ethical implications (Adams and Purtova, 2017).

My aim here is to highlight how social media visibility is increasingly more subjective and oftentimes has little to do with criteria which links to job specifications and roles. Surprisingly, little is known about management attempts to scrutinise employees through these platforms. In extant literature, there is some critical reflection on the likelihood of surveillance occurring, yet there is little reflection regarding the actuality of management practices or approaches in this domain. Given the rise in subjectivity through online observation, the accounts in this text will substantially recast this by highlighting how this may include widening forms of hegemonic management practices and bias. Such forms of management (mal)practices are rarely discussed or challenged.

Through my discussion and empiricism, I seek to illustrate how there is very little scrutiny of management approaches in this domain per se, and furthermore, there is very little challenge on their surveillance approaches using social media to subjectively monitor employees. Simply put, these activities are forgotten, left well alone and subsumed into everyday management practices (Islam, 2012; McDonald et al, 2016; Moussa, 2015; Taylor, 2018; Taylor and Dobbins, 2021).

Critically, this implies that forms of social media surveillance are left unchallenged, reified, and forgotten about by wider HRM practices and senior leader ship in corporations. Reification involves: "...seeing people in 'thing-like' terms, treating their aspects as inert properties rather than as subjective expressions" (Islam, 2012: 41). Reification reduces employment relations practices to the allocation, deployment, and cost of human capital involved in the production of tasks (Islam, 2012). This perspective denies human emotion and infers that all employees are supposedly self-disciplined, including management. This conceptualisation fails to acknowledge how social media surveillance practices contribute to an undermining of employee morale, fostering a deepening mistrust between workers and management (Kizza and Ssanyu, 2005).

The growing impact of surveilling employees via social media is much more invasive than we think. Employers are accessing deeper biographic and personal materials where our online identities are more on show (Moussa, 2015). Corporations legitimise such surveillance practices under the guise of improving effective and productive use of company time. The purpose is to minimise issues such as work-related gossip, cyber-loafing, pilfering, and emerging workplace deviancy such as online gambling, accessing pornography, to name a few (Moussa, 2015).

Clearly, there is a growing trend in complex varieties of worker (mis)behaviour which is only just being debated. Moreover, the narrative on misbehaviour rarely discusses how management actors may also misbehave; my aim is to build on these discussions and suggest management are equally capable of criminal, irregular, subversive, and abhorrent behaviour in work and online (Ackroyd and Thompson, 2003; Taylor, 2018). The surveillance practices captured in this text build on existing literature, including pre-profiling, observation, and monitoring of work-related blogs and posts.

Pre-profiling involves gathering information from individual social media profiles or search engines. This occurs typically during pre-recruitment processes where personal, online, biographical materials are used to supplement background information checks on recruits (McDonald et al, 2016). This extends the visibility of prospective recruits beyond the utilisation of the traditional curriculum vitae or online application processes (Harrington, 2009; Tripathy and Kaur, 2012).

Accessing personal online content asserts an employer's right to legitimately protect organisations from negligent hiring (Blackwell, 2004; Shea and Wesley, 2006; Zeidner, 2007). Significantly, many employees are potentially unaware of pre-profiling practices (McDonald et al, 2016; Taylor, 2018). We are rarely asked if we give consent for the employer to view our online content. This is not necessarily a personal violation as much of our content is in the public domain. My point here is to highlight a greater need for individual users to consider what they wish to share in the public gaze (Ehrenreich, 2000/2001). Moreover, it is understood that if our online material or posts are considered defamatory, corporations may take decisive action regarding our employment. I wish to illustrate how social media profiles and posts are often used as evidence in HR processes to identify discrepancies between the information supplied by existing employees, such as feigned illness, absences, appearance, and horseplay issues (Taylor, 2018).

Online monitoring is rooted in employment law and embodied in social and economic infrastructures of our societies (Ehrenreich, 2000/2001). Sadly, employees have little protection from such employer practices or procedures, particularly if monitoring and observation of social media is cited in organisational policies (Biro, 2011).

Controversially, given that most UK social media case law cited an infringement of privacy, there is no universal definition of workplace privacy (Ehrenreich, 2000/2001; Jeffery, 2002a; Miller and Weckert, 2000). Furthermore, in the UK, there is currently no fully formed guidance for employers on how to establish ethical surveillance practices. Therefore, there is no recognised best practice motif for how surveillance practices are applied (Taylor, 2018). Indeed, Clark and Roberts (2010) suggest surveillance practices are potentially harmful for society. This debate is especially more important since the incorporation of the Online Safety Act (2023, UK) where observation, monitoring, and surveillance practice are called for, thus potentially leading to an increase in these practices. Therefore, alongside this legsislation workers should have the right to seek clarification on when and how management monitoring of social media takes place. More importantly, what punitive action will be taken should management breach protocols (Taylor and Dobbins, 2021).

These activities illustrate deeper mental fences which workers must overcome (Zerubavel,1991). Previously, it was possible to delineate and segregate professional and personal hemispheres of life (Rothbard and Ramarajan, 2009). Our use of social media has created a bleed or seepage between these hemispheres to the extent they collapse into each other (Wesch, 2009). Little is known about social media monitoring and the impact this has on how traditional workplace boundaries are managed (Malaterre et al, 2013). A prominent discussion in this debate is how corporations manage and take punitive action over risqué or controversial social media content.

**Discussion box 6: Pause for reflection**

Who do you interconnect with at work?

Are any of your interconnections your manager?

Do you ever feel your manager or other senior leaders are watching you on social media?

Discuss the ethical issues of your manager judging you by your online social media content.

Critically reflect on how you may wish to adjust your settings on who can see some of your activity online.

Are you aware of any HR development programmes in your place of work or study which focus on how to develop practices to observe employees?

Discuss whether such programmes should be developed.

Often our social media content becomes more akin to gossip-mongering (Kuo et al, 2015). We now use social media for strategic means, including we also use this to socially compare each other and gain instant cultural information. This may include cues about what we look like to create archetypes or reducing ourselves to one-upmanship over fellow employees (Manaf et al, 2013). These contribute to emerging forms of online worker resistance or (mis)behaviour (McDonald et al, 2016). Importantly, this allows management to further use social media content to categorise employees as things of beauty or recalcitrant, disobedient workers (Ackroyd and Thompson, 2003). Equally, we become eyewitnesses and informants on each other. Thus, contributing to wider understanding of social media (mis)behaviours was important in this text.

One such area is the use of facades or masking on digital technologies. Social media allow individuals to remain cloaked using anonymous blogs or fake personas. These are often created to put forward defamatory or irreverent online content. This is harder to police and has led to an increase in abhorrent social behaviours, such as misogyny, sexual harassment, and coercive behaviour. This illustrates how social media allows us to create multiple persona. We may also have an ulterior persona which is more controversial, and we may enact both simultaneoulsy online. We may have everyday visible identities such as a director or accountant, and we may enact these online. We need to get better at detecting this.

Equally, when we may choose hidden identities such as an avatar, catfish, or troll these are not widely understood. Thus, I have tried to provide some greater exploration of these behaviours to address the overlap in workplace contexts where employees are the subject of harassment or subjugation in digital contexts. My aim here is for future HR practitioners and managers to be more vigilant and skilled in alternative, ulterior practices. Moreover, to understand and be more cognisant of how such workplace conflict may manifest itself. Therefore my aim is to develop discussion how essential it is to develop better support measures to address the long-lasting psychological damage these instances may have on good workers.

Subversive use of social media, if caught, may lead to criminal cases and dismissal from work (McDonald et al, 2016; Taylor, 2018). Employees can try to challenge disciplinary legal action by appealing against dismissal in employment tribunals. The main line of defence tends to rest on how what they posted fell outside working hours. However, employers may consider any online activity and conduct regardless of when this was posted falls within their jurisdiction, regardless of working boundaries. Therefore, a burgeoning issue with the increased use of these technologies is the implications for intensifying management practices, additional work pressures, and unclear reporting boundaries.

Equally, these issues further depersonalise work by further altering a sense of justice and adding to wider inter-organisational inequalities. This may include the loss or creation of new jobs, affect and tilt the balance of power dynamics between differing stakeholder groups, and create the shaping of new organisational forms (Bondarouk and Brewster, 2016: 2664).

This sections highlights scepticism, tensions, and conflicts associated with forms of management surveillance and disciplinary actions (CIPD, 2013b, 2013c; Jeske and Shultz, 2015; McDonald et al, 2016; Van Gramberg et al, 2014). Yet surveillance practices provide a mono-account of social media use. Therefore, I introduce a wider debate by illustrating emerging *veillance practices* where social media use allows workers the capacity to reverse the digital, panoptical gaze on those in power.

## Social media sousveillance and employee voice

A failure in the discussion of surveillance is that it widely assumes employees are passive and submissive (Taylor, 2018; Taylor and Dobbins, 2021). Chiefly, such assumptions ignore how employees engage on social media to air their disgruntlement at work. Equally, the issue I have is that this assumption also largely ignores how social media allows employees to interconnect and converse with corporate elite, which means, significantly, workers can and do observe and monitor those in power through their use of social media. Workers, therefore, may use social media to specifically challenge or resist hegemonic management practices and observe management (mis)behaviours (Marler and Parry, 2015; Martin et al, 2015; Taylor and Dobbins, 2021).

Employee voice (EV), conceptually, has many definitions which involves a variety of processes or alternative structures in work, including the ability for employees to contribute to decision-making in organisations and to air their concerns about work (Bingham, 2016; Boxall and Purcell, 2022; Budd, 2014). Conventionally, EV channels are devised by management who scope conditions for both communication and engagement in workplace issues (Holland et al, 2016). This incorporates a variety of domains and topics such as procedures, policies, compensation, workplace conditions, and work methods (Wilkinson et al, 2020).

EV conceptions in literature are often narrow, differ by discipline, and are located from a unitarist lens (Barry and Wilkinson, 2016; Wilkinson et al, 2020). This offers an asymmetrical, imbalanced perspective of power where workers have limited capacity to engage in EV channels. Yet HRM practices for EV are deployed to mediate conflict, control behaviours, and e-communications for both the employer and employee in this context (Ulrich, 2010). Definitions of EV are therefore often unsatisfactory due to the emergence of digitised contexts, which do not account for how employees may controversially speak out about work experiences via social media networks, offering strong opinions or alternative views of the employer online (Bingham, 2016).

Simultaneously, corporations use social media to positively engage with employees and allow real-time dialogue to address workplace issues (Martin et al, 2015). Management, in this scenario, purposefully use the immediacy of social media responses to harness employee opinions to advance the organisation

(Holland et al, 2016). This requires management and leaders' preparedness to incorporate social media as part of the employment deal (Martin et al, 2015). There is a paucity of research on how leaders incorporate social media for positive organisational communication and EV purposes.

Additionally, trade unions utilise social media to recruit, campaign, and organise workers (Geelan, 2015). This illustrates how social media devices enhance EV to include dialectical interactions which are oppositional to corporate views (Martin et al, 2015). Social media has been used to shape societal protest and collective disputes which management or the government are not necessarily able to control. Examples include the Junior Doctors Strike UK (2016), Black Lives Matter Campaign (2013), the storming of Capitol Hill, Washington, USA (2021), and protests against the Police, Crime, Sentencing and Courts Bill (2021). Employees have also used social media and mobile devices to capture dire working conditions and oppressive work regimes in major corporations, such as Amazon, Foxconn, and Sports Direct (Chan and Pun, 2010; Briken et al, 2017; Taylor and Dobbins, 2021). In this context, social media offers employees and people greater power and capability to invert the process of surveillance and power.

This allows an alternative perspective and veillance practice of *sousveillance* to emerge. Sousveillance is where the observer becomes the observed using digital technologies (Mann et al, 2003). The etymology of sousveillance is again derived from the French "*sous*", meaning below and "*veiller*", as before, meaning to watch and observe. Sousveillance, therefore, allows employees to observe management or those in authority (Taylor and Dobbins, 2021).

Mann et al (2003) were not specifically referring to social media when they discussed sousveillance. They suggested mobile technologies could be used to film, photograph, and record data. I have simply extended this view to include social media as a growing space for employees to record, monitor, and take control of workplace or societal concerns using these devices. Thus, sousveillance problematises conceptions of surveillance and employee acquiescence. Moreover, employees may use social media to observe management to collate evidence of management (mal)practices. Thus, sousveillance increases the equity between the surveiller and those being surveilled (Taylor and Dobbins, 2021). As a divergent approach, sousveillance affords workers to be both masters and subjects of a panoptical gaze and is considered a wider form of worker resistance.

Foucault failed to adequately construct a theorisation of resistance which is defined as a "…constant process of adaptation, subversion and reinscription of dominant discourses. This takes place as individuals confront, and reflect on, their own identity performance, recognizing contradictions and tensions and, in so doing, pervert and subtly shift meanings and understandings" (Townley, 1994).

Sousveillance, therefore, further develops a subtle re-conception of communicative worker voice conflicts adding to a micropolitical view of resistance

(Thompson, 2016). Resistance manifests itself in all forms of organisational behaviour. This highlights competing efforts to shape and fix meaning on expected worker behaviour norms (Mumby, 2005). Thus, social media use is stimulated by complex, contradictory, and alternative subject positions, which highlight oppositional discourses and differing individual interests in work (Thomas and Davies, 2005). This, therefore, is a core fundamental issue for employee relations and HR practices.

Sousveillance contributes to a much deeper narrative about worker control, which, in my view, is never absolute, as employees will "... constantly find ways of evading and subverting managerial organization and direction at work" (Ackroyd and Thompson, 2003: 47). Lastly, little is known about the extent or practices of sousveillance which adds to the intrigue. I have sought in this text to uncover some truths in its growing use.

**Discussion box 7**

Were you were aware of the concept of sousveillance?

Do you think HRM needs to be more aware of this concept?

Do you think management is aware that employees could use social media to capture evidence of management misbehaviours?

What management training and development do think is required to develop greater awareness of this?

## Dramaturgical performances on social media

An important trope in this book is that social media platforms represent differing online "auditorium" or stages which we use theatrically as individuals to dramaturgically shape identity and advance personal power (Kerrigan and Hart, 2016). Dramaturgy uses notions of theatre as a metaphor by suggesting that human interactions are stage-like performances (Goffman, 1959). Performativity links to a rehearsed discourse of power which produces the phenomena it regulates and allows beliefs to be formed (Butler, 1993).

The theorisation of dramaturgy suggests that it incorporates ideological concepts of a front- and backstage persona which we create at specific times for differing on- and offline audiences (Butler, 1993; Goffman, 1959). On social media, we can create personas, characterisations, and identities which are less delineated and performed more fluidly online (Kerrigan and Hart, 2016). In this context, we have multiple versions of ourselves in targeted online platforms which are used as visible front stages to present desirable, staged images of the self (Bullingham and Vasconcelos, 2013).

My aim here is to suggest that this creates falsehoods and adds to a more sinister version of the looking glass self (Taylor, 2018). Like Narcissus, we gaze on ourselves constantly online. We develop overly staged and aesthetically pleasing online personas which we refine and edit to look more appealing. We have a growing neediness to have a constant feed of likes. This fuels excessive positioning and posting to vie for attention in different fora.

As managers and HR practitioners, we need to be more aware of the asinine allure and impact that the staging of the self may have on workers and colleagues. We also need to unpick more carefully narcissistic, socio- or psychopathic personality disorders, which are increasing in prevalence and may require support or, conversely, discipline.

Therefore, we need to have more awareness of how social media activity allows us to create more liminal digital personhoods. The idea of ulterior identities interlinks with notions of conflict. Liminality is defined as a transition of being which occurs as actors' move between and betwixt differing states (Turner, 1960). Our different states involve the creation of professional personas or more ulterior sense of self online. There is little empirical evidence on how such online transitions manifest themselves or how these are managed in work.

As social actors, we use social media to incorporate four dramatic techniques to enhance power as follows: scripting, staging, performing, and interpretation (Benford and Hunt, 1992). We exploit our identities, using them to create pastiches of the self in order to survive work (Carbado and Gulati, 2000). This involves adopting strategies to signify hard work, team orientation, personal goals, and trustworthiness. These are positively observed and liked off- and online. For example, we use LinkedIn to script or stage a positive narrative of career successes and triumphs. This enactment of self-identity is important, as it lends itself to labour processes as part of our employment relationships. Equally, our social media profiles act to conceal evidence or contradict official constructions of the self (Raghuram, 2013; Hunter-McDonnell and King, 2013). This links to the use of masking, where we hide and manipulate differing interpretations of the self, yet another theatrical gadget or metaphor (Goffman, 1959).

Significantly, our dramaturgical performances link well to performativity in specific professional roles. Each role performance is a blended and pre-agreed version of identity in work. Organisations provide actors with different settings to perform, experiment, or even enforce roles (Benford and Hunt, 1992; Simpson and Carroll, 2008). This intensifies how workers engage in impression management to stage or dress their sense of self online.

We all love to be liked. Social media contexts seemingly fuel a need for mass adoration. This links to costuming and properties and other theatricalised gadgetry. There is a rise in individuals who obsessively post images of themselves, using software to filter and enhance aesthetic qualities or appearance. We post scripted soliloquies as leaders, managers, or workers to gain notoriety and increase or boost our profiles. This is referred to as a discretionary effort made by actors to control information used to influence perceptions about themselves or organisations by others (Giacalone and Rosenfeld, 1990; Goffman, 1959; Richey et al, 2016; Schlenker and Wowra, 2003).

## Online emotional and aesthetic labour

Our unconstrained online conversations and identity portrayals allow employers to participate in making subjective evaluative comments about work-related issues, including what we look like. This has led to a rapid rise in forms of emotional and aesthetic labour (Nath et al, 2016; Hochschild, 1983). Emotional labour is defined as the *management of feeling creating a publicly observable bodily and facial display* (cited in Ashforth and Humphrey, 1993).

Aesthetic labour is defined as "characteristics, embodied capacities and attributes which are possessed by workers (Nickson et al, 2001), which are then commodified and mobilised to fulfil corporate expectations but which essentially focus on how employees look, sound, and dress in work. Thus, aesthetic labour consists of the appraisal of workers who look appealing a (Warhurst and Nickson, 2001, 2007). Thus, social media further commodifies workers by assessing our delivery of emotive and aesthetic performances at work (Witz et al, 2003). The pressure to perform for large audiences online demonstrates a worrying trend in emotional and aesthetic labour, worker appearance, and body modifications in organisations (Nath et al, 2016; Timmings, 2015).

We, therefore, use emotional labour to manipulate the feelings we experience within work routines to create appealing, observable facial and physical displays (Hochschild, 1983). These online manifestations objectify workers in more visible ways. This illustrates a murkier, shallower side to social media use and wider societal assumptions on what is deemed objectionable or un-aesthetic about employee appearance, behaviours, and our identity, which requires further ethical debate.

## Identity exploration and sense-making

Identity is conceptualised as a set of central, distinctive, and enduring characteristics that typify a person or a line of work (Albert and Whetten, 1985; Ashforth, 2001; Kreiner et al, 2006). Identity incorporates how we choose to represent ourselves and is core to our sense of being (Erickson, 1964). Individual identity exploration in social media contexts is an interesting part of this debate. Primarily, because, as previously discussed, our identity portrayal is more fluid and increasingly staged. This is due to the constant renegotiation of our identities in the variety of differing platforms (Kerrigan and Hart, 2016). Therefore, identity fluidity poses significant challenges for HRM and management to understand and more relevant to this discussion control (Cooper and Inglehearn, 2015; McDonald et al, 2016).

My aim here is to highlight how observing and monitoring employee identity differences in online contexts is nuanced, highly complex, and open to interpretation. Actors in key management and HR roles must, therefore, be more discerning to ensure that they are not bigoted and do not breach wider legislation such as the Equality Act (2010). This legislation harmonises several laws which seek to protect different individual characteristics, such as sex, sexuality, race, religion, gender, disability, and age. The identification of identity, therefore, links to concepts of the self in relation to distinct categorisations which impact on work, role, and our demography (Brewer, 1991; Hogg and Terry, 2001; Oakes, 1987; Webb, 2006).

Erickson (1964) suggested that identity exploration required being true to one's actions. Yet being true and authentic online is problematical, particularly when social actors use social media to develop identities which are dictated by corporations. These may be conflictual with our own personal expectations and perceptions, which in part are driven by our own individual need to be distinctive. We seek to cultivate, craft, or elevate differing identities to boost audience interaction. This has implications for our employers, particularly, in how we choose to both interact and present self-identity across these multiple levels (Van Gramberg et al, 2014). A core tenet is whether these multiple versions of the "self" lie in tension with the professional self.

Clearly, as we have witnessed in the last few years, prominent social actors in the world of entertainment have produced online content which has caused a furore. Such online comments jar with employment requirements to be impartial and objective, and for us, as employees, not to harm corporate reputations.

Josselson (1996: 28) stated: "Identity is what we make of ourselves within a society that is making something of us". This links to the employment relationship and how we are regulated at work. Our identity therefore influences our work experiences, addressing two central questions: "Who am I?" and "how should I act?" in work (Cerulo, 1997).

This involves a critical appraisal of the self to construct a coherent and positively valued work identity (Alvesson et al, 2008). This involves "...forming, repairing, maintaining, strengthening or revising the constructions that are productive of a sense of coherence and distinctiveness" (Sveningsson and Alvesson, 2003: 1165). In creating a coherent sense of self, we are required to sense-make of identity work. This is particularly complex during individual liminal transitions or online crises where our identity work involves a radical transformation of the self (Ibarra, 1999). These variations in self-identity create a perceived need for corporations to increasingly control our identity beyond work to ensure the corporation looks and sounds great (Webb, 2006).

Sense-making is something which emphasises the importance of understanding and discernment for HR and management actors. This requires them to understand the fragile interrelationships between knowledge and information and to act within a non-judgmental code of conduct.

This is defined as "meaning making" or "feeling making" and requires individuals to reflect on and make sense of behaviours and social-emotional human experiences of interaction (Schwandt, 2005: 182). Weick (1995: 20) claimed the "maintenance of identity is a core preoccupation in sense-making". This is problematical in digitised contexts. Managers and HR practitioners need to understand more nuanced digital identities. Actors in these roles must make sense of newly acquired information about each other constantly, as they interact and observe each other in real time online. The CIPD (2023) has developed a code of conduct and ethics which requires HR practitioners to be competent in promoting workplace cultures where ethical values and behaviours are embedded. They suggest practitioners make difficult decisions regarding work and therefore must think carefully regarding the implications and consequences of decisions and actions taken. This suggests that sense-making is hugely important and has a need to respect key virtues in work which champion and create positive working practices which are fair and equitable for all.

Schwandt (2005) suggested sense-making processes are dependent on the development of a sense-making framework and characteristics of the sense-making process itself. This occurs by developing understanding from social cues. However, sense-making of online identity may exhibit large variances between where meaning is attributed to. This may include making greater moral or ethical judgments about fellow co-workers, which requires further moral courage.

Identity theory in corporate contexts focuses on the: "...categorisation of the self as an occupant of a role, and the incorporation, into the self, of the meanings and expectations associated with that role and its performance" (Stets and Burke, 2000: 225). Sense-making is critical when moments of tension, paradox, or ambiguity occur or where the sense of the environment is affected by a disruption. Sense-making of identity in this context is vital, as managers and powerful elite will use cues within these organisational environments to make "expedient and decisive actions" (Schwandt, 2005: 177).

Additionally, extant literature suggests actors in elite or management roles author hegemonic identity narratives which are refined and shaped by reactions from co-workers (Humphreys and Brown, 2002). Identity formation therefore adds dimensions to the staging of power displays at work. In doing so, this builds tensions where social media narratives act as both a central and subplot in the ongoing dramatic achievement of the self. We don't truly author a set script for the staging of self online. Thus, any deviations and improvisations of selfhood are fraught with major problems which pose problems for sense-making accuracy in how actors are understood at work (Reissner, 2010).

This is linked to the development of a moral identity, which is a psychological function concerned with living a moral life (Blasi, 1995; Damon and Hart, 1992; Erikson, 1964). This is not easily reduced to possessing the requisite skills of sophisticated moral reasoning or being committed to the attainment of moral goals, as my later *Acts* will show. A moral identity cannot be simply reduced to personality traits or linked to prosocial behaviour such as conscientiousness, agreeableness, or generativity, traits which require greater action (Hart et al, 1998: 515). Developing a moral identity is a further complex undertaking. This requires individuals to possess moral standards and impose self-sanctions which are considered important predictors of a person's moral behaviour (Bandura, 1999; Bandura et al, 1996). This conception requires individuals to critically reflect on their own discourse and behaviours and, importantly, to use moral reasoning when observing co-worker's online posts, identities, and behaviours, which straddle private aspects of life. Such critical reflection in online contexts is rare.

## The missing practice of critical reflection

Critical reflection enhances organisational learning and significant change (Høyrup, 2004). Social media networking is positioned as an aspect of work which requires both. Appraisal of the literature demonstrates social media is used increasingly in cybercrimes (BBC, July 2016), such as revenge porn and harassment. The Crown Prosecution Service (CPS, 2016) reported a rise in *Violence against Women and Girls* and cites social media use as a growing area of sexual criminal activity. Since this report little has changed and the UK justice system has been accused of failing women (www.endviolenceagainstwomen.org.uk)

Social media surveillance and sousveillance are used for gathering evidence and to make public disclosures on abusive activity in organisations such as national care homes, prisons, or grooming informants (BBC, 2012 House of Common Select Committee, Child Exploitation Report 2013–14). These case examples illustrate key failures in HR and management practices to challenge inappropriate on- or offline behaviours. Thus, the development of a more moral identity, reasoning, and critical reflection should have been used to address these techno-misbehaviours.

Reflective practice (RP) is a determinant of HR professional behaviour. The Chartered Institute for Personnel and Development (CIPD) suggests RP requires critical awareness, capability to make well-informed decisions, and to challenge assumptions (CIPD, no date: produced by Owen and Fletcher, last accessed 2017). Further studies on RP, which focused on part-time MSc Students who worked in HR, suggest these HR practitioners view forms of self-reflection with a great deal of scepticism and feel RP is too introspective (Bull and Taylor, 2014). This suggests practitioners dislike reviewing their own behaviours. This text is positioned, therefore, to encourage and provide space for greater critical reflection and thought about HR and management practices in the ever-growing digital terrain of work.

**Discussion box 8**

What do you think about critical reflection for HR practitioners?

How do you think RP could improve HR approaches and interventions?

How could corporations and professional bodies ensure HR practitioners and management engage in authentic RP to establish and champion better working practices?

These bodies of literature were presented to foreground and explore the complexity of social media use. They have been carefully positioned to elucidate on the different perspectives surrounding contemporary employment relationships in this context and the implications this has for worker control.

The next section focuses on the empiricism used to underpin this text.

## Behind the scenes: The social actors and their staged worlds

This text is supported by empirical research, which is now briefly outlined. The methodological approach was developed to triangulate a multi-perspective of social media use in work within several large UK corporations. Interpretative phenomenological analysis (IPA) was used to allow a deeper exploration and to develop understanding of key professional social actors and their experience of managing how social media devices were integrated, regulated, and managed in each context.

The key social actors who took part in this study held distinct corporate professional roles in HR management, operational management, and frontline operational roles. These roles are perceived to form the bedrock of contemporary employment relationships. This approach allowed a deeper sense-making into the social actor's sense of agency in these corporate roles. The study purposively explored how each actor used social media as part of their corporate existence collectively, personally, socially, and professionally (Smith and Osborn, 2003. The approach sought to understand their professional roles in shaping practices to develop rules and control the use of social media. Further, it aimed to understand how they individually adhered or circumvented these regulations, leading to greater understanding of emerging forms of misbehaviour and discipline in this domain. Furthermore, this approach explored how social media was used to enhance forms of EV and resistance in work.

To do so, the in-depth study comprised of thirty five semi-structured interviews. The interviews were conducted using a purposive sampling approach. Each interview lasted between 30 minutes and 2 hours; these were recorded, transcribed, and analysed using an iterative, hermeneutic process which captured four superordinate themes which underpin the subsequent chapters in this text.

Each interview took place in several differing corporate environments, adding further dramaturgical dimensions to the staging and the use of social media. The difference in using and regulating social media in each context, and by the individual social actors, was cross-compared to highlight divergent approaches. These provide a greater critical reflection of the social media phenomenon.

## Phenomenology

Phenomenology refers to the study of phenomena, which are described as anything appearing within or to a social actor as a conscious experience (Gill, 2014; Moran, 2000). In this text, the phenomenon studied was the use of social media by corporate social actors, and how each organisational context attempts to control or manage this type of work to ascertain what can be learned and understood from each environment.

Phenomenology is core to interpretive research paradigms (Denzin and Lincoln, 2000; Geanellos, 1998; Gill, 2014; Koch, 1995; Le Vasseur, 2003; Lopez and Willis, 2004). As a philosophical perspective, phenomenology focuses study on the fundamental nature of human experiences, seeking to more deeply understand how actors live through differing phenomena. This involves their human wholeness and ability to care (Geanellos, 1998; Moran, 2000; Tymieniecka, 2003; Wojnar and Swanson, 2007). This was important for ensuring understanding ethical and moral issues associated with management of social media use in work.

Phenomenological enquiry is similar to an artistic endeavour, as it allows a "linguistic description that is holistic and analytical, evocative and precise, unique and universal, powerful and sensitive" (Van Manen, 1990: 39). This suited both the research endeavour and the underpinning of this text. Linking to the belief that when we use social media, we are staging and acting out a variety of characterisations in dramatic and creative ways.

IPA links with a Heideggerian philosophy and conceptually frames phenomenology as "the science of the being of beings" (1926: 35). A Sense of being is hugely important to a hermeneutic understanding of social actors and their life-worlds which does not occur remotely from their temporal, social, and cultural contexts (Geanellos, 1998). Hermeneutic enquiry uses scaffolds and structures from human creations as an armature which enables possible creative self- interpretations (Guignon, 2012). This links with how we fluidly create fluid identities online.

## Dasein or there-being on social media

A factual sense of worldliness and reality becomes present in this study through a sense of *Dasein* or *there-being* in the world (Heidegger, 1926). Humans act on differing possibilities or desires to satisfy urges, such as impulsivity [*epithemia*]. Impulsivity is important when considering the social media phenomena. Social actors post online impulsively, viscerally, and lovingly. On social media, our impulses are often improvised and use dramaturgical approaches which cause great impact on corporate environments. Hermeneutic enquiry was used in this study to explore how each key social actor navigated impulsivity on these devices, requiring grounded reasoning for action via their own reflections.

*Dasein* is not an instrumental device; it is achieved by being thrown into the world, which may or may not be of our choosing. This culturally fits with social media contexts. These devices potentially shape who we are. They inform the places we work, the professions we choose, and/or the characteristics we adopt to create our personalities, identity, or alternative personae (Guignon, 2012). The principles of *Dasein* and *being* are applied to the specific organisational roles to create a scaffold of understanding in how individuals interact with each other on- and offline. This draws reference to human agency in institutions and corporate environments (Alvesson and Skoldberg, 2009).

## Importance of professional role

Three key professional roles were focused on in the programme of study. These are inextricably interlinked in work, as they anchor employment relationships and have transferability to most corporate environments. These roles are now briefly outlined.

*HRM:* These roles are typically entrusted with creating strategies for coordinating the effort and control of people in organisations. These roles link to the nature of human agency and being a subject in work. HR roles are integral to shaping the construction of organisational rules, policies, procedures, productivity, employee performance, and expected work behaviours. This includes particular use of corporate ways of being associated with appearance, language, symbols, and mechanisms which shape people management practices. HR practitioners play a key role in disciplinary processes, coordinating investigations into misbehaviour and supporting management to develop disciplinary or grievance outcomes. HR roles interviewed to underpin the empiricism in this text were employment and social media policy development leads, HR directors, HR managers, HR business partners, and HR development and employee relations specialists.

*Operational management*: Management roles are of central importance within organisational life. Management is a broad term; however, largely, individuals in these roles are perceived to embed and enforce regimes of control and lead the performance management of workforces. Management roles are apparent across all corporations in functions, such as marketing, finance, production, etc. HR practices are routinely devolved to wider operational management. Thus, management takes on HR practices such as the coordination of labour processes and involves the appraisal, performance management, observation, calculability, power, control, and surveillance of employee offline and online behaviours (Townley, 1994).

The empiricism sought to observe how actors in management roles develop their own agency and interpretation of social media policy and practices. Management roles are synonymous with establishing disciplinary tactics to control and manage worker effectiveness and productivity, including the discipline of worker distractedness and misbehaviours, which links with the misuse of social media (Moussa, 2015; Moqbel et al, 2013). The corporate roles interviewed to support the empiricism in this text included top-tier operational and supervisory management actors in a variety of functions such as production, manufacturing, IT, customer support, marketing, and sales.

*Frontline operational roles*: Workers who hold operational roles are expected to adhere and comply to regimes of control and management practices (Townley, 1994). Employees in frontline roles pose a challenge for management and HR where it is often assumed that employees are perceived to break regulations, particularly when using the social media. The empiricism therefore sought to explore employee experiences and perceptions to develop a critical social construction of how management controls and develops rule-setting agendas which impact frontline operational workers. A key aspect was to capture employee actor understanding of the social media rules. Additionally I sought to explore how workers may use this digital landscape to voice concerns regarding issue and surveillance at work, both in offline and online interactions with management. This was purposefully done to develop understanding of wider ethical considerations for management and HR. Employee roles interviewed in the empiricism to support this text included assembly workers, support officers, administrators, sales advisors, and union activists who have dual roles. Trade union representatives are vital in work contexts, as they often mediate on the development of regulatory processes and provide support during disciplinary or grievance procedures, workplace negotiation, and consultation. Actors in trade union roles are significant as they protect wider employee rights which are vital in the growing use of social media. The operational actor narratives, therefore, are used to add greater critical perspectives on approaches for EV and union partnership working.

Professional roles are often dismissed as archaic or clichéd (Mangham, 1996). Yet, professional roles are deeply embedded in a social constructionist view of the world. These were deemed to be useful in developing a framework for understanding role agency and performativity. How we embody our role and make sense of the professional practices which are needed to effectively perform at work and within strict codes of professional conduct.

Our sense of role informs the ordering and purpose of the self in organisations (Townley, 1994). Importantly, the status of professional roles may determine and inform our view power dynamics in work. Immersion in our professional role is akin to a dramaturgical performance. We may don the robes of power or adopt many masks to survive work; developing ongoing constructions and notions of the self (Goffman, 1959). Our identity enactment and embodiment of role make institutions come alive, often through our improvisation. We don't always follow ready-made scripts for our roles. We use unwritten librettos which are drama or play-like (Berger and Luckmann, 1966). Therefore, professional role was consciously built into the development and scoping of this text, as roles are something it was felt we could all relate to. We all have a manager or operational colleague in work. We will have had interaction with HR or people management roles through recruitment, appraisals, development, and other work-based interactions.

## Corporate staged environments

The commercial settings of work are hugely important in shaping performativity, identity, and ways of being (Webb, 2006). Corporations are classed as physical entities in social theory and are often considered beings or actors themself (Rowland, 2008). Each corporation in this text is positioned as a stage or auditoria as they contextually comprise ergonomic, scenic spaces, logos, imagery, uniforms, and cultural "scripts" used by workers which further shape corporate culture and the enterprise aesthetically (Johnson and Scholes, 1999; Strati, 1999). Significantly, each corporation manifests themselves as digital entity with a presence online, where the organisation stages itself across many digital platforms to vast audiences, further adding to the sense of theatre.

Eight differing corporate contexts are presented in this text to highlight differing employment relations frame of reference, management styles, and cultural ways of being in work through their social media use. Each corporation was anonymised to protect true identities. The corporations used in this text are as follows:

1 Aedis Housing – A UK social housing provider.
2 Alumno University – A modern university.
3 Charta – A UK office supplies provider.
4 Pala Communications – A global telecommunications corporation.
5 Pharma PLC – A global chemical engineering corporation.
6 Senes PLC – An international healthcare technology provider.
7 Tiro Hire – A leading UK recruitment agency.
8 Vita Care – A leading UK healthcare provider.

These organisations operated in the UK and are sizeable national, international, or global employers employing between 3,000 and 700,000 employees. Each organisation had an established HR management department. Corporate size and scale are shown here to emphasise the legitimacy for the organisation to develop social media regulations in an effort to protect brand or service reputation online. Reputation illustrates the corporate standards which are assumed or often taken for granted (King and Whetten, 2008).

## The cast of characters and corporate settings

Literary and theatrical works use a cast of central characters who bring central themes, tropes, intrigues, and relationships to life. This was a major driving force in developing this text, where I have sought to bring greater humanness into human and employment relations practices. These are not imagined characters. These are real social actors: workers, managers, and human resources professionals who participated in the in-depth study. They work amongst us.

Extant management and HR literature uses the terms *Leader, Manager, Worker.* These are devoid of humanness or emotional affiliation. This text purposefully brings these characters to the foreground, repositioning them as agentic in the utilisation of the social media. My aim was to help readers connect and identify with these characters as people, rather than as abstract terms. Each actor was given a pseudonym to protect their real identity. A brief biography of each actor is now provided and includes an overview of their role, qualifications (if known), credentials, and experiences as follows:

### Aedis

**Alex**: HR Manager, CIPD accredited. Qualified in MSc occupational psychology. Alex appeared to be quite reflective and had experiences of differing HR contexts. In their role, Alex had developed corporate values and behaviours in fast-changing organisational environment. Alex had experience of coordinating social media misbehaviour and disciplinary cases. Alex held a unique perception that social media corporate policy was unnecessary to control employee use. Alex used LinkedIn and Facebook.

**Alan**: Head of Property Services, managing a facilities operational team. Alan held a strong managerial ambition to build a cohesive team. Alan was studying at MSc level to supplement management knowledge. Alan managed several cases of social media misbehaviour and harassment in the team. Alan used highly informal networks to control his team. Alan used LinkedIn.

**Anne**: Engagement Coordinator. Anne had experience of using social media in various roles for collective and community participation, internally and externally. Anne's approach was highly radical and causing tension with management. Anne was frustrated by a lack of forward thinking in the organisation and was using social media to enable housing tenants to have a voice. Anne used Facebook and LinkedIn.

### Alumno

**Davina**: Head of Policy Development, CIPD accredited. Davina had experience of addressing social media misbehaviour cases in public sector. Davina was involved in partnership working with trade unions. Davina was responsible for coordinating the social media policy development group. Davina limited her personal use of social media choosing to "lurk" and observe friends and peers online. Davina used Facebook and LinkedIn sparingly and manipulated her online activity to stage a professional identity.

**Debbie**: HR Policy Development Manager, CIPD accredited. Debbie had experience of managing online misbehaviour cases. Debbie was the co-chair of the work policy development group. Debbie managed formal discussions with recognised trade unions. Debbie felt that she used social media to positively support the organisation. Debbie used LinkedIn and Facebook.

**Dahlia**: Operations Manager, MSc qualification. Dahlia had experience of investigating and disciplining social media misbehaviour and loss of productivity. Dahlia incorporated management methods of observation, monitoring, and developed performance management techniques to control use of these devices. Dahlia was frustrated by a perceived lack of corporate social media policy and guidance, which she viewed as a *grey area*. Dahlia chose to develop her own interpretative approach to these regulations deviating from wider policy. Dahlia used Twitter and LinkedIn, which she used strategically to develop professional connections.

**Darcy**: Senior Officer, MSc qualification. Darcy supervised a support team. Darcy used social media to reflect the aims of Alumno. Darcy had experience of addressing employee social media misbehaviour and misuse, which caused tensions within her team. Darcy felt she lacked management support and needed further development. Darcy used Facebook, LinkedIn, and Twitter.

**David**: Academic, PhD, entering retirement phase. David was an ex-trade union chair and representative. David was involved in negotiating and developing social media policy at university level. David was a member of the policy development group. David was reflective on how social media policy development affected the protection of union members, their human rights, freedom of expression, privacy, and punitive discipline approaches, which he was seeking to challenge. David used LinkedIn in a very limited way.

### Charta

**Fiona**: HR Manager, CIPD accredited. Fiona used social media to interconnect for personal and work purposes. Fiona had led social media disciplinary cases. Fiona felt social media policy was dictated by other stakeholders such as marketing and ICT departments. Fiona was frustrated by the lack of social media training and development to support appropriate use. Fiona connected widely online with colleagues at all strata or functions within the organisation on the social media. Fiona heavily utilised Facebook and LinkedIn to showcase her identity.

**Flo**: Learning and Development Manager, CIPD accredited. Flo felt frustrated by the lack of corporate scope to utilise learning and development to improve and strategically develop employee social media use. Flo felt the organisation used a hegemonic management approach. Flo mainly used LinkedIn.

**Frances**: Credit Control Supervisor. Frances incorporated a transactional, hard HRM managerial approach to establish team performance. Frances incorporated regular surveillance and observation of her team. Frances improvised management tactics to control employee mobile device use and social media, including a mobile phone amnesty (taking peoples phones away from them). Frances used Facebook and LinkedIn.

**Freya**: HR Officer. Freya had retreated from social media altogether due to psychological experiences of grooming, which affected her personal self-esteem. She perceived not using social media suited her wider long-term HR career plan.

### Pala

**Claire**: HR Director, CIPD accredited, MSc in Leadership. Claire had a wide range of directorship experience, leading large HR teams. Claire was highly focused on leadership development. Claire was involved in scoping, reviewing, and developing social media policies. Social media use was high across the organisation due to the nature of the sector. Claire's personal use of social media was minimal and restricted. This seemed at odds with her strategic role requirement. Her role required her to create corporate communities of practice online and develop regular HR blogs. Claire was not comfortable using social media and was involved in addressing corporate cases of social media misbehaviour. Claire used LinkedIn and Facebook.

**Charles**: Operational Manager, recently changed roles from operations to HR. Charles had stopped using social media due to the new HR role. Charles was involved in addressing cases of social media misbehaviour, which informed his lack of use. Charles had experience of consulting with trade unions on social media regulation, HRM practices, and disciplinary processes.

**Charlotte**: HR Consultant, CIPD. Charlotte had vast experience of handling social media misbehaviour and disciplinary cases. Charlotte used case outcomes to contribute to wider organisational learning on shaping appropriate use. Charlotte was not a regular user.

**Clive**: Sales Director, BSc, an aspiring leader with a long service employment record. He was responsible for a large commercial team. Clive used LinkedIn and Facebook widely for client relationship building. Clive followed management guidance on social media use. Clive felt social media blurred the boundaries between work and privacy. He had involvement in addressing employee misuse and technology breaches.

### Pharma

**Georgia**: HR Manager, CIPD accredited. Georgia had vast HR experience in differing sectors and employee relations environments. Georgia was keen on developing trade union partnerships. Georgia stated that social media policy was developed by corporate marketing. Regulations focused on limiting personal use of Facebook. Georgia disliked LinkedIn but did have a presence. Georgia felt corporate learning to develop social media use strategically was limited. Georgia used Facebook for personal use.

**Greg**: Operations Manager, BSc. Greg had a strong managerial ambition and discussed using a control and command, highly disciplined management style. Greg used LinkedIn sparingly. Greg made constant comparison of social media rules with his previous employer. Greg perceived social media use should be highly restricted for all employees.

**Gary**: Assembly Worker, Skilled Labourer, and Trade Union Representative, which gave him great pride in his work. Gary had a strong personal dislike for social media, preferring traditional face-to-face communication. Gary did not use social media to engage with his constituent union membership. This was associated with his substantive role where corporate restrictions were placed on assembly workers from using mobile phones for health safety purposes on the factory floor. Gary was involved in collective bargaining, negotiation, case work, and supported social media disciplinary cases. Significantly, Gary had not been involved in social media policy development.

### Senes

**Erica**: HR Director, CIPD accredited. Erica was an avid social media user, using platforms to build HR and employer branding. Erica developed policy and learning and development for social media use. Erica had led disciplinary cases on social media misuse. Professionally, Erica was a keynote speaker advocating social media use. Further, Erica sought to build leadership and social media skills to develop a prominent HR profile and identity. Uniquely, Erica experimented with multiple online identities such as an avatar critiquing HR practices. This caused tensions with perceptions of professional identity in work.

**Elizabeth**: HR and Corporate Social Responsibility (CSR) Officer. Elizabeth used social media mainly for work purposes, involving promoting the organisation for CSR purposes. Elizabeth sought to get employees to widely use social media to showcase CSR activity. Elizabeth had managed breaches in social media use.

**Elana**: IT Manager, BSc. Elana was an avid social media user and very passionate about interconnectivity and digitalisation, internally and externally. Elana used social media to develop her identity and for knowledge creation. She loved the fact that social media could be used for on-the-ground public journalism to challenge societal issues. Elana was responsible for social media development and training. Elana used a plethora of platforms, including Facebook, Pinterest, Instagram, and LinkedIn.

### Tiro

**Beatty**: HR Regional Officer, CIPD accredited. Beatty used LinkedIn to develop her professional identity. Beatty managed social media misbehaviour cases. Beatty incorporated some social media development training in her role. Her approach was a traditional personnel command and control management style. Beatty regularly used social media to pre-profile recruitment applicants and surveil current employees. This was not documented in corporate policy.

**Beth**: Director, BA. Beth led large recruitment sales teams across the UK. Beth managed differing cases of social media misbehaviour and nefarious digital activity. Beth uniquely had been a victim of social media abuse by employees in her team. Beth was not a regular user of social media, which she perceived was for younger generations. Beth had some development to encourage her to use social media to increase productivity, sales revenue, and business connections. Beth used employee observation and physical proximity to workers to control productivity and discourage distractedness.

**Brittany**: Sales Recruiter. Brittany was disciplined and reprimanded for social media misuse in a previous company. Brittany resigned prior to the disciplinary outcomes. Brittany used social media for personal interaction and friendships and relied mainly on Facebook. Additionally, Brittany used Facebook interchangeably to attract and place agency employee applicants. Brittany used LinkedIn for similar recruitment purposes. Brittany had little understanding of the repercussions of her misuse. Brittany had little understanding of relevant digital policy, guidance, and disciplinary processes. Brittany had little training on social media use and had little legal knowledge of recruitment practices, general data protection, or the protected characteristics in the Equality Act.

### Vita Care

**Greg**: Director. Greg used social media to interconnect with the workforce for participatory and EV purposes. Greg was responsible for leading developments on social media policy, guidance, and training.

These organisations and the characters who work within them are used in the remaining sections of the text to provide discussion and insights into the issues associated with integrating and using social media in differing corporate contexts. These demonstrate the intrigue and fascinating individual motifs for using, leading, managing, and controlling social media in work.

**Section 2**

# Act 1

## Adopting, shaping, and staging social media use in organisations

# Act 1. Scene 1 Hegemonic forces

## How organisations adopt, stage, and use particular social media in work

This section focuses on the backstage approaches and strategies used by corporations to integrate social media in work. The coordination and control of social media work is one of the most contested terrains of work due to the duality of use. The aim, therefore, with this scene is to develop a greater understanding of management expectations and practices associated with controlling access to social media in the workplace. Sociologically, this is used as a starting point to understand how these devices impact on power dynamics, dominant values, and the arrangements for social media use in the differing corporate environments to identify how discipline emerges in this field of work. This endeavour enables a greater discussion on both HR and management practices which seek to coordinate worker's effort when using these devices. These insights interlink with how employee's conflict, resistance, and (mis)behaviour begin to unfurl in these contexts, which lead on to the next chapters.

**Key learning points**

1. Integrating social media in work differs in each corporate context.
2. Corporations determine and consent which social media platforms are accessed in each context. Some corporations operate strict regulations controlling access and use. Conversely, some corporations have no apparent regulations or policy to manage or control use.
3. Using social media is not an activity afforded to all employees. Employees in elite positions are more freely able to access these devices, whereas employees in lower frontline, operational roles are least likely to have access to use social media at work.
4. Social media and other digital technological networks, therefore, create a digital hierarchy adding to pre-existing power dynamics at work. This forms the basis of an interesting subplot focusing on wider structural inequalities which manifest themself in work, education, and society.

DOI: 10.4324/9781003137269-4

5 Individual subjectivity and personal perceptions of social media influence whether we choose to engage with them at all.
6 Lack of online engagement may be informed by a sense we are observed or surveilled, bringing forth an Orwellian subtext.
7 Laissez-faire approaches to social media use had significant legal and disciplinary implication in each corporate setting.

## Hegemony and social media in work

*Hegemony* is defined as "Political, economic, or military predominance or leadership, by one member of a confederacy or union over other states" (OED online – last accessed 29/09/23). In this text, hegemony is used to explore how leadership and management, who hold dominant power in organisations, develop and define parameters to control social media use in work. Focus centres on how social media are integrated and the approaches used to constrain or coordinate worker effort in this context. The aim is to explore more closely the differing ways workers are regulated in this area of work in corporate and digitised environments. Reviewing current practices will enable readers to discover ways to enhance social media use and engagement and, importantly, to critically reflect on these arrangements.

To understand the *adoption, shaping, and staging of social media* we need to first understand the lived experiences and agency of social actors. To do so, the social actors in the three integral corporate roles were asked three key questions:

*1 How does your organisation embrace social media?*
*2 Which social media sites does your corporation use? And for what purpose?*
*3 Which sites do you use individually and for what purpose?*

These questions allow a greater sense-making about the differing structural, cultural, and phenomenal characterisations of social media used in differing work contexts. The empiricism used in this text elucidates on the variances which occurred between corporate and individual social media practices, the latter of which is explored in the next scene. Each scene, therefore, identifies some unexpected behaviours which emerge and may cause conflictual issues in work for readers to reflect upon.

Understanding how social media are incorporated in work shows what happens on a daily basis in corporations. This draws attention to how these devices are agentically repurposed as a dramaturgical device (Goffman, 1959). The aim here is to provide insights into the idiographic use of social networking to enhance greater understanding of the *potentiality-of-being-oneself* online (Heidegger, 1926: 257). This helps to establish a growing nexus between digital contexts and human agency online where the individual self is much more contentious, fluid, ethereal, and nebulous.

As we become more interconnected, our online interactions contribute to a plethora of workplace and societal tensions, which percolate within our employment and social relationships (Taylor, 2018). Our identity fluidity, therefore, may jar with corporate expectations. This scene creates a wider awareness of workplace issues which are becoming more apparent.

Inappropriate use of social media is on the rise. This has a major impact on brand reputation and individuals in the workforce. This is, therefore, harder for management to lead, control, and coordinate. Therefore, HR practitioners must ethically consider how to control these devices, giving greater consideration for issues such as freedom of expression and how to work with social media within the greater blurring of boundaries which exist within and beyond work. This section allows us to reflect on developing organisational coordination and learning to address these factors to support future approaches for the regulatory nature of social media work which is equitable to all.

## Corporate adoption of social media

Essentially, no two companies will integrate its use in the same way (Headworth, 2015). This section explores how social media platforms were incorporated in the differing corporations and the extent to which social media sites are integrated in work (see Table 2.1).

Table 2.1 illustrates how key social actors in HR, management, and operational roles perceived social media was profoundly or minimally used by workforces in the different corporate contexts to highlight how integrating social media occurs.

The differing social actors in these corporations described how social media use in their different professional environments was both ad hoc and piecemeal. This highlights some confusion regarding the strategic integration of social media within working practices and further that social media is considered to be a primary concern for most workers or recognised as a true element of work.

*Table 2.1* Organisational preferences for social media

| *Organisation** | *Social media platforms used* | *Adoption level* |
|---|---|---|
| Aedis | Facebook, X (formerly Twitter), LinkedIn | Low |
| Alumno | Facebook, X, LinkedIn, Yammer, blogs | Medium |
| Charta | Facebook, X, LinkedIn | Low |
| Pala | Facebook, X, LinkedIn, blogs | High |
| Pharma | Facebook, X, LinkedIn | Low |
| Senes | Facebook, X, LinkedIn, Pinterest, Instagram, YouTube, Yammer, blogs | High |
| Tiro | Facebook, X, LinkedIn | Medium |

* Names changed to ensure anonymity.

Exploring this more thoroughly, most workers perceived social media use was operated by marketing functions and was used to promote the corporation, brands, and services.

**Discussion box 9**

**Pause for thought:**

In your own organisations, is there a distinct strategy for who uses social media?

What purposes do these individuals use social media for? Is this clear?

Or, is social media used primarily by marketing teams?

Discuss whether you feel how workers use social media in your place of work needs clarity.

**Reflect on:**

Why do you think managers and HR practitioners are reluctant to view social media use as part of their functions of work?

Do you think corporations should allocate social media work to key individuals?

The daily reality is all workers across all functions in your place of work are encouraged to use social media to push aspects of the corporation to users and consumers of your corporate services or brands. Culturally, we will use social media to develop and use these as frontstage spaces to showcase our own individual talents.

Thinking about your own role, have you been encouraged to push corporate initiatives, maybe for recruitment, brands, or services or even to celebrate individual or department achievements? Herein lies an underestimation regarding our own labour effort in this field of work.

Greater reflection and clarity are, therefore, required on how we are expected to integrate, establish, and shape professional use of these devices. This raises the key issue for organisations to rethink and ensure that corporate reputation is upheld. This requires business function leaders to think and develop a strategy regarding the following:

1 Who has access to use social media in your business?
2 How can we develop the requisite and desired skills for use?
3 How do we regulate and control this area of work ethically?

## Strategic leadership of social media

In different organisations, both management and HR practitioners must articulate a distinct corporate strategy for social media use. Empiricism in this text illustrates how employers do not appear to have a coherent plan on how to integrate and purposefully shape social media use to promote the organisation, brands, or services. This incoherence and lack of clarity will affect the conventions of corporate digital performance and employees' social media engagement and expected online behaviours.

These perceptions correlate with wider literature suggesting that corporations are still unclear and vague about how to coordinate worker effort in this domain. This presents a key challenge for future executive leaders, HR practitioners, and management: So how do we develop digital skills and performance management tools for this type of work? Importantly, if workers are unclear about their role in developing social media use, it will impact on corporate communications and reputations via social media.

Additionally, if the stratagems for social media use are unclear, this will impact on how the workforce understands and makes sense of social media policy, regulations, rules, processes, and practices. A lack of coherent strategy for social media use in work will therefore undoubtedly problematise control of this type of work. Therefore, a starting point in the backstage preparations for developing social media strategies is to create a scaffold on how these devices are integrated as part of new ways of working which are apparent to all within the workforce for the rules of online engagement.

## Reliance on major platforms

Most organisations will be reliant on a small number of the main major social media platforms (see Table 2.1). This is unsurprising; however, it is worth reviewing from a strategic perspective. Primarily, use of social media platforms are dictated by information and communications technology (ICT) or marketing departments. This has transferability to many corporate contexts. Typically, the dominant brand platforms used in these workplaces are Facebook, X (formerly Twitter), and LinkedIn. There is a perception that these platforms are more "corporate" when promoting the corporation and brands, goods, or services. These sites are also used to simultaneously stage influential key employees as "thought leaders" in their respective industry sectors. This establishes how social networking platforms are used to accumulate power in organisations. This further influences power dynamics in work.

These platforms are multidimensional constructs which straddle society, economy, and work (Castells, 2000a). This highlights how power, societally, continues to rest with the ruling political elite, governmentality, and the role of law (Edwards, 2003; Townley, 1994). These devices, therefore, propagate, manipulate, and increase the span of power control where leaders may espouse cultural values, which may be positively or negatively received. Worryingly, use of deep fake and artificial intelligence (AI)-generated material may distort what leaders do and say. My aim here is to draw attention to how organisations and HR practices need to get a stronger angle of the unrealities that also shape social media use.

## Increasing corporate power through social media

Each corporation accumulates an economy of wealth and knowledge through online data gained on consumers and workforces via social networking sites. We are constantly observed via the algorithmic use of these platforms. This has created a new era of surveillance capitalism designed to exploit our preferences. These data can be used to further influence, manipulate, and more widely control our societal actions. We have observed this in the ability to influence how we politically vote. This commodified power, visibly, shows where digital power emerges and percolates within pre-existing societal and corporate structures (Townley, 1994). Therefore, there is a need to be more aware and shrewder of growing forms of corporate power (Zuboff, 2019).

We need to be more sceptical in how these platforms feed off our human experiences. This premise is used to question the everyday practices and tactics associated with this area of work which has often remained veiled. This could be harmful for differing types of workers. Social media use is still evolving, and what becomes more apparent is how most organisations are still "experimenting" with a variety of commonplace platforms to market brands, services, talent, and recruitment. Table 2.1 further illustrates that some organisations rely on the main platforms and others are developing use of Snapchat, Pinterest, TikTok, Instagram, and YouTube. This will naturally evolve as newer platforms become available, so societal habits change.

Each of these is also used by workers personally, so there is an appreciation that our work and private lives are now more intertwined, which cause issues for HR practices. Our online performances appear to be improvised in nature. Therefore, leaders often feel these sites are more unprofessional, social in nature, and may not represent the corporation or key workers in a positive way. The improvised nature has implications for how social media are integrated and controlled across the workforce. There is a precedence for corporations to be more mindful in developing expected online social mores, behaviours, skills, and competences to establish desired appropriate use of these devices.

**Case vignette 1: Using social media to exploit untapped potential**

In one case organisation, Senes, a healthcare corporation, chose to embrace a wider range of social networking sites (SNS). The corporate aim was to extend marketing reach to a variety of differing users. They were seeking to use social media to extend untapped marketing territory and potentiality for business development. Yet they were unclear how each platform requires differing voices or marketing approaches to develop productivity and consumer interaction. They were also not collating data on how these platforms yield results.

*HR Director:* *We don't really have a major strategy for each social network that we use, we leave this up to the different departments to decide. We encourage workers to post things on social networks. We don't really collate data or information on how successful this is.*

As a corporation, this illustrates how they were still finding their feet on how to fully gain traction on social media.
Questions

1 What problems can you foresee with this approach to corporate social media use?
2 How would you develop a framework to encourage different disciplines to develop a strategy for social media to promote the corporation, brands, or services.
3 In what ways would you collect data to analyse evidence on which platforms are working for your organisation?
4 How could you develop a coherent corporate strategy for social media use?
5 How would you review HR development needs to support employees to use social media appropriately to promote the organisation?

## Corporate perceptions of social media

Consideration is often given to how social actors in corporate environments in HR, leadership, and management roles hold deeply rooted perceptions of social media use. In this text, as I observe practices from an HR and employment relations perspectives, the dominant view is that key social actors in organisations will perceive social media to be riskier for corporate modes of communication.

In the empirical findings, many of these actors questioned whether social media was an actual element, skill, or competence of work. Therefore, social media activity is perceived to be a major distraction for workers from their key work remit which again correlates with extant literature (Moussa, 2015; Moqbel et al, 2013). Is it not time to change this perception, particularly, as the next generation of workers will be way more immersed in digital communications. Interestingly, in the case study, organisations used to underpin this text actors suggested that there was little prolific levels of social media adoption by social actors across the workforce.

In each case organisation, the social actors suggested that only elite workers or marketeers regularly used social media with any kind of prominence. Significantly, the empiricism highlighted that workers in operational or manual roles were more likely to be restricted from accessing social media or mobile devices in work. The main reason for restricting manual and operational workers from accessing social media is the perception that these workers are more easily distracted by these devices and are more likely to misbehave when doing so. This perspective demonstrates a healthy, mistrust of frontline workers, further strengthening the *us and them* mentality in work. This presents a challenge for HR practices to galvanise methods of integrating social media fairly and to radically improve the development of workforce digital skills.

## Restricting social media use

Restricting the use of social media platforms at work is commonplace. This is a simple strategy used to increase employee productivity and to try and reduce online misbehaviours which may affect corporate reputations. This approach was particularly prevalent and, therefore, highly transferable. Firewalls are commonly used by corporations to limit access to named websites and social media in controlled ways. Firewalls and control mechanisms are discussed further in Act 2.

However, I wish to state upfront that limiting access to social media and other websites is unlikely to stop unexpected online behaviour or address issues of unproductivity. This somewhat naïve perception suggests that we can demarcate and compartmentalise work in this domain. My aim here is to encourage management practitioners to rethink regulatory practices, rather than creating a barrier or rule which will definitely be broken to focus more on developing professional and ethical digitalised practices.

An important issue to take note of regarding restricting access to social media is that these rules are often not fairly applied across the organisation. Leaders, management, or HR practitioners have much freer rein to access these sites. This perception reinforces a belief that social actors in elite roles rarely misbehave or are distracted from work. This is rarely discussed, and as you will see in the next chapters, this is far from the reality. My aim here is to disavow the glorification of management, so we can be more realistic about social media policy, training, guidance, and discipline in this area of work. Moreover, with the proliferation of leaders who use social media to both abuse and accumulate power, my aim is to radically address this imbalance.

## Accessing and using mobile phones in work

It will not surprise readers that HR practitioners and wider management in commercial environments seek to control or limit use of personal mobile phones at work through relevant policy. This is loosely discussed to demonstrate regulations on mobile phone use are interlinked with our individual capability access to social media. I am not being contrived here. Often regulations and policy for both social media and mobile phones are shown in extant literature to be ridiculously hard to find, vague, or hidden in corporate settings. This demonstrates corporate failures to set parameters of use and clear rules guidelines for employee behaviour, etiquette, or rules in these areas.

So, how enforceable is it to control employees in their use of social media or their personal devices in this setting? There is a rising plethora of legislation which should link to development of online practices. If left unaddressed by the corporation, over a period of time, such laxed approaches become more subsumed into everyday practices. Therefore, embedding regulations becomes harder. The mechanisms to control social media become highly misunderstood and allow managers to author individual approaches to address differing forms of misbehaviour that are now creeping into organisations, which are more complex to manage. These are discussed later in the book.

**Discussion box 10**

- Discuss whether your place of work uses firewalls or restricts the use of mobile phones?
- Who in your organisation has access to freely use social media at work?
- Is this applied fairly to all different levels of the organisation?
- Does this create additional power dynamic and issues with transparency and fairness over social media use?
- What impact do you think restricting social media use will have on worker behaviour?
- Do you think this effectively stops workers from making online comments about the organisation or their colleagues?

## Strategic learning, training, and development for social media use

Given an apparent lack of structural ordering and control of social media work, I have sought to explore what corporate programmes of learning exist which aim to enhance appropriate social media use and online behaviours. This included exploring any policy development on management approaches for monitoring, observation, and surveillance of employees through their use of social media, or, more broadly, for workforces training on understanding corporate expectations, social media etiquette, online communication competencies, or skills.

Training and development are a fundamental HR activity, involving planned corporate interventions, which aim to facilitate organisational and individual learning in organisations (Stewart and Rigg, 2011). HR development functions may link with ICT or marketing departments who jointly develop programmes of learning for enhancement of digital skills, including AI and professional social media use.

A major empirical finding highlights a major lag in learning and development programmes which aim to shape digital competencies in this area. In the differing corporate contexts, there was no distinct across-corporation training or organisational learning for social media or digital skills for HR, the workforce, and management. Lack of development or learning for managerial advances to control social media use reinforces a laissez-faire approach, which sends out a peculiar message about acquiring professional digitalisation skills or embedding positive online behaviours. Similarly, with little practical or applied learning for the workforce to acquire improved digital skills over time, this may restrict organisational innovation in this area. Corporate failure to develop professional skills in this context may lead to wider corporate (mis)behaviours, which ultimately affect brand reputation.

Significantly, there was a perception that management and HR practitioners needed relatively little development in this work context. This inferred management and HR practitioners are seamless in this area of work and, more importantly, would not breach regulations or practices in this digital context. A discussion on management misbehaviours is largely missing within HR and management literature, with the exception of a few careful writers (Ackroyd and Thompson, 2003; McDonald et al, 2016). Yet, societally, we know powerful elite abuse social media to manipulate and serve their own interests. This has become more obvious recently with the antics of political leaders across the globe who use social media to influence the masses. This under-discussed issue of work illustrates how social media infiltrates and shifts power dynamics in this context. Furthermore, minimal corporate attempts to address inappropriate leadership behaviours on social media is becoming more prevalent. HR practices must evolve from avoiding taking evasive action to control management per se in this context. Of relevance to this discussion is how corporate elite actors may flaunt legislation or corporate social media rules, which form part of a wider corollary on management misbehaviours, as observed later in this text.

Responsible, ethical HR practitioners and senior corporate leaders now, more than ever, need to be more alert to forms of elite corporate subterfuge and misbehaviour. Corporations must listen when workers give details on issues associated with leadership unprofessionalism and abhorrent forms of behaviour. Contextually, this is important for budding HR practitioners, who should be encouraged to question and challenge unethical leadership and management behaviours in general. A number of workplace issues have become apparent where those in power have used social media for abhorrent social practices, such as sexual harassment, racism, violence, and manipulation. These affect corporate reputations and hit media headlines which highlight the need to address social media behaviour requires fundamental change.

## The role of HR in developing social media regulation and use

HR practitioners are perceived to own, embed, and develop the scaffolds which support the regulatory nature of work. A key finding in the empiricism and extant literature suggests that HR functions have little role in developing ICT or social media policy. Indeed, the differing corporate case studies presented in this text show that HR had little or no input into determining or embedding social media regulations. This is considered to influence how wider regimes of digital control manifest themself in the ordering and control of the workforce at work (Foucault, 1970; Townley, 1994). A lack of HR involvement highlights how removed or distant HR or people management practices may be becoming within digitised aspects of work or rule-making (Beer et al, 1984; Kaufman, 2015).

Disjointed approaches to rule-making are perceived to shape greater propensity for employee misunderstanding of social media use. The less employees understand regarding these dimensions of work, the greater the prevalence for (mis)behaviours to occur online. Significantly, if human resource management (HRM) practices are not fully involved in the filtration of rule-setting agendas for social media use, then somehow regulations maybe rendered invisibilised or obsolete. What became apparent in this context was that this created an environment for management to develop bastardised rules. This is where in the absence of or perceived deficiencies in rule-making, management simply take the law into their own hands making decisions on how discipline should be used, which was never fair or evenly applied in the workforce. This suggests a growing need for HR departments to work cohesively with relevant stakeholders to develop clear policy and rules on social media and digitalised aspects of work.

## Social media is not for me!

A significant empirical finding suggests that social actors in key HR roles did not see the purpose or value using social media in their or other professional roles. Naturally, this may resonate with other elite professional roles. May aim here is to say social media has a dividing nature and is not for everyone. This does have some implications for wider narratives on embedding and integrating digitalisation skills in work and, more broadly, for the HR profession.

For HR professionals, my aim here is to suggest how such perceptions may have a direct influence on corporate behaviours and potential social media skills development per se. This may feel as though HR is making a judgement about worker (mis)behaviours and identity creation before they have fully understood the value of social media work.

Interestingly, The Chartered Institute of Personnel and Development (CIPD), the UK professional body for HR personnel, has developed a skills pathway and profession map to determine key professional HR competencies, core knowledge, behaviours, and specialist categories of HR work, which they require to be an exemplary HR practitioner. The CIPD places importance on developing greater skills and understanding of digital technologies. The CIPD states that digital technologies enhance corporate communications, collaboration, and organisational agility. Furthermore, they view digitalisation as a mechanism to engender positive workforce communities and increase capacity for staff engagement and employee voice mechanisms in work (CIPD, 2024).

Additionally, the CIPD accentuates the role of employment relations as key specialist knowledge area for HR practitioners. Employment relations secure and operationalise positive working relationships between corporations and their workforces, demonstrating a symbiosis between digitalisation and the development of superior workplace cultures.

Despite the growing positioning of digital expertise in people management, the HR social actors in this study had relatively little personal expertise or experience of social media use. This finding contributes to deeper debates about HR development of professional capabilities, practices, or behaviours in this context. HR actors were more likely to feel dislocated and lagging in their social media use. As a consequence, they simply avoided or undervalued social media use as a true dimension of work. Therefore, consideration must be given to how HR practices evolve to avoid being out of touch with differing forms of digitalisation and social media use.

## To give employees social media access or not? That is the question

A clear area of confusion for HR and Management professionals in the differing corporate contexts was the need to shape regulatory approaches and employee access to social media. A key theme which was the cause of much debate centred on which group of corporate employees should have capacity to access and trust to use social media in their work. Uncovering truths about workforce access to use social media allows us to observe greater disparities and social divides which manifest themselves within corporate entities.

In these case study organisations, only white-collared and elite workers were often able to access SM. This encourages a widening of different stratifications in workforces to emerge within already pre-formed corporate hierarchies. Therefore, currently, digitalisation and use of social media add to the complexity and dynamics in hierarchical corporate structures and power. A disconcerting finding was that HR professional actors gave little critical reflection to how digital devices added to this antagonism. Little afterthought was given by HR practitioners as to how these devices could enhance employee engagement. Conversely, extant literature highlights how social media enhance employee voice (Hodder, 2020).

An appraisal of this showed how HR and management actors showed little interest in integrating digital devices as mechanisms to interconnect or engage with workers, hear workplace concerns, or use within decision-making processes. This is transferable to wider corporate contexts, particularly those where management uses highly traditional, top-down approaches for wider workforce communications, which often include one-dimensional traditional approaches such as use of fliers, posters, newsletters, or formal workplace meetings with line management. Yet corporate leaders and HR directors often struggle to focus efforts to engage or communicate with workforces. This suggests a cultural lag or innovation for employee voice.

## Elite blogging and social media

A growing significance is how corporations expect elite workers and leaders to shape their authority using personal blogs, vlogs, and accounts, either internally or externally, to voice strategy or to communicate with their workforce. Personal tweets/posts/vlogs/blogs are dramaturgical devices from where we can individually develop “front stage” personas for powerful corporate elites (Goffman, 1959; Kerrigan and Hart, 2016).

This draws attention to how leaders use social media to orate key corporate beliefs, shape aesthetic labour, and create model employee archetypes. Social media platforms obviously extend the range for us to develop our social capital and identity. Influencing vast audiences adds new dimensions for power, hegemony, white privilege, and gendered elitism within organisations. The visibility of specific elite corporate individuals ensures that the wider workforce receives cultural and aesthetic cues which shape, inform, and reinforce perceptions of leadership. We are subliminally moulded by what we access and observe in online contexts at work. These engender wider inequalities to manifest. Leadership archetypes in work settings are predominantly male and white. This continuation online highlights a gender blindness and may have implications for establishing diversity and inclusion in top-level roles.

Blogging and giving air to one’s voice in work via digital means increase the idea that managing employee voice is integral for emerging leaders. This suggests leaders must allure and hold appeal with the workforce. More importantly, these leaders, if using these platforms, must listen and hear the diversity of employee voice and engage in meaningful discussion on a range of issues. Significantly, they must respond and address these issues in real time to avoid wide circulation of issues going viral.

## Establishing employee voice on social media

When scoping online employee voice mechanisms, organisations must enable workers across all levels to have equal access to contribute and participate in voice forums, including digital platforms, both internally and externally. A greater question, therefore, is whether organisations allow employees full use of social media to express their thoughts and concerns about work for EV purposes.

The empirical findings in Table 2.1 demonstrate only two case organisations (Senes, Alumno) used internal platforms to interconnect across the organisation. Yammer was the chosen device used by these corporations. These were integrated for participatory online forums which sought to increase employee engagement and voice (Martin et al, 2015). However, the discourse regarding this online engagement suggested that participation was ad hoc, and further findings revealed that these sites were not well integrated or used coherently. Additionally, findings highlighted how management actors perceived these sites to be "moaning shops" for workers rather than mechanisms to hear concerns and explicitly address workplace issues. Interestingly, in all case organisations, some employee groups were unable to participate or regularly access internal employee voice platforms during the working day. This disproportionately affected workers in manual, operational roles where use of PCs or mobile phones were not allowed or used for work activities. This reinforces how some workers may feel disempowered by participatory voice mechanisms, contributing to a perceived unfairness in decision-making and being heard when raising concerns at work. Therefore, digital technologies in work may contribute to wider subdivisions and structural tensions in contemporary employment relationships.

## Factors influencing social media adoption

The following factors, therefore, influence the adoption, integration, and engagement with social media use in work.

### *Factor 1: Clear strategic aims for social media use*

A key theme for critical consideration is how organisations lack a clear strategic direction for adoption and participation of social media use. This structural factor is evidenced in the following participant quote:

> We have a Facebook page …We've got a Twitter account, but we've not got any strategy behind that, so we are not clear on why and how we use it [social media]…Facebook seems to be a moaning ground for our disgruntled customers.
>
> (Aedis, Alex, HR Manager [p. 1 line 3–6])

This view contrasts with wider literature which suggests social media is used constructively for business purposes. In this case study, the social actor, Alex, an HR manager, illustrates a confused strategy and integration of social media in work. This perspective is not unique. Therefore, leadership and management must figure out how they develop strategic use of social media to communicate to their workforces and consumers. Importantly, corporations must develop routes which integrate professional and equitable use of social media for all.

This case study Aedis, a social housing organisation, had no visible strategy to integrate social media within the business portfolio. The quote illustrates how use of social media was highly confused and had become a contested area of work (Edwards, 1979). The online platforms were being commandeered by consumers as a complaint's forum rather than a corporate engagement platform or branding initiative. This provides a key insight into how corporations must carefully integrate social media to avoid a negative market position and impact on corporate reputation.

#### *Factor 2: Developing social media skill sets*

Discussion in this section highlights how employees require greater training and development on social media or online with peers, consumers, and wider organisational stakeholders. This should resonate with all organisational professionals. Incorporating structured programmes to educate workers in online environments will potentially minimise risks for organisations, particularly if the parameters of use are more clearly defined.

This draws our attention to potential legal issues as social media interactions increase the likelihood of conflict between consumers and employees who may defend their work or the organisation online, as illustrated in the UK case British Waterways Board v Smith (UKEATS/0004/15, August 3, 2015). HR departments must not simply create regulatory approaches to stop employees from using social media. They must reflect and develop approaches that enable employees to reflect on how to respond positively online. Establishing professional behaviours better protects the corporation and individual worker reputation from making inappropriate or litigious comments online (Holland et al, 2016; McDonald et al, 2016).

Social media interaction relies on the voluntary nature of use. Greater corporate expectation is now placed on employees to self-regulate, modify behaviours, and use common sense when posting. In my experience, common sense is neither common or sensical. Logic does not prevail in these circumstances as case law attests. HR practices need to cement greater implementation of organisational learning and goal setting in this context to develop effective digital behaviours and practices (Høyrup, 2004; Martin et al, 2015; McDonald et al, 2016; Nyhan et al, 2003).

***Factor 3: Developing a strong market position and labour resource on social media***

Social media was used mainly to create growing opportunities for business growth, securing talent and marketing opportunities. Social media activity is, therefore, synonymous with varieties of capitalism and obey a wider imperative to renew labour production (Hall, 2010). This quote illustrates this view:

> They are looking to expand the team that deals with social media. They feel it's an untapped resource. They think they are not up to scratch ...and that they're not exploiting it to its full advantage.
>
> (Alumno, Davina, HR Policy Development [p. 1 line 1–8])

This discourse emphasises the growing role of human agency and performativity in social media work (Townley, 1994). Digitalisation is driving radical change in labour production and increases growing pressure to rationalise structural factors at work (Briken et al, 2017). Growing emphasis is now placed on exploiting social networking to increase corporate presence and market share. In this quote, Davina draws attention to how social media activity may lead to greater work intensification. Developing social media skills is often placed on and shaped by individual workers, not specifically captured within job specifications or descriptions. There is often nothing definitive captured about the effort or effectiveness of this type of work, unless associated with a core digital marketing role.

Yet corporations capitalise through our social capital and wider digital networks. As shown, social media increases the visibility of key personae or corporate entities on a local, national, or global scale. Having an online presence for key individuals, brands, or services is vital. Core elite workers are encouraged to participate in marketing or corporate branding activity via social media. Yet there is little control or rule setting regarding what this type of work would look or feel like for individuals. This suggests this is still a confounding area of work where calculability of labour processes or activities in this domain is not eschewed.

HR and management practitioners must place greater emphasis on how to establish best practice criteria or measure online performance against key performance indicators in this work.

This prompts several clear questions for readers:

- What does social media effectiveness look like?
- How will social media ineffectiveness be observed, viewed, or monitored?
- If an individual was perceived as underperforming in this area of work, how would this be reviewed and addressed?
- What would punitive action look like for social media use?

- If employees did not have a predilection to use social media, would they be forced to go into more digitised worlds? Or, would they be dismissed if they refused?

***Factor 4: Increase the adoption-innovation of social media***

A key narrative reveals social media use is not broadly adopted by employees across all stratifications of the organisations. This illustrates how fragmented and unplanned social media use is in organisations. This demonstrates how developing interconnectedness on social media across organisations is challenging. An HR director, Erica, elaborates on fragmented use in her organisation as follows:

> It [the organisation, Senes] has embraced it [SM] on a very mixed level ... I tend to think of the adoption-innovation curve when I think about Senes, … that is so true about social media here. There are some early innovators who see the opportunity and have been trying to push it for some time. There's a chunk of people who are the kind of late majority and are starting to now get it, but we have some laggards who are still doing the whole "this has got nothing to do with me".
>
> (Senes, Erica, HR Director [p. 2 line 2–6])

This reveals how employee adoption of social media use is affected by individual, personal preferences to embrace digital devices. Some employees will view social media use as a strange uncharted territory of work or their social lives.

Therefore, social media is not for everyone. Indeed, some people will only use devices sporadically. Some may find social media frustrating or find the whole experience off-putting. My view here is that we should not force people to use social media. Equally, we should think carefully about who we want to be the adopters and practitioners in this area of work. This should not be just limited to "young employees"; in general, we need to be much more integrative and diverse in encouraging individuals to use social media, this in turn will who showcase and value the different employees in our workforces.

I wish to add that there are clear valid reasons workers will choose not to use social media. Principally, ethical personal choices and preferences suggest some social actors really disliked and feared being on these devices. This is still an underdefined, highly unspecified niche area of work. The rise in case law adds to a sense of nervousness and potential precarity in this context.

In this case study, Erica, the HR director, conceptually links social media use to the Everett Rogers (1962) model of adoption and innovation. This conception was referred to in three separate HR actor narratives, signifying a growing marketisation of digital work.

Most workers are highly unclear about whether using social media is, in fact, a full part of their role or not. Therefore, more tangible expectations of social media use in employment is perhaps required. The discourse suggests that many social actors felt social media use impacted on their privacy and right to express themselves freely (Taylor, 2024). This is transferable across all global corporations. Social actors have differing motivations to use these devices personally or professionally and are indeed wary of use due to a fear of employment repercussions, particularly as legislation is tightening on issues such as freedom of expression in this area.

Significantly, personal choice to use certain platforms may conflict with a professional and private sense of self. Some platforms are quirkier. Tinder, Grindr, Snapchat, TikTok, and Only Fans have all influenced recent employment case law where use of these sites contradicts expected in-work behaviours. Such activity has led to an increase in corporate power to monitor, observe, and surveil personal use of such sites.

Corporations, therefore, have a duty to educate and protect workers. Some sites indulge in online content which is subversive or harmful to others in society. For example, content observed on Only Fans is perceived to be exploitative, manipulative and represents wider societal misogyny. We need to ensure we educate workers to be more mindful and reflect on this before engaging on these sites. Additionally, secondary forms of employment through these sites will undoubtedly impact on individual and corporate reputation. This conflict of interest needs to be made much clearer for workers to avoid confusion regarding contractual obligations.

***Factor 5: Integrating social media for recruitment or marketing purposes***

Most organisations acknowledge social media activity is aggregated into two distinct areas of business: marketing and recruitment of key personnel as the following quote illustrates:

> The company only uses social media only from the part of recruitment and marketing… they'll use LinkedIn, they'll use Facebook, they will tweet and we probably have different directors through the business that tweet as well.
>
> (Charta, Fiona, HR Manager [p. 2 line 2–5])

It is commonplace for organisations to primarily use these devices for the purposes of marketisation and attracting talent. Corporations will readily use social media for employer branding and to showcase the organisations as a great place to work. This is an important subtext for HR practitioners.

Corporations can be rated for employment matters on social media sites such as Glassdoor. This has implications for attracting and retaining talent. Employers must, therefore, become shrewder on how to manage employment relationships to avoid being negatively critiqued in online forums by angry ex-employees.

For recruitment, LinkedIn and Facebook are regularly used. Yet, there was no distinct mention of an overarching recruitment strategy on these devices. In fact, most organisations simply posted jobs and career advancement in an ad hoc and random way online. Significantly, all HR and management actors "observed" candidates in a very untargeted, undefined ad hoc ways, primarily via LinkedIn and Facebook, which were used to scrutinise or judge applicant profiles (McDonald et al, 2016). This was explained as a method to root out undesirable behaviours or to protect organisations from negligent hiring (Biro, 2011). However, this activity was conducted in a very unstructured and unregulated way which was perceived to be highly subjective, biased, and may lead to potential breaches of applicant privacy. Importantly, there was confusion in methods to judge applicants and what should corporations do if applicants could not be found via LinkedIn; does this render the persona non grata and deemed untrustworthy by their lack of presence? Such subjectivities are problematical for HR practices. More research and development is needed to scrutinise this issue further.

#### *Factor 5: Employee representation*

This trope focuses on the perception that social media use requires greater regulation to ensure employees represent the organisation positively. The following quote made by an HR officer illustrates this point:

> …how do you represent the business when we want you to and then how do we rein it in when it gets out of control.
>
> (Tiro, Beatty, HR Officer, [p. 2 line 3–7])

In this context, the social actor intimated a corporate need to protect the organisation from the risks of employee online comments. This actor consistently highlighted legal tensions which now exist in this context. This perspective implies employee online activity regularly goes out of control. This subtly alluded to a perceived organisational need for greater monitoring of social media (Briken et al, 2017). This elucidates on growing corporate surveillance and discipline in this context.

Beatty used a metaphor to *rein* in SM use. This denoted the physical act of disciplining and harnessing animals. The metaphor is interpreted to mean a clear organisational need to restrain employees from making unprofessional social media comments. This perspective exposes subtle hegemony, where unnoticed levels of subordination and punishment appear within this context. This highlighted the precarity, subjugation, and advancement of management control in this context (Blyton and Turnbull, 2004). Most elite actors in this study used social media to observe, monitor, and surveil co-workers or future applicants via their online activity. Only one HR and management actor interviewed stated they would responsibly and ethically avoid making subjective judgements of workers. In my view this position is harder to maintain. The aim here is to suggest we must encourage HR practices which are more vigilant to the increasing subjectivity used by managers and recruiters who now rely more heavily on social media surveillance activities when hiring workers.

***Factor 6: Lurking, monitoring, and surveillance***

New forms of surveillance are more prevalent and emerging in this context as the following quote illustrates:

> They have been looking at how we [employees] use social networking and in particular the views that are portrayed on there.
>
> (Pharma, Georgia, HR Manager [p. 2 line 4–7])

Georgia, an HR manager, highlights the intangible nature of emerging surveillance practices in these contexts. This is linked to power relations and the corporate need to control or punish employees (Foucault, 1975; Townley, 1994). This was alluded to in the narratives of actors in HR and management roles regularly. These actors commented on surveillance activity being undertaken by remote third parties to ensure that employees represent organisations positively (Taylor, 2018). Yet surveillance in this context was a very little understood area of regulation and devolved practices for all actors.

Observation and surveillance link to Foucauldian discourse on power and the concept of panopticon (Foucault, 1975), as discussed in Section 1. These disciplinary approaches are perceived to impact on relational dimensions of trust and communication in the employment relationship (Kizza and Ssanyu, 2005).

Thompson (2016) suggests that the contemporary work contexts facilitate use of technology as an electronic panopticon which employees will naturally seek to resist. This illustrates how conflict, resistance, and misbehaviour in work will become more present in this domain.

Surveillance by managers and leaders in this study played a dominant role in their dramaturgical performances (Goffman, 1959). The narratives demonstrated surveillance activity was informally achieved and largely unnoticed:

> I find that I am an observer rather than an active participant.
>
> (Alumno, HR Policy Development Lead, Davina [p. 9 line 3])

The practice and technique of surveillance is achieved by the actors' discretion. In this case, this was characterised by the conception of lurking or silently observing peers online. Lurking is the act of simply watching without actively participating with co-users. This is perceived to be an increasingly active part of our day and will intersect within all employment relationships. I simply emphasise this to suggest this activity is opaque and highly unregulated. Lurking is of interest as it suggests a veiled and obscure form of observation which supports a reification of emerging forms of wider veillance practices to more greatly observe workers (Taylor and Dobbins, 2021).

The notion of social media as a digital panopticon is interesting as our online observation tower may also be used to subvert the surveillance process. Foucault stated:

> He who is subjected to a field of visibility, and who knows it, assumes responsibility for the constraints of power, he inscribes himself the power relations in which he simultaneously plays both roles, he becomes the principle of his own subjection.
>
> (Foucault, 1975: 202)

What I love about this perspective is how it illustrates the contradictions, reality, and actuality of social media users who are under constant observation. Paradoxically, as actors, we are both the observer and the subject. This means that leaders and HR practitioners are also under more scrutiny if they use social media. Thus, there was a growing fear of the wider repercussion of any perceived digital forms of misbehaviours which become more visible even for those in power which conceptually link to sousveillance (Mann et al, 2003).

Lurking as a concept led to an emerging pattern across the study. All actors suggested that they used social media voyeuristically to observe wider peer groups or to observe actors. Nine HR actors consistently referred to observing images of online nudity and debauchedness. This further strengthened a perception of a strong moral HR identity which is considered distinctly different to ethical codes of HR practice (Bandura, 1999). Sceptically, this created a fissure between those who were judging employees fairly and perhaps those who held more biased or stereotypical views which was more discriminatory of younger co-workers.

Lurking links to dramaturgical aspects of work. The art of spying on one another for the purposes of manipulation is akin to the role of Iago in Shakespeare's play Othello, who used trust, observation, and manipulation of contexts to gain power. Therefore, HR practitioners need to be aware how social media allows workers to create knowledge and power through their increasing use of digitised environments.

My teenage children would say this is *snakey* behaviour. Being *snakey* replicates showing coldness, venom, or deceitful cunning behaviour. We therefore may use social media profiles to snitch on co-workers. For example, if we are "supposed" to be in work and call in absent with a feigned illness and are then observed on Facebook to be socialising in a "restaurant or bar" inevitably our co-workers will naturally feel aggrieved. The anger this causes will then allow indviduals to exercise their right to snitch or tell-tales to management for the purposes of retribution. Therefore, social media adds to the complexity and intensity of work and trust within employment relationships. This emerging form of misbehaviour is discussed in Act 4 Scene 2.

Interestingly, social media *veillance* practices are often not captured in social media policy. This is confounding and perceived to impact more broadly on employee privacy (Miller and Weckert, 2000). This raises issues on the subjectivity and regulations applied to surveillance, sousveillance, forms of observation, and monitoring in this context. Forms of surveillance are included in legal advice and guidance (GOV.UK 2024). This suggests management may observe employees to ensure social media and work compliance. Monitoring and observation were only formally captured in three policies within this study (Pala, Alumno, and Charta).

This section highlights a variety of complex issues which circulate around the integration and controlled use of social media at work. My aim here is to highlight greater considerations regarding the purposes of social media use in work. This requires a coherent strategy, and all social media use needs to be articulated more broadly in employment contracts and policies. This may include rules for professional engagement, who has access to use social media, and how do we control and monitor employees.

I wanted to position the different mechanisms and approaches for integrating social media in work, thereby adding to new areas of debate. This section shows how this domain of work is applied in ad hoc, subjective ways with little strategy to scaffold appropriate social media use. The next scene focuses on the individual and unique ways workers adopt and use social media.

# Act 1. Scene 2 Players and voices

## How differing organisational actors adopt, stage, and use a variety of social media in work

The exploration into social media use has so far focused on the way the corporation integrated these devices into work with mixed effect. In this scene, I focus on how the individual social actors in the differing corporate contexts chose to use, adopt, and stage themselves on social media. These actors hold fundamental professional roles within human resources, operational management, and frontline work. This is important as HR and management roles are integral to the agenda setting, decision-making, and regulatory practices for controlling, managing, and establishing work routines which incorporate how we as workers use social media or digital devices in work.

By focusing on the individual preferences for using social media, I aim to highlight the divergence of use between individuals in the workforce and that of the desired corporate employer preferences. Understanding the differing personal characterisations of using social media allows us to understand more deeply held knowledge and perceptions of the disciplining self in this domain (Townley, 1994).

Extant literature has focused on the need for effective control of workers seeking their compliance and autonomy. Yet due to changes in the formal and informal organisation of work, more subtle kinds of behaviour are emerging which are more difficult for management to control (Friedman, 1977, Ackroyd and Thompson, 2003). My aim in exploring the personal use of social media is to establish where the antagonisms and fissures emerge in this digitised context of work. This will allow us to more greatly understand the impacts this has on our employment relationships more significantly (Taylor and Dobbins, 2021). This scene, therefore, acts as a foreground for how conflict, resistance, and (mis) behaviour in work become more apparent.

**Key learning points**

- Individual social media use differs from corporate use.
- Age, gender, and status affect personal social media preferences.

DOI: 10.4324/9781003137269-5

- Low or no use of social media affects employee voice and impacts on wider stakeholders in the employment relationship such as trade union representation.
- Social media allows power and control to become more visible and unequal.
- Critically, violence and sexualisation on social media impact on female workers more significantly, forcing them to withdraw from online interactions.

## Social media and individual employment relationships

This scene captures the formality and informality of rule setting, policy, and practices which are applied by individuals to their social media use in and beyond work. Informality is of utmost interest, as we use social media for more than simply work. The blurring of boundaries between our private lives and employment is hugely complex, particularly for corporations trying to regulate and control social media use, which moves beyond working hours. This space allows corporate management and HR actors to observe an increasing fluidity in worker identities which appear after the working day, which are more visible and may be non-conformist to corporate expectations. This allows for new forms of (mis) behaviour to emerge. This has far-reaching consequences and presents greater challenges for managing the once traditional boundaries which previously existed. As a consequence, the gap between these hemispheres is narrowing, causing competing tensions in work relationships (Holland and Bardoel, 2016). Little is known about the effects social media have on individual employment relationships. This scene aims to gain greater understanding of these individual motifs and focuses on how actors in key roles may adopt and use social media themselves.

## Adoption of social media by professional role

Understanding individual preferences for social media use is important and provides greater insight into sociocultural dimensions of work. Exploring individual motifs establishes how social actors in differing roles may adopt, experience, or even reject social media. This links to ethicality, morality, and the harmful exposure these sites may cause workers and draws attention to how we use and access social media in their profession or personal lives.

Whilst large corporations have an online presence, we need to be more alert about how workers experience digital contexts to reflect on the psycho-social and well-being impacts these devices have on individuals. From an employee relations and human resource management (HRM) perspective, we need to understand whether the rule-setting agendas and performance management processes are effective in this area of work. This is much more nuanced due to the boundary-spanning nature of social media. Furthermore, we need to more deeply understand the complexity of this type of work and the discretionary effort of employees who use digital devices in their roles. In order to drive responses to this theme, each individual actor was asked two associated questions:

- *Which social networking sites do you use?*
- *What purposes do you use these sites for?*

The following sections focus more deeply on the worker preferences in these key roles.

## HR practitioners' social media adoption and preferences

This section uses the empiricism to illustrate how social actors in key HR roles stated they use social media in and beyond work. Typical roles these actors held were HR directorship, HR business manager, HR business partner, employee relations policy lead, learning and development experts, and HR advisory and administrative. These roles are fairly transferable in large corporations. These roles are integral in developing and shaping HRM, people management, and workforce strategies. These roles combined are largely responsible for the development of workforce policy, guidance, and a variety of practices to support people management in corporations, including how to develop and enhance social media practices at work.

Table 2.2 demonstrates HR practitioners' social media preferences and levels of use.

*Table 2.2* Individual HR actor preference and adoption of social media

| *Organisation* | *Name** | *Social media platforms* | *Adoption level* |
|---|---|---|---|
| **Aedis** | Alex, HR manager | LinkedIn, Facebook | **Low** |
| **Alumno** | • Davina, HR manager | LinkedIn, Facebook | **Low** |
| | • Debbie, policy development manager | LinkedIn, Facebook | **Low** |
| **Charta** | • Fiona, HR business partner | Facebook, LinkedIn | **Medium** |
| | • Flo, organisation development manager | Facebook, LinkedIn | **Low** |
| **Pala** | • Claire, HR director | LinkedIn, closed Facebook group, Facebook | **Medium** |
| | • Charlotte, HR consultant | Facebook | **Low** |
| **Pharma** | Georgia, HR business partner | Facebook, LinkedIn | **Low** |
| **Senes** | Erica HR director | LinkedIn, Facebook, X (formerly Twitter), external blogs, Avatar blogs, Yammer, Pinterest | **Extremely high** |
| **Tiro** | Beatty, HR advisor | LinkedIn, Facebook | **Low** |

* Names changed for anonymity.

The findings shown in Table 2.2 may be understood in several ways. First, it could be said HR practitioners perceived social media use to hold little value in work. Many HR practitioners stated they personally were low adopters of social networking platforms. Furthermore, these actors perceived these devices to be more socially motivated devices, not business tools.

Significantly, their HR role in discipline and grievance procedures and observing growing patterns of misbehaviours at work had influenced their perceptions of social media. They discussed their unlikeliness to engage in wide use of social media for the fear that they may observe acts of workplace misbehaviour or deviance online. Thus, most HR practitioners were found to shy away from interconnecting or making "friends" with work colleagues, as they perceived this would undoubtedly add to their workloads in disciplining members of the workforce.

The empiricism suggests HR practitioners are mainly likely to use LinkedIn to interconnect with other HR peers. This was primarily for their own continuing professional development (CPD) to gather HR information and advice or for recruitment and selection processes or personal networking purposes. This correlates with conceptions of homophily and a perceived need to interconnect with like-minded peers (Christakis and Fowler, 2009).

LinkedIn is therefore used as a dramaturgical device to reinforce and stage their individual professional HR identities. This *stage* was used to highlight and share their individual personal expertise and social capital as part of their roles. Examples of this were recruitment leads connecting with potential candidates, head hunting specialists, or recruitment agencies to source candidates or applicants. Other uses of LinkedIn were to gain external advice or share ideas on new innovations in employment legislation, policy adaptations, or wider HR practices and issues.

Recruitment sourcing is an emerging trend where social media is used to search, assess, or identify engagement with potential talent (Headworth, 2015). This is of great interest. Sourcing focuses on interacting with non-applicants with the aim of persuading users to become viable candidates for specific organisational jobs. A concern with this digital recruitment trend is how it may widen the threshold for potential discriminatory practices in recruitment to manifest. Extant literature suggests this practice dangerously violates equality legislation, inclusive processes, and practices, affecting marginalised groups who are most at risk from being discriminated in recruitment processes (Kroll, Veit, and Ziegler, 2021).

Advice on sourcing suggests this activity gives access to those in organisations who are perceived to have a potential kind of market value (Headworth, 2015). This rests on using key word searches such as job title, company, skills, and location, and more concerning is that guidance suggests using images to source people. Wider bodies of research have raised concerns regarding the conception of sourcing and pre-recruitment profiling, which have come under wider moral and ethical scrutiny (McDonald et al, 2016). This suggests hidden levels of bias exist in HR professional practices.

Sourcing links to the concept of aesthetic labour, where we judged on our individual appearance, voice, and attributes for the purposes of recruitment or career prospects (Nath et al, 2016). The act of scrutinising online profiles prior or during recruitment may use our profiles to make sense of who we are. This is perceived to have many subjective levels of bias (Taylor, 2018). Individuals may also use cybervetting, a form of candidate screening using the evaluation of online information sourced about candidates, applicants, and non-applicants using internet and social media searches (McDonald et al, 2022) to avoid negligent hiring (Biro, 2011).

**Case vignette 2 Pre-profiling and vetting job applicants**

Beatty, an HR Business Partner in a large organisation, has recently advertised a job role for a receptionist through a recruitment agency.

On receiving the applications, Beatty uses the personal information gained via the application process to cross-compare with social media profiles to vet the job applicant.

Beatty uses this information to ascertain whether the applicant details, experience, and skills are verifiable. When looking at the first applicants shared Facebook material, Beatty notices they have a neck and sleeve tattoos. She also notices they are posting a lot of images of them in bars and nightclubs. These images perturb Beatty, as the advertised receptionist role will meet and greet the recruitment agency applicants and key employers. Beatty thinks the looks and appearance of the applicant may put their agency clients off. She decides to do wider probing into the client. She searches on several different social media platforms to see whether the images and behaviours correlate. Other images show the applicant out at other alternative events where the dress code is more provocative.

Beatty feels she cannot pursue the application.
Questions:

1 What do you think to the HR practice of pre-profiling?
2 Do you think there are any ethical issues in judging applicants by their appearance and behaviour using their online profiles?
3 What do you suggest corporations should do to address issues of unconscious bias and subjectivity?

Such practices infer HR and management practitioners require or use a high degree of moral reasoning and fair criteria to shape these labour market and recruitment processes. The empirical findings illustrate that this is increasingly more subjective. My point here is to query who challenges HR practices like this in organisations, given HR is the moral compass in many organisations. Who decides what is moral or amoral in this context given that this is usually positioned within HR.

Corporations place an awful lot of trust on HRM practices and in HR social actors to be objective and unbiased. This unearthing poses an ethical conundrum for the HR profession. To illustrate these concerns, I now delve deeper into findings regrading HR practitioner's use of social media.

## The unsocial media self

A pattern emerged when cross-comparing individual HR actors. Most acknowledged they were unlikely to widely interconnect on a variety of social networking sites (SNS). Unsurprisingly, all HR actors discussed a need to control their individual digital profiles and content (boyd and Ellison, 2007). Many HR actors also rejected the more socially oriented social media platforms such as Facebook or Instagram (see Table 2.2). The reason these actors gave for avoiding Facebook was that they perceived it to be more difficult to manage multiple online personal identities. They were further concerned that content would bleed across these sites causing an issue between their professional and more personal sense of self. This conceptually links to the phenomenon of social media leakage (Kerrigan and Hart, 2016). This is where use of different sites begins to seep into one another. The HR actors felt their use of social media may erode or distort their otherwise clean, professional identity. This in itself is interesting. On one hand, this is pragmatic and suggests we can protect our private lives. Yet, on the other hand, as practitioners, they were making subjective judgements about applicant lifestyle choices.

This demonstrates HR actors perceived sites like Facebook were synonymous with a more socially uninhibited sense of self (Taylor, 2018). Whilst HR professionals suggested they rarely used Facebook personally to post, contradictorily, these actors were simultaneously using Facebook to regularly lurk, monitoring, judging, and subjectively determining the actions and behaviours of employees, applicants, or candidates. These sites, therefore, held great allure for HR actors to more widely observe co-workers.

This illustrates that surveillance activity by HR actors occurred in highly veiled ways. This covert type of online (mis)behaviour was often forgotten and over time has become reified (Islam, 2012). This is an important finding. This suggests corporate rules for monitoring or observation are ignored or more concerningly do not apply to HR professionals. Remember, HR practitioners, in essence, are the regulatory, ethical, and moral compass of the organisation.

Often, employees are totally unaware that pre-profiling activity was going on around them. This brought the asymmetry of power and knowledge into sharper focus. This is not simply occurring in small pockets in organisations. Facebook and other sites are used to regularly harvest information and data about us. Artificial intelligence (AI) and wider digital technologies used to judge us are big business. There are ethical concerns about such calculability which renders innocent individuals at the mercy of practitioners (Zuboff, 2019; Taylor and Dobbins, 2021). Moreover, these findings illustrate how pre-profiling is an invasion of privacy by people with very little discernment or training in observing online behaviours. Importantly, this sheds light on how practitioners may not be using fair methods of skill analyses to measure online performances with relevant job criteria.

## Personal branding

As with all users, HR actors suggested they adopted certain platforms to build their social capital and showcase their individual identity for the purposes of career advancement as this quote by an HR director illustrates:

> I think there's a personal benefit to individuals. So there is the personal branding thing. Personally, I've developed my career through social media, so many of the people I know and collaborate with today, those relationships have come through social media and transitioned into real life relationships.
>
> (Senes, Erica, HR Director [p. 5 line 33–36])

This highlights how adopting social media networking more broadly enhances employability prospects for any aspiring HR elite actor. In this case, Erica relished her chance to stamp her leadership identity within this virtual corporate auditorium. Erica discussed how she enjoyed participating in digital activities where she could be observed and heard by her peers across the organisation. Staging herself on social media had developed her own unique personal brand on a much wider, more immediate scale and had enhanced her networking capacity and professional friendship circles.

Erica was not alone; other HR actors spoke of how these platforms are crucially important dramaturgical devices to stage and marketise their professional capability as this HR actor suggests:

> The lightbulb moment, actually, you know, was this is about marketing me as an individual in the organisation. And then as an individual who maybe looking for work, I see it as a promotional tool for me.
>
> (Aedis, Alex, HR Manager [p. 13 line 18–20])

Using LinkedIn is commonplace; we all use this as a mechanism to reinforce a positive construction of self and promote our individual labour as a marketable commodity. In the above case quote, Alex uses the metaphor of a *lightbulb*, suggesting a eureka moment and realisation that these platforms are hugely powerful for potential career advancement.

I have illustrated cybervetting, profiling, and touting for work are emerging as subtle forms of behaviour/(mis)behaviour. Using social media to vet and pre-profile applicants builds on previous extant literature (McDonald et al, 2016). In this text, I hope to show how HR actors are knowingly using profiles being subjective and eliminating applicants based on flimsy evidence. In the second issue, touting for work is perceived as a form of workplace disloyalty. Using LinkedIn to tout for work forms a central tenet in employment law where a great emphasis is placed on the battle for corporations to harness commitment. In Whitmar Publications v Gammage (Section 2.13), use of these devices for self-promotion was a catalyst for wider tensions in the employment relationship where one can ultimately be dismissed for touting for employment. Any mention that you are seeking work elsewhere is likely to go down badly with an employer.

This is also an interesting dilemma for HR practitioners where their remit is to retain and harness talent, including their own. So is Alex breaching corporate expectations? This will be dependent on the corporate culture. Ultimately, if we are to advance our personal careers, we are ensnared in building a sleek digital profile in order to advance and become a member of the corporate elite. This requires us to understand the social mores and cues dictated by corporations in this context.

Moreover, this is a contradictory situation. Leaders and key corporate experts must now develop core digital skills from which to stage and orate corporate views, actions, and behaviours. These often complement wider organisational marketing initiatives and employer branding exercises to showcase workforces' talent digitally. It is, therefore, likely that corporate social actors may get head-hunted for their skills. I will add developing slick profiles was not perceived as a core skill and was viewed as a personal endeavour. Not one of these case study corporations held workshops to support individuals in developing their digital persona and identities. I also surmised that some actors, regardless of role, disliked the idea of acting or "showing off" in both on- or offline settings to vast audiences. My point here is HR development (HRD) is required in organisations to aid workers to showcase themselves and the corporation on social media.

**Discussion box 11**

**Discuss:**

In your place of work or study, are there any social media development programmes?

Do these include how to shape your online professional profiles?

Do you think workers need support to develop professional profiles?

**Pause for reflection:**

What is your view on workers who reject social media use in work?

If workers refuse to use or develop social media profiles in their work role, how would this impact on performance management and disciplinary measures in work?

## HR blogging and influencing

As suggested in the previous *scene*, many organisations require elite leaders to shape prominent online profiles through social media influencing and to develop professional blogs, vlogs, and podcasts. Two actors in this study, Clare and Erica, held HR directorships. They both discussed how blogging and influencing were an emerging part of their role, professional status, and career advancement. Clare discussed the process she goes through to develop her online presence:

> I think about what I might want to put on my profile…what articles I have come across that I think will be good for people in terms of learning. But I am also conscious that the things I post are typically the things people would associate with me.
>
> (Clare, HR Director, Pala)

Clare articulated how she sought to establish her role, status, and power using socials to blog about her career and thought leadership. This visibly represented a forced sense of being. Clare, illustrates how she ponders the themes of her posts. There is an expectation of appearing "interesting".

Younger generations of workers actively follow, engage, and communicate with influential users who hold similar personal beliefs and career aspirations. Very little is known about the impact of these online interconnections. Corporations are capitalising on this behaviour; they cajole business leaders into using social media to influence worker and societal perceptions of the corporation and business settings. Clare described this activity in mechanistic terms, diary noting when to post. This felt depersonalised and routinised. It felt as though she was developing a script form which to perform by and thus the activity became more akin with acting. The corporate expectancy suggests leaders must author scripts and perform to large audiences. This case illustrates this activity is more nuanced. Clare was going through the motions rather than being authentically her. This was perceived as trying to retain some self-privacy by removing true personality from this activity. So, does this truly give us a "connection" with the individual?

Furthermore, Clare expressed she did not feel she possessed the requisite skills to be fully competent at blogging. This narrative relates to conceptions of emotional labour which is where we regulate and manage emotional expression within our professional role. In this case, Clare is forced to portray forced positive emotions in their working roles (Hochschild, 1983). Further, Clare did not feel confident about this activity and alluded to imposter syndrome. This activity may disproportionately affect women. Thus, greater development, coaching, and mentoring are required to enable employees to sculpt their digital space and be more fluent on platforms to promote their skills.

## Role modelling

The use of blogging emphasised an emerging pattern where HR actors felt a growing expectation in their employment relationship to act as a role model online. Two differing types of role model emerged: *avid* and *restricted* social media users.

### *Avid user role model*

The following case example highlights how individuals who were avid social media users champion their online expertise and engage with others in work:

> I'm role modelling it and I like to think that it makes me really accessible for people as well, 'cause HR in the past here wasn't accessible. So I like to think that's one way we could say: "we're real people and we're nice".
>
> (Senes, Erica, HR Director [p. 3 line 10–12])

Erica's discourse highlighted her passion for social media use. Strategically, Erica discussed how this may change historic perceptions of HR. Through the use of social media, Erica perceived she was increasing accessibility to the wider HR department and herself as a leader (Leonardi et al, 2013).

Erica's narrative reveals an interesting repetition of the word *real* in her discourse about HR personnel. This was interpreted to mean HR is often perceived as cold and remote. Social media in this case was used dramaturgically to authenticate and stage a more "friendly" approachable appearance of HR to wider work peers (Goffman, 1959). There were comparable findings with other HR actors, five of whom felt wider perceptions of HR departments were negative:

> We are a team and there is an open-door policy… we really have tried…it can be challenging.
>
> (Pala, Beatty, HR Manager [p. 8 line 49–53])

Displaying and staging identity allows employees to witness key people in potentially "real" terms. Thus, digitisation may help position HRM functions in differing ways, albeit slowly and with a degree of mixed success. A cross-case analyses highlighted how HR departments were slow in embracing social media or e-HRM. This may, in part, be due to the second categorisation of role modelling which involved individuals restricting or rejecting social media use.

***Restricted user role model***

Restricting personal use of social media was considered to be a conscious personal choice which signified both responsible autonomy showing a restraint using social media and to be perceived as a professional role model. Adopting strict self-protocols held huge significance to most of the HR actors interviewed as shown in this participant quote:

> I am an example to other people in the HR department.
>
> (Alumno, Davina, HR Policy Development [p. 3 line 7])

The cross-case analyses indicated that nine HR actors did not participate frequently on social media. Moreover, they chose not to portray their sense of self on a variety of platforms or to widely network. This established a clear pattern of restricting or rejecting social media by HR actors. This has a degree of transferability with other professional roles. Headworth (2015) suggests this is a wide-scale issue affecting organisations where the uptake to integrate digitally skilled workers is unusually slow.

So why do some HR actors limit their adoption and presence on social media. Chiefly, this was associated with what they witnessed online. Their discourse consistently alluded to observing peer nudity, drunkenness, and horseplay content. This demarcation was conceptually linked to the moral and ethical dimensions of self (Hart, 1992). These individuals were, therefore, influenced by dominant HR or working cultures which are heavily informed by the disciplinary and regulatory nature of work. This perception stemmed from HR involvement in disciplinary cases and legal guidance (Biro, 2011) as this quote suggests:

> I don't think it's appropriate that I see everything that you do in your outside world.
>
> (Pharma, Georgia, HR Manager [p. 5 line 3–8])

In this case, Georgia was reflexive about her stance to restrict her online interaction. She drew reference to the need for her personally to create a boundary between herself and wider colleagues in online contexts. This was perceived as a moral justification to socially disengage (Bandura, 2002). This action may enhance their role model status and showed a capacity to "empathise" as a key part of their sense of being (Heidegger, 1926). This highlights how HR actors may be seen as closed off from their workforces in current contexts.

## Positivity and identity reinforcement

A key discovery was that HR actors felt an inherent responsibility to portray their selves positively online:

> I never ever comment about work on Facebook, I comment on positive things. I might say that I have had a great day at work.
>
> (Alumno, Debbie HR Policy Development [p.8 line 18–21])

This discourse suggested HR actors are more likely to use social media for positive-only displays of self to reinforce their professional identity. This conceptually links to impression management (Richey and Coupland, 2016; Schlenker and Wowra, 2003). This dramaturgical representation of self in the digital contexts highlights the ongoing construct of emotional labour where actors only display positivity (Goffman, 1959; Hochschild, 1983).

Such portrayals reinforce a unitary perspective of organisations who seek to create and display a harmonious workforce online (Cradden, 2011; Fox, 1966). Using positive posts corresponds to the regulatory nature of social media policies. These may outline the tangible obligations and behavioural expectations underpinning employment contracts and contemporary employment relationships in this context (Blyton and Turnbull, 2004).

Performances of positivity online are unrealistic and are deemed as evangelical in terms of corporate life and worker behaviour (Ackroyd and Thompson, 2003; Cornelius, 2010). These portrayals further signify tensions in what constitutes positivity and may create wider breaches which now exist in employment relationships (Edwards, 2003; McDonald et al, 2016; Thompson, 2016). This creates a subjectivity in how role agency is influenced by interactions at work. This relates to Foucauldian analyses regarding institutions and, particularly, the growing emphasis placed on displays of structural relationships where actors appear more involved rather than a concretion of policy (Hatch and Cunliffe, 2013; Townley, 1994).

## HR adoption-innovation of social media

As we can see, so far HR actors seemingly adopted social media and were influenced by their elite individual status and the expectations set out by the corporation in their role. Whilst Erica derived a lot of pleasure and benefitted from using social media, Clare, HR Director at Pala, felt differently:

I confess. I'm a laggard. I'm not out there… only in a closed user group.
(Pala, Clare, HR Director [p. 4 line 24–25])

Clare's discourse revealed that she minimally used social media. Clare's dialogue was highly reflexive regarding her individual position. Clare diligently participated via posts, blogs, or communities of practice. But she felt she lagged in her capability. This demonstrated high expectations placed on her within her employment relationship (Blyton and Turnbull, 2004).

Clare was perceived to be donning a mask to carry out such activities. Her dialogue revealed confessional tones of guilt as she reminded herself to complete such digital activities. This conceptually links to the impact leaders have on influencing organisational interconnectivity and adoption of social media (Headworth, 2015; Martin et al, 2015). I interpreted her tone to mean she was fearful of breaching expectations in her employment relationship (Edwards, 2003; McDonald et al, 2016; Spooner and Haidar, 2006).

This discourse conceptually links to the adoption-innovation curve (Rogers, 1962). See Figure 2.1. The model demonstrates the propensity to adopt or resist products. In this study, 22 actors were perceived to be located in the *late majority* or *laggard* quartiles. Only one HR actor (Erica) was perceived to be an *innovator* and three actors were perceived to be *early adopters* (Clive, Anne, and Elana).

A key area influencing an early adoption of social media by HR actors was linked to their understanding that social media offered a fabulous mechanism

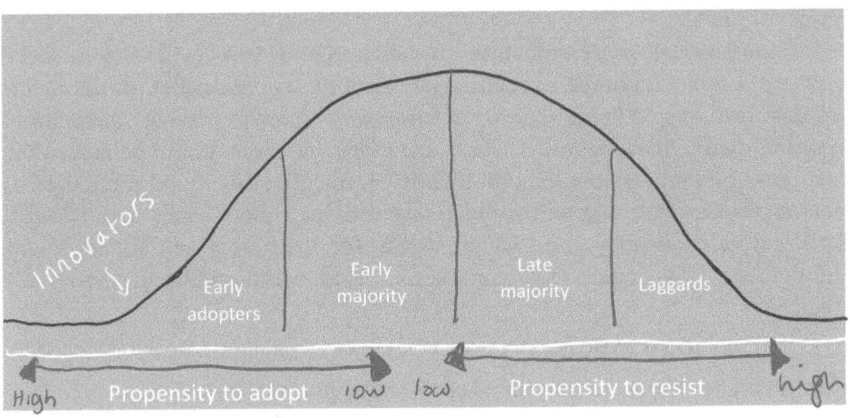


*Figure 2.1* The adoption-innovation curve.

Source: Rogers (1962).

for engaging with workers and for employee voice purposes, as this quote demonstrates (Martin et al, 2015):

> … if you're an HR person, you've got your ears to the ground and you're sufficiently out there and not sat in an ivory tower. You should know most of what people are saying to you anyway, but it does present you with another way of getting your employee voice.
>
> But I also think there's a wider element to employee voice generally, not just employees to leaders within their own organisations but through things like Glassdoor, where prospective employees, pissed off former employees are going on and talking about your company and I think it has a role to play in the trade union side of it as well … the millennials or the genzeds or whatever they're talking about … these are people who are digital natives…this is how they communicate, so you gotta be there as well.
>
> (Senes, Erica, HR Director [p. 13 line 13–21])

Erica raises the importance of embracing an online presence to engage with employees of all age groups and workers who have key stakeholder roles such as trade union members. This has become more pressing in the current context as we are witnessing more workplace conflicts due to the rising number of collective action in the last few years in the UK.

Interestingly, in Erica's dialogue she raises the thornier topic of how social media extends the parameters of the employment relationship where ex-employees use platforms like Glassdoor to comment on work experiences. This does significantly impact on employer branding and how past and future applicants rate or perceive the workplace. This illustrates how HR practices need to adapt to counteract the negative press these posts may have on corporate employer brands.

In summary, HR professionals are considered to be low-level users of social media. These actors opted to regularly restrict or segregate their social media use as a form of role modelling. Restriction was linked to personal perceptions of social media misbehaviours which are more prevalent and to enhance their own sense of a professional, moral identity. Ironically, this was contradicted by their high use of lurking and subjectively judging others using social media. Furthermore, how they used social media for their own self-advancement, highlighting how social media marketises and commodifies the self more readily.

## Management role social media adoption and preference

In the study, seven management actors were interviewed. Table 2.3 outlines their individual preferences and adoption levels of social media.

*Table 2.3* Individual management social media adoption and use

| *Organisation* | *Name* | *Social media platforms* | *Adoption level* |
|---|---|---|---|
| Aedis | Alan | Facebook | Low |
| Alumno | Dahlia | X (formerly Twitter), LinkedIn | Medium |
| Charta | Frances | Facebook, X | Low |
| Pala | Charles | Withdrawn from sites | None |
| Pharma | Greg | LinkedIn | Low |
| Senes | Elizabeth | Facebook, LinkedIn, X | Medium |
| Tiro | Beth | Facebook, LinkedIn, X | Low |

* names changed for anonymity.

The cross-case analyses demonstrated a similar level of social media adoption between HR and management actors who also minimally used social media. The main platforms used by these actors were Facebook, LinkedIn, and X (formerly Twitter). Equally, the management actors interviewed in this study also tried to segregate their social and professional use. Interestingly, one management actor had completely withdrawn from using social media altogether as they perceived this would compromise their role (Charles).

Resistance to use social media in work contexts is not unique. Archibald and Clark (2014) and Headworth (2015) suggest employees are unaware of the applicability and benefits of social media to collaborate and develop best practice. Again, this may relate to workplace cultures where control and disciplinary regimes are more hegemonic. Rarer still was how management actors in this study used platforms to communicate with workers for employee engagement or voice purposes. This shows how in the current climate management fails to use social media as a pulse-check for workplace issues, tensions, and conflict.

In the main, the findings illustrated that most management actors appeared to be perplexed by social media use. It is worth noting like their HR counterparts that the management actors were often wary to interconnect with peers or colleagues. They often opted to restrict developing workplace interconnections because of their role in performance management and disciplinary purposes. The choice to reject social media was perceived as a rigorous management rationality driven by their need to increase productivity (McDonald et al, 2016; Moqbel et al, 2013; Moussa, 2015), and more broadly, does not observe co-workers misbehaving beyond the workplace (Taylor, 2018). This demonstrated how online presence further shapes regulatory processes of labour production and collaborative endeavours at work (Briken et al, 2017).

A critical evaluation of the management actor perceptions suggested that they held highly traditional views about social media use and were unsure of the benefits of using these technologies which appeared to be an experimental enigma in work. A key point here is to reflect on the need to develop digital capability of management, as these devices continue to become part of the fabric of business (Castells, 2000b). Avoidance is perhaps not the best strategy for enhancing employee engagement.

## The generation game

Some management actors felt social media held little appeal for their generation:

> …the younger people clearly use it [SM] far more effectively …my colleague doesn't even have a Facebook account, she's 45, but the young ones who've grown up with it they come in and go "oh just put it on Facebook"... I don't want work stuff on my Facebook, it's not about that it's about keeping in touch with people I haven't seen for 30 years.
>
> (Tiro, Beth, Sales Director [p. 2 line 6–11])

These perceptions highlight how some managers may perceive that social media is for younger workers. These views, if unchallenged, further reinforce stereotypical views which dominate digital contexts. The perception that young people are more immersed on social media is prevalent in extant literature, as previously discussed in the conceptual chapters of this text (Rosen et al, 2010). Research suggests millennials, children born in 1990s, have differing levels of connectivity and work values to those born in the 1960s. This discourse was apparent in this study. Contradictorily, the youngest participant in this study (Freya) had withdrawn from social media altogether. Thus, there is a need to be wary of stereotyping use and not to ostracise any demographic in work.

Furthermore, the discourse in this case illustrates how Facebook is perceived to be more social. Again, contextually, these sites are used interchangeably. Thus, perhaps management actors may need to recast their views and hold multiple profiles so as not to close themselves away from co-workers.

## Retreating from social media use

A commonality occurred became apparent in the cross-case analyses regarding the cultural implications of social media use which forces some HR and management professionals to rethink about participating on these devices at all:

> I was [on Facebook] and I was on Twitter but I logged out of both.
>
> (Pala, Charles, Manager [p. 10 line 32])

Withdrawal from social media is now commonplace. This may coincide with a change of career, such as moving from a commercial roles into HR. This ironically reinforces how social media adoption is culturally espoused (Castells, 2000b). This further demonstrates strategic gaps in interdisciplinary use (Martin et al, 2015; Nyhan et al, 2003).

This creates a micro-political view of social media use where some management actors rejected interconnections on certain platforms:

> I wouldn't touch Facebook with a bargepole… My life is busy enough.
> (Alumno, Dahlia, Manager [p. 8 line7–8])

The management actor discourse demonstrates how social media sites such as Facebook has a somewhat polarising effect. Some actors perceived this platform impacted on the staging of a professional identity (Benford and Hunt, 1992). Dahlia used the metaphor of a *bargepole* – a long pole used to push a boat away from dock side. Her tone illustrates a strong distaste for Facebook due to the strong perceptions that it lacks certain credibility. A re-reading of this narrative inferred a perception that all social media use increases workload (Bondarouk and Brewster, 2016). This is interesting from an employment relations perspective where increased digitisation clearly adds to labour effort and creates greater complexity over what constitutes fair work (Briken et al, 2017).

Furthermore, Weil and Rosen (1997) suggest individuals re-establish boundaries when using technology to protect personal space and minimise stress. This narrative, therefore, highlights that for some social actors there will be a constant interrogation between the private and professional self-identity. In this day and age the ability to remain segregated online is complex. Thus, being online may be a potential workplace stressor for some employees who wish to retain a degree of privacy (Kerrigan and Hart, 2016).

The rejection of social media by actors in HR and management roles is perceived as a form of resistance which could link conceptually to dissent and disengagement at work (Thompson, 2016). This is unusual given that Castells (2011) postulated digital networks create power and capacity to enhance the role of leaders. Power drives a moral context where individuals are responsible for an agency to be effective in organisations; therefore, to be powerful in this context requires individuals to decide where to focus attention (Lukes, 2005).

Not being on social media is problematical for management, as they hold powerful strategic positions in corporations and additionally should ensure the appropriation and integration of social media use in work. Westaby et al (2014: 67) defined this position as *centrality*, suggesting this is an important metric for use. Management positions in this context are used as a central entity where social networks act as an additional hub and spoke structure. Yet management actors in this study chose to operate a more *panoptic* position, where their engagement with social media was seen as an extension and mechanism for tighter observation and employee control rather than for collaborative work activities. This conceptually links to Foucauldian concepts of power in management practice

(Townley, 1994). Conversely, if management actors resist using social media, this can be perceived to tilt the status quo of power balance. In the latter sections of this text, I show how employees do cast management aside from their social media groups. Furthermore, such resistance could be deemed as form of recalcitrance or interpreted as a form of underperformance which links to an emerging form of management misbehaviour This is highlighted to show how social media creates complexity and precarity for all roles.

## Selectiveness and in-groups

The cross-case analyses highlights a similarity between all actors in terms of their selectiveness in interconnecting with others. This is again problematical from an employment relations perspective as this creates the notion of in-groups and could lead to colleague in-fighting and perceived favouritism and cronyism in work as shown:

> I am friends with some employees.
>
> (Charta, Frances, Credit control manager [p. 2 line 9–11])

This highlights a potential trigger for further conflict and forms of misbehaviour to occur between work peers. The choice to interconnect with selected colleagues may unwittingly create perceived favouritism or cronyism. The ability to evaluate the merit of in-groups requires a high degree of mental processing (Tajfel and Turner, 1979). This again highlights a micro-political situation in work where some peers are favoured more than others. This could be misinterpreted by other team members as a management tactic to create power, favouritism, and compliance (Edwards, 2003; Lukes, 2005; Townley, 1994).

Self-monitoring theory suggests people differ in how they regulate, control, and present themselves in interpersonal relationships or social settings (Fang et al, 2015; Snyder, 1974). This suggests managers may lack skills to express themselves in the digital settings which require greater interpersonal navigational skills. This had a strong resonance with both management and HR actors in the study.

In summary, there are similarities between HR and management actors who often delineated use of social media to protect their assumed professional identities. This does have implications for interdisciplinary interconnectedness and power dynamics. A key predictor of low adoption by managers was their role in discipline and performance management. Significantly, management actors perceived social media to be a device for younger employees. This adds to emerging debates regarding stereotyping and bias. Moreover, the lack of digital engagement could impact on collaboration between intergenerational workforces. Further, the creation of in-groups is likely to add to wider workplace conflict and politicking in organisations.

## Employee and trade union role in social media adoption and preference

In the study, eight employee actors were interviewed, and two workers held trade union roles. Their social media preferences are captured in Table 2.4.

The cross-case analyses demonstrated employees also had varied and limited use of social media. Only three employees used social media to widely interconnect with peers and external communities (Anne, Elana, and Clive).

Two actors in trade union roles were very reticent to use social media. This was primarily due to their role in supporting employees in disciplinary hearings. One trade union representative, Gary, who worked in the manufacturing sector, coined the term *never-user* as he had not engaged in any form of social media use. Gary had a traditional preference for face-to-face communication. The other trade unionist, David, was retiring from their role as a senior academic. David saw little potential to increase use of social media for professional union activism or work purposes. These individual motifs have transferability to other corporate settings due to role, preference, and, in some case, their age (Headworth, 2015).

From a participatory, trade union, and employee voice perspective, it was interesting to observe how these two trade union social actors were not engaging

*Table 2.4* Individual employee actor preference and adoption of social media

| *Organisation* | *Name** | *Social media platforms* | *Adoption Level* |
|---|---|---|---|
| Aedis | Anne | Facebook, X (formerly Twitter), LinkedIn | High |
| Alumno | • Darcy<br>• David (trade union) | Facebook, LinkedIn<br>LinkedIn | Medium<br>extremely low |
| Charta | Freya | Withdrawn | None |
| Pala | Clive | Facebook, LinkedIn, X | High |
| Pharma | Gary (trade union) | Never user | None |
| Senes | Elana | Facebook, X, LinkedIn, Instagram, Yammer, YouTube | High |
| Tiro | Brittany | Instagram, Facebook, X, LinkedIn | Medium |

* Names changed for anonymity.

on social media. This has further ramifications for trade union engagement with workers. This correlates with wider extant literature on the potentiality to use social media to engage with new or younger members (Hodder and Kretsos, 2015; Hodder, 2020). These findings corroborate how adoption and participation are linked to a discourse on power dynamics found to exist in these digital contexts (Foucault, 1975/77), Lukes, 2005; Townley, 1994).

## Stratification of social media use

An emerging pattern of social stratification and categorising of employees was shown to exists in digital environments and thus perpetuates the notion of *Us and Them* in work between management and the workforce. The findings revealed most employee actors demarcated who they interconnected with on social media. Unsurprisingly, this was often colleagues in similar status peer groups:

> I'm on Facebook…but my manager and the Associate Director I'm not friends with them because there is a certain line to draw.
>
> (Tiro, Brittany, Recruitment Sales [p. 2 line 4–7])

This illustrates how social media adds to the already present subdivisions which tangibly exist in different strata at work. This has transferability to all organisations and has implications for strategic integration of interdisciplinary and collaborative working on social media (Nyhan, 2003). This demonstrates the complexities in establishing digital interorganisational relationships, which may add value to the business, are more complicated. Simply put, this reinforces the barriers which exist between elite and low-level employees which are routinely and further perpetuated through social media (Ehret et al, 2013). This demonstrates wider schisms in employment relations, reinforcing historic discourses of power relations in organisations (Edwards, 2003, Townley, 1994). This infers social media use is reliant on voluntary interactions and interconnectivity (Culnan et al, 2010).

## Trade unions and social media use

Interestingly, two employee trade union actors felt social media activity was a waste of time. This highly traditional view coincides with intergenerational perceptions in this study:

> …there are loads of people interested in contacting me though Facebook. I get endless emails about it…I just delete them... I'm never going to contact them.
>
> (Alumno, David, Academic/TU representative [p. 4 line 9–18])

The trade union representatives (TUR) in this empiricism were both male, white, and over 50+ years. Neither TUR actor used social media for union organising purposes. Both their narratives suggested that they felt using social media was puerile and tantamount to time theft (Moussa, 2015).

This was interesting due to the duality of their roles. Their preferences pose interesting challenges for trade union representation, organising, and membership growth (Woods, 2014 as cited in Hodder and Kretsos, 2015). This demonstrates unions with older generational leaders may need to rethink strategies on how to integrate social media to redress power dynamics or enhance employment relations in work (Lukes, 2005).

Social media has the capability to reach and attract younger memberships as adolescents are increasingly using digital rather than print forms of media (Geelan, 2015 as cited in Hodder and Kretsos, 2015; Hodder, 2020). Digital networking allows greater interpersonal connections and may create a broader base for worker solidarity, community groups, and unions to interconnect. This was addressed with David:

> ...our traditional methods of communication were not very effective. And that's been a constant theme for us I think over many, many years...because we've got low attendance at branch meetings, we rely very heavily on email and email isn't a great form of communication for that dialogue and exchange, for sharing these ideas. And we've lost something significant there. So it's a question of whether we can find that again. Social media possibly could be a way to do it. But then it requires everyone to think that that's a good way to do it. And unfortunately, that's not the position.
>
> (Alumno, David, AcademicTU Representative [p. 5 & 6 line 51–13])

Undoubtedly, social media help unions to communicate to mass target audiences at a central level and to assimilate power (Castells, 2011; Hodder and Kretsos, 2015). Whilst at a local union level, there is more work to be done in in encouraging older TU representatives to engage with social media. Whilst David did endorse use of social media more unilaterally to develop union activity locally, it was interesting to hear how this conflicted with his personal perceptions of social media. This seemed to counteract with the growing expectations of his TU role.

Further problematising this issue is the decline in trade union memberships per se. The traditional norms of unionism often lack appeal with younger workers, and, moreover, they feel concerned about the costs of trade union fees (Hodder and Kretsos, 2015; Hodder, 2020). Perhaps trade unions need to use social media more at a local level to encourage younger workers to participate and join unions. Interestingly, not all young people are immersed in using social media, as the following case attests.

## Societal impacts of social media on employees

The analysis unearthed startling, idiosyncratic, biographical experiences of social media use and activity. This revealed why some young, female actors may reject being online because of the psychological impacts it may cause them:

> Once you're out there you can't come back.
>
> (Charta, Freya, HR Administrator [p. 2 line 13–15])

In this case example, Freya, a young teen worker, had withdrawn from all social networking sites. This was due to how these devices are increasingly used as mechanisms for personal comparison, sexual exploitation, and grooming. This form of sexualised misbehaviour had a significant impact on her psychologically.

Freya's narrative echoes research on adolescents whose low self-esteem is caused by a constant comparison between their self and others online (Royal Society of Public Health (RSPH) report 2017). Relationships between social media platforms and self-esteem are incredibly complex, with differing patterns and a variety of explanations. It is argued that social media use does not affect self-esteem for most users, yet some individuals may experience negative side effects of using these devices. Research calculating person-specific side effects suggests the relationship between self-esteem and use of social media devices is influenced by individual susceptibilities which determine this is more person-centric (Cingel, Carter, and Krause, 2022).

There is a degree of concern regarding the negative impact social media use has on body image and personal appearance-based discrimination, so much so the UK government launched a House of Commons inquiry into this issue (March 2021). Findings detail growing statistics of adults and children who are negatively affected by online settings. This is also found to affect those with protected characteristics, such as age, sex, race, gender, and disability, disproportionately where our online commentary increases forms of lookism, sexism, and racism. Freya's narrative revealed the darker, more psychological perspectives associated with social media use. I am positioning this to suggest HRM practioners need to critically reflect more deeply on the impact social media use may have on some employees and to ensure greater online safety for workers (Hørup, 2004; Yanow and Tsoukas, 2009).

It has also been reported that the millennial generations are more susceptible to poor mental health despite being perceived as the most interconnected; they are conceived as the loneliest generation (Guardian, 2024). Our need to be liked and the increased competition for vast audiences and greater interconnectedness has not necessarily helped us feel any happier or positive about interrelationships. Thus, management and HR need to be more vigilant about the well-being impact of social media, which could affect psychological states such as presenteeism, induce stress, or lead to absence from work due to the poor mental health associated with its use.

Freya's withdrawal from social media contradicts the stereotypical view of younger generations. It is pertinent to note Freya was pursuing a career in HR. This case demonstrates that differing forms of observation exist which are more pervasive and have a huge impact on more vulnerable types of workers.

## Act 1 summary

This act focused on exploring and developing understanding of the structural nature of social media use at work. The aim was to develop a more holistic and revealing understanding of social media experiences in work from a multi-perspectival view from within contemporary employment relationships. The aim was to show how use of social media is constructed and scaffolded, thus affecting an individual sense of being.

Act 1 Scene 1 focused on the differing ways social media are adopted and integrated and the strategy behind their use in work. This shows the approaches are still quite improvised and evolving.

Act 1 Scene 2 focused on the individual ways social actors in key roles adopt and integrate social media. This shows these devices are dividing practices.

A key driver for success in developing social media network use in work is the corporate capability to interconnect individual actors across the different layers of the organisation stratifications (Nyhan et al, 2003) and centres on a digital effort to ensure that organisations develop a strong online presence (Ackland and Zhu, 2015). This showed how all organisations dictate which platforms are accessible to employees. These represent differing dramaturgical stages to manipulate and portray the organisation and key actors aesthetically. The cross-case analysis often revealed social media use is highly segregated and hierarchical.

Online interconnectedness was sought by all the participating organisations. However, it is argued that a lack of strategic integration impacted on both communication and interdisciplinary working on these devices. Therefore, integrating digital platforms and their use requires careful strategic planning, management effort, communication, and ongoing training. Learning and development was rarely utilised to support the greater embedding skills or hone professional online behaviours. This illustrates how there is a distinct skills shortage in this domain. This places greater emphasis on HRD interventions to drive professional use and talent as we become more reliant on these devices (Headworth, 2015). This may now include the use of AI as they both significantly intertwined.

Only one organisation in this sample established a programme of some form of limited training for social media use for some staff groups and championed its use (Senes). The remaining organisations provided training for management or

HR only on areas of social media policy. This implies HRD is used to reinforce a managerial discourse to maintain effective control to protect the interests of the organisation and establish some degree of compliance (Humphreys and Brown, 2002). This approach is associated with low-trust management regimes and lacks efficacy of the social media strategic purposes. Moreover, as you will see in Act 4, these forms of training were inadequate in addressing forms of misbehaviour.

Low-level skill sets also inhibit wider purposes of marketing, networking, and employer branding which are perceived to impact on organisational learning more broadly. Nyhan et al (2003) developed four factors of consideration for organisational learning; these are now considered:

1 *Coherence between the tangible and intangible dimensions of the organisation to reconcile with individual learning needs.*

Six organisations struggled to make sense of the tangible benefits and purpose of social media. This becomes problematical for sense-making and created a paradox for HR and management actors who did not consider social media use as a mainstream business activity. This is still prevalent today, as online activity is often an afterthought by most or the responsibility of marketing teams. Clearly, we can no longer afford to have this view. Focus, therefore, must centre on how social media could be more broadly integrated into organisations and, importantly, within the HR portfolio.

Social media will supersede use of websites and internal intranets (Bennett et al, 2010); there was evidence in the empiricism to suggest this trajectory was beginning slowly with the integration of Yammer in two organisations (Senes and Alumno). Some organisations incorporated blogging or communities of practice to enhance organisational learning. However, this was a low-level activity. The findings suggest how blogs reinforce the status and hierarchy of elite organisational actors. There are growing expectations for senior executive actors to perform visibly online (Benford and Hunt, 1992). Therefore, we use social media to stage an evolving identity and power status. This finding has transferability and conceptually relates to Foucauldian concepts. Social media creates a panoptic effect for elite actors who also may be widely examined and observed in their use. Critically, this may diminish power thresholds by use of sousveillance (Foucault, 1975/77; Mann et al, 2003; Townley, 1994).

2 *Stimulating or challenging work is a prerequisite for implementing a learning organisation.*

It can be argued that our relationship with social media creates stimulation as some individuals were avid users. However, many actors struggled with the concept of social media use. Let's face it, it is not for everyone. In this context, HR actors used online activity and content as a basis for learning about misbehaviours. The reason I posit this perception is that many HR and management actors centred on learning about what not to do online and to emphasise policies. This encultured view perpetuates conceptions of risk adversity for HRM. There was little evaluation or production of knowledge on whether policy and regulation was effective.

Only two HR actors were involved in developing learning projects such as communities of practice. This implies management and HRM could more broadly embrace social media to advance communities of practice more robustly or as a cost-effective mechanism for HRD purposes (Martin et al, 2015). This has transferability for organisations and HRM to champion social media use (Ulrich, 1997, 2010).

3 *The provision of support and guidance*

There was little evidence of coherent HRD support and guidance which sought to enhance positive engagement and appropriate social media use. Development was used to create understanding of policy and regulation for selected management, trade union elite, and some key HR actors. Development rarely covered how to engage all workers to use social media for business practices, employee voice, relationship building, or developing employees more broadly (Martin et al, 2015). This contributes to a managerial agenda of securing acquiescence and compliance. This rationalises notions of right and wrong and legitimises self-interest linked to role (Humphreys and Brown, 2002). This also reifies how HR treats employees as resources, particularly when incorporating social media (Islam, 2012). This offers a critical view of HRM and suggests a need to develop recognition for nurturing positive work relations which support employee dignity in the digital context (Briken et al, 2017). This should include use of social media as an employee voice mechanism which would not only aid organisational learning but also allow employees to contribute to decision-making processes in organisations using such technology (Martin et al, 2015). Importantly, this may also be used in closed groups to address mutual employee concerns about work practices (McDonald et al, 2016).

Ironically, perhaps support and guidance should critically focus on HRM use of social media, particularly, focusing on the unethical practices associated with pre-screening and surveillance of social media material. The findings demonstrated how HR recruitment practices using social media did not necessarily comply with equality legislation and were often prejudicial (Nath et al, 2016; McDonald et al, 2016; Moussa, 2015). Such recruitment techniques were hugely subjective which is problematical for the ethical application of HR practice in this area (Islam, 2012). This is a serious concern and involved judging people on their looks and use of body art (Timming, 2015). This view contributes to a growing body of knowledge and suggests reflexivity is required to step back from such bias. This builds on pre-existing knowledge regarding HR practitioners which suggests they avoid reflective practices (Bull and Taylor, 2014). This is positioned to suggest that HRM endorses more critical reflection to address prejudicially encultured views that HRM has created for itself.

4 *To address organisational learning, there is a need for crossing boundaries and interdisciplinary partnerships between the vocational education and training and HRD communities.*

Crossing boundaries and creating interdisciplinary partnerships in the social media context was found to be complex. There was some evidence to suggest that organisations were trying to be integrative; however, the findings highlighted existing conflicts between control and ownership of social media policy and how to interconnect between strata of the organisation. The context provided little opportunity to widely work on social media across different project groups. Islam (2012) states this creates a greater need for HRM to develop deeper ethical considerations of the workplace and to redress the imbalances in infrastructures. Islam (2012) also suggests this creates ongoing labour conflict which is punctuated by a struggle to defend ways of being. This is positioned as a mechanism for greater interdisciplinary working. In order to address social media use, HRD must work collaboratively with key organisational partners to shape and support workers to integrate the use appropriately. This illustrates why there may be a higher prevalence of online corporate misbehaviours which are discussed later in the text.

Scene 2 further highlighted the divergence between corporate and individual social media use. Engagement and participation with social media are affected by a range of factors such as psychological experiences, age, and status role. The discussion and findings reveal social media is viewed with a degree of scepticism by HR, management, and trade union actors who rarely engaged on social media. Furthermore, many actors were not fully clear on how to integrate social media in their role. This will not have changed radically. This inferred digitalisation had changed at such a pace in some organisations and how key actors were unsure and potentially daunted by these new territories. Much of the discourse highlighted an employee resistance to use these platforms.

Actors in trade union roles had strong preferences for traditional face-to-face communication, indicating the impact this has on the collective and participatory nature of social media and work. Conversely, elite HR actors found social media adoption increased the visibility of their status, networking capacity, and employability. This act therefore reveals an inherently institutional view of social media practices which are conservative and culturally determined. Table 2.5 brings together a cross-comparison of the three key roles.

*Table 2.5* Cross-case comparison of adoption and participation on social media

| | *HR Roles* | *Management roles* | *Employee roles* |
|---|---|---|---|
| **Type of SM use** | • HR elite roles are expected to use and champion SM as part of widening organisational expectations placed on them<br>• HR elite have a key role in creating communities of practice.<br>• Most likely to use LinkedIn to professionally interconnect with likeminded HR peers or HR networks<br>• Least likely to interconnect with employee groups outside HR functions.<br>• Most likely to connect with peers in a leadership role<br>• Use of LinkedIn to self- promote skills and for employability purposes.<br>• Minimal or self - restricted use of SM to protect professional identity which was viewed as role modelling<br>• Role influenced the self- restricted use of SNS<br>• Aesthetically manipulates online images to portray professional identity. | • Most likely to use LinkedIn to connect with like-minded peers<br>• Minimal SNS use in work, disconnect between marketing initiative and labour effort<br>• Least likely to connect with work colleagues from different strata in the organisation<br>• Use of LinkedIn to self-promote and for employability purposes<br>• Minimal use of Facebook and X (formerly Twitter)<br>• Role in regulation and control influenced their perception of SNS | • Most likely to use Facebook to connect socially with family and friends<br>• Most likely to connect with peers in a similar role and status<br>• Most likely to use LinkedIn to gain business connections and seek employment<br>• Gender, age, role, and sociocultural experiences influenced whether they used SNS at all<br>• Restricted on SNS use by use of firewalls |

(*Continued*)

*Table 2.5* (Continued)

| | *HR Roles* | *Management roles* | *Employee roles* |
|---|---|---|---|
| **Level of Adoption by group** | • Limited use of differing SNS<br>• Resistance and significant withdrawal from SNS<br>• Distinctive idiographic cases used SM to develop identity for growing HR leadership role, career and professional profile | • Limited use of SNS. Wide resistance and withdrawal from SNS | • Limited access to use of SNS<br>• Some rejection of SNS |
| **Purposes of SNS use** | • Self-promotion<br>• Lurking<br>• Surveillance of others<br>• Pre-screening of recruitment candidates' employees<br>• Networking<br>• Learning and development<br>• Career enhancement | • Surveillance of others<br>• Pre-screening of recruitment candidates' employees<br>• Networking<br>• Learning and development<br>• Career enhancement<br>• Affiliation and Friendship | • Affiliation and friendships<br>• Sousveillance<br>• Networking<br>• Learning and development<br>• Career enhancement |
| **Influencing factors in the restriction of SNS use** | • Role identification<br>• Age<br>• Regulation, rule adherence and legislation<br>• Case work as a predilection for minimal use<br>• Moral identity and justification | • Role identification<br>• Age<br>• Time wasting<br>• Rule adherence<br>• Firewalls | • Harassment (sexual)<br>• Gender<br>• Age<br>• Role identification<br>• Rule adherence<br>• Firewalls |
| **Adoption/ Innovation** | • Innovator if in elite role. If not laggard/ late- majority. Significantly high propensity to resist SNS of a social variety i.e. Facebook. | • Late majority/ laggard significantly high propensity to resist SNS of a social variety, i.e. Facebook. | • Innovator/ late majority/ withdrawal |

SM, social media; SNS, social networking sites.

Act 2 focuses on the discourse of power, control, and surveillance in digital contexts. The theme centres on the differing mechanisms and practices used for the purposes of controlling, discipline, and punishment of social media use.

# Section 3

# Act 2

## Digitised regimes of power: How control and surveillance are established at work

So far, we have explored how corporations and key workers integrate and use social media. These were deliberately positioned to highlight the impact this has on developing regimes which aim to control social media use in work. This section develops this corollary and centres on the visible managerial regimes, styles, competencies, and mechanisms sought to control social media use in work to highlight the many ethical complexities which exist in the context of power (Lukes, 2005).

In society and work, certain key individuals may possess some element of power or who may be powerful (Ball, 1976). In general, it is argued that the working classes are largely denied power (Morriss, 2002). We tend to oversimplify and reinforce this conception. This infers we are passive, further implying that societal and managerial elites hold all the command and, in doing so, act responsibly when in power. Further, we do not fully comprehend the role of social media in this mix which may tilt and distort notions of power and control. We must, therefore, greatly understand how social media are used by management to extend their field of vision to influence, reinforce, or challenge power dynamics. Further, to establish their own personal approaches which may enhance or detract from the established mechanisms of control in work.

Act 2. Scene 1 begins to rectify this gap. This is interesting from an employment relations perspective, particularly, where power may intersect with the moral duty as part of a leadership or management role. This scene explores how key corporations and the actors within them authored scripts of power and identity by improvising or reinventing corporate regulations for controlling social media use and the impact this has on the workforce, which is rarely discussed.

DOI: 10.4324/9781003137269-6

# Act 2. Scene 1 Discipling discourses

## Social media rules and regulation

This scene provides a unique insight into the individual management styles, approaches, mechanisms, and techniques used by the key social actors to control use of social media and digital devices in their differing work contexts. The scene explores corporate mechanisms used to limit access to social media and mobile devices such as Firewalls, GPS tracking, analytics, mobile phone amnesties, and other forms of visible and calculable control. These approaches aim to create the order of things in work. They provide greater insight into the nature of discipline, regulation, and rules in work. Additionally, I focus on how workers may adhere to these processes and practices and explore where they may resist management desires, creating the impetus for differing forms of (mis)behaviour to manifest in work.

### Key learning points

- Employee relations management styles influence power dynamics and how social media use in work is controlled which often protects the workplace rather than the employee.
- Firewalls are unlikely to fully contain employee use of social media.
- Social media policies are hard to find and difficult to understand by both management and workers alike.
- Forms of social media surveillance are regularly integrated to observe employees. This is often informal and not fully articulated to the workforce or future applicants.
- Individual managers create their own techniques and rules for controlling worker use for social media.

### Control, discipline, and power

Digitised terrains have extended what we understand to be the working day and with them the introduction of an extended working week. Alongside these,

DOI: 10.4324/9781003137269-7

social media has further interrupted and blurred the boundaries which existed between work and privacy. Ultimately, this context has altered how power and control are exercised in corporations which undoubtedly has become more pernicious because of these devices.

Lukes (1974 as cited in Lukes, 2005) suggests there is an imperative to understand *how and what can we learn from the study of power*? I, therefore, wanted to dedicate space to how power is exercised in these differing organisational and social media contexts. Townley (1994: 52) stated human resource management (HRM) practices define the nature of work, coordinate the differing dimensions of the labour process, and control the effort required of workers and noted that often these parameters and the practices which sit behind them are not greatly understood.

These scenes therefore aim to address a further research question:

> How are organisational rules for regulating and controlling social media shaped, managed and understood by the actors?

The discourse centres on management approaches used in these corporations to regulate online activities, including digitised forms of gatekeeping which alter the nature of HRM practices and pose challenges for the manager–employee focus in the employment relationship (Van Buren et al, 2009). Understanding the realities of how management carry out these activities enables one to reflect more deeply on whether the approaches and related management competencies have wider repercussions and ramifications for misbehaviour, identity, discipline, and punishment at work.

Many writers have pondered and conceptualised power and control. These involve both creative and repressive conceptions which suggests power is ambiguous (Townley, 1994), and even more so in increasingly digitised contexts. Thus, understanding how the power to control is exercised is evermore alluring as this creates even greater vexation and contestation in life and work.

Mills (1956 as cited in Lukes 2005) inferred power is positional and affects the everyday lives of ordinary people. This suggests societal elite occupy strategic command posts which are located in the hierarchy of our social structures. This conception has greater traction in work and digitised contexts where corporate elite occupy a greater panoptic span of control which, as shown, includes social media. This is therefore becoming more manipulative and enacted in much more veiled ways. Therefore, we need to more greatly understand the management methods which sit behind this. As a parent, educator, and manager, this is becoming more complex to navigate. There is very little discussion or challenge to whether such fields of vision or power are responsibly exercised or morally, ethically right. Trying to understand how social media devices are culturally assimilated and controlled by operational management, and the range of competency in doing so, is therefore of importance.

Dahl (1958 as cited in Lukes 2005) suggests power is both intentional and active, therefore suggesting it is down to the preferences of the ruling elite to dictate decision-making situations in corporations. Social media influences and seemingly overlaps with this domain. This conception infers one group is more referent, subordinate, and obliging to the ruling influence of an elite few. Naturally, this context is familiar in work and may create a conflict of interests between likely stakeholder groups such as the workforce and their management. This theorisation typifies how we see and make sense of corporate hierarchy. However, this context can be distorted through social media where our wider power structures are not simply or neatly contained through distinct groups anymore. This may affect who holds power in both offline and online contexts simultaneously. This is explored in the later acts.

Schumpeter (1962 as cited in Lukes 2005) stated individuals acquire power through a competitive struggle for a peoples vote. This conception suggests people are the subjects of an elite leader, which we follow passively accepting their decisions. This is relevant to how we vie for attention in both on- and offline contexts. On social media, we compete to gain audiences, vast troops of willing followers, and likes, propping up our notoriety and position of power.

Elite influencers hold highly instrumental positions which span across digitised contexts in which they may also seek to influence perspectives on work, politics, and societal issues. Again, any person hoping to influence online audiences is at their mercy. We can simply turn off and cop out of interacting with them. As Bacharach and Baratz (1970, as cited in Lukes 2005) suggest, power, therefore, is not reflected by such concrete decision-making. They state certain individuals or groups consciously or unconsciously reinforce barriers to the airing of public conflicts. Schattschneider (1960, as cited in Lukes 2005) suggested this stimulates bias in favour of the exploitation of conflict and the wider suppression of others. Social media is located at this intersection, used to exploit us and simultaneously challenge barriers by raising awareness of gross inequalities in society or work, which we are seeing happening more and more.

Foucault (1983) suggested power manifests itself conceptually through the very notion of being a subject. To be a subject in work is to be dependent, controlled, or tied to an identity by self-knowledge or a conscience. These elements again draw attention to how power is embodied through our sense of self and suggest that we author a narrative to portray differing forms of power. This maybe within an assigned corporate role where we develop a script for our identity endeavours both off- and online where we expound our knowledge to influence others' perceptions. This is relevant to the discussion in this scene.

Lukes (2005) further suggested we can predict the measures of control which exist around us as we carry around a map of human agency and power in our heads. This enables us to better understand the disposition and ability of those we interact with and how they may affect our interests. Thi case explores how management acquires and exercises power. Using this premise, I focus on how actors dramaturgically shape and author their role in power dynamics to develop insights into how they shape corporate mechanisms to control social media and our identities in work.

Many previous studies have focused solely on developing a quantitative understanding of policy, practice, and regulation in this context. These studies provide high-level themes on determining whether employees have an awareness of social media regulation (Broughton et al, 2010; CIPD, 2013b; Deloitte, 2009). This oversimplifies the context and suggests social media use is more controllable than it actually is. Further, such themes fail to make sense of the emerging nature of discipline in corporations or how tensions may arise regarding the control of social media. Using qualitative empiricism, therefore, allows us to more deeply ascertain how power is asserted in this context by management.

Management approaches, in general, are assumed to be responsible and equitable to workers. This suggests management are competent and have observable, positive skill sets. My discussion observes more closely how such practices create a much contested terrain. The following section focuses on the apparent management styles and employment frames of reference operating in each environment. These set the tone and determine the characteristics for how we are treated in work. My aim here is to illustrate the contextual differences between how employees in the case organisations may often be treated as commodities rather than valued assets (Islam, 2012). This suggests management competence is often mechanised, and as a result, the softer side of HRM is minimised; therefore, it creates greater issues in work.

The empiricism is used to show how employee voice channels and strategies are predominantly used for the benefit to management (Kaufman, 2015; Taylor, 2018). Often minimal opportunities for formal employee voice interventions. This highlights how a tightening of the managerial agenda may impact on employee satisfaction and engagement experiences at work. Additionally, the discussion illustrates how little workers are involved in meaningful consultation about the rules which affect them (Cuillane et al, 2012).

## Managerial styles in action

Each organisation will adopt differing managerial styles and approaches. These demonstrate conceptually how employment relationships are essentially governed in each context (Purcell and Ahlstrand, 1993). Dundon and Rollinson (2011) suggest individualism is the extent employees are regarded as important resources within organisations, whereas collectivism is the extent employees are involved in decision-making processes in organisations.

Figure 3.1 (overleaf) plots the management styles observed in the differing case study organisation. These are adapted from the conceptual model developed by Purcell and Ahlstrand (1993).

The impact of these management approaches are now explained.

**Employees as a resource**

*Individualism*

| | | | |
|---|---|---|---|
| **Employee Development Focus** | Sophisticated Human Resources<br>• *Aedis*<br>• *Tiro* | | Sophisticated Modern (Consultative)<br>• *Alumno* |
| **Paternalism** | Paternalist | Sophisticated Modern (Constitutional)<br>• *Pharma*<br>• *Senes* | Modern Paternalist<br>• *Pala* |
| | Traditionalist<br>• *Charta* | Standard Modern | |
| **Cost Minimisation** | **Unitarist Focus** | **Adversarial** | **Cooperative** |

**Employees as a commodity** ***Collectivism***

*Figure 3.1* Management styles in action.

Source: Adapted from Purcell and Ahlstrand (1993).

## Shades of individualism

Three of the case organisations incorporated individualised management approaches.

1 Charta operated a *traditionalist* style of management which incorporated hard HRM approaches which views employees as resources to be "used dispassionately and in a formally rational manner" (Storey, 1992: 26). This strategic HRM approach focuses on cost reduction rather than substantial investment in the workforce. The emphasis at Charta focused heftily on revenue generation and profitability. In this model, employees are considered little more than overheads. The participant findings highlighted employees were offered little development opportunities, including social media use. This is ironic given these devices are used to market company brands and services. Management actors at Charta focused on utilising highly aggressive management styles which were observed to infantilise and subjugate employees.

2 Aedis and Tiro operated a more *sophisticated human relations* style. Discourse in these two organisations focused on managerial regimes which incorporated softer HRM approaches to galvanise the workforce. A soft HR approach is considered to foster environments of employee commitment, motivation, and development (Legge, 1995b;1995c). Management in these corporate environments focused on enabling some innovations which sought to create participation and communication with their workforce (Beer et al, 1984a; 1984b; Boxall, 1996; Guest, 1990; 1991; 1992; Noon, 1992; Walton, 1985). This activity saw the inclusion of operational workers shaping the development of core organisational values to establish expected behaviours in the workplace. Yet minimal development of social media use was offered to staff, HR, and management actors. Furthermore, the access to use social media by all across the organisational stratifications was not fully ratified. Similar to Charta, workers in Tiro were under a commercial pressure to perform.

**Shades of collectivism**

The remaining organisations operated collectivist approaches. Yet these highlight varying shades of pluralism are observed. I focused on understanding how employees and trade unions were included in decision making processes for social media use in work. These again were minimal. Decisions to involve employees in developing regulation were often carefully orchestrated by management and HR departments.

1 Alumno used clear processes of negotiation with trade unions and management on social media regulation. This is perceived to be a *sophisticated modern consultative* style of management. HR Actors at Alumno alluded to scenes of discussion on social media use. Their narratives suggested where they relinquished a degree of power sharing to develop social media regulations and activity. The negotiations for social media integration were of interest. The discourse demonstrated dramaturgical techniques to display power within these key role constructs. Attention was drawn to the *staging* of "partnership" working. Whilst Alumno allowed trade union employees to be included in consultation and discussion, there was a definite hierarchy of power which was displayed in the formal meetings.

The scripts of HR actors were heavily loaded to suggest social media rules were there to direct, control and manage employee dissent. The discourse inferred trade union representation was antagonistic and remained a challenge to management desires. So rather than reflecting a plurality of interests in the organization this highlighted notions of conflict and resistance which existed in the employee relations terrain (van den Broek and Dundon,

2012; Thompson, 2016). HR actors sought to control trade union activists by trying to dissuade meaningful discussion regarding issues of freedom of speech. Conversely, the trade union actors enjoyed the debate.

These scenes of power demonstrate how a corporate cast of characters are crucial in the staging, posturing and development of employee relations contexts. These scenes highlight polarising views on establishing and coordinating social media use.

Barry and Wilkinson (2016) suggest open forums for employee voice allow the organisation to develop motivations for constructive change. In this context it may be argued management sought to hold power and often tried to silence or marginalise employee concerns regarding social media use (Dyne et al, 2003). This is primarily because HR actors tried to galvanise sentiment about opposing use of social media. This draws attention to low HRM approaches where employees are not to be trusted. This is perhaps a stereotypical perception of structurally connected stakeholders and demonstrates how strategic HR needs to stand back from such subjective views.

(Islam, 2012)

2 Senes and Pharma operated a *sophisticated modern constitutional* style of management as trade unions were reluctantly conceded in these organisations. The managerial regimes in these corporations therefore had more direct control of the workforce (Ackroyd and Thompson, 2003). The dialogues regarding policy development suggested management strategies directed employee behaviour (Dundon and Rollinson, 2011). Implementation and development of ICT and social media regulation was demarcated and reserved for management to integrate at their discretion.
3 Senes, however, remained unique in this sample as they were passionate about the strategic purpose of social media, driven through their HR director. A wide range of development was made available to employees and certain SNS were unrestricted to employees. This conceptually links to Purcell and Ahlstrand (1993) who state management styles reflect the human resource strategy. HRM in this organisation operated a more engaging and high trust modus operandi of employees. This is perceived to be influential in how social media work is treated or valued.
4 Pala was located as a *modern paternalist* where the style of management incorporated a strong involvement with trade union representation. The HR actors focused on a strong sense of social responsibility in social media use due to its sector. Thus concerns about social media use were not just internally motivated. They incorporated training and development which added to a more inclusive participative managerial regime.

(Ackroyd and Thompson, 2003)

The consideration of management styles demonstrates a shift in shades of pluralism to greater depth. Employee voice has significance for employment relations environment and sectors of work (Bennett, 2010; Holland et al, 2016; Martin et al, 2015; McDonald et al, 2016; Prowse and Prowse, 2007). Indeed, employee voice practices were observed to have developed to the extent that there is a representation gap where employees in this study had very little say beyond work tasks (Dundon and Rollinson, 2011). There was little recognition of the plurality of worker interests to the extent that even within pluralist, collective environs the employee voice channels remained at the shallow end of the spectrum of pluralism (Marchington and Wilkinson, 2008). This further demonstrates how social media creates more hegemonic approaches. Ackroyd and Thompson (2003) suggest managerial styles develop systems of production which inhibit or build trust and thus they are more contestable. They suggest managerial strategies of direct control do not eliminate misbehaviours; they simply lead to greater employee innovation on resisting or being more uncooperative with management.

## Perceptions of risk and need to control social media

Management styles have established a link with how policy and practice for social media in organisations will evolve. In the main, something which is evident today is the fact that social media poses significant risks to people and organisations.

The case vignette is based on a conversation with an influential HR director. The discussion aims to highlight that we have always had risks and issues with employee misbehaviour. The difference is the way in which we do this. The forms of media have changed over time. The main issue is how do corporations manage this issue so that we enable use of social media as a business tool and encourage people to behave positively together online. The problem therefore ostensibly rests with how we see the use of social media as a problem or do we see it as an opportunity.

A way to establish more informed ways of working with social media is to develop corporate practices with the workforce. If they can co-create and facilitate the development of policy, processes, and practices, surely this will enhance how we incorporate these devices into the everydayness of work life. One way to achieve this is through employee stakeholders such as trade unions.

## Trade union involvement

Employment relations often advocate the integration of partnership working with trade unions. Management rhetoric here suggests this approach creates a more positive depiction of work. Trade unions allow workers capacity to

**Case vignette 3 Social media is hazardous for corporate reputation**

In many organisations social media is still seen as a highly risky. International news, *People Today*, and other HR magazines and news platforms have focused on widely reporting the issues of discipline and employee misbehaviour on social media.

An HR director explains this view:

We only get to hear about social media when it goes horribly wrong. We only get to know about stories where employees have used social media to share inappropriate pictures or say something about their place of work in a negative way. These both get retweeted or reposted and build a trajectory where these become major memes. Then there is the reputational damage. What a lot of organisations did initially as a result of this was set out rules. Many organisations simply said you're not allowed to use social media; you simply can't do it; you can't identify who you are and then set out more rules which focus on what you mustn't do, all these sorts of things. You can sort of understand this as a sort of natural reaction. These people were concerned about the issues around organisation and personal reputation. They were worried about breaching of information or how self-expression may impact on the business. I took the view that there are some risks with using social media. But there are risks in things in everything people do. This has always been the case. People will discuss work or colleagues on a bus and someone would overhear them and report it. Only in years gone by, you would receive a letter of grievance and complaint. You would investigate it and deal with it.

Moving forward, the internet came along and became more accessible to people. We began to use e-mails. Again people send inappropriate e-mails and share pictures through this medium. Again with the advent of the internet, people would become distracted and look at shopping sites, news channels, and more broadly, inappropriate sorts of things like porn that they had previously done in their own time. So people have always breached the rules; it's just the media that's changed.

feel supported and heard. So it seems natural that working with these key stakeholders may enhance social media use in work.

Focusing on the case organisation, Alumno gave further insights into stakeholder relations in this context. This organisation was focused on because this institution purportedly had developed a strong relationship with their formal recognised trade union through a well-established partnership working agreement.

David (a trade union representative at Alumno) was the only actor in the study who was given access to participate fully in any formal employee voice channels due to his union role. Conversely, Gary (Senes), also a trade union representative, experienced minimal employee voice opportunities. The HR approach in the Senes case organisations did not consult with the recognised union on anything wider than pay. This further demonstrates how *consultative* management styles may impact on power sharing features and trade union involvement which are often associated with high-calibre employee voice mechanisms (Cullinane et al, 2012; Holland et al, 2016; Kaufman, 2015). Thus, as Ackroyd and Thompson (2003) suggest, if employees are not included in developing regulation, this creates a more corrective, punitive approach to discipline and offers employees wider potential to dissent.

Interestingly, as discussed in the previous section, neither trade union representatives used social media to collectively organise or stimulate member discussion in their respective corporate environments. My aim here is to reemphasise that trade unions must rethink stratagems to increase collaborative networks for organising (Heckscher and Carre, 2006). The findings suggest that this is a complex undertaking and highly dependent on the preferences of the actual trade union representatives.

Importantly, these management styles shown on this scene demonstrates how power is further concentrated with management and HRM and therefore perpetuate more unitary perspectives (Edwards, 2003; Humphreys and Brown, 2002; Lukes, 2005; Townley, 1994).

The HRM subjectivity found to exist in the empiricism is used to question the suggestion made by Ulrich that HR managers operate as a voice for employees in management discussions (1997). This discovery suggests HR actors perceive their self as an agent with power to perform and act for the organisation (Islam, 2012; Townley, 1994). This is important, as Edwards (2003) noted a power to control employees is rarely given much attention in industrial relations texts.

The next section focuses on two major themes:

1 *Development of social media regulation:* Explores differing permeations of governance and coherence regarding regulations for social media use.
2 *Mechanisms of control:* Explores the differing mechanisms developed by corporations and which are authored by management to control social media use.

## Developing social media regulation

This section provides an overview of the type of social media regulations and policy which were incorporated in these differing workplaces. Table 3.1 highlights the lead department considered to "own" social media regulation and summarises the major methods used to control social media access. Additionally,

*Table 3.1* Development and typology of social media policy and regulations in the case study corporations

| *Organisation and ER frame of reference* | *Typology of policy* | *Department ownership of SM policy* | *Trade union involvement in the development of SM policy* | *Use of Firewalls* | *Use of training and development to embed SM behaviour or compliance* |
|---|---|---|---|---|---|
| **Aedis (Unitary)** | No SM policy. Code of behaviours or harassment policy used to address issues | HR | No (derecognised) | Yes | No |
| **Tiro (Unitary)** | SM policy | HR | No | Yes | Yes (management focused) |
| **Pala (Pluralist)** | SM policy plus wider policies on use of SM communication | HR | Yes (2) integrated in discussions on SM policy | yes | Yes (management focused) |
| **Alumno (Pluralist)** | SM policy | HR | Yes (4) integrated in discussion on SM policy | No | Yes (HR focused) |
| **Senes (Pluralist)** | SM policy | HR | Yes (1) not integrated in discussion on SM policy. | Yes | Yes |
| **Charta (Unitary)** | SM policy | ICT | No | Yes | No |
| **Pharma (Pluralist)** | SM policy | Marketing | Yes (1) not integrated in discussion on SM policy | Yes | No |

SM, social media.

the table highlights the level of involvement from other key stakeholders such as trade unions capturing who else was involved in the scoping and decision-making of social media regulations. Finally, the table captures whether training and development were integrated to develop online skills, behaviours, and compliance. These provide some insights into how organisations attempt to develop rules and begin to exercise some degree of control through organisational training and development interventions.

The table illustrates four participating organisations had recognised trade unions as part of the employment deal (Alumno, Pala, Pharma, and Senes). Trade unions are important stakeholders in employment relationships. Trade unions and their constituent members contribute to productivity, meaningful business decisions, and provide recognised vehicles which contribute to employee voice, engagement, and development (Blyton et al, 2012; Martin et al, 2015). Whilst this shows these organisations are more *pluralist* in their approach, there were differing degrees of engagement with representative unions on the development of social media control, policy development, and punitive actions. This depicts how some organisations are typically more *unitary* in their management style. Further, the table illustrates which organisations did not officially recognise trade unions (Charta and Tiro Aedis).

It is apparent that there was very little or no training and development investment provided for employees on social media use. More broadly, minimal development was given to management or HR actors. This has two implied meanings:

1 This reinforces the main belief in organisations that management and HR are competent, more compliant, and least likely to break rules. This assumption massively underestimates the capacity for staff in these groups to misbehave, which is rarely discussed. I address this gap in Acts 3 and 4.
2 HR and management development centred on how to investigate online misbehaviours and to outline corporate disciplinary, punitive measures rather than skills development. This infers the general workforce will fail to follow regulations rather than developing appropriate behaviours or positive online etiquette.

This correlates to extant literature (CIPD, 2013b Social Technology Report) which states employees are not skilled in their use or control of social media. This is still relevant. We still have little angle on how social media impacts on management and workers. This highlights both are left very much to our own devices. This highlights a laissez-faire approach, leaving things to unfurl.

This highlights how HR development fails to centre on instilling skills or competence for management on issues such as ethical surveillance, monitoring techniques, or how to address forms of online conflict and resistance. For workers, more broadly, this fails to develop online competencies per se. This means we can predict a higher degree of propensity for misbehaviour to appear which I expand to show that this is not always those in frontline operations.

## Rule-setting agendas

The empiricism highlights is commonplace for social media regulation to be developed by either marketing or information, communication, and technology (ICT) functions. There was often little involvement with HR departments. This illustrates differing residual organisational locus of control for corporate regulation. Further, where ICT and marketing functions lead strategies for the creation of digital policies, these are less widely understood by employees (Taylor, 2018).

Policy ownership, dissemination, and concretion in organisations are important. If this is confused, this adds to a lack of coherence regarding regulation and control of social media use. This was also coupled with internal interdepartmental conflict and bureaucratic control in organisations. Indeed, my findings demonstrate two HR actors in this study (Fiona, Erica) commented on interdepartmental battles over competing interests to control and regulate social media use. Interestingly, only two organisations consulted with unions on social media regulations (Alumno and Pala) which suggested how management largely seeks to protect their power as an employer.

## Mechanisms of social media control

Making the methods of control visible in this context shows how organisations seek to restrict social media use. These are considered as properties which aid the staging of power in the employment relationship. Illuminating on empirical findings shows how these create problems for management control of digitised activity and in some cases render the rule obsolete. May aim here is to rethink strategies to support better use of social media and to say restriction is unlikely to succeed.

## Firewalls; don't give them access!

As discussed previously, use of firewalls is a primary mechanism in all organisations which aims to restrict access to use named sites and social media. This correlates with wider research (Billington and Billington, 2012). Controlled use of social media is perceived to reduce the effects of presenteeism, which is defined as being in work but with low productivity (Moqbel et al, 2013). Thus, if we stop workers accessing social media, they cannot be distracted and thus will be effective in work. This is more closely explored.

Firewalls are often cited in policy, so staff should be aware of these rules potentially. Firewalls were found to not be uniformly applied across all

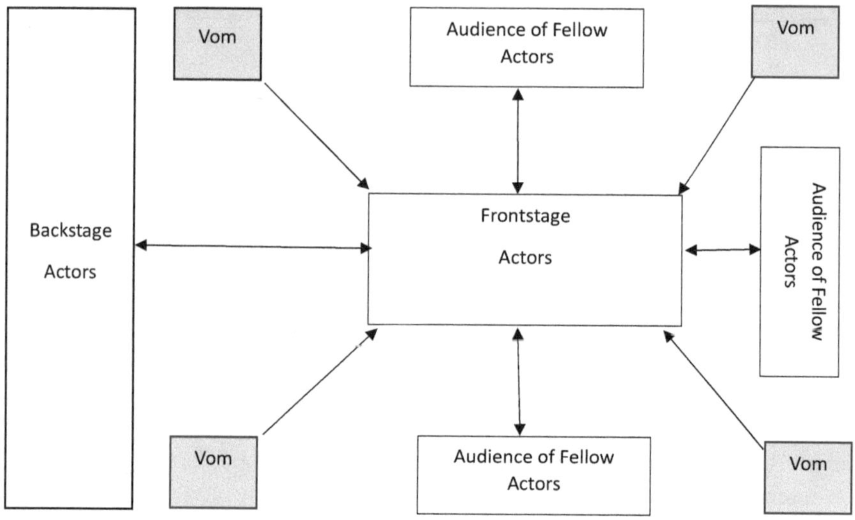


*Figure 3.2* Social media represented as a stage, including vomitoriums.

stratifications of in the participating case study organisations as the following quote demonstrates:

> We don't allow normal folk access to the likes of Facebook, Twitter other than before eight o'clock in the morning and after six o'clock at night.
>
> (Aedis, Alex, HR Manager [p. 9 line 4–5])

Firewalls replicate a dramaturgical device called a vomitorium which is a technical design feature of a theatre stage. Vomitoriums are used to physically control the exits or entrance points to the stage for actors and stage workers. They are often hidden and provide a tunnel or hiding point (www.tdf.org/on-stage/theatre-dictionary/search-by-letter/voms/ /last accessed 20/08/2024). See Figure 3.2.

The illustration depicts social media as a metaphorical theatre with a thrust stage and incorporates the technical, architectural feature of the vomitoriums, voms for short. Vomitorium devices often lead under the stage, this is perceived to be akin to organisational control of social media use through use of Firewalls (Moussa, 2015). This suggests employers create a closed arena which they believe they can stage and dictate when and how we access social media. Firewalls are used to control and restrict employee access to certain websites, mainly for the cast of employees in lower stratifications in organisations. Conversely, actors in elite roles are rarely restricted and are allowed greater capacity to access social media (Taylor, 2018).

Firewalls are installed on personal computers. Yet my findings showed how all actors found these are easy to breach and circumnavigate access rules simply by using their mobile phone devices. Just like a theatre vomitorium, social actors create a mechanism to hide and use devices to access social media. Thus, regulations in this domain are very weak. Therefore, these must interlink with wider corporate protocols for other digital device use in work.

Four actors, Beth (Tiro), Charles, Clive (both at Pala), and Greg (Pharma), discussed how they personally or their employees used their own personal phones to breach Firewalls. Significantly, workers in lower operational roles are under greater scrutiny and regulation in this context. Conversely, actors in elite professional roles were rarely observed or surveilled (McDonald et al, 2016; Moussa, 2015).

This demonstrates the differing levels of mistrust which exist in contemporary employment relationships and further evidence of growing inequalities in work where frontline employee social media use is viewed with a higher degree of scepticism. Thus, corporations more greatly dictate how worker online identity should be shaped in strict time frames (Goffman, 1959; Kerrigan and Hart, 2016; Webb, 2006). Thus, Firewalls pose an interesting paradox in the discourse on digitalisation of work.

**Discussion box 12**

**Discuss:**

In your place of work or study, are there restrictions or Firewalls to stop you from accessing social media?

Do you think these are effective?

**Pause for reflection:**

Have you accessed your own mobile device when you should have been working?

Reflect on what happened? Did management reprimand you?

Are the rules fairly applied in this context?

## Digital natives

In the empiricism, all the actors sought to sound progressive and discussed being transparent and supportive of employees using social media. All of them wanted employees to be digital natives, a rhetoric which was supposed to mean the advanced use of technology in work. Three actors in one case organisation coined a phrase:

> digital by design
>
> (Aedis, Alan, Property Services Manager [p. 12 line 3])

A discourse of transparency and of aiming to be more "digital" in this context is intriguing. A previous quote by Alex, also an HR Manager in this organisation, discussed how approaches to integrate greater digitalisation and social media did not apply to *normal* employees. This has multiple connotations. This is interpreted to mean Firewalls are installed to maintain cooperation, productivity, and restrict workers in the lower operational ranks of the workforce. This contributes to a distinctly hierarchical view that social media participation and adoption is a privilege for elite actors as they achieve positions of power. This contradicts any discourse of being *digitally inclusive*, the reality is that for most workers, organisations will try to tightly control their social media access.

Furthermore, the narratives revealed management in these organisations were aware of Firewall breaches. Thus, as Ackroyd and Thompson (1999/2003) suggest management decide and address whether breaching rule is perceived as a misbehaviour and make decisions over whether to tolerate or take action. Some of the mechanisms to control our access are now discussed.

### *Digital employee checks*

In order to address any potential digital misbehaviours, some management in some of the case organisations performed regular digital employee checks on personal computers, company-owned mobile phones, and associated expenses claims. My point here is to be aware that access to certain platforms are scrutinised and monitored to ensure that these have applicability to routine work. Actors in the Pharma and Pala case organisations stated that the employer calculated lost time and data charges incurred by employees. These were used as evidence in disciplinary procedures. This further demonstrates wider calculable labour strategies to scrutinise both employee performance and technology use (Townley, 1994).

However, five case organisations did not utilise calculable methods of social media scrutiny. In these organisations, the employer was totally reliant on discretionary management effort to observe lack of productivity and time theft due to social media use. Ackroyd and Thompson (2003) state that calculable methods of surveillance should also include observation of management wrongdoings in these contexts.

Not one organisation reviewed management actions in these contexts. My point here is to raise awareness of any potential unfairness and unethicality present in the employment deal. Moreover, the point is to highlight the proliferation of the view that management are incapable of misbehaving. As my findings show, they just as likely to breach Firewall protocols and other social media regulations. This raises an important question over who is observing management.

## Social media policy

Pre-existing literature and case law emphasise the need for social media policy and guidance. This suggests employers should provide clear disciplinary rules for social media use (Biro, 2011; Broughton et al, 2010; Dessler, 2015). Empirical findings highlight organisations do tend to have specific social media policies and online behaviour codes (Taylor, 2018).

As the following quote suggests:

> …it's a brand that you're trying to protect and when you've got x amount of employees saying whatever they like all over the worldwide web, that gets harder to protect.
>
> (Tiro, Beatty, HR Manager [p. 5 line 22–28])

This emphasises how most corporations and HR actors within them will perceive that there is a need to protect the employer. This is not being questioned and links to ACAS guidance and UK best practice in this area (Broughton et al, 2010; CIPD, 2013b; 2017).

However, the discourse in the empiricism suggested shaping of social media policy was more complex due to the duality of its role professionally and privately. Social media use allows individuals to reimagine liminal and multiple individual identities visibly showing "who am I?" (Cerulo, 1997). Management are, therefore, increasingly interested in controlling our identity (Webb, 2006). The dominant discourse in this domain suggested how HR and management actors perceive online behaviours, and our multiple identity exploration online sits in tension with the organisational view of "who do you want me to be?" and "how should I act?" (Cerulo, 1997). This requires new rule-setting agendas which align to the sense of being a subject at work and wider corporate regulations *for how we do things round here* (Foucault, 1983).

### *Lack of policy*

Despite legal advice, some organisations may not possess enforceable social media policies (Broughton et al, 2010). Onc case origination (Aedis) failed to have any relevant social media policy. This is transferable to smaller enterprises who may not have a fully developed regulatory framework as shown in this quote:

> They've not developed a policy, and if there were issues around what employees put on Facebook then we would probably cover that under other policies.
>
> (Aedis, Alex, HR Manager [p. 1 line 12–15])

The context of UK case law demonstrated in the introductory conceptual section showed how a lack of presence of any form of regulatory policy diminishes employer powers to protect their interests (Biro, 2011).

Social media policy is effective in balancing the employers' need to regulate and the employee's need for privacy interests (Biro, 2011). Yet the above narrative by the social actor Alex highlights how regulation of social media is still a grey area for HRM practices. Greater emphasis is, therefore, placed on employers and HRM approaches to create unambiguous privacy boundaries (Moussa, 2015). McDonald et al (2016) highlight how such ambiguity adds to changes in the workplace norms which impact on privacy and work intensification. A lack of policy is problematical and majorly reliant on a significant individual responsible autonomy and self-regulation (Ackroyd and Thompson, 2003; Fang et al, 2015).

The need to have a distinct social media policy and zero tolerance approaches was explored with the actor, Alex who stated:

> I don't buy that ... if we've got a company Facebook page then I would like our employees to be putting comments on that page so if there are discussions around what the organisation does then I'd want the employees to understand that and also to support the organisation publicly. So, I don't see that it should be zero tolerance... that's why they've not gone down the social media policy because it can be very restrictive and it's not adding value to a business.
>
> (Aedis, Alex, HR Manager [p. 3 line 6–11])

This shows how some HR actors believe hegemonic punitive action is not needed, which is fantastic from an employee perspective. However, having little or no social media policy regulation may be limiting employee understanding regarding the expected behaviours. This finding is interesting. This same actor clearly contradicts their previous statement regarding restricting access for *normal* folk. Here, they suggest they want employees posting on their organisation site. This draws attention to the conflictual and contradictory nature of regulation and control in work and the confusions this may unwittingly create.

Management have discretion and power to direct and define behaviours at work, including categorising and developing procedures for misbehaviour identification and what they find unacceptable (Ackroyd and Thompson, 2003). This case illustrates how some HR actors are in fact adding to confusion regarding shaping compliance and competence in work. My aim here is to suggest that this adds to the complexities and challenges for employers.

Importantly, a lack of clarity regarding online behaviour and social media engagement rules enables employees to contest disciplinary measures as they arguably do not know what is expected of them (Biro, 2011; Broughton et al, 2010; Lucero et al, 2013; Moussa, 2015). In the current context, contesting disciplinary measures for employees is compounded by the associated legal costs of defending themselves should they seek recompense through employment tribunal processes.

Lack of policy is one issue compounding all employee behaviours, but what is the actuality of social media policy? Access was sought to review these documents. These are not published to protect the anonymity of the organisations in this study.

### *Policy wording*

Social media policy content, pretty much like many policy documents, is lengthy, written in an inaccessible tone or verbose language. My point here is to suggest that this makes regulations difficult to understand by all the workforce. This is perceived to add further complexity in how employees interpret regulation and determine characteristics for acceptable behaviours. This may adversely affect diverse employees.

The following quote intimates how complex some social media policies are:

> There is a lot in that policy that states what you should not do … its things like “make any views that could be deemed as the company’s”. So you have to say “I” and not “we”, as the organisation. There is a lot of stipulation in there about if ever you are doing anything which is linked to [Pharma]... people know it is your personal view … there’s a lot of stuff about general disciplinary rules around not bringing the company into disrepute…like “the manager’s getting right on my nerves this week.”
>
> (Pharma, Georgia, HR manager [p.6 line 1–10])

This particular actor describes how full and busy the social media policy is. Whilst this may give direction, the narrative suggests employees must use specific styles of grammar and personal pronouns. This requires a higher analytical and English language skill.

This is significant given the differing educational levels and diversity within UK workforces where English may be an additional language. This draws attention to a growing concern: regulating social media behaviour at work requires greater training and, in some cases, significant educational support. I repeatedly found no large-scale training was provided in these case organisations for employees to develop their analytical, language, or digital skills. This correlates with extant literature suggesting that the lack of social media development is a growing issue (Headworth, 2015).

Only one organisation had created a very simple and easy-to-understand social media policy, which consisted of six bullet points. Employees at the organisation could recite the policy in a somewhat sing-songy Von Trappian way. I am not critiquing this approach. It made the rules of online engagement clear, much more memorable, and what appeared to be engaging for workers. To ensure positive adoption of social media, I explored how this organisation (Senes) took this uniquely simple approach to shape positive online behaviours as the HR director describes:

> *I proposed a completely different policy it fits social media. ... it seriously raised some eyebrows from certain quarters; not least actually our global HR Director who said to me: We don't really write policies like this ...I can't remember how I actually got them to put their signature to it but I must have been very persuasive.*
>
> (Senes, Erica, HR Director [p. 5 line 1–13])

All the actors interviewed in this company discussed how the simplicity of their policy made it more effective and widely understood by the workforce. The HR director, Erica was engaging and passionate about advancing use of social media. She personally championed use of social media in work. Her strategy for increasing use was underpinned by the orientation of policy development and incorporated widescale training support for all in the corporation. The approaches focused on the benefits of using social media rather than the punitive and restrictive measures in all the other corporations. This correlates with wider research on the role of leaders, establishing social media participation and employee voice (Martin et al, 2015).

Having previously worked in HR development, where you are trying to engage workers behaviourally with policy, I understand and know that anything you can do to make policy come alive, is well worth it. This also takes management effort to embed policy. The HR team in this organisation were all incredibly passionate about social media. So this also added to the traction.

## Policy visibility

What usually occurs at work is that there is a proliferation of ICT, social media, and behaviour policies which further appear to add to worker confusions over how they may use or access social media. This further makes any relevant policy difficult to understand, and moreover, in larger corporations there are a plethora of competing policies which lack visibility to both workers, management, and HR practitioners, as this quote illustrates:

> Unless they fall upon it [SNS policy], I'm not sure how they would find it?
> (Charta, Fiona, HR Manager [p. 4 line 20])

The cross-case analyses highlights locating relevant policy is an issue in all the organisations. The invisibility of policy poses a challenge for the defensibility of the employer (Moussa, 2015). Policymaking per se is complex and will be dependent on the actors in the organisation and the institutional reasons for developing rules and behaviours (Cairney, Heikkila, and Wood, 2019).

**Discussion box 13**

**Discuss:**

How effective are all your social media and digital device policies in your place of work or study?

Do these policies elaborate on how to formulate wording for posts and tweets, etc.?

Do these policies incorporate rules on surveillance, monitoring, and observation of employee use of social media?

**Pause for reflection:**

Reflect on how organisations can make policy and practices for social media behaviours more positive?

***Surveillance in policy***

Not all organisations explicitly capture the right to observe and monitor employee social media activity in policy. Only three organisations made this clear by having a line within their policies which stated that they reserved the right to monitor employee social media (Charta, Pala, and Alumno).

These findings suggest surveillance through digital platforms is rarely made apparent to employees. This has wider sociopolitical implications for the freedom of privacy as outlined in the Human Rights Act (1998). Smith (1993) states privacy is rarely captured in policy. Ultimately, this demonstrates how corporate policy is positioned to protect the rights of the employer, not the employee.

### Protecting the employer

Policy is a strategic device to protect the employer from employee misuse of social media. This further demonstrates how management assert their might and power against the worker. Interestingly, the discussion regarding social media regulations in some contexts showed how employers would exercise their might to use any policy to reprimand employees at any cost, as the following quote demonstrates:

> We were almost trying to fudge our way through those regulations to find a point where we could have them [employees] on basically.
>
> (Alumno, Davina, HR Policy Development: [p. 2 line 7–11])

This emphasised how HR actors will manipulate social media or wider policy to catch employees out. This quote by the social actor, Davina, illustrates how organisations are often *fudging* their way through regulation. To *fudge* is an interesting metaphor. This is an action which avoids making a clear decision (Oxford Dictionary, OED Online www.oed.com/dictionary/fudge). This has differing connotations. This can be interpreted to mean corporations will manipulate social media policy to deliberately ensnare employees. This provides a greater insight into the visceral regulatory nature of employment relations. This conceptually relates to coercion in corporate power dynamics which seek to standardise and coercively control employee behaviours (Fox, 1966; Townley, 1994). Fudge is also thick and sticky. This was interpreted to mean that HR actors were also very unclear about how to address social media behaviours.

This means more can be done to develop, interpret, and embed clear rules for all.

**Discussion box 14**

Discuss, in groups, how HR practices use policy to seemingly catch employees out and *fudge the rules?*

How might this impact on perceptions of HRM in organisations?

**Pause for reflection:**

Do you think this is fair? And how should management and leaders challenge HR approaches and encourage workplace practices to be ethical and more fair to the workforce?

***Employee challenge to policy***

In many disciplinary processes, employees may seek to challenge being reprimanded using social media policy. This is particularly prevalent if they are being disciplined for social media misbehaviour which they felt or deemed to have occurred outside of working hours. As the following participant quote suggests:

> … they copied their manager in … well where does it state that you can't put anything on Facebook in your own time?… apart from the obvious, it's common sense, there was nowhere that stated that … it's like having a policy that's generic enough to capture everything… common sense in line with the policy.
>
> (Pala, Charles, Operations Manager [p. 4 line 6–17])

This shows how employees will freely express themselves on social media beyond work. The issue is this is often not in line with expected in work behaviours. What is interesting is the actor infers that all worker behaviour should be guided by common sense, trust, and controlled responsible autonomy (Ackroyd and Thompson, 2003). However, HR and management actors often perceived that employees do not use logic or common sense when online. This is irresponsible autonomy.

Common sense is neither common or has a sense of appropriateness (Taylor, 2011). Common sense implies individuals self-regulate and adapt their behaviour (Fang et al, 2015). This is not the case where social media is concerned, probably due to the blurring of the boundaries between work and privacy. Clearly, workers have held onto the belief that they can say what they want in their own time. THIS IS NOT THE CASE. I have put this in capital letters to make readers aware of this issue. We cannot misrepresent our employers or imply via social media that the corporation holds our beliefs; this is relevant where racist and misogynist commentary has become rife online. Simply put, don't post or air these views if you want to keep your jobs.

## Developing professionalism

Thus, it is important to note that we cannot say what we want online even after the working day has finished. There needs to be more emphasis on this issue. Codifying online behaviours and conduct is expanding our notions and understanding of what constitutes workplace professionalism and appropriate behaviours (McDonald et al, 2016; Taylor, 2018). As a result, corporations have recast and redrawn the boundaries of work. This is redefining notions of control which is now beyond work and what is deemed acceptable in terms of behaviour. This exploration of social media use in work suggests HR and manager actors rarely reflected on why employees found social media regulation and use problematical.

What apparent was how they tried to instil forms of professionalism.

### *Lack of trust approach*

The empiricism continually highlighted a growing lack of trust in employee digital and social media skills by HR and management actors. To counteract any issues with social media performativity in the case organisations, some tried to overcome this issue by requiring employees to secure formal authorisation to use and participate on online sites externally.

In two organisations (Alumno and Pharma), individuals were asked to send suggested posts to be pre-checked by a third party, such as corporate marketing or communications teams, before posting. Such activity is aligned to Foucauldian concepts (1977) of standardising procedures and documentation to allow managers to make comparators on performance.

Standardisation of digital and creative work is difficult to achieve (Will-Zocholl, 2016). Trying to standardise social media content is perceived to affect the degree of autonomy and control individuals have (Taylor, 2018). Furthermore, this simply adds to unnecessary levels of corporate bureaucracy and is considered to adversely limit creativity and affect interconnectivity. I have to say that this approach would probably drive most workers crackers.

Somehow we need to strike a balance between worker control and freedom to express what we want online. This is hard to navigate, but increasing development in this area could reap benefits, particularly for worker autonomy, trust, and corporate online marketing.

### *Championing social media use*

Having a champion who is passionate about digitalisation and social media use is worth having. These individuals will drive workplace innovations. This was explored with one unique individual. Erica an HR director had a unique perspective which bucked the trend across the sample of HR participants. Erica discussed how she got traditional management to embrace integration of social media on a more wholesale scale. Erica detailed how she put forward a strong business case for social media use:

> I had an argument … it's about networking, it's about sales; it's about the brand message… I could make other realistic arguments about why it was useful…I guess, from a Facebook perspective, I didn't have a very good argument; there was a huge amount of concern that people would waste time on it, so, if I'm honest, I kind of left it 'cause I thought I've won the battles that I really need to win... I let it go and I've never fought the battle again.
>
> (Senes, Erica, HR Director [p. 4 line 14–12])

This discourse highlights carefully the value of key platforms and how businesses can use these to promote the corporation. Erica describes the development of a strategic *business case* for each platform, drawing attention to the marketisation and capitalistic enterprise where social media adoption will be used to show a return on investment as part of the labour process. However, the narrative demonstrates a perception that Facebook was an issue and may cause distraction from work (D'Abate and Eddy, 2007; Moussa, 2015).

A central construct in this narrative was the focus on internal "battles" that key leaders will and may have with fellow directors to integrate certain social media platforms. Erica revealed how she fought for the case to widely integrate social media. She discussed the depth of feeling regarding such experiences in championing use.

There was a visible resignation in her discourse regarding the whole approach. This is a cautionary tale. If you have a role model or champion battling any form of new innovation or policy approach, this can be tiring. They will need management and leadership buy-in. This may affect their perception of collegiality in work. Therefore, we need to create a web of folk who will champion new ways of digitally working.

Challenging peers to avoid working in silos on social media work draws attention to the polarising effect digital and social media adoption has on individuals. Erica's steadfastness ensured that this was driven through the corporations. This is a central tenet of power dynamics perceived to impact on future work approaches, cultures, and employment relationships (Edwards, 2003; McDonald et al, 2016; Townley, 1994). A lesser person may have given in.

**Discussion box 15**

Discuss, in groups, whether your workforce has an workplace champions who encourage wider digital practices?
Do you think having *Digital and Social Media Champions* would impact positively on digitalisation and social media behaviours?

**Pause for reflection:**

How might using champions benefit the whole organisation?

This section illustrates how a coherent strategy to develop social media use can be advantageous. Moreover, a greater awareness of regulatory mechanisms and policy will more greatly help the workforce to understand what is expected of them. Conversely, it can be argued that the majority of employees are still majorly unaware of ICT and digital or social media policies (McDonald et al, 2016). A disproportionate number of employees in all corporations were highly unclear of the implications of social media, its misuse, and any sanctions which may be applied should they breach regulations. This demonstrates social media policy lacks translation and embeddedness throughout organisations. Some employees are, therefore, more at risk as they are not wholly informed of what constitutes corporate code for behaviour or misconduct (Biro, 2011; Broughton et al, 2010; McDonald et al, 2016; Moussa, 2015). If this is the case and your employees don't get the rules, they are definitely more significantly at risk.

The less participative approaches involving employees as key stakeholders to developing regulation were shown to have an adverse effect on workers. I go so far as to say that this may contribute to ongoing misbehaviours at work (Ackroyd and Thompson, 2003; McDonald et al, 2016).

Importantly, many employees are unlikely to have the requisite skills to use social media appropriately because most organisations fail to articulate what this looks like and rest on our ability to use our common sense, which I think, we can agree, is not common or sensical. Further, there is a lack of HR development to offer any relevant corporate training programmes which positively demonstrate what behaviours, skills, and competence look like in this domain. Further, the very rules organisations create to restrict use are often breached. Simply put, Firewalls are not a full deterrent for distractedness. These are discussed in the next section more broadly. This further contributes to a wider sense of confusion over social media regulation, engagement participation, and skill sets. Moreover, there was little to no regulation of management and their approach to surveillance and monitoring skills; again this is expanded on in the next scene which focuses on the unique personal management approaches the actors used to control and discipline unexpected social media use.

# Act 2. Scene 2 Digital panopticons

## Towers of surveillance in social media use

The purpose of this scene is to delve deeper and reflect on how individuals in key organisational roles use social media to monitor, observe, and judge workers. This contributes to wider discussions and awareness of how certain individuals in key roles exert power using social media. The purpose is therefore to give greater emphasis on management scrutiny in this context as this activity has become more pervasive.

All individuals in organisations are subjects of power. Clearly, management are employed for their judgement and skill to harness productivity in the workforce. Their role in power dynamics is to enforce control and discipline. There is very little debate about the actuality of management competences, methods, or systems of exerting control over workers in HR texts. A growing body of literature is aiming to rectify this gasp and focuses on how power is asserted using monitoring, observation, or emerging surveillance practices of workers (McDonald et al, 2016). These seminal pieces of work depict how such management activity is fraught with wicked problems which require greater analysis. I therefore have sought to add to this debate to more deeply make sense of how such interaction takes place and to understand the impact this has on organisational contexts.

***Scene 2 summary***: This scene uses empiricism and social actor narratives to focus on how key players in organisations incorporate forms of surveillance and develop more invasive managerial regimes to control workers. The scene observes how the actors adopt different approaches to control and discipline in each context. Further, the scene focuses on how these individual use their key positions to extend the range or flaunt their positions of power using social media to extend the boundaries which previously existed between work and privacy.

The intention is to reflect on and illustrate the use of social media surveillance and the impact this may have on employees.

This scene focuses on two key themes as follows:

DOI: 10.4324/9781003137269-8

1 *The strategies and techniques of controlling social media use:* This scene explores the variance in individual strategies deployed by management actors who embed rules and take disciplinary control of social media use.
2 *Personal power dynamics in the employment relationship:* This section focuses on the idiosyncratic power strategies deployed by individuals in key positions of power in organisations to gain worker compliance. It focuses on where power was shared through employee voice (EV) mechanisms to consult with employee stakeholders and how these affected ongoing relations. This further reveals how key actors dramaturgically develop identity performances to establish their power and control.

This is of importance as Jacobson and Tufts (2012) state that little empirical research has focused on management practices in this domain and the impact this has on employment relationships.

## Individual techniques of controlling social media

Whilst much has been written around management styles, there is very little which focuses on the varied individual approaches key social actors adopt to control their workforce. I have sought to focus on the varied strategies for using social media for surveillance purposes to specifically observe employees or how this is achieved. This is a growing phenomenon.

This section, therefore, seeks to illustrate and unpick the performances of management practices in this area to provide a fascinating insight into emerging displays of power in this domain. The empiricism aims to reflect on actors' individual perceptions and need to establish more power to control employee performance in their teams. These are used to draw attention to the variability in how key actors shape regimes of control.

## The panoptic effect of social media

An emerging discourse in the corpus of data from the empiricism suggests that most actors use social media to observe worker performance. The case study narratives revealed that all management actors used surveillance through covert and informal means which has differing implications both for the regulatory use of social media and for the control of (mis)behaviour in organisations. As we are all more visible, I start with the worry of being watched on social media.

### *Fear of being observed*

This case highlights how workers fear being observed by their co-workers or indeed management. This may impact on how we interconnect or communicate in organisations. The social actor here discusses the physical effects of being watched and observed by co-workers or leaders via their social media and the impact this has:

> I went on to Facebook I saw my boss who doesn't normally use Facebook, was on Facebook. I'm like, "stop panicking"… . I literally cacked myself [pause] … Then I was like, grow up! As if she's going to call me in tomorrow and say, "I saw you on Facebook at three o'clock yesterday" … I'm so terrified of big brother.
>
> (Tiro, Beth, Sales Director [p. 10 line 30–36])

The actor in this case is a director who openly discussed how they felt when they realised they were on a social media platform when they should not have been. My aim is to highlight how easy it is for all workers to breach their own corporate rules. The social actor in this case explained and understood workers in this corporations should access Facebook during lunch periods (12–2 p.m.). This has transferability to many organisations.

The social actor in this case went on Facebook outside the Firewall. The quote illustrates the fear effect of being observed on social media by a fellow director. The actor in this context clearly links forms of observation and monitoring to Orwellian concepts of surveillance. This is taken from the book penned by the writer George Orwell, whose novel *1984* depicts themes of mass surveillance, totalitarianism, state control, and oppressive regimentation of people and their behaviour in society.

We are all aware that social media has the capacity to increase how we are watched or observed by powerful third parties. The narrative creates a dramaturgical and sinister undertone, linking back to a Foucauldian discourse of power. This shows how digital devices are used increasingly and allow a panoptic visibility of employees at all levels to emerge. The dialogue infers the fear of being caught and notions of corporal punishment. Beth's reaction infers she *cacked* herself at being observed by executive management. This is a Yorkshire colloquialism meaning to defecate oneself. This highlights a pathological anxiety and physical response to surveillance situations (Steimer, 2002). Beth, implied she was not necessarily conscious that fellow directors would observe her via her social media platforms. This highlights how actors in senior positions may also misinterpret policy and drew attention to the fact that managers maybe unclear about organisational regulations and highlights they too are prone to more visibility and forms of surveillance.

This has resonance for performativity and calculability at work (Moussa, 2015; Townley, 1994; Will-Zocholl, 2016). Importantly, this case demonstrated the subjectivity inherent in these surveillance practices. It revealed that rules on observation and monitoring and circumnavigating Firewalls are not routinely applied to all stratifications of the workforce (Ackroyd and Thompson, 2003). As Beth held a directorship, this is perceived to influence how she was treated differently to employees in lower-ranking positions within the organisation. Those in lower-ranking roles were more severely reprimanded for their misuse of mobile phones, circumnavigating Firewalls, and accessing social media at unspecified times in the day. This exposes the often-unfair contradictions in the application of the regulation processes in this domain (Dessler, 2015). This raises important ethical considerations regarding how management protects their interests and agendas (Moussa, 2015). More importantly, this shows how management are capable of forms of indiscretion and (mis)behaviour.

***The watchtowers***

Foucault (1975) stated that discipline assumes the mechanisms of power and a greater need to observe agents in the workforce. Surveilling employees in work emerged as a strong discourse for management actors who focused their narratives on techniques they deployed to watch, monitor, and observe workers in their daily routines and practices:

> I'm always on the lookout for people who might be swinging the lead, I do think I am quite observant and I am always keeping my eye out.
> (Charta, Frances, Credit Control Manager [p. 5. line 18–21])

The particularity of this case highlighted the keen-eyed observation deployed by some management. The social actor Frances consistently referred to her work teams' addiction and attachment to their mobile phone use. This was of interest. Extant literature and new media commentary suggest our addiction to social media and mobile devices are epidemically growing which suggests compulsive use. This manifests itself in behavioural addiction symptoms which include salience, tolerance, conflict, withdrawal, relapse, and mood modification (Hawi and Samaha, 2017; Griffiths, 2005).

During discussions with the actor in this case study, Frances used a metaphor of *swinging the lead*; this describes her perception of how she believed her team had a propensity for work avoidance. The phrase is translated to mean the act of shirking or malingering at work (*Oxford Dictionary*, 2016). In this case, Frances felt workers in her team were procrastinating over their work and therefore wanted to control their daily routines and increase their productivity more rigidly.

Ackroyd and Thompson (2003) state direct control over employees is a habitual practice of management. Conversely, they suggest an habitual attitude of employees is recalcitrance and misbehaviour. Clearly, this case example highlights how Frances embodies this view. Frances was developing strategies which involved a panoptic-like view of her employees. Her discourse alludes to the metaphor of the watchtower. The narrative simply illustrates how some managers author regimes to metaphorically gaze down on and scrutinise employees

(Foucault, 1977). The regimes of control in this case were improvised and informed by a perception Frances' team would:

> ...take the mick
>
> (Charta, Frances, Credit Control Manager [p. 5 line 26])

This is a UK colloquialism which links to a form of ridicule and recalcitrant (mis)behaviour. The language used highlights the perception that workers are both dismissive or contemptuous of the need to be productive. In this organisational context, Frances and her colleagues described a reliance on hard human resource management (HRM) techniques which were symptomatic of the wider organisational culture where they worked. The organisation was controlled by venture capitalists. The sole focus for all teams, therefore, was to produce and increase calculable revenue performance and deter forms of worker distraction (D'Abate and Eddy, 2007; Moussa, 2015). These cultural approaches increased the likelihood of more physical forms of observation. These types of worker control strategies were apparent and normative in two highly commercially driven organisations (Charta and Tiro).

Management actors in these two case organisations used displays of power which involved eyeball management and physical proximity, such as standing over employees to make them focus on work. In the following quote, the actor describes this activity and what she would do when seeing employees who are distracted by their personal mobile devices as this case quote suggests:

> I will just go over and say "Oh what are you doing?... Anything interesting?"
>
> (Beth, Sales Director, Tiro [P12 L18])

These actions are attributed to a discourse of power where such disciplinary practices have real consequences for employees (Thompson, 2016) as this actor further elaborated:

> Seeing them on the phone is like a red mist to me. So I have been known to go up to people and say "if I see you on your phone again I will throw it out the window".. literally like they have been warned and warned and warned
>
> (Beth, Sales Director, Tiro [P12 L18])

These illustrate offline forms of surveillance which are more oppressive. These forms of performance are full of theatricality. They reveal a greater depth of subjugation and power dynamics being played out in the employment relationships in these settings. In this case, the employee would have been dismissed for repeatedly being unproductive.

Further analysis unearthed wider mechanisms and disciplines which management actors authored to organise and more deeply control their colleagues and co-workers. These are now elaborated upon.

### *The wall: Keeper of phones*

The empiricism highlighted how some management actors held a deep cynicism and mistrust of employees in their workforce. As discussed, this was, in part, due to the reinforced belief employees are distracted or addicted to their mobile phones, social media, or malingering in work. Exploring this notion revealed unique techniques designed to stop mobile devices being used at work. The most striking case was again shared by the actor Frances.

This actor forced her team to relinquish their phones at the start of the working day. She had developed a bastardised rule which required workers to hand over their devices. She made them place their phones on a window ledge at the other side of the office building. I have termed this ledge "The Wall". In my reflection of the empirical interviews and observations of the management styles in this organisation, the window-ledge signified a dramaturgical device used by Frances to exert power. I felt this was reminiscent of a boundary or force-field very much like "The Wall" which is depicted in the book and TV dramatisation of *Game of Thrones* (G.R.R. Martin et al, 1996). The Wall is a fortress or boundary which is designed to be inaccessible. This self-imposed phone amnesty was an "unwritten rule" developed by Frances and stemmed from her deep mistrust of her immediate subordinates. The hope here is that by taking mobile devices away from her team members Frances may increase their productivity.

**Discussion box 16**

**Discussion:**

Discuss in groups whether you think taking away personal mobile devices away from workers in your place of study or work is likely to be a deterrent to stop distractedness?

Discuss positive ways that you could utilise and incorporate use of digital devices and social media in work to benefit workers, management, and the corporation?

**Pause for reflection:**

Discuss whether you feel this would improve worker productivity and engagement?

These sentiments were echoed by other actors in this study, an individual view which conceptually fits with the Theory X notion of the lazy worker (Ackroyd and Thompson, 2003; McGregor, 1960). The actor Frances further elaborates on the development of wider rule regimes she developed to manage worker distractedness from use of mobile phone issues:

> …you can't have any personal phone calls; you can't have your phones on your desk… I don't want to micro-manage people; that's not my style.
>
> (Charta, Frances, Credit Control Manager [p. 5 line 27–31])

Ironically, Frances revealed she did not wish to operate a "micromanagement" approach. This is perceived to mean she does not wish to infantalise her teamworkers. Her technique links to management styles which are an important canon in employee relations contexts (Edwards, 2003; Purcell and Ahlstrand, 1993).

Management styles add to the perception managing conflict is inherent in the employment relationship and incorporate differing methods of worker control. This case organisation was operating a traditionalist management style. This highlighted how managers in this organisation injected their own philosophy and ideas to legitimise poor labour conditions and management approaches (Dundon and Rollinson, 2011). Frances was highly focused on her desire to encourage hard work. This script and performance enactment is perceived to be a hallmark of more transactional management practices which are associated with low trust management regimes (Edwards, 2003; Ackroyd and Thompson, 2003). I approached this issue with France to explore how she sought to address the issues of mobile phone misuse and distractedness via social media use. Frances stated she would:

> I generally send out a blanket e-mail to everybody of my expectations, I try not to single you out.
>
> (Charta, Frances, Credit Control Manager [p. 5 line 7–19])

Frances explained how she sends out an email to her team. The use of written communication to map out desired behaviours generically was highly interesting, primarily as she is not physically addressing the issues with the actual perpetrator which seems unusual. This has multiple connotations. First, this approach may be designed to reduce stigmatism of perceived misbehaviour or avoid singling out any one individual (Ackroyd and Thompson, 2003). On the face of it, this action seems fair. Second, this approach may be used to reinforce expected phone etiquette and behaviour with the rest of the team. However, it may also signal the manager in question is visibly avoiding individual performance discussions to avoid confrontation.

There was a similar habitual pattern of avoiding confrontation with staff by all management actors in the study who discussed their reticence to approach or discipline employees for fear of repercussions or escalating the situation. This demonstrates a need to support management more broadly to strengthen their competence to tackle unconventional behaviours at work.

This relates to wider research which suggests managerial regimes have an impact on further rule-breaking (Ackroyd and Thompson, 2003; Edwards, 2003; Rollinson et al, 1997). Use of email as a form of discipline simply records the issue as evidence. However, this may be highly unlikely to address forms of recalcitrance and may be counterproductive in inducing appropriate workplace behaviours. We need to enshrine more humanistic approaches which drive improved relations and impact positive work behaviours, not simply control or command. We need to drive better approaches that use opportunities to address conflicts to affect change.

## Employee voice and consultation

This section focuses on how wider employee relations concepts are applied in differing work contexts. These are used to illustrate corporate attempts to share power and how this is sought within the employment relationships. HR actors are directly involved in shaping workplace policy development, regulation, and behaviours across the organisation and are often instrumental in the inclusion of employee voice mechanisms to develop such regimes. This section explores the extent to which HR actors acknowledged or utilised EV mechanisms for consultation on social media use and development of control or discipline with wider stakeholders such as trade unions.

This draws attention to the backdrop of tensions which may occur at work and within the dramaturgical performances of key work roles who are supposed to work in partnership to develop working conditions in these domains.

The following case study centres on formal EV arrangements with trade unions and includes how discussions were used to shape rule-setting agendas for social media uses in work.

### *Trade union relations and perceptions*

This case shows how the differing interests emerge in the playing out of power relations in the employment relationship. My discussion focuses on how we perceive key stakeholders and the impact this may have for the idea of leading and control the workforce. A central construct for some HR actors is the relationship they have with their trade union counterparts as this case quote illustrates any form of resistance is rarely welcomed:

> ..Trade unions are true to type, they have an issue about surveillance monitoring and the freedom of speech... they [trade union leaders] were more reluctant to subscribe to anything. We thought we had got to a point where we

> thought we had agreed the policy and they fed it to their regional branch and … they were saying that we don't want this for our members so there was a bit of issue there with the dynamic between how region were imposing their way to a local consultation and discussion …we said to them "come on we have local negotiation here and good partnership".
>
> (Alumno, Davina, HR Policy Development [p. 2 line 8–20])

The narrative focuses on perceived challenges to power during the processes of consultation on social media policy. This is perceived to add further antagonism and tensions in employment relationships where coalitions and personal interests became more prominent. A central dynamic for HR is the need to balance each side of the opposing debates on ethical approaches for social media regulation (Barry and Wilkinson, 2016; Bingham, 2016; Edwards, 2003). This statement highlights the intricacy of discussions which were being played out at a regional and local level. Bingham (2016) suggests this perpetuates a unitary view where management is unlikely to concede power to wider organisational members and leads to an assertion of management power.

Barry and Wilkinson (2016) suggest forms of pluralism should incorporate social values which recognise employee rights to have an effective voice, regardless of any consequence to management. They suggest there is a blindness to systemic issues of power. Critically, this demonstrates the time, thought, and effort which needs to be given to hearing all sides and interests in this context. This further demonstrates how EV processes may impact upon the employment relationship.

Discussions on social media use in organisations principally focuses on the employee right to freedom of expression and speech. This area of legislation poses challenges for an interpretation of law due to differing philosophical viewpoints (Steel, 2012). Organisations must navigate between liberal and draconian notions of limiting "freedoms" on digital platforms. These must not breach societal needs, protection of the business concerns, and individual (Biro, 2011).

This correlates to our previous discussions regarding privacy and monitoring of employee behaviours through technology (Moussa, 2015). This has implications for the employment deal where employers strive to strike a balance between regulating behaviour and mitigating rights of the employees (Reddington, as cited in CIPD, 2012a). These rights are potentially diminishing. The use of the dark net gives rise to further concerns societally as it offers space for anonymous solidarity and nefarious activity (Rudesill et al, 2015; Van Gramberg et al, 2014). More broadly, employers worry about how our activity either in and beyond work can affect corporate reputations. So corporations may, in future, try to limit what we can do and say online by developing harsher remedies.

Consultation forums at work allow employers and trade unions an opportunity to air concerns over such issues. These fora discussed by the actors and create corporate scenes in which dramatic techniques of power are displayed. In these meetings, individuals develop scripts to more widely stage their ideas, norms, beliefs, and values in organisational discourses (Benford and Hunt, 1992). These portrayals of identity and characterisation link to edifices of power relations. These scenes exist as subplots to managerial regimes by allowing EV to contribute to legitimate decision-making in organisations (Martin et al, 2015).

In EV approaches, power is essentially pluralist and two dimensional in nature (Cradden, 2011; Edwards, 2003; Fox 1966; Lukes, 2005). EV mechanisms offer employees an opportunity to articulate alternative visions of power arrangements, challenge management by raising concerns about work, and have involvement in corporate decision-making. Whilst extant literature suggests HR practitioners are inculcated to represent the interests of both the organisation and employee (Kochan, 2004), the empiricism in this study suggested HR actors follow a distinctly more managerialist approach. The quote highlights how the actor Davina states "come on" to the trade unions trying to cajole them to accept management terms.

Van Gramberg et al (2014) state the digital context presents a timely need for the advocacy of ethical HRM practices, arguing HRM activities should more coherently champion the needs of employees and not just corporate ones. The primary concern raised by trade unions in this case centred on issues of surveillance and retributive steps taken by management to punitively address perceived online digital misbehaviours.

### *Freedom of expression and censorship: The management view*

What is of central issue is how HR actors give little reflection to the acknowledgement of worker issues associated with freedom of speech and privacy. The narratives highlighted how these interactions led to a polarisation of views between HR and trade union actors in this context:

> They were like WHY!?… Particularly the academics who said its freedom of speech, we are allowed to say whatever we want to say. ... We were faced with "too tight guidelines" and "you are being too controlling", "you are watching us and policing us".
>
> (Alumno, Debbie, Policy Development [p. 1 line 23–30])

This draws attention to corporate frustrations over the apparent challenges to management heterodoxy made by trade union stakeholders, and, more importantly, for this institution, how this may collide with academic freedom and expression. This understandably demonstrates a potentially detrimental implication for consultation, negotiation, and ongoing joint partnership working efforts in higher education institutions. This drew attention to how HRM in these institutions sought to galvanise corporate opinion and sentiment (Benford and

Hunt, 1992). Whilst this comment feels innocuous, it highlights the challenge to the essence of academic freedom and links more spuriously to the idea of censorship.

Docherty (2024: 252) suggests that there are growing tensions for academic freedom and expression. This is becoming more prevalent in the current context where academics are being asked to limit their sense of self to "strictly parolled and parochial debate, making no great claims for the effect or purchase of their work". The point emphasised is universities have a commitment to preserving academic freedoms, but this has come at a price where saying what we think has become a minefield. I highlight this debate as this has a crossover with social media use and where some institutions have asked academics to professionalise their content, both on- and offline, or face punishment.

**Discussion box 17**

**Discussion:**

Discuss your perceptions of *Freedom of Expression?*

Discuss how clear you think social media policy and practices are in articulating employee duty and responsibility regarding Article 10 on the European Convention on Human Rights?

Do you think it is fair to limit and censor what employees say on social media?

Do you think educational institutions should *police* and censor what teachers and academics say?

**Pause for reflection:**

Discuss how this can be misinterpreted?

## Freedom of expression and censorship: An academic view

A major area of discussion for all organisations centres on establishing limits for online speech and permissibility. The dynamics and issues associated with both the control of social media use and the impact on academic freedom of speech were explored with the actor David, a trade union representative:

> Personally, I wouldn't feel my need to express my academic freedom would require me to have any access to social media at all!... the major tension for me was I wasn't that keen on the idea of a policy at all because the point

> about policy generally, when I'm taking a union perspective … and looking at what HR are doing, is to say "this is about having some way of penalising people if they do something wrong". I'm very happy to have a policy which is a supportive policy, which says "We'll help and encourage you to do the right things". It's what the sanctions are if they don't?
>
> (Alumno, David, Academic TU representative [p.3 line 13–38])

This, therefore, centres more on wider competing tensions which arise between trade unions and the employer who decide the parameters for freedom of expression and punitive sanctions for social media use.

A concern for the trade union was the articulation of punitive sanctions which were not designed to be supportive of employees and how these may be applied to forms of perceived misbehaviour. This correlates with guidance on this thornier issue as a moot point of clarification (Biro, 2011). Moussa (2015) suggests social media policy regulations should include protection for academic freedom and use of social media for pedagogical work.

Jansen (2024) suggests each democratic community will set out legal parameters for freedom of expression which includes a variety of exceptions such as defamatory speech. However, it can be further observed there are sensitivities regarding academic freedom of expression which may bring unfavourable attention on individuals or educational institutions, potentially threatening funding, reputation, and ranking (Steel and Petley, 2024). This raises institutional concerns regarding the civic duty of an academic to provide thought-provoking discussion and research.

There is a rising issue in universities who are now seeking to censor academic speech, monitor classroom activities, and allow students to make complaints about teaching, which some students find disagrees with their personal views or should be disciplined in some way (Docherty, 2024). Whilst academics are provided some protections enshrined in law, there is a need to support academic freedom of speech. This has been observed recently in the UK. A senior academic used data which an international student found objectionable. This led to the institution cancelling a module. This raises concerns regarding marketisation and student capabilities to influence course content which may question or test political, economic, or managerial ideology and hegemony in certain geolocational contexts. Conceptually, this links to Lukes (2005), who states organisations seek acquiescence in power relations and firmly draws attention to the dominant interests of the parties in the employment relationship. Renton (2021 writing in the Guardian UK) suggests this intentionally gives right-wing groups the right to attack universities under the guise that any radical speech is an attack on these ideologies.

### *Minimising employee voice*

A way to circumnavigate trade union or employee challenges to management agendas was to simply minimise EV processes and avoid meaningful consultation with key stakeholders on regulations for social media use. This was explored with other HR actors in the sample:

> We consult with them on disciplinary grievance and not much else.
>
> (Senes, Erica, HR Director [p. 12 line 17])

This demonstrates a full exercise of power between HR, management, and trade unions. It shows how HRM may exclude forms of EV, thus rendering unions more amenable to regulation in a formulaic and prosaic way (Townley, 1994). This focuses attention on the differing shades of pluralism and the ongoing asymmetries in employment relationships (Dundon and Rollinson, 2011; Edwards, 2003; Bingham, 2016). This suggests forms of consultation may be less meaningful in some organisations. I seek here to suggest that such dramaturgical performances could be perceived to be used as a motive for coercing compliance and signify further means of oppression (Lukes, 2005). Critically, these approaches challenge idealistic strategies for HRM posited by Ulrich (1997: 149) who stated HR managers should be "The employees' voice in management discussions" and assure "employees that their concerns are being heard". The empiricism clearly shows the opposite to be true in these organisational contexts.

A significant finding in this empirical study is that HRM across all corporations sought to suppress EV. This creates a nexus with employee silence, where social actors, for a variety of differing reasons, offer no vocalisation of workplace issues or they are effectively silenced by the corporation (Dyne et al, 2003). This discourse reveals how HR actors dramaturgically display loyalty to role and swear allegiance to organisationally constructed definitions and norms (Benford and Hunt, 1992). This is of interest as this exposes how actors develop, enact, and secure commitment to their organisational agentic and professional identity. This also relates to the concept of self-censorship where the individual voluntarily or intentionally withholds, constrains, or limits information to protect the self, others, and wider stakeholder (Bar-Tal, Nets-Zehngut, and Sharvit, 2017).

## Management's right to manage

These contexts clearly establish a premise for management to exercise the right to control social media and freedom of expression. However, when trying to rein in use of these devices, management actors discussed how they could not locate regulations or policy used to manage such situations:

> I started to look for a policy on it and I couldn't find one so I know our Head of [Services] has just produced something or had somebody produce something but it is quite, as a lot of our policies are, quite big and it doesn't really drill down to the level that I wanted ... It's still open to interpretation ...I will be supplementing that policy myself.
>
> (Alumno, Dahlia, Manager [p. 4 49–51])

The absence of visible rules and policy in this area drew attention to how managers will seek to develop their own rulebooks without being constrained. Regulations, therefore, are dramaturgically used as draft scripts which are adapted and exchanged in favour to suit a manager's own ideology of control (Dundon and Rollinson, 2011).

In this case study, the management actor perceived the social media policy was too broad (Dessler, 2015). In the earlier quote, the actor, Dahlia, stated policy did not drill down to the specificity of her needs, which is often cited as a common error in policy development (Lucero et al, 2013). However, the central issue here is the ease with which management seeks to improvise with corporate rules, creating their own hybrid versions. This is problematical for establishing fair treatment and support at work for employees (Ackroyd and Thompson, 2003). This is worrying given the levels of institutional surveillance are on the rise thus privilege wider work inequalities to emerge.

Further, extant literature on measuring digital work suggests that policy is further compounded by inadequate methods to articulate, quantifying or qualifying what social media activity, therefore, intensifies control of labour in this domain (Pfeiffer, 2016 as cited in Briken et al, 2017; Will-Zocholl, 2016). In the case narrative, a Twitter project had not been fully scoped by the management actor. There began a process of growing conflict between expected management outcomes and employee achievement of calculable goals. In terms of procedural approaches to address forms of online misbehaviour, the management actor was struggling to understand what punitive or disciplinary action to take.

Belcourt et al (2008) suggest employee monitoring involves a range of differing management tactics, involving monitoring internet links, emails, telephone use, video surveillance, and the storage and recording of employee performance. Pfeiffer (cited in Briken et al, 2017) suggests these instruments of atomisation. These require a commitment to a performance of power and the development of strict protocols (Benford and Hunt, 1992).

The approach to performance management and discipline was explored with this actor, who stated:

> I'm quite at liberty to get a report from IT if I feel that I'm suspecting there's you know inappropriate use … I don't feel justified. I couldn't go there now based on what I know. I think that would be almost kind of you know victimisation really. (Alumno, Dahlia, Manager [p.4, line 33–36])

The actor, Dahlia, appears reticent while articulating what unproductivity and misbehaviour in this context look like. This emphasised managerial concerns which sought to protect her actions from being perceived as a form of employee *victimisation*. This highlights growing psychological anxieties over how managers approach the discipline of employees. This was perceived to be a reflexive approach and demonstrated a subtle discretionary effort required by management to investigate issues using empathetic approaches (Ackroyd and Thompson, 2003). This relates to her sense of being and how she used empathy and caring (Heidegger, 1926).

Yet this could have been different within more unitary, hegemonic forms of management or where management maybe culpable in the dire articulation of work activities, task orientation, and goals or expected outcomes. This highlights how disciplinary processes rest on the persona of the manager and the employment relations between key actors who are involved in the coordination of formal or informal processes (Saundry et al, 2011).

## Master of whispers

The surveillance of employees unearthed some interesting findings on management behaviours in general. This incorporated other dramaturgical devices relating to employee observation and gossip (Kuo et al, 2015). To gain knowledge and power over employees, some management actors lurked in the workplace:

> You hear them in the corridor saying similar things ...there are people who feedback things and there's ways to find out what's been said.
>
> (Aedis, Alan, Property Services Manager [p. 14 line 6–20])

This portrayal by Alan drew comparison to characters in theatre and literature, such as Varys, the spymaster, in Game of Thrones (G.R.R. Martin et al., 1996), or Iago in Othello, who both use dramaturgical devices to observe and remain concealed from fellow characters. Similarly, this real social actor used a veiled position to create knowledge and manipulate power over his co-workers. This illustrates how gossip and social media are synonymous with each other. Content and obscured behaviours, including lurking in and beyond workplace surveillance practices, are, therefore, concreted in work and are manipulated by management as a dramaturgical attempt to secure power.

Gossip as a phenomenon affects all of us and creates cynicism at work (Kuo et al, 2015). Research has centred on understanding the functions and motives of gossip at work. This may involve exchanging and evaluation of information about absent third parties (Dores Cruz et al, 2019). This is prevalent with social media use where colleagues show content to managers for one-upmanship on peers. Further, in this case study, Alan appears to use a network of wider co-actors who are complicit in this schema and vie for positions of power with work structures.

This poses ethical issues and relates to knowledge of truths, which, in essence, is a contested concept. As Kizza and SSanyu (2005) state, such management activity could undermine morale and create suspicion which causes wider strain within employment relationships. Gossip emanating in the office or from social media can therefore act as a cement and essential survival factor of work (Beersma and Van Kleef, 2011).

Use of informants is clearly sought after by management to prop up their position of power. I am highlighting how observation is both varied and open to interpretation. It further highlights how both office spaces and social media are used as panoptical stages from which to closely observe each other (Mann et al, 2003). Further, some management may capitalise on this activity at their discretion (Ackroyd and Thompson, 2003). However, such propagandising in work is likely to backfire in the long run. I wish to suggest management need to ensure they focus on positive inter-team relations to minimise the likelihood of greater infighting and conflict occurring. I wish to add not all workplace cultures operate in such an insidious way. I am merely demonstrating the case some management use gossip to anchor power and manipulate teams to suit their own means which destabilises performance and productivity. I observed how this affected co-workers when facilitating workplace mediation cases and restorative development sessions for dysfunctional teams, where many issues stemmed from gossipmongering and backbiting.

**Act summary**

This act focused on how social media yield new opportunities to exercise power and develop techniques for controlling employees. The strategies observed in the empiricism perpetuate traditionalist styles of management. This highlights a divergence from aspirational approaches posited in extant literature which suggests management capability should encourage collaborative behaviours in this context (Nyhan et al, 2003).

The findings reveal a number of unique approaches and mechanisms for trying to cement employee compliance. These routinised approaches are rooted in creating fear and minimising EV mechanisms. These contradict best practices advocated by CIPD, UK and wider literature in HR texts.

Internal ownership of policy often made social media and digital device policy structurally difficult to find and therefore affects how employees and management regulate and control use. Furthermore, some organisations still do not have a distinct social media policy which enables employees to challenge regulations in social media contexts.

Firewalls are a common device used to regulate employee access to social media. The analyses on Firewalls provided insights on digital methods to classify workers which perpetuate organisational hierarchies and create further asymmetry in the employment relationship.

Organisational elite actors had liberal access to use devices and social media whilst those in lower strata were often denied use at certain times, affecting the collaborative nature of social media and trust between colleagues. Such tactics to control use contributed to new forms of misbehaviour and a growing repertoire of management techniques to counteract mobile device use, thus rendering Firewalls redundant.

Only two organisations used limited EV processes to try and approach social media use and compliance. However, these narratives demonstrate that consultation on digitalisation regulation was not always meaningful. In some organisations, trade unions were not invited to participate in these discussions at all, highlighting that differing shades of pluralism are alive and well in organisations.

These scenes of discussion reinforced *characterisations* of identity portrayal by actors to show their alignment to traditional organisational ideals. Their agency was shown to galvanise corporate hegemony which now dominate employment relationships. Furthermore, imbalances in the infrastructures had implications for the democratic aims of EV mechanisms (Martin et al, 2015; Thompson, 2016).

Some of the case organisations in this study sought to be more transparent and digital by design. This is perceived to be management rhetoric because these channels were integrated and observed to perpetuate distinctly management agendas, further more as access to digital platforms were not fully integrated for all organisational actors this affects the breadth and scope for all employees to actually air their voice (Cullinane et al, 2012; Kaufman, 2015).

This suggests HRM approaches are needed which act more responsibly to align and cultivate approaches which provide greater democracy for EV which is a strong *raison d'etre* to utilise and enhance engagement with workers (Hodder and Kretsos, 2015; Holland et al, 2016; Martin et al, 2015). This finding has transferability; launching digital channels of communication would represent the differing needs of the organisational population.

Managing out EV on social media has a number of implications and may affect the flow of information that management relies upon for decision-making in this contemporary context (Holland et al, 2016). This is perceived to be a likely cause of conflict and resistance in contemporary employment relationships (McDonald et al, 2016).

It is unlikely some employees are likely to cooperate or add to voice channels on social media. What was surprising was how this affected actors in key stakeholder roles, such as trade union representation, where two actors in union roles were resistant to use platforms or social media due to an encultured and traditional view of organisational communication (Biro, 2011; Broughton et al, 2010; CIPD, 2012a; Hodder and Kretsos, 2015).

This adds to psychoanalytical literature of social media use by Turkle (2015), who suggests that there is still a strong need to reclaim true conversations. This is of interest psychologically, despite more methods to communicate in organisations. The art of meaningful conversation and engagement with workers is still highly favoured in shaping work interrelationships. This is a key consideration for leaders when communicating intergenerationally across organisations (Holland and Kretsos, 2015).

The managerial regimes observed to control social media use demonstrate that hard HRM techniques prevail in this context. These approaches contributed to perpetuating misbehaviours as they are shown to subjugate and infantilise employees. These practices included standing over employees, ridiculing them, and taking their mobile devices away from them. This brings a perception of a naughty child and worker syndrome.

*Table 3.2* Key constructs of power and control

| *Constructs of power* | *HR role* | *Management role* | *Employee role* |
|---|---|---|---|
| **Regulation** | Lead role in developing SM regulation which may reinforce organisational ideals. | Embeds and improvises on SM regulation which may deviate from the main policy. | Subjugated by regulation and surveillance. |
| **Strategies for SM control** | Shapes discussion on SM controls via EV mechanisms. Uses their key role as aesthetes to shape and embody agents in organisations using pre-screening which perpetuates unitary view of organisation. | Adapts control methods to suit own needs and agendas. | Ability to challenge control where regulations are unclear, non-existent, or less transparent. |
| **Dramaturgical devices to enhance power** | Consultation forums used to stage key HR roles in power dynamics, procedure, and process. Use of panoptic approaches and surveillance to recruit idealised agents. | Use of panoptic approaches, spying, surveillance, and physical displays which subjugate and infantilise employees. Manipulating network of employees to create a web of power. | Use of sousveillance as a reversed panoptic device. |

EV, employee voice; HR, human resource; SM, social media.

This drew attention to a need to more carefully consider management techniques in this domain, particularly as employees may increasingly use *sousveillance* to observe management to counteract such treatment. This is discussed in the next scenes.

The variability in individual techniques heralded deeper ethical implications of social media use for HRM practitioners. A clear issue to address is surveillance and pre-screening which revealed a subjective nature inherent in social media use and reinforce the unitary nature of organisations.

Table 3.2 summarises the key constructs of power and control existing within this study.

The following chapter focuses on the evolving identities and dramaturgical performances observed by social actors.

# Section 4

# Act 3

## Evolving identities and dramaturgical performance online

Sociologically, how we shape and accumulate our identities in increasingly digital contexts is hugely interesting. Historically, we are conditioned to believe that our sense of being and self are constant and static. Yet our relationship with social media has made our identity evolution more visible, complex, and, at times, unfathomable. Therefore, the concept of identity in this text centres on the idea that we are multidimensional. The discoveries I put forward relate to the evolving personal sense of self and our identity online. I wanted to show how self-identity is much more experimental, and how this may diverge from corporate expectations of professional role identity, particularly, where employers may seek to further control identity or mould us as subjects (Alvesson and Willmott, 2002).

DOI: 10.4324/9781003137269-9

# Act 3. Scene 1 The multidimensional self

## Identity and new ways of being online

***Scene summary:*** This scene focuses on how key actors use social media as a front stage area to portray ad shape their self-identity through differing dramaturgical performances. The intention is to show how identity work in this space is much more contradictory, unexpected, and much more illusory which may deepen antagonisms in work. The aim is to emphasise how this may create complications for addressing discipline of (mis)behaviours in the workplace, particularly the challenges we have when dealing with actors in elite work roles. Whilst these are attributable to actors in three key roles, these can be transferred to workers in other professions.

**Key learning points**

- Social media dimensions provide multiple platforms for us to project a whole array of selves.
- Using social media incorporates a highly iterative process of self-discovery, invention, and reinvention for self-identity creation.
- Ulterior identities are prone to leakages, affecting followership, leadership, authority, and power of elite actors who choose to experiment with self-identity online.

Social networking platforms represent different "stages" to dramaturgically and theatrically perform and play out differing identities and characterisations of the self. This heightens the notion that the self and our identity in this context is highly fluid. Who we present at any given time across these spaces may differ from the perceived identity we portray in work (Kerrigan and Hart, 2016).

Learning about how we view leader and co-worker identity in digital spaces is of paramount importance to HR management practitioners. Particularly, if the development of our identity flaunt rules, regulations, or includes the use of anti-ulterior identities which are contrary to expected professional work identities. This is rarely discussed, so my aim is to address this gap and highlight how elite

DOI: 10.4324/9781003137269-10

professionals may develop subversive digital identities and the impact this has on working relations.

From an employee relations perspective, this creates a further contested terrain of work (Edwards, 1979). It is, therefore, of great interest, ethically how corporations legitimise subtle control of all worker identity and behaviour in digital contexts, not just those in frontline roles. The discussion shows the contradictions in this pursuit.

Dramaturgy is used to reflect on how social actors in these key roles present their sense of self-identity in on- and offline interactions (Goffman, 1959). Dramaturgy is informed by a sense of reflexivity and introspection, even more so on social media where we are exposed to a much more critical gaze of the self online by others. This context allows the individual to be a greater subject and object of both power and knowledge. The empiricism shows gaps in our knowledge, highlighting that we do not fully understand the profound nature of identity and in this domain. This scene, therefore, corresponds with a search for truths and discoveries about individuals, where the subject is much more hidden (Townley, 1994). I, therefore, delve deeper to uncover some amazing truths about identity work and offer a greater exploration of how social actors scope out their identity performances online. The case studies offer insights on emerging identities in key professions and potential forms of misbehaviour. These may be used as blueprints to reflect on how we may need to adapt approaches, processes, and practices to manage such paradoxes.

The scene focuses on three subthemes:

1 *The evolution of HR professional role and identity:* This section focuses on HR actors' sense of commitment to professional role identities in this digital context. It reveals how HR actors define the identity of others and their own. It explores how senior HR actors are not as they appear in their role, and how this may impact on power dynamics and discipline in their roles.
2 *The evolution of management role and identity:* This section focuses on management actors' commitment to a managerial identity, and how actors use this to articulate power and control in their roles.
3 *The evolution of employee, trade union role, and identity:* This section focuses on actors in operational employee and trade union roles and explores how interconnections and power relationships shape and control identities in digital contexts.

## The evolution of HR professional role and identity

Exploring how HR actors used social media and the emerging dramaturgical techniques used by these actors to shape their identity, role, and power was fascinating. I looked at their approaches for scripting, staging, performing, and interpreting their own and others identity (Benford and Hunt, 1992). As expected, much of the discourse shows how HR actors strongly identified with developing positive, professional identities. This was an endeavour to affiliate with their organisational role, which is integral to the employment relationship. This added to their sense of being a subject and is greatly aligned with their role in shaping regulatory processes and discipline.

### "It's in the blood": HR cultural perceptions of social media

Identity is shaped within cultural contexts and, therefore, may lead social actors to perform within their role commitments. This process is increasingly aligned with our growing reliance on social media which enables us to modify multiple versions of self-identity for different audiences (Benford and Hunt, 1992; Castells, 2011; Taylor, 2018). This section explores how HR actors use on- and offline contexts to shape their identity.

A key construct emerging in the discourse of HR actors was how they developed a script which related to their institutional, agentic roles. The central dialogue focused on their role as a subject of power, embodiment, and commitment to HR techniques. This was enmeshed with their sense of duty and associated work in developing corporate mechanisms for discipline and control. This provided an everyday sense of how these actors viewed their self in relation to social media activity and interconnectivity:

> … when you are in HR… it is part of your genetic blood … you just don't [go on social media].
>
> (Alumno, Davina, HR Policy Development [p.7 line 34–35])

This quote highlights how developing a professional identity involved showing a strong sense of self-discipline. This was achieved by limiting or rejecting use of social media as discussed in Act 1. This case reinforces how rejecting interconnectivity with wider work peers or other social actors is a central tenet for an HR actor's sense of self-identity as a moral individual.

The narrative used by the actor, Davina, centres on a biological metaphor of restraining her social media use. This was interpreted to mean that rejecting use of social media is culturally espoused. This has transferability to many professional roles. For instance, barristers or solicitors who may wish to hide their online social identity, limiting interconnection or perhaps using avatar profile names or pictures to protect the identity of themselves or loved ones from being discovered. Additionally, to ensure that their posts do not impact on their professional sense of self. In this case, Davina's script is shaped by a concern their social media pose a significant risk to the institution and others.

The notion of limiting digital identity is seen as a legitimising identity (Castells, 2011). This dramaturgical mechanism of abstention or remaining hidden enforces their position in the corporation and is shaped by their disciplinarian role in knowledge, power, and truths (Foucault, 1975/77); Townley, 1994). This suggests workers are actively engaged in self-regulation and censorship online and are capable of controlling their behaviours (Thompson, 2016). Further, this suggests that employees are able to segregate and manage the public–private boundaries. An individual approach to managing identity is now discussed.

### Commitment to segregating the self online

All actors in the empirical study made a conscious effort to stage a professional identity. This involved tailoring and manipulation of online performances:

> When I joined here and people asked me to be friends… I went back and edited my photos because it had gone back over 10 years... i.e. flicking the V [gesture / swearing] … falling over [drunk] on a hen do! I don't want this to be the side of me they see… I don't want to project this image to anyone.
>
> (Alumno, Davina, HR Policy Development [p. 9 line 14–18])

Editing images and posts is of increasing interest in the current context. This is due to speculations regarding a recent royal photo released in the UK for Mother's Day 2024 due to the fact this image was edited. My point here is to state authenticity is a much wanted and important societal value. Yet across all levels of society, we actively engage in editing and touching up online images and content. We manipulate images to make us look glossier. Therefore, uncovering truths from online images is much harder to do in the current context which may cause great impact.

HR actors similarly were keenly involved in editing their online profiles to manipulate the views others have of them. In the process of study, I was given access to personal profiles. I observed one HR actor was constantly absorbed in updating and revising their profile photos and sharing images of themselves constantly on their daily feeds. This involved airbrushing and photoshopping content to the extent the individual had significantly altered their appearance by whitening teeth and visibly altering prominent facial features to appear more aesthetically pleasing. Psychologically, this showed an extreme neediness to be liked and, to a degree, a vulnerability. However, making such changes is a constant effort and a transitory state which we cannot hope to sustain. The simple truth is, in reality we may never hold such appeal or allure when people see us physically, they will note we look nothing like the online version of ourself.

The increasing level of criticality with which we are gazed upon is indecipherable. We don't appear to fully understand the psychological impact on individuals or give this much thought or concern as a phenomenon, despite it being so culturally commonplace. Some may say addictively so as we get a dopamine hit from these interactions.

This activity seems very looks based. From a dramaturgical perspective, this is akin to make-up and costuming. We dress and stage ourselves to gain adulation from vast audiences – some making careers out of this activity. Prioritising looks is worrying in this context where surely competence and skill, which are more lasting, should be more prized.

This demonstrates a fear of our own self-identity. Manipulation of online profiles is therefore used to present an idealised gestalt, but not entirely authentic version of the self. This dramaturgical technique is used to rescript identity and links to impression management (Goffman, 1959; Kerrigan and Hart, 2016). This creates a dilemma as we are caught into a never-ending cycle of aesthetic labour, which is discussed in the next scene. My point is to raise concerns about the more unhealthy relationships we have with our digital self. Moreover, this may allow cynicism and scepticism to creep into our social relationships, where falsehoods appear and may lead others to critically "call out" individuals regarding their inauthenticity.

The HR actors more readily discussed how they tried to segregate their online profiles to contain or hide their past identities. This illustrates how our online identity is, therefore, more conflictual with work expectations. We reimagine our profiles, reflexively reconstructing a new, emergent professional identity in order to look good and sound great (Kerrigan and Hart, 2016; McDonald et al, 2016; Nath et al, 2016). This establishes a further agency problem for HR actors in this context, primarily because our online content could mismatch with the perceived role and identity identification in the offline context (Hatch and Cunliffe, 2013).

## The critical gaze of others in online contexts

In some cases, we are forced to engage in a greater level of introspection and self-censorship to address contradictory identities and behaviours so our online behaviour does not impact our professional roles (Yanow and Tsoukas, 2009). We now edit our photos to appear more professional and befitting of our work status, as this quote highlights:

> I am also conscious that … I am management level …should I have a picture of me with that last Pina Colada looking inebriated at the bar because I am a role model.
>
> (Alumno, Davina, HR Policy Development [p. 9 line 7–9])

This reflection demonstrates how social media forms part of the architecture in how we now make sense of ourselves. Social media holds a mirror up to our sense of self so we may gaze on ourself and use content to see ourselves through the eyes of others. This helps us reflect upon the two differing hemispheres of our private or public sense of self in relation to our role and status.

We have, therefore, become an aesthete, trying to navigate, adapt, and manipulate how others view us (Nath et al, 2016; Strati, 1999; Taylor, 2018). This suggests we consciously act this way because we are performing to audiences online (Kerrigan and Hart, 2016).

The appraisal of the self is used both for an interpretation of performance and to secure power relations (Benford and Hunt, 1992; Taylor, 2018). Thus, social media are used to shape a self-identity which adheres to social conventions and rules. This is purposeful for inspection, judgment, comparison, and correction of the self online. However, this may be used more prejudicially and critically demonstrating the panopticist nature of these devices (Foucault, 1980; Lukes 2005; Townley, 1994).

In this case, Davina is distinctly trying to segregate and protect herself by creating a boundary around her past and more uninhibited self (Ashforth et al, 2000; Zerubavel, 1991). The editing of pictures and content aims to protect herself from the wider judgements of co-workers and increase a managerial sense of power within her role. Boundaries are purposeful to confine the temporal, physical, emotional, and cognitive aspects of our self. A clear issue is whether such online material can truly be segregated or even deleted, as case law has shown people copy and post on materials. The tendency to compartmentalise the self online is all but diminished. Our digital material therefore may seep into differing spheres of our lives (Kerrigan and Hart, 2016; McDonald et al, 2016).

Increasing visibility of our identities online means we are prone to greater forms of regulatory surveillance which destabilises public–private boundaries of the self and allows contestations in the employment relationship to arise (McDonald et al, 2016). Deletion of online material allows actors to develop a mask which is used to demarcate between the private and professional areas' self-identity (Rothbard and Ramajaran, 2009). This increases the emotional labour we invest in to portray the best version of the self in an online contexts (Hochschild, 1983). We devise a range of *dramatis personae* or parts which we develop and play in differing situations (Benford and Hunt, 1992).

This critically serves to remind us of our human fragilities, and we are subject to our own contradictions in digital contexts. Redefining our sense of being tells truths about how we feel regarding this constant manipulation as the actor further stated:

> …it is a shame... these are only snapshots of our lives and can never truly be the whole picture of who you are…
>
> (Alumno, Davina, HR Policy Development [p. 9 line 31–32])

Undoubtedly, social media is a mechanism for reflexive learning on and in our actions which is of paramount importance to our employability (Yanow and Tsoukas, 2009). Yet HR actors are actively involved in scrutinising and decoding profiles for recruitment purposes. This opens opportunity to use social media for wider methods of workplace control (Briken et al, 2017) and how HR render workers as subjects (Barratt,2002); Kerrigan and Hart, 2016; McDonald et al, 2016; Townley, 1994; Webb, 2006).

Modifying the self revealed an inner conflict. In this case, Davina mourned the loss of her authentic true individual identity and conveyed sadness about losing her past identity. Performance online is therefore linked emotionally with our life biographies as we develop overtime. Our profile content captures key life events, different friendships, and loved ones. These importantly allow us to flourish in happy, positive environments. The images and commentaries serve as an album for differing aspects of our identities and are part of the representation of our wholeness. At this intersection, employers use our past online content to judge who we are in recruitment and selection processes. Our past therefore collides with our future. This may create precarity for employment and career progression.

Empiricism has raised concerns about the rise in using online content to judge workers (McDonald et al, 2016). My work echoes these sentiments, primarily, over the approach and validity in how online content is decoded, which is a key issue. Our online activity is massively inspected and interrogated with growing popularity. There is little inspection over the efficacy of these methods where all actors engaged in online screening and pre-profiling to inform judgements on potential recruitment candidates. I am emphasising to readers that there is a greater need to pause and reflect on how we view editing, manipulation, self-regulation, and authenticity and the impact this may have on the ethicality of profile screening (Fang et al, 2015). This is discussed more broadly in the next scene.

**Discussion box 18**

**Discussion:**

Discuss how much you are prone to edit your own profile content and pictures?

How obsessed are you about seemingly looking perfect?

Do you regularly adapt your appearance to make your teeth, facial features, or body seem more aesthetically pleasing?

What are your views on people who do this?

What are your views about making judgements about peoples' appearance for the appraisal of work?

**Pause for reflection:**

Reflect on whether our online profiles are misleading?

Reflect on what are the ethical repercussions of making judgements about people in online contexts?

This shows we have become more obsessed with our identity and appearance online. This has ramifications for work and personal lives. Thus, managing the boundary between these two hemispheres has become more complex.

## Management of the two hemispheres

The complexity of managing and negotiating identity strongly emerged in the HR and management actor discourse. This highlighted the challenges for managing the boundaries between the differing portrayals of self. Their role as a subject of discipline made them more acutely aware of a perceived incompatibility between the two hemispheres of the public and private self.

Management of these two hemispheres of life was addressed further with the actor, Davina:

> I think I can't dissect one from the other I think the person you are in work trips over into your home life and your home life trips over in to your work life unless you are a complete robot. But I guess it is the extremes for me, so the "true me" that my friends will see at 11 o clock on Friday night is not what you will see on social media or what I will be in work…That is just how I want to be perceived.
>
> (Davina, Alumno, Policy Development Lead [p. 10 line 34–38])

Davina's narrative emphasises how navigating the transition between the social and professional self is more complex. This demonstrates how our liminal identities may compete with one another. The metaphor of the robot was interesting. This was interpreted to mean dissecting the socio-emotional self would create an impersonal view of individuals. This offered a dystopian view of work where employers seek to harness a mono-identikit worker Barratt (2002).

Staging the self on social media involves hard work, requiring effort to prune, coordinate, manage, and direct materials (Benford and Hunt, 1992). This requires skills to decide which aspects of our lives audition to get "stage-space" online. One method to try and compartmentalise is to create a professional identity on LinkedIn, considered to be the largest career- and professional work-oriented site. My point here is that many recruiters use this platform. Therefore, this may increase the likelihood of us crafting a highly staged performance designed to interconnect the "self" with a cast of specially selected characters. This is a further method of identity construction (Cover, 2012) where "cast" members support the reinforcement of professional HR or work identity. This was the case for HR actors in this study who tried to showcase a virtuous self by recrafting their digital content.

### Virtuous HR identity

A convergence in HR narratives suggested actors retreated or demarcated use digital platforms and interconnections. This is perceived to link to the construction of a virtuous identity (Dutton et al, 2010). The virtuous identity advanced as actors described performing to the criteria of being an *HR subject* which added greatly to their sense of being at work and online (Creed and Scully,2000).

In this case study, Debbie described how she reprimanded fellow colleagues for their less professional online dialogues:

> I took it upon myself to go and say to that individual "do you know who are your friends in this department?" They just had not thought.
>
> (Alumno, Debbie, HR Policy Development Team, [p. 7 line 11–12])

Debbie used her HR role to inspect her "friends" online content. Debbie saw this activity as a form of coaching and mentoring of co-workers gently getting them to reflect on the appropriateness of their posts. This position of power was used to cultivate modifications to online behaviours and to help shape professional identity. This was perceived to be done with empathy for individual co-workers freeing them from judgment by wider peers (Foucault, 1983; Heidegger, 1926). Components influencing Debbie's identity were her affiliation to her HR script used to demonstrate a construction of self which was informed by a need to act as a moral arbitrator. Her discourse was imbued with symbolic meaning through her benevolent behavioural approach (Dutton et al, 2010; Goffman, 1959; Park and Peterson, 2009). This form of peer observation conceptually links with sousveillance and panopticism (Mann et al, 2003). Debbie used this construct as a dimension of power knowledge (Lukes, 2005; Townley, 1994).

It is not clear whether her "friends" or co-workers interpreted these actions as friendly advice or a form of suppression, or tittle-tattle. Whilst it may be perceived as a form of integrity linked to the virtue-laden identity (Dutton et al, 2010), such behaviours are likely to trigger conflict with fellow colleagues if they resisted suggestions for any ascribed identity norms which may affect team relations.

Critically, this form of identity development reinforces a hegemonic rhetoric. It renders individuals as a subject of the organisation rather than an unrestricted construction of self. Castells (2011) suggests this relates to resources and stratagems which allows individuals to survive institutional power struggles. Identity work in this context is therefore more culturally ascribed and regulated by the organisation (Alvesson and Willmott, 2002; van den Broek and Dundon, 2012). This crystallised how identity work is related to labour processes at work. This approach has psychological implications for how we cross-compare self-identity with peers (Fineman, 2006; Hackman, 2009). This further emphasises how self-identity in work online contexts may be perceived as hackneyed, contrived, and less authentic.

Positive dialogue online is a dramaturgical device which is like storytelling (Sims, 2005). The online dialogue represents the meaning we create of ourselves and others. Content is fairy-tale like, where identity creations are full of illogicality. We teach children not to tell fibs, yet our online content is so staged and may involve an over-generosity with (un)truths regarding identity, aesthetes, and skills. This adds to the precarity in this context, particularly if we cannot achieve fairy-tale expectations of the self (Sims, 2003).

We underestimate how the different versions of "ourselves" in digital spaces as content control is harder to contain. This next case focuses on how our social media may lead to leakage and how this may seep into offline worlds (Kerrigan and Hart, 2016). I now discuss how this occurred for an HR actor who experimented with highly liminal and subversive identities using an avatar or parody of the self. This is problematical for the elite HR actors who are ideally supposed to be a paragon of virtue and restraint in organisations.

**Discussion box 19**

**Discussion:**

Discuss how important it is to segregate or demarcate between work and privacy?

Do you think this is achievable in the current social media context?

Discuss how you might try to segregate your different online profile content and pictures?

**Pause for reflection:**

Reflect on whether corporations should make comparisons between our online and offline identity and use these to inform judgements about whether these impact on work?

### The avatar: Multiple online selves

One unique case highlighted how an elite HR actor creatively experimented with their identity through their social media use. This case demonstrates the highly conflictual nature of identity work, where we create an ulterior identity online, which collides with the expected professional identity and leadership roles. The issue was this type of contradictory behaviour was least expected by an otherwise exemplary character in work. This added greater tension and precariousness of trust of leaders within contemporary employment relationships.

Surprisingly, this HR actor openly discussed how they created a satirised account which mocked work:

> I have another Twitter account [Now X] that is a parody account, It's got its own blog which is a parody… only somebody didn't see it as a parody here.
> (Senes, Erica, HR Director [p. 9 line 49–52])

The particularity of this case was interesting. The actor held an HR directorship. It is understood that the actor knew this account may misrepresent the HR profession. Therefore, we need to understand and explore how social media affords individuals the opportunity to create anti-identity constructs (Carroll and Levy, 2008).

This is becoming more commonplace as artificial intelligence (AI) and certain social media platforms allow us to actively experiment with the self as a caricature. This also forms the bedrock of UK case law. This demonstrates a corporate need and skill sets for management to be more shrewd at discerning the duality of identity in this space, which creates a more distorted conflictual sense of self.

This case emphasises how co-workers unearthed the parody social media account. The workforce therefore critically scrutinised the actions of this leader. In this sense, the position of power is eroded. The wilful misunderstanding that use of this parody account would be seen as a bit of fun to lampoon work was not shared with their fellow colleagues. This was a somewhat naïve decision. This affected their followership and position as their activity mutated into resistance which ultimately challenged the spoof and behaviour of the director. This illustrates how such discoveries are used to level the playing field of power as workers raised issues about the X account and perceived management (mis) behaviours with wider directors.

In this case study, Erica was experimenting with her sense of self and trying to appear humorous to a differing audience. However, this dis-identification of the self caused problems with an otherwise virtuous HR self-identity. This is interesting given the social actor's HR role. This actor disconcertingly thought this account would remain anonymised and hidden. This has repercussions for responsibility of individuals in work and is perceived to be a form of (mis) behaviour.

On reflection, the perception of the parody self may have appeared more secure because the actor perceived this was contained as a bounded self on a bounded site (boyd and Ellison, 2007). This is an unstable approach and demonstrates how all social media activity is discoverable and prone to leakage (Kerrigan and Hart, 2016). Erica's reflection drew attention to how we think our performance online is dramaturgically played out in a stage-like realm and that our characterisations are understood like a comedy or pantomime. Yet audiences are discerning. They too are moral beings. Thus, avatars and parodies present subversive alternative versions of self. These *dramatis personae* may offend observers as they are being more contradictory and a somewhat more rebellious version of ourselves in an online context.

This again has obvious links to dramaturgical devices in Shakespeare. Characters use disguises to fool other actors in plays like *King Lear*, *Midsummer Night's Dream*, and the *Tempest*. The illusions of character are used as a means of trickery, control, power ,or resistance (Benford and Hart, 1992). This has ramifications for leaders where the evolution of a digital identity runs contemporaneously alongside the real, professional self. In this case, there was a conscious effort to mask and cloak their identity, which appeared to wider colleagues as underhand. This experimental aspect of shaping identity pushes the boundaries within the professional role and what is expected behaviour at work. This may be perceived as an act of defiance or form of misbehaviour (Ackroyd and Thompson, 2003, van den Broek and Dundon, 2012).

This was confounding as HR actors are expected to commit to dramaturgical disciplines and conventions which are more professionally oriented (Benford and Hunt, 1992). These actors set the tone for work. They develop rules, processes, and practices for performance in work, including responsible autonomy, where we control our actions' behaviours within skilled groups (Friedman, 1977). This case was unique; however, it highlights spurious decision-making and contradictions in professional behaviour.

Lastly, I wish to point out that the actor was lightly reprimanded for their behaviour. This highlights how little challenge elite actors face if they misbehave, and how they are more leniently disciplined in work. Something we may need to reflect upon. Moreover, this case relates to how leaders are more observed by employees through an emerging veillance practice, sousveillance, which is discussed more deeply in Act 4 Scene 1.

**Discussion box 20**

**Discussion:**

Discuss whether your organisation ever scrutinises HR leaders and management actors in their use of social media?

Do you think or believe that these types of workers are capable of forms of misbehaviour or are they more disciplined?

Discuss whether to your knowledge HR and management actors are ever disciplined in work? What penalties did they receive? Were these less severe than workers in frontline positions?

Discuss whether this creates a fair and level-playing field for all in work?
**Pause for reflection:**

Reflect on whether corporations should make comparisons between different levels and hierarchies of workers.

Reflect on how this impacts on the nature of discipline in work.

How might these inform and perpetuate incorrect judgements about certain types of workers and whether these impact on work?

What can HR and management do to address this imbalance?

The next section focuses on management actors and how they utilised social media as part of their identity construction.

## The evolution of management role and identity

There was a strong correlation between the management and HR actors in the cross-case analyses, where management actors also sought to demarcate social media use to reinforce their professional identity. Like their HR counterparts, management actor identities are assigned against a backdrop of power relations and labour production processes (Briken et al, 2017; Edwards, 2003; Jenkins, 1996; Webb, 2006). Further characteristics suggested managers developed an enterprising identity (Watson, 2008). This relates to principles of agency theory where managers are controlled to ensure that they act in the best interest of the organisation (Lukes, 2005; Hatch and Cunliffe, 2013).

## The disciplined and productive self

Management actors used social media to create an objective interest in their identity which linked to their strategic purpose in work. In this case study, Dahlia discussed how she strategically reviewed online friend or interconnection requests to rationalise the purpose and potentiality of interconnecting with them:

> Can you explain what you think the benefit of this connection would be.
> (Alumno, Dahlia, Service Manager [p. 10 line 16])

This demonstrates an instrumentality in the managerial discourse which is used to reinforce their individual managerial identity (Webb, 2006). This highlighted the dynamics of class and economic consciousness which relate to a managerial output. Conceptually, this links to the enterprising nature of identity, where actors seek to use interconnections so that forms of capitalism may flourish (Watson, 2008). After all, it's who you know that counts.

Dahlia discussed how she unfollowed other users if they failed to meet their objective. This demonstrated a highly strategic process and a more visceral nature of identity creation on social media. Interestingly, Dahlia inferred she did not interconnect widely with her team. When asked why, she stated:

> ...What would I do if something outrageous came up... how would that cloud my judgement really.
>
> (Alumno, Dahlia, Manager [p. 9 line 23])

Demarcation from peers was used to distance the self from observing work colleagues. This emphasises the ordering of subjects and how social media are used as mechanisms of power (Barratt, 2002; Lukes, 2005). Dahlia felt that she would feel confused if she saw any perceived misbehaviour. This links to panoptic effects of observing employees online and represented the need to develop an ideological boundary between her public and private hemispheres in digital work. In this sense, social media constitutes a sense of cultural and social continuity at work. For management actors, this meant there was no escaping from their role of discipline and power which extends beyond routine employment relationships into the omnipresence of social media contexts (McDonald et al, 2016; Moussa, 2015). Demarcation or rejection of interconnecting with co-workers seemed an oddly arcane strategic decision, particularly as managers are now more involved with employee engagement where social media could play a vital role in building relations.

I also argue that management actors, if they choose to interconnect with co-workers, are under greater scrutiny from employees due to how social media allows forms of sousveillance, where they as the observers are also more readily observed (Mann et al, 2003).

## Subversive in-groups and the renegotiation of self

The narratives of management actors showed how their online interrelationships are more fragile due to the emergence of social media which impacts on their sense of self. In the following case, the dismissal of a work colleague caused a flurry of negative comments. Social media was used to discuss the sacking of their peer and to name-call a director. The actor recalled the comments made about her:

> Oh there's a snake in the grass, we all need to stick together now, you can't trust anybody.
>
> (Tiro, Beth, Sales Director [p. 8. line 43–44])

This narrative emphasised how management disciplinary action is dissected and commented upon within online groups, whilst the power that may reside with leaders' offline, social media platforms are is utilised by employees to test the equilibrium. This shows how employees may use social media to subvert how power is distributed (Lukes, 2005). This drew attention to how online interrelations overlap with disciplinary processes. Managers, therefore, must discursively navigate and interpret their identity performance which is now more visibly scrutinised. We rarely discuss the impact of significant HR processes on leadership, and I feel this is something we need to review so that support can be provided, particularly if approaches veer towards forms of harassment and bullying.

Derogatory comments form the basis of case law by ridiculing the individual. I explored how the comments affected the actors' sense of self-esteem:

> ..Somebody else rang me and said off the record that "last night you should have seen what he was putting on Facebook"… we knew what he was up to and it was clear he was slagging me off… horrible, vindictive, nasty, manipulative and unprofessional behaviour. He's connected with lots of people. This was very negative about me … we went through a quandary of how we dealt with it. In that instance, because of who his network was we decided not to do anything about it.
>
> (Tiro, Beth, Sales Director [p. 8 line 27–38])

This case discussion illustrates how we now use social media to form subgroups and wider collectives. The discourse demonstrates the huge effect reading these online comments has on individual feelings, image, and identity. These are used to deliberately exclude people from the online dialogue. In this case, the subgroup on Facebook Messenger was used to tip the balance of power and erode the status of the director. This demonstrates the emerging complexity social media have on workplace conflict, forms of resistance, and the effect this has on contemporary employment relationships.

The impact of not being included in online groups or being "unfollowed" on social media has a melodramatic effect. This dramaturgical technique has similarity to Shakespearean mytho-drama, where actors are subjected to false friendships and cast aside. This is apparent in plays such as Shakespeares play *Othello*, where actors feign friendships in order to fully manipulate power dynamics. This has implications for ongoing identity construction and capability to dramaturgically play a strong role in performance management and discipline (Benford and Hunt, 1992).

This creates a further paradox in work. Corporations fully expect management to engage and interlink with teams across the organisation to enhance their leadership identity. Clearly, the boundaried nature of subgroups diverts this process. The private–public schemas of social media identity in this context therefore sullies inter-team relations. This activity conceptually relates to new forms of worker resistance and a further potential construct of misbehaviour (Ackroyd and Thompson, 2003; Lukes, 2005). The case emphasises how a subgroup was formed and became quite powerful which posed challenges for disciplinary processes. The actors described how the corporation mulled over what to do with the key individual who was leading the resistance and challenge.

In this scenario, the individuals' social media capital and strength of their role competence became of paramount use. The case illustrates how power was redistributed as no course of action was taken over the employee's use of derogatory comments. This demonstrates how the economic power of the employee gained through their network was used to great effect (Castells, 2000a). Their economic performance is treated as an area of negotiation in the power to discipline (Townley, 1994).

My point here is to look at the fairness of disciplinary processes. We are at a juncture where use of subgroups is more prevalent, as demonstrated in a number of high-profile cases in the UK, where co-workers use closed online groups. These are perceived to circumvent corporate rules in certain professions such as the police. If discovered, the online commentaries in these so-called private WhatsApp or Messenger groups affect the reputation of major institutions. More broadly, this relates to gender discrimination where female workers are often left unheard when they raise issues of harassment by subgroups in corporations. Thus, more needs to be done to address and challenge inappropriate behaviours in this context.

**Discussion box 21**

**Discussion:**

How would your place of work or study address the inappropriate use of a social media subgroup, for example, workers who may use WhatsApp to discuss colleagues or working practices without including other workers or management?

How might this affect power dynamics between workers and management leaders if management is not included in the subgroup or WhatsApp group?

Do you think this may adversely affect harmony and team relations?

Is it feasible to tell workers to not use these subgroups?

Does your organisation discipline workers who have effectively harassed someone both off- or online.

**Pause for reflection:**

Should workers who achieve work targets and appear to be productive ever be subject to discipline?

Reflect on how this further impacts on the perceived fairness of discipline in work.

**Regimes of hierarchy, agency, and identity**

The narratives of management actors focused on their role in the performance management, control, and regulation of others which relate to a subjective managerial discourse and identity (Karman and Alvesson, 2004). The discourse suggested they use their sense of duty and obligation to develop power dynamics within the employment relationship:

> My expectations are high and I accept that not everyone will meet my expectations. It is difficult because you set yourself up for failure because I can't always meet my own expectations [laughter].
>
> (Pharma, Greg, Operations manager [p. 6 line 52–55])

This case study illustrates a managerially inspired discourse relating to high achievement. In this case, Greg is complicit in accepting power structures and his position to obey (Milgram, 1974). Interestingly, this highlighted how certain management practices may encourage work intensification and significantly impact on employment relations if calculable performances are not achieved (Townley, 1994). This dramaturgical performance of identity links to calculable outputs, economic relations, and how power is operationalised in the employment relationship.

Management actors further articulated how they coped with differing expectations and developed identity templates in order to create conditions which empowered subjects (Barratt, 2002; Linstead and Thomas, 2002; Sveningsson and Alvesson, 2003). However, this developed a wider polarisation in relations at work which affected online engagement as this narrative suggests:

> there is a "them and us" culture between the trade staff and the management team.
>
> (Aeidis, Alan, operational manager [p. 7 line 46–47])

This emphasises the ever-present power dimensions which are still inherent in organisational cultures. These are used to reinforce management identity. They further highlight the perpetuation of ongoing class struggles which appears in the subdivisions of labour in organisational contexts. This identity template shows how differing interests in the employment relationship create tensions and attitudes within differing work roles (Hatch and Cunliffe, 2013).

Paradoxically, the conflictual nature is observed to affect employee engagement and online participation between worker stratifications. This may explain why employee engagement on internal platforms are low, particularly where workers are distrusting their leaders. Therefore, loyalty and trust in this domain are more difficult to attain. If you can remember, this organisation highly restricted social media use for frontline workers which adds to minimisation of the dimensions of trust in contemporary employment relationships. Therefore, in all probability, the corporation was never likely to get many workers to engage in online forums if they felt mistrusted offline.

This also contributed to strong management resistance to use social media in work, as shown in the following comments:

> If you're at work, you're at work …I struggle to see how Facebook would be useful in your working environment. … people in marketing might say well it is part, you know, your role might determine if you need to use it. In my team … I don't see why you need to be on social media during your work time.
>
> (Pharma, Greg, Manager [p. 8 line 52–57])

The management discourse was punctuated by a perception that social media are not purposeful to the organisation or work outputs. This is a highly traditional view and creates a wider conundrum for corporations who want employees to utilise social media to promote brands, services, or for engagement purposes. This shows how a managerial identity is shaped by role agency, acquiescence, and commitment to highly traditional performance rules.

Managers fostered views of their self to legitimise individual strategies through their own narratives (Humphreys and Brown, 2002). In this case, the subjectivity views social media technology as a distraction. The resistance to adapt and integrate new forms of working may create discipline, yet this may paradoxically affect business innovation.

The final section focuses on the employee actor use of social media and how this impacts upon their identity formation.

## The evolution of employee role and identity

The employee actors demonstrated a varied, but limited, experience of social media use. Significant factors included access to engage online, age, and life experiences of the actors in this group. This yielded surprising findings on how this affects identity performance. The experience of using social media for some employee actors was not always positive. These are briefly discussed to highlight broader concerns about social media use, more broadly, and its impact on well-being, identity, and wider human resource management (HRM) practice. The analyses are presented as individual cases with the relevant illustrative quotes.

## Career development and the online identity project

A similarity arose between employee and HR actors who experimented with a variety of differing social media platforms to project and dramaturgically shape professional identity (Benford and Hunt, 1992). The following case demonstrates identity is anchored by differing assimilations of the digital self to construct a positive work identity:

> I relate more to the business objectives around what we want to get out, whereas my personal thing is my objectives are different.
>
> (Senes, Elana, ICT Coordinator [p. 2 line 16–18])

Elana discussed how the digital context presents employees with the possibility of achieving both business and personal goals. This affirms a strong role commitment (Allen, 2011). Elana was hyper-connected. Her identity was porous and permeated across a range of differing networks (Kerrigan and Hart, 2016). This was unique in the employee actor group. Elana's narrative focused on how she used networking and interconnection to create knowledge, reinforcing professional work identity in this context (Goffman, 1959; Nyhan, 2003):

> I think the connectedness is a really interesting one. It's knowledge, isn't it … I like the idea of the hive mind, but I guess that also has a downside, doesn't it in terms of the people responding in a measured way to stuff.... so there is a flip to that… I think the way that you can develop ideas by connecting with other people is really interesting.
>
> (Senes, Elana, ICT Coordinator [p. 7 line 16–20])

Social media in this empirical case study had a positive impact on individual employee identity and their sense of self. Elana links social media to the conceptual notion of the hive mind. This is defined as collective intelligence using technologies to develop knowledge, network, and to provide feedback (Glenn, 2009). Elana uses a metaphor which links to the collective nature of worker bees. From an employee relations perspective this was interesting. The duality of meaning infers the infinite possibilities to collaborate and to build self-development. Further, this can be interpreted to reinforce roles and hierarchy established within bee colonies which are replicated in work. This placed an emphasis on work roles and relates to concepts of teamwork and solidarity which have a colonising effect on identity (Casey and Schellenberg, 1997).

This is purposive to HRM and renders the worker as a subject at work (Barratt, 2002; Townley, 1994). This shows social media are beneficial for establishing power dynamics (Castells, 2011) and labour production (Barratt 2002; Townley, 1994). Whilst Elana derived pleasure from her ICT role, this demonstrates corporate cultures ensnare individual identity to accomplish control in organisations (Alvesson and Willmott, 2002; Webb, 2006).

**Retreating from social media**

A further pattern emerged in the empirical analyses which highlighted how a significant number of employee actors were rejecting or retreating from social media. This was principally influenced by a commitment to their professional HR role (Allen, 2011). The following case illustrates how adolescence represents a critical transition for individuals and a crucial axis point for identity formation online.

Social media are perceived to be vital for millennials in terms of social groups, culture, music, shared experiences, and defining who they think they are (Rosen et al, 2010). Freya, a younger employee, highlighted its significance:

> just purely because you know what everyone's doing and you are not missing out on anything.
>
> (Charta, Freya, HR Admin Assistant [p. 3 line 15–17])

Social media provides constant access to perceived friendships, affiliation, and structural ties to peer groups (Cover, 2012). If you have teenagers, you may have noted how much time they appear to interact online. The pressure to gain popularity seems to be a measure of social capital in the current context.

Temporally, as Freya matured, she shows how her need to constantly access social media had shifted. I explored this further with the actor:

> On Facebook you can be very unrealistic, you can be in this unrealistic world where you can put things on, pretending that you're someone else and you're really not. Like to be fair if I looked at Facebook, some of the stuff I probably was putting on I'd think "Why did you do that?" That's not even the type of person you are…
>
> (Charta, Freya, HR Admin Assistant [p. 7 line 13–17])

This highlights the more fragile and porous nature of identity construction in online contexts for adolescents (Baxter-Magolda, 2003; Kerrigan and Hart, 2016). Freya discussed how she perceived her profile to portray a false sense of self. Her dramaturgical performance had become more masked and staged to create a pastiche of the self. Contextually, the speed of technology creates a need for deeper reflection as we mature (Baxter-Magolda, 2003). This demonstrates adolescents are reflective regarding the enormity of their social media use and the complexities this involves when developing multiple, illusory online identities, as Freya discussed:

> I don't want people judging me on what I do in my spare time.
>
> (Charta, Freya, HR Admin Assistant [p. 2 line 42–46])

The findings showed that all the actors used social media to surveil the content of current and prospective employees. Freya was aware both her career and friendships may possibly be affected by online interactions. This reinforces how organisations, HR culture, and social media influence identity (Castells, 2011).

## The impact of online abuse and trolling on identity

A significant life experience online may also further impact on workers. In this case, a social actor discusses the major effect online abuse and trolling has on her self-esteem. This led to a renegotiation of identity. In the discussion, Freya referred to a situation of being trolled and groomed. *Trolling* is defined as: "A deliberately offensive or provocative online post with the aim of upsetting someone or eliciting an angry response from them" (Oxford online Dictionary, 2016). Freya discussed how this experience had a profound effect on her friendships and herself:

> She was getting a lot of abuse … what seriously have you got going off in your life that you actually have time to sit and bully someone through a social network?
>
> (Charta, Freya, HR Admin Assistant [p. 3 line 18–23])

This case reveals how observing and scrutinising tipped over into victimisation and online issues of harassment. This led to the actors experiencing a degree of self-estrangement with their self and their social media use.

In society, there is a worrying increase in sexual harassment in both online and offline contexts. Recent CPS reports in the UK highlight violence towards women and girls using social media are rising (2018/2019). This context demonstrates wider societal issues of social media use which impacts on gender and identity formation online. Sexuality is a way of expressing shaping identity (Ackroyd and Thompson, 2003). However, this may tip over into forms of subjugation, including forms of sexual harassment, sexting, upskirting, and revenge porn which we can assume may occur in work. There is a growing area *sextortion* which is a form of online misbehaviour, harassment and abuse. Recent media reports show how easy it is to access online materials such as detailed manuals and guides for the purposes extorting money from teenagers who are tricked into sending intimate pictures of themselves to fraudsters who threaten to share images if they do not receive payment (Guardian UK, 2024).

This is relevant to HRM regulations and disciplinary practices in this context. If these platforms are increasingly used as vehicles to wreak havoc on individuals, then this puts pressure on HR and management to address and manage these issues. These are becoming more prevalent forms of misbehaviours, particularly as these activities may take place during working hours or involve employees. This relates to growing issues associated with identity threats (Caza and Bagozzi, 2009) which draws attention to an emerging need for HRM-related skills to professionally handle sensitive cases for employees.

The current context highlights a growing need for vigilance regarding sexual harassment which has pervaded many corporations. The recent scandals such as the murder of Sarah Everard must now force HRM to institutionally adapt and hear the voices and concerns of people who experience these types of issues. Primarily, but not solely, this may disproportionately affect female workers. We need to enable workers to confidentially raise issues in work which may affect their sense of being or sexuality and to address these claims fairly and sensitively with appropriate procedures. These may link to wider policy on sexual harassment in work. This highlights the significant threats and fragilities which now exist and must more readily be addressed.

## The looking-glass self

As discussed, some actors actively use social media as a mirror from which to review and reconstruct their adult identity. Actors perceived that their dramaturgical performances were influenced by the perceptions others had on their sense of self (Goffman, 1959; Richey et al, 2016; Schlenker and Wowra, 2003). Freya, as an adolescent, discussed how her online content was used to develop her self-esteem and identity. This noticeably had a sexual undertone:

> I thought if I put something on Facebook and a lad liked it kind of thing that would make me feel better about myself.
>
> (Charta, Freya, HR Admin Assistant [p. 8 line13–17])

Conceptually, the discourse links to notions of the "looking-glass self", where our online content is used to garner adoration from followers. The interactions and views of others online are used to renegotiate identity to be more sexually appealing. This has transferability regarding the importance we attach to criteria such as appearance or behaviour (Martey and Consalvo, 2011). The metaphor of a mirror in this theme is fitting and demonstrates how we narcissistically use content to make sense of ourselves from a third-party perspective.

Impression management is further used to develop online material which is targeted specifically to be liked and gain popularity (Leonardi and Treem, 2012).This gives insights into the gendered experiences of young people. This emphasises how using social media is used to establish more sexualised identity creations. Moreover, the way we portray and stage ourselves may specifically drive more overt attraction which is targeted for audiences to drive self-esteem. This is problematical to address as we are aware sexualised behaviour in work has become more prevalent in work and society. This can be anything from cleavage gazing to more physical forms of assault (Ackroyd and Thompson,

2003). This case contributes to wider discussion and suggests that this is not just within the office now, it is also on the social media which adds to this issues.

**Discussion box 22**

**Discussion:**

Discuss the extent to which you witness and observe more sexualised behaviour in digital and social media?

Do you think this has become more normalised?

Given that forms of online harassment is on the rise, discuss how would your place of work or study address the inappropriate use of social media for the purposes of trolling or sexual harassment?

What support is available to effectively address the psychological impact of being harassed by someone, both offline and online?

Do you feel your current approaches help workers in this context?

**Pause for reflection:**

What can HR and management do to address sexualised behaviour in work?

This scene focused on exploring how actors assimilate a variety of platforms which they use to prop up and reconstruct their identity in online contexts. The scene demonstrates how actors use dramaturgical performances online and offline to strengthen a sense of self and professional identity. The scene explored how key social actors were found to mould an image of the "self" and multidimensional identity creations using social media. These were found to be socially co-constructed and relate to images and expectations which both organisations and society develop (Gioia et al, 2000; Webb, 2006). This influenced how these individuals felt that they should act both online and offline, a conception which relates to identity work and the question of "how should I act in work" (Cerulo, 1997). Similarities existed between how all actors tried to demarcate and set boundaries for their profiles to extend the range of power dynamics in organisations (see Table 4.1).

Inhabiting our professional role is dictated by status, position, and social context (Simpson and Carroll, 2008; Callero, 1994). Use of social media adds to this mix and was observed to significantly shape both identity and role performance. A core facet of an evolving sense of being in this context centred on how social actors have a strong affiliation to their professional role.

*Table 4.1* Cross-case comparison of evolving identity

| *Role:* | *HR* | *Management* | *Employee* |
|---|---|---|---|
| **Basis for identity construction** | • Virtue is used to shape identity<br>• Retreat and segregation of self<br>• Role and identity boundary management to protect a sense of self<br>• Multiple complementary and virtuous identity creations<br>• Cultural assimilation of identity in role.<br>• Reflective and reflexive about SM | • Managerial discourse shapes identity<br>• Partial retreat and segregation of self. Boundary between co-workers to protect the self<br>• Cultural assimilation of identity in role<br>• Reflective about SM | • Identity is controlled by managerial ambition<br>• Generation and tradition shape identity. Retreating from SM identity to reach an ideal sense of self<br>• Identity is developed through the hive mind and associated with the learning process<br>• Reflexivity on identity construction |
| **Impact on SNS activity** | • Moral engagement with role<br>• Created a positive construction of identity<br>• SNS is used as a device for lurking and observation | • Commercial and colonising effect of identity<br>• Power dynamic within identity<br>• Individual create selves that align to internal and external standards | • Individual progressively engaging with SM and identity.<br>• Colonising effect of identity.<br>• Life stages and learning are equivalent to SM use and ongoing identity construction |

SM, social media; SNS, social networking sites.

HR actors were observed to wield tremendous power which now incorporates greater panoptic observation of co-workers through pre-recruitment surveillance and lurking. These performances were legitimised by the actors' perception that they were developing a virtuous identity (Dutton et al, 2010). To shape a virtuous online identity, HR actors create dramaturgical online performances which demonstrated their worth as a responsible professional elite.

Staging a virtuous online identity included use of positive-only posts to demonstrate a more principled quality of character (Dutton et al, 2010, Humphreys and Brown, 2002; Park and Peterson, 2003/2009; Peterson and Seligman, 2004), whereas some HR actors retreated from social media to illustrate personal qualities of wisdom, courage, humanity, justice, and temperance. This highlights an increasingly subjective view HR actors may have on their wider co-workers when on social media. This was observed when HR actors discussed increasingly observing profile content and aesthetic images which highlighted employee sexuality, drunkenness, and nudity. These views may therefore sit in tension with the Equality Act (2010) and are considered to have significant implications for HRM practice in recruitment and profiling (McDonald et al, 2016).

HR actors legitimated online surveillance and pre-profiling activity because of the public nature of social media, and therefore, virtue is used to reify HR actions which are open to interpretation (Islam, 2012). Critically, these narratives highlighted a further subjectivity which rarely included assessing their own actions. This correlates with extant literature which suggests HR practitioners dislike reflective practice and feel introspection is dangerous (Bull and Taylor, 2014).

Retreating from social media was profoundly important to HR actors to demonstrate a strong affiliation they had with their role commitment and to further portray a positive, professional identity online. Sadly, in some cases, retreating from social media use was related to wider forms of sexualised behaviours, such as trolling and grooming. These experiences impacted on women in the study. This may lead actors to remove their online identity altogether to protect their own sense of being. This emphasises the profound impact social media experiences have on identity construction and the self, particularly from a gendered viewpoint.

Some social actors gained significantly more positive work-related identities because of their adoption of social media expertise and experimentation within their repertoire of skills. This is a progressive and evolutionary aspect of identity.

Some elite actors experimented with social media in more subversive ways, creating parody accounts and altering their identity using an avatar. This highlights the evolution of an anti-identity which may significantly impact the employment relationship. This demonstrates how social media allow us to shape evolving, liminal identities (Kerrigan and Hart, 2016). Figure 4.1 is used to demonstrates the evolutionary states of identity and being in this context.

Using multiple versions of the self online enables actors to relinquish any preformed sense of identity. This further contributes to debates about the shifting nature of identity using social media. A growing number of dramatic techniques were used by actors to improve appearances, mask the self or, as shown in some cases, taking on the mantle of someone else (Goffman, 1959; Kerrigan and Hart, 2016). This provides an interesting counter debate regarding conceptions of a moral, virtuous identity and shows HR actors contemporaneously are capable of developing an anti-identity (Simpson and Carroll, 2008).

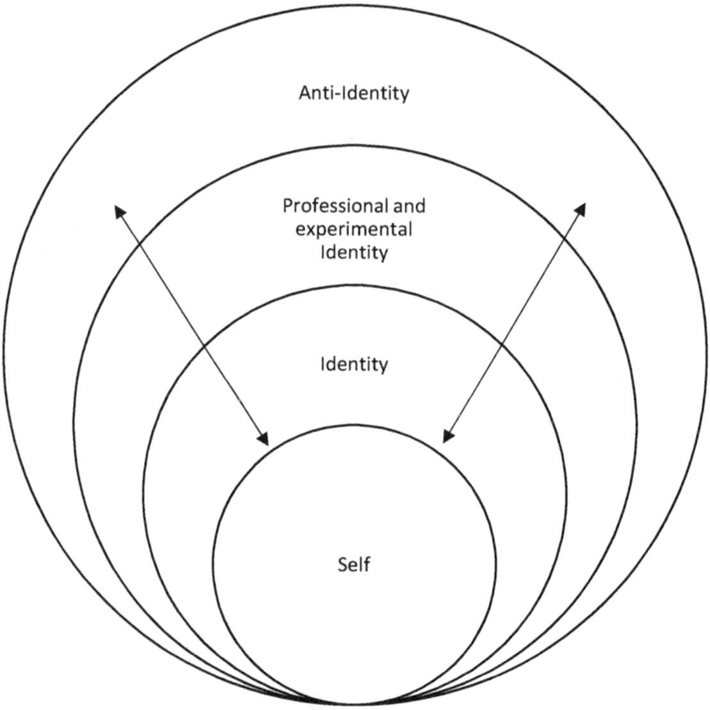


*Figure 4.1* Evolving identity.

I seek to highlight an ulterior identity creation can be seen as playful or simultaneously, they may highlight a darker side of identity construction which allows individuals to reflexively develop new ways of being or seeing the self in online contexts (Lundgren and Poell, 2016; Yanow and Tsoukas, 2009). This experimentation with "being" contributes to further understanding on the conflictual nature of (mis)behaviour in this context.

The use of avatars demonstrates how some employees perceive they have a right to retain a private ulterior identity within their social media use. Yet this is perceived to add to emerging forms of peer-to-peer conflict which may now exist in employment relationships (McDonald et al, 2016). Further, such parodies and misbehaviours reveal a discourse of subversion where social media are used to tilt power dynamics in work.

A contemporary understanding of the management role often views them as persons of consequence: "strategists", "leaders", "culture-creators", "visionaries", *or* "entrepreneurs" (Sveningsson and Alvesson, 2003). Therefore, one would expect to see developing a managerial identity as a creative, iterative process where individuals develop differing identity positions (Kerrigan and Hart, 2016). There were a variety of interesting identity and dramaturgical performances developed by each manager in the empiricism. These were found to be more traditional and included strengthening their hub position using cast members of their business function and social media accounts to act as a web of spies to inform managers of (mis)behaviours at work (Goffman, 1959; Rooney et al, 2010). This creates social media as an object of positional power (Mann et al, 2003). These are further techniques which develop conceptions of panoptic observation in the workplace. This provides a novel twist to notions of conflict, manipulation, and gossip in the workplace (Kuo et al, 2015).

Observation of profile content affected the identity of some management actors negatively. This was observed when decisions to control and discipline misbehaviour spilled over into social media contexts. This allowed employee in-groups to develop using WhatsApp, etc. This contributes to greater understanding of identity devaluation where online interaction leads to workplace conflict and altercations which occur simultaneously in both online and offline contexts. This shows how social media impact on a crises in identity foundation (Dutton et al, 2010). Conceptually, this relates to the temporality of identity and shape a sense of being thrown chaotically in the world (Heidegger, 1926). This dimension adds the greater complexity to workplace conflict where forms of digital misbehaviour now trigger managers to cognitively reflect on aspects of their role, identity, and, perhaps, loss of power.

Therefore, the role of management and their identity is more precarious and conceptualised as a variety of social masks used in the ongoing construction of self (Goffman, 1959; Sveningsson and Alvesson, 2003). This relates to a Heideggerrian sense of existence and a metaphorical sense some social media identity is "being-towards-death", signifying the ending of an online self and metamorphosis of the next iteration, particularly where we retreat or come off social media.

The findings in this study highlight how some employees limit how they interconnect with each other (Christakis and Fowler, 2009; Rooney et al, 2010). Cover (2012) states this is a specific strategy to gain friends or demarcate who we wish to interact with. In most cases, online interactions were formed with those who are similar to us in order to create highly personalised networks. This has multiple connotations; predominantly this reinforces notions of hegemony in organisations as employees are subjected to more categorisation in work (Humphreys and Brown, 2002; Townley, 1994).

Furthermore, this relates to place identity which is perceived as an affiliation to physical settings and the people we function with (Rooney et al, 2010). Thus, management may seek to capitalise on this using it to develop a colonising effect for identity (Webb, 2006). Simultaneously, workers may resist such work practices in order to survive work and may develop subgroups to develop a collective social identity (Hogg and Terry, 2000; Lukes, 2005; Rooney et al,

2010). Thompson (2016) extends this view suggesting that workers use this position for forms of dissent, employee voice, and to seek solidarity from over-oppressive work regimes.

Cover (2012) states identity is shaped by the views of others and that actors manipulate content in order to be "liked". The narratives in this study observed how we use social media to develop a uniqueness of self and for impression management purposes (Bullingham and Vasconcelos, 2013; Goffman, 1959; Richey et al, 2016). The majority of actors created online content to manipulate how others observe them, particularly the employer. Manipulation of online material for impression management and identity work can have a huge impact on social actors. The particularity of one case, Freya, an adolescent, demonstrates how social media are incorporated to manipulate a sense of beauty, sexuality, and belonging.

Organisations capitalise on this position, driving wider conceptions of aesthetic labour to ensure employees look good in this context (Nath et al, 2016). Social media therefore are used as a contemporary looking glass to reflect a fragile and aestheticised sense of self. These were often found to be at odds with the interior sense of self (Kerrigan and Hart, 2016). Therefore, identity navigation is now more complex and is a response to feelings of competing with fellow actors to create positive impressions (Cover, 2012; Reagle, 2015; Richey et al, 2016; Rosen et al, 2010; Turkle, 2015). In terms of impression management online, we attract and court critique of others through their comments. This helps us shape how we make sense of ourselves and how we use wider dramatic techniques to adapt how we look, changing our appearance to be more pleasing.

Conversely, retreating from social media may help us to evolve a more positive sense of self and to avoid such comparisons to protect the self (Dutton et al, 2010; Bullingham and Vasconcelos, 2013). Social media help us to confront a new sense of being and to help transition to a new phase in life and how identity is temporally linked to provide a sense of self-esteem.

Our profiles and online content are becoming more provocative. These are a focus of both organisational inspection and cultural statements about beauty and aesthetic judgement (Nath et al, 2016; Strati, 1999). Identity construction and dramaturgical performance therefore link with Foucauldian analysis, gendered power dynamics, and aesthetic labour in work, which are discussed in the next scene.

# Act 3. Scene 2 Keeping up appearances

## Aesthetic labour in digitised working contexts

This section focuses on how social media are used to stage the employer brand to emphasise a working context where workers seem happy and perfect. This both stages a positive effective working environment and employee morale to consumers and to attract future employees for recruitment and selection purposes. The scene then focuses on how social media forces both corporations and us individually to be more obsessed with appearance and aestheticised versions of ourselves and the impact this has on our labour effort.

**Scene 2 summary**: The intention of this scene is to illustrate the growing importance organisations give to window dressing, scene-setting, and further discussion on the conceptual idea of aesthetic labour (Nath et al, 2016). I explore how social actors in the three key roles develop organisational regimes for employee appearance, including how we look, dress, sound, and portray personal images online. The scene discusses how organisations form and develop aesthetic cues which are used as technologies and factors for decision-making in pre-recruitment, selection, and career progression in work. Ostensibly, how social media are used as a means to observe future workers accessing data on individuals which goes beyond the curriculum vitae and application forms (McDonald et al, 2016), which are much shallower measures and do not necessarily focus on job criteria, knowledge, skills, and competence.

I have discussed how pre-profiling is much more commonplace in HR recruitment practices (McDonald et al., 2016). This is an evolving and somewhat veiled practice which impacts on workers' careers. Therefore, a greater enquiry and exploration into the way human resource management (HRM) inculcates this process is needed, so that we may challenge the impact this presents for ethical recruitment and selection practices (Aguado et al, 2016; Bartosik-Purgat and Jankowska, 2017; Headworth, 2015).

This section provides some greater insights into this emergent form of worker surveillance and observation. Focusing on the empiricism illustrates the subjectivity applied to informing judgments regarding applicant or employee suitability to job roles.

DOI: 10.4324/9781003137269-11

### Aesthetics in organisations

Briefly, our organisational life involves some form of human agency and knowledge which rests upon us using our senses such as sight, smell, touch, or taste. These further allow us to judge and make sense of the beauty of something (Strati, 1999). Aesthetics are also linked with how we describe and code aspects of the beautiful in corporate life. These are, therefore, highly linked to imagery and the imagination rather than the logical. In doing so, we take a corporate direction which centres on the sensory to judge what is pleasant or not.

As social media are used to depict and showcase corporate life, they primarily drive further notions of aesthetics in work. We use content imagery in activities to depict workplace endeavours and further we now use these to make judgements about individuals for recruitment and selection practices using profiles. Little is known about how these practices occur. I have used the empiricisms to explore how social actors formed and developed aesthetic codes to further judge us and the impact this has on aesthetic labour effort to contribute to wider discussion on this emerging domain of work.

Whilst aesthetics may relate to tangible objects which exist in organisations such as artwork, furniture, or décor, these may also be closely associated with online corporate portrayals of the business. Online materials provide imagery and sensory aspects considered to be of "beauty" through websites, intranet sites, and other digital forms of communication. This, I believe, is used and includes how corporations brand themselves as an employer of choice.

These online images and content highly aestheticise corporations carefully constructing aesthetic codes which we use to make sense of corporate cultures and the perception of harmonisation in the workforce which we derive from these platforms. We therefore accumulate a sense of understanding of what is pleasant for an organisation and their workers. We may use these sites to inform decisions when applying for job roles and subliminally pick up on these aesthetic regimes or not. They inform whether we see ourself represented in the workforce or not. This has wider implications for equality, diversity, and inclusion in work.

At this intersection, these aesthetic cues are used by management and HR practices to inform judgement on whether future applicants are suitable for work within the corporation. This includes making sense of whether applicants fit a desired employee, if you like the sculpturing and creation of an archetype, who may fit their corporate mould. This approach has become worryingly subjective since the advent of social media. Greater debate about such activity is required as this may contradict the very essence of ethical HR approaches and CIPD codes of behaviours.

**Aesthetic labour and online presentation of beauty**

Earlier in the text, I discussed how employees are subjected to forms of aesthetic labour where they manipulate their social media content to look good and sound right (Warhurst and Nickson, 2007). This process of judgement allows employees to be more greatly commodified on the basis of their identity, visual appearance, looks, and timbre of voice (Nath et al, 2016). Aesthetic labour, therefore, focuses on the management of appearance in employment and informs the prescribing of physical image norms in work.

Evaluation of employees in this context is based on the organisational development of implied, informal, or precise organisational standards in relation to several factors such as dress sense (Spiess and Waring, 2005), accessories (Pettinger, 2005), voice/accent (Nath, 2011), body art, and physical appearances (Timming, 2015). These are more readily observed through our varying association on social media platforms and for the purposes in this context on corporate websites used to entice us as future employees of a corporation. Thus, employer branding (EB), online identity, and aesthetic labour collide to develop the construal of individual attractiveness which may be psychologically impactful (Taylor, 2018).

There are growing concerns, particularly in recruitment practices, that corporations are observing people in "thing-like" terms (Heidegger, 1926). We consider "their aspects as inert properties rather than as subjective expressions" (Islam, 2012: 41). This perspective both forgets and reifies the subjective nature of our identity and increasingly how our humanness is judged, a process which has seeped steadily into HR practices, with very little control or challenge.

These practices may include forms of unconscious bias. This is often termed implicit bias and is considered a form of learned stereotyping which may influence our behaviour (Noon, 2018). This develops over time and is deeply ingrained and based upon our attitude (Guynn, 2015). Importantly, any bias we may bring into recruitment approaches may have little correlation to judging employee skill set, competence, or work experiences. Given that it is increasingly difficult for individuals to protect the self with boundaries on social media to inhibit users from accessing more private aspects of our lives, it has become all too easy for employers to exploit and mine social media data to pre-profile future employees (Kerrigan and Hart, 2016; McDonald et al, 2016).

The process of commodifying the workforce aesthetically begins with online EB. Corporate websites and social media are used purposefully to attract prospective employees to secure workforce talent (Eger et al, 2018). In this context, these devices are used to digitally stage performativity and display employee attractiveness. The online portrayal of the workforce is choreographed to create a "gestalt" or beautiful image of workforces or individual key employees (Taylor, 2018).

The imagery in this context subtly informs applicants about required organisational aesthetic codes. These are used by HR or management practitioners to deepen notions of aesthetic labour, which is conceptualised as "a supply of embodied capacities and attributes possessed by workers at the point of entry into employment" (Warhurst et al, 2000: 1). Furthermore, this subtly creates an employee archetype which is used to protect the corporation from negligent hiring (Biro, 2011); McDonald et al, 2016; Taylor, 2018).

Aesthetic labour links with both staging the self for the purposes of future employment and career progression. The images we post of ourselves are now more readily used in pre-profiling exercises which are undertaken by key social actors involved in the recruitment of the workforce. My discussion aims to build on extant literature to demonstrate that this is growing in scale and the impact this has on workers.

Pre-profiling activity broadly involves management and HRM practitioners using social media devices and other content to accumulate biographic data secured from online materials. These are then used to make comparison regarding an individual's behaviour and appearance (McDonald et al, 2016). Aesthetic labour in this context, therefore, advances forms of implicit bias and surveillance behaviour by management and HR practitioners. Social media allow practitioners to judge applicants on their more embodied physical attributes to ensure that the individual "fits" with predefined corporate expectations of appearance (McDonald et al, 2016). This hardly seems fair as social media allow us to experiment with our identity. In doing so, we may present multiple identities, some of which maybe conflictual with non-virtual worlds (Bullingham and Vasconcelos, 2013).

As my discussion shows, there is very little challenge or training on how to use social media, and this includes undertaking social media pre-profiling and worker surveillance activities to mitigate against forms of unconscious bias.

In larger corporations, management involved in recruitment maybe asked to complete online training to address or reduce forms of unconscious bias. Significantly, this has little focus on using social media profiles and thus may have little impact on approaches.

In the context of social media, we are so used to clicking in daily to see what is going on. I have already highlighted how this includes observing and lurking to watch in more veiled forms of worker observation. This activity therefore has been subsumed without due consideration. Therefore, this could have an impact on both individual identity exploration and our career or employability, particularly if our identity does not align with prescribed corporate codes for appearance, dress, or behaviours which is problematical for ethical HR practices (Taylor, 2018; Taylor and Dobbins, 2021).

Little is known about how aesthetic labour informs recruitment pre-profiling activities or how practitioners use physical appearance to inform labour activities. This section explores this notion to further bridge this gap by contributing to an ethical debate regarding subjective labour processes and HR recruitment practices (McDonald et al, 2016; Thompson, 2016).

This section addresses a further conundrum: *How do HRM and management practitioners use social media during pre-profiling processes to judge or commodify applicant suitability and adding to ongoing aesthetic labour effort?*

## Employer branding and aesthetic codes

All organisations are perceived to use artistic processes to construct aesthetic codes (Gagliardi, 1996). Awareness of aesthetic codes is less obvious to innocent job-seekers and employees. These become apparent through online EB, an activity that includes key marketing principles and used within HR initiatives (Edwards, 2010). EB is a process of building an employer identity aimed at existing employees and targeting future ones (Sivertzen et al, 2013). Marketing methods are used to position and create a unique employer identity to differentiate corporations from their nearest competitors (Backhaus and Tikoo, 2004).

Brand and corporate reputation are essential commodities for organisations seeking to lure and attract the best, new candidates to create employee engagement or position the organisation as an employer of choice (Berthon et al, 2005; Cappelli, 2001; Headworth, 2015). In this sense, organisational attractiveness is compared and used by future employees to evaluate their own image, identity, personality, and values with that of potential employers (Backhaus and Tikoo, 2004). These elements inform perception of an attractive, employee archetype (Taylor, 2018).

Many studies do not explore individual sense-making regarding the aesthetic labour or measuring attractiveness in recruitment practices. This is primarily because management theory of organisations is idealised or portrayed with rationality. Corporations are perceived as non-sentient entities with no soul or feeling. Strati (1999) suggested this provides theoretical foundations which are devoid of beauty, eroticism, sensation, and attraction. Aesthetics, therefore, allow for a fuller definition in this context to informan acquiring of knowledge gained through the senses (Strati, 1999; Taylor and Hansen, 2005; Elias et al, 2018). Through EB, these are much visible through the use of the internet and social media sites. These allow employers to construct aesthetic codes where digital images of their workforce are populated with artefacts which represent the workforce and organisational culture. Similarly, so are our online content, which can be used to match with corporate desires.

Consumers and prospective employees use these corporate digital images to construct a "schemata of perception and taste, models of vision, 'lenses' through which to look at reality" Gagliardi (1996: 572). These artefacts are technologies which inform, influence, and shape belief (Sorenson, 2010). Aesthetics, therefore, powerfully influence a subject's perception of reality (Hancock, 2005). Extraordinarily, these aesthetic codes and images are, therefore, a rich resource for recruitment coordination where employees sense-make about requirements from an employer perspective and vice versa.

Aesthetic codification enables corporations to discipline perceiving subjects within an "aestheticized regime of meaning or pathos" which subtly reinforces beliefs, norms, and cultural values (Gagliardi quoted in Hancock, 2005: 38). Further, Strati (1999:117) suggests we use language and sentiment to depict emotions and beauty which involves words which focus on the *beautiful, ugly, grotesque, and tragic.* These more derogatory notions are further picked up as codes within our own social media. We may judge people as they seemingly don't fit with perceptions of beauty; these also form the basis of case law.

We adapt our profiles to be seemingly more happy or beautified. We use emoticons and face altering technology to imply we are more beautiful; these may also involve emoji responses to show we are complicit in suggesting an individual is symbolising beauty with hearts, faces, or smoking hot emojis, etc.

The constant readaptation of the self, our physical appearance, and identity through applications which allow us to alter ourself has raised major concerns from legislators and advocacy groups worldwide. The concerns centre on the unrealistic perceptions they create of beauty. There are criticisms of major sites for driving content which causes anxiety and depression in audiences, particularly those who are more impressionable. The Royal Society for Public Health report (2017) found that Instagram was fundamentally detrimental to adolescent mental health. In light of these concerns, Norway and France have called for amendments to social media legislation requiring users to state when they have retouched their appearance, this is in an attempt to make it clear that we can never attain such aestheticised versions of the self. I have tried to focus on the essence of this to say suggest we perhaps need to review practices in the UK.

### *Happiness and the harmonious workplace*

In all cases, EB online will use social media to portray aesthetic representations of happy co-workers. These images further reinforce unitary perspectives of work (Cradden, 2011; Nath et al, 2016). This form of aesthetes is used to stage workforce harmony, unity, and cohesion and to show forms of what we consider to be beautiful about work. This is observed in the following quote made by an HR director:

> So when people apply for a job, we put … comments to them: "why don't you go and have a look at our Pinterest board?"… we're doing lots of pictures of smiley, happy employees, suggesting that this is a brilliant place to work.
>
> (Senes Healthcare, Erica, HR Director [p. 1 line 24–32])

We have probably all looked at pictures of organisational workforces and EB when we are researching for a new job. We see images of all the workforce in front of amazing shiny buildings. We see pictures of leaders with hazy images of either other forms of architecture, art, ergonomic office space, or by planting to seem content, relaxed, and happy or perhaps powerful and strong. Such depictions give a brief indication of supposed organisational culture and life. What a great company, come be with us!

It would be naïve and counterintuitive to think organisations would post pictures of miserable, unhappy employees. We need to scrutinise corporations through many different lenses and not rely on synthesised contrived pictures. However, this form of staging can be false advertising. My point here is for future applicants to dive below the surface.

Equally, social media imagery and discourses provide in-depth depictions of contemporary working life (Strati, 1999). They capture the subtle cues and codes, such as dress or visual appearance norms (Nath et al, 2016). Erica's discourse demonstrates a language which suggests social media are loaded with these values. Yet this narrative gives rise to an undertone of cynicism using the word "*suggesting*" which intimated a more false and potentially disharmonious view of work. This is interpreted to question the authenticity of the EB.

***Deceitful representation***

As discussed, we are now caught in a trap of constant readaptation. We see more of us trying to stage the self aesthetically on social media, often editing and manipulating looks. We use social media asa front stage to craft how we look – an covey that we are happy, smart, sexy – which are used to stage and to push our joyous employment experiences to vast audiences. This is for the purposes of suggesting what a great worker I am. This seems innocuous, but it is also very nuanced and subjective.

For some HR actors who were more pragmatic the way we readapt ourselves and constantly overtly showcase our employment achievements was seen as deceptive and insincere. In the following case, the HR actor's narrative focused on the strong dislike of using LinkedIn platforms and profiles because of the manipulated imagery and content as this HR manager suggests:

> It's where people blow smoke up their own backside.
>
> (Pharma, Georgia, HR Manager [p. 4 line 1])

Georgia uses the metaphor of *smoke.* This was interpreted to mean how individuals use these platforms to inflate their sense of self. Furthermore, this emphasises how dramaturgical aspects of online identity are linked to impression management in online contexts (Goffman, 1959). The metaphor of smoke adds wider theatrical connotations. In theatre productions dry ice is used to create a smokescreen which eerily masks characters on stage, usually the villain. Georgia intimates a similar effect, which highlights how our profiles are more misleading and may misrepresent the authentic self. My point here is to acknowledge our staged online representations and identity may be interpreted in differing ways. This sends out a message that we need to act carefully. Equally for those who are recruiters this is to noteworthy and suggests we may not be as we appear to be. Thus, we need to be more aware of such fallacious self-advertising.

The notion of staging the self online conceptually links with the role of a craftsperson or aesthetes. We constantly carving and manipulating our social media images. We now observe those users who addictively recraft and post content to renegotiate their sense of self as perfect and wholesome. Why do people manipulate how they look online to appear younger, slimmer, have whiter teeth, cuter noses? This seems to gild the lily. In reality, such appearances can only ever exist online. As soon as one meets these people, let's say for the purposes of an interview, those recruiting you will observe the less subtle, more natural, and imperfect elements of who they are. Surely, this false advertising and may lead to disappointment, which could negatively impact on the attraction we have with these people. My main emphasis is to suggest none of this activity lends itself to protecting the organisation from negligent hiring if applicants are inauthentic. Moreover, this demonstrates greater subjectivities and complexities in the hiring process and the psychological development of temporal online identities (Kerrigan and Hart, 2016). My point here is for HR and management practioners to be wary of social media profiles or making judgements on future co-workers particularly those who are reliant on airbrushing and artificial intelligence (AI) to doctor their identity and looks. These will not help gain "truths" about the suitability of applicants. Additionally, as HR practitioners we need to pay more attention to the well-being of those who are trying constantly to be liked and to be too perfect, as this clearly leads to concerns about rising mental issues which may further impact in work.

### *Pathos, tragedy, and hate online*

Where we discuss beauty, we must also discuss the tragedy as part of the emotional and aesthetic digital landscape. This is because as humans we don't just portray our beauty. We also stage our sadness and ugliness. There is a pathos in what we post which is both quite tragic and heartbreaking. This has left us with a wider societal issue where we feel too sad, too compared, too ugly, too fat, too old, etc. Moreover, in terms of pathos or tragedy, we appear to share more intimate details about our lives which can also be judged by both co-workers and those recruiting or advising us in HR as part of our everyday work survival strategies. My point here is we rarely discuss pathos and tragedy. Perhaps these are things we hardly consider. From an ethnographic point of view, we probably all have had interactions and online altercations. These show our vulnerabilities and some may say unattractive elements. This may include those who overshare.

Importantly, this form of perceived unattractiveness may link with forms of vitriol and hate speech (Taylor, 2024). Our use of social media allows us a fertile ground on which to express ourselves more freely. This has become more concerning to corporations, countries and their and governments as hate speech is becoming more prevalent online (Miˇskolci et al, 2020).

In one scenario the HR manager explained they had a situation where an individual had a disagreement with their manager in work and then later posted on Facebook that they were going to "put their manager in the boot of their car". This language is a form of aggression which intimates they are going to violently dispose of their manager.

The HR manager understood this individual was ranting about corporate management. They discussed how this impacted on perceptions of both pathos and reputation. This was perceived to be a growing work-based issue particularly where freedom of expression boils over into hate speech and is deemed more menacing, ugly, threatening, and aggressive.

One HR actor discussed a situation where a member of staff had posted about their partner, who also worked in the same organisation. This individual had an affair with a co-worker which left the person bereft. They had posted their anger and vulnerability online. This impacted on and separated the workforce into differing camps over who were upset, shocked, and disgusted by the actions or those who thought it was funny and gossip. This tragedy shows how we get involved in wider personal issues where the aesthetic codes of tragedy as this are publicly played out. The impact was discussed with the HR social actor who stated:

> Personally I think they should keep it to themselves…you know they put comments on about an ex…how they hate them and they are glad they got rid of them.
>
> (Fiona, HR manager, Charta)

I explored how HR approached this situation and the support given to the agonised individual so that this did not affect the supposed reputation, beauty, and harmony in the organisation. The individual was dealt with a director who requested to remove the post. Further, the HR manager stated that no further conversations were had and openly stated:

> I don't want to do the tea and sympathy, that's not what I am here for… but occasionally its necessary.
>
> (Fiona, HR Manager, Charta)

On the face of it this is quite a blunt statement. This infers as workers we are to act and behave in thing-like ways. We are expected to be constant and happy. We dislike the notion of anger at work. Whilst we have codes of conduct, we rarely discuss the human centricity where all emotions are present. The issue here is that this often fails to map over into policy. This needs greater articulation so workers do not fall foul of any discipline associated with more hostile and aggressive forms of sour behaviour and language, particularly in online content.

This activity links with how we may be perceived to be *unattractive* in work. Our humanness therefore may impact on our long-term career. One of the individuals in this scenario left work. Had this post been left online, this could have affected how other employers viewed our online content and further impacted on the ability to be recruited elsewhere.

**Discussion box 23**

**Discussion:**

Discuss the extent to which you witness and observe hate speech in digital and social media?

Do you ever confront these people and ask them to take it down?

Do you think we are too tolerant of this type of behaviour because it has become more normalised?

Do you think your workplace or place of study challenges this type of behaviour effectively?

Do you feel your current approaches help workers in this context?

**Pause for reflection:**

What can HR and management do to address forms of hatred and hate speech in work?

These forms of online discussion are now more interlinked with pre-recruitment and wider forms of surveillance practices now discussed.

## Pre-recruitment veillance practices

I think by now we are aware that we are all being watched, observed, and judged online. This becomes more heightened at the entry point of recruitment and selection practices. The empiricism in this study explored this activity. All the actors discussed the greater need for employers to surveil, manage, and control employee identity, appearance, and behaviour beyond the working day (Moussa, 2015; Moqbel et al, 2013; McDonald et al, 2016; Taylor, 2018). Management and HR practitioners used differing veillance practices for pre-profiling employees.

This allowed them to purposefully and dramaturgically shape and aestheticise workforces.

Additionally, using our profiles this allowed corporations to uniquely sanitise unpleasant or "unaesthetic" aspects of working life which management may find unpalatable (Nath et al, 2016; Strati, 1999). This is an ethical issue for contemporary HR practices which seek to direct approaches to aesthetically control labour (Taylor, 2018). Strati suggested:

> Declaring that an organisation is beautiful or ugly, that the work performed within it is beautiful or otherwise, that its members are beautiful or otherwise, is to pass judgement on the organisational life constructed and reconstructed from day to day. This is aesthetic judgement.
>
> (Strati [1999: 102])

I believe workers must be more vigilant about how aesthetic judgements of our virtual world merge with our current and future working lives. Importantly, if we are now expected to invest in emotional and aesthetic labour practices in order to survive work and create beautiful, pleasing profiles, then we must seek to understand how management discern ugliness through these surveillance tactics to manage and ensure our career (Strati, 1999; Taylor, 2018).

#### *Profile evaluation and judgements*

Literature suggests pre-recruitment surveillance is the norm and often expected by applicants in the digital context (Moussa, 2015). Whilst this is the case, further, empiricism suggests online content was observed without individuals being aware or more ethically informed their profiles were being surveilled or used in recruitment decision-making (McDonald et al, 2016; Taylor, 2018; Taylor and Dobbins, 2021). Primarily, I discovered, future applicants were often unaware that their aesthetic performances in online contexts were being judged. This raises questions over the temporal use of social media and whether the presentation of self, over a period of time, can be justified. Importantly, management and HR practitioners were not making applicants of employees aware of monitoring or privacy policy, and there were very little regulations or procedures for this type of work (Dillon and Thomas, 2006; McDonald et al, 2016; Moussa, 2015). Therefore, we must debate the realities of corporate practices associated in this aspect of work.

Interestingly, observation of positive, professional posts informed how HR actors observed and made sense of other users' images and online content. Conversely, if we use platforms for mainly our social events, this presented an ethical dilemma in how HR actors perceived and utilised our online profiles for decision-making in recruitment and career advancement:

> We make judgements on somebody's suitability for a role and if they look like they're out partying all weekend are they going to be a hard worker.
>
> (Tiro Recruitment Beatty, HR Manager [p. 3 line 29–31])

Surely, management and practitioners are more discerning. If we are out partying to celebrate a success, a loved one's birthday or a life changing event – does this make us bad workers? Without wider interrogation, are individual profiles the best evidence to ascertain our suitability to a role? There needs to be a deeper understanding of the individual. Worryingly, we seem to scroll all too quickly through content as now discussed.

## Snap decision-making

The social actors were asked if they ever made snap or gut decision-making when trying to discern whether applicants were suitable for a position. One recruitment director informed me that:

> I think it is fair to say you make your decision in reception, don't you… .. I was interviewing people who I didn't have to work with, it took me a long, long time to understand what good looked like and who was placeable and who wasn't placeable.
>
> (Beth, Recruitment Sales Director, Tiro)

This highlights that pre-profiling is the first stage in assessing our appearance and how look and sound in the workplace. We are then judged again in the reality of the workplace. The director went on to explain further judgements on what they found regarding our appearance. This discussion involved making a judgement regarding an applicant for a reception role in a factory. The discussion centred on wider sensory assumptions and aesthetic codes which discern a perceived ugliness:

> Well you know we wouldn't have them working here, her hands are dirty and she had teeth missing and she smoked a lot. People do make decisions"… . We call it the halo and horns effect.
>
> (Beth, Recruitment Sales Director, Tiro)

In this scenario, the applicant is judged on her cleanliness and her habits. The good news is the applicant was given the post. The director had undergone some development in the psychology of interviewing and meeting people. However, in some case, our bias and subjectivity may impact on whether the individual would have been offered the position. Such subjective judgements about our content and our social habits are used to inform recruitment decisions.

***Intoxication***

The focus so far has shown that much of the judgment centred very little on seeking images or content which corresponds with competence or job specifications. This shows how HR actors legitimise "searching" through online profiles seeking an embodiment of a wholesome individual. This not only involves observing aesthetic perfection this activity also involves how these actors justify making judgments on whether we appeared inebriated or debauched, images which ultimately confirm opinion and may decide our employment fate as this case attests:

> if they look like they're falling over drunk all the time or you know, from the clothes they wear and unfortunately whether we like it or not, snap judgments are made all the time and they're specifically made by our clients. So if we're you know, recruiting candidates or recruiting, we've got the same kind of snap judgement that our clients are going to have.
>
> (Beatty, HR, p.2 line 50–55)

Subjective judgements of individuality do not necessarily work within the bounds of relevant equality legislation in the UK which aims to create a more level-playing field for people from diverse backgrounds. These modes of observation were perceived to be snap judgements regarding our appearance or increasingly more about social aspects of life. Importantly, these actors rarely reflected on such superficial judgement, particularly when they discussed our social habits, drunken behaviour, or appearance.

In one case, an applicant was being considered for a job opportunity. The recruitment process involved checking through their profile. This unearthed content which the applicant had posted regarding drugs and drug-taking as described:

> I've just Facebooked him and his photo on his profile is of a cannabis plant and all his stuff is cannabis everything.
>
> (Beth, Recruitment Sales Director, Tiro)

I therefore raise this theme to suggest we need to educate workers to be more discerning of their individual content which they deem to be for a "private" audience and to understand our online materials are going to be more deeply scrutinised in much greater detail. Therefore, multiple contemporaneous identities and changing behaviours on issues, such as intoxication and drug use within given contexts, can impact on our ability to gain employment or improve our career trajectory.

I also wish to add that perhaps these images can relate to being on holiday in destinations where drug-taking is legalised. We may not be the party animal people consider us to be! So again recruiters need to be more pragmatic. The director in this case further commented on being realistic in this situation. They stated they carefully considered decisions where images such as these were concerned and felt that they tried to not let these affect their judgment but ultimately inferred:

> if every picture of them is of them out partying, wrecked all the rest of it, it would put me off.
>
> (Beth, Recruitment, Tiro)

This suggests that whilst those involved in recruitment may try not to be too subjective and critical, our content is etched in their mind. This has an everlasting impression on these individuals. No matter how hard they try, their own opinion and judgement will inform and could sway their final decision-making.

**Pressure to look good**

One case example highlighted the pressure to constantly look good and sound great occurs from a young age. The actor discussed how they felt consistently having to portray beauty from the age of 13, which correlates to wider research as follows:

> your pictures have got to look a certain way and they've all got to be edited. So your dimples on your face, for me, are not there, kind of thing.
>
> (Freya, HR administrator, Charta)

This exemplifies how young people are caught in a cycle of comparison with their peers. The actor stated they personally edited their pictures to get rid of their perceived imperfections, including features in their physical appearance such as dimples, in order to craft their own idea of beauty. This is concerning. The actor, an adolescent, further explained how they aesthetically manufactured their appearance to feel more perfect:

> with just growing up and being that age, you felt like oh your hair's got to be perfect, your makeup's got to be done. You've got to have your nice shoes on and your nice jeans and your nice coat.
>
> (Freya, HR administrator, Charta)

This intensifies aesthetic labour and the need to be perfect. As a parent and educator of young teenagers, this feels worrying. Whilst this is just a conversation with one individual, I work with young people who are more concerned about posting the perfect picture, the need to have a high proportion of *likes* from followers thus, the phenomenon of being liked and portraying perfection has grown. The constant need to be flawless is a heavy burden. Moreover, who arbitrates and gets to decide on what beauty and perfection is. Significantly, very little reflection was given by HR practitioners on whether glossier images of applicants or employees were manipulated for impression management purposes rather than actual skill set. This appears to throw a veil over a wider societal ethical crisis which involves stereotyping and bias (Bandura, 2002). This often occurs at different stages in the recruitment process.

***Screening out***

A key theme which emerged in all interviews was a growing reliance on pre-screening applicant online profiles during recruitment processes. Pre-screening online profiles has long been debated in literature (Broughton et al, 2010; McDonald et al, 2016). This has serious repercussions for HRM and management practice. It is of interest in relation to principles of privacy stipulated in the Human Rights Act (1998) and ethical considerations as part of the Equality Act (2010). Screening out potential candidates is a clear power statement regarding individual identity:

> I can give you 20 examples of times when we have screened people out ...recently, we were showing somebody out of an interview, we took him into reception and said thank you very much for coming in, loved him, gorgeous he was... After he'd gone the receptionist said, "You might just want to Google him. I've seen something on Facebook [about the person]... So we Googled him and he'd just done two years for following students home on the night bus and then mugging them. Not once, but a multiple offender and he'd just done time. We'd looked him in the eye directly and said, "Have you got any criminal convictions declared unspent with the Criminal Convictions Act 1974 and Rehabilitation of Offenders Act 1974?" ... We screened him out ... Facebook has stopped us making far worse mistakes.
>
> (Tiro, Sales Director, Beth [p .6 line 22–36]

This case highlights how we unconsciously use terms associated with beauty. The actor in the physical interview deemed the individual to be both *lovely* and *gorgeous*. This was interpreted to be associated with a form of beauty. The recruitment team was then advised to more deeply scrutinise the individual through pre-profiling. This was used to unearth material evidence on the applicant. All actors articulated they used pre-screening regularly and legitimised its use. In this case, a spent conviction is uncovered which the applicant had not declared under the Rehabilitation of Offenders Act (1974). This information is therefore powerful and changed the decision-making process. The findings highlight that candidates need to be transparent regarding issues which may affect their employability.

***Body art***

The use of pre-profiling also revealed an interesting discourse of implicit bias and stigmatisation of people who have body art by some HR actors:

> ..Tattoos for example, I once was recruiting using a telephone interview and I was looking on Facebook and there was a young lady and she was going to be front of house and she had a tattoo on her neck… you really can't because its judgement … I didn't take that candidate any further.
>
> (Tiro, Beatty, HR Manager [p. 3 line 2–8])

Most actors in this study focused on an aesthetic code which involved making judgements regarding forms of body art which includes tattoos and piercings. The narratives suggested when pre-profiling, these HR actors preferred applicants who had more traditional looks and wholesome images. This illustrates how our online images are used to judge, stereotype, and label individuals by HR actors who may deem applicants unfit for certain job roles based on their aesthetic appearances (Nath et al, 2016; Timmings, 2015). There is a plethora of research which centres on how our labour capacity is impacted by our appearance and a myriad of issues associated with protected characteristics such as race, disability, gender, and age (Van Laer and Jansens, 2011; Hoque et al, 2018; Bell et al, 2002); Kunze et al, 2011). These can be challenged with the Equality Act (2010).

This case illustrates the subtle wider forms of employment discrimination which are harder to legislate against which now impact our careers. The empiricism links with body art, such as tattoos and piercings. Warhurst et al (2009) suggest this is a form of lookism. This is of interest as tattoos and body art are not related to skill sets. Therefore, pre-screening is becoming more biased. This conceptually links to notions of organisational aesthetes and a quest for employee beauty norms in dress codes, image, and body art (Nath et al, 2016; Strati, 1999; Timming, 2015).

This drew my attention to how HRM approaches may use negative judgement of body art and thus violate parts of the Equality Act (2010). Tattoos and body adornment are an expression of identity, not capability. Clearly, in this case example, Beatty viewed body adornments as conflictual with her individual perception of normative dress conventions at work. Timming (2015) found HR practice is prejudicial to applicants with body art. ACAS (2016) are keen to eliminate such stereotyping and released guidance which reflects more ethical recruitment practices. An exploration of how this approach fitted with this key piece of legislation was discussed with the actor:

> If I'm absolutely honest, it probably really doesn't which is why it's not explicitly written but we all make judgements all the time…I know the times are changing now, it hasn't been a candidate driven market so we've been able to be more picky.
>
> (Tiro, Beatty HR manager [p. 3 line 28–32])

There is, therefore, a requirement for greater scrutiny of HRM recruitment practices which fail to adhere to key legislation or, in more veiled ways, show how this is being breached. This type of activity is transferable. There are dedicated sites on Instagram and Pinterest which promote the uniqueness of these forms of adornment. We therefore need to adapt to focus less on looks in this scenario and embrace how people wish to change their appearance. More importantly, body art may have wider cultural value associated with our indigenous race. This has been observed recently when Oriini Kaipara became the first person to become a primetime news anchor in New Zealand with a cultural marking or moko kauae, traditionally worn by Māori's. I point this out as Oriini has had an incredible amount of online hate regarding her facial tattoo. She challenged this beautifully, outlining that her body art did not mean any intent to cause harm, and that she did not wish to be treated with such contempt.

We therefore need to be more respectful of any form of body adornment. It appears we have become so used to reviewing online images and have forgotten wider societal moral codes which value our difference. As McDonald et al (2016) suggest, this raises concerns from an employee perspective which includes how qualified are employers to make such decisions.

### *Nudity*

A reoccurring construct with aesthetic coding in the dialogue of HR practitioners was how they reviewed content to look for images of inhibition and drunkenness. The following case centres on online pre-screening content involving the judgement of nudity online. As discussed in the last section, our content may increasingly contain gendered and sexualised images. This suggests many prospective and current employees are unaware that their content is being scrutinised and is more widely practised by employers.

Research suggests that group norms dictate sexualised behaviour in online contexts. It shows an increasing number of adolescents are sending and receiving nude images online (Baumgartner et al, 2010). This case is positioned as a key issue for management recruitment practices. The supervisor, who was presented with a semi-nude picture of a newly recruited member of her team, explains how this impacted on her impression of her new recruit:

> somebody's clicked onto his Facebook page … his bottom's out with his underpants pulled down… He's starting with us next week, so that's my lasting impression of this new guy.
>
> (Alumno, Darcy, Support Officer [p. 4 line 4–9])

The representation of the "self" using nude images is interesting and has multiple connotations. This emphasised how boundaries between our personal lives online are more open to judgement by employers and work peers (Malaterre et al, 2013).

Our expressiveness is juxtaposed with how social media are reconstituted for surveillance and the awareness online content maybe shared socially or in a work context. This case highlights a growing need for actors to set strict access settings. This also requires training on self-censorship, assessing whether nude or provocative images could be detrimental to their career prospect. Limiting access to personal profiles does not necessarily diminish the chance of anonymous people scrutinising online materials. My aim is to draw attention to the fact that applicants and employees appear to have little awareness of how to contain online content, or how these are used to judge individual appearance and behaviour in work. Displaying nudity can be aesthetically and artistically achieved. Yet this could lead to stereotyping of people who are more confident or overt about their body or appearance. This has potential implications for sexuality under the Equality Act (2010).

I sought to understand how the actor made sense of the image:

> I'm trying not to judge what I've seen but I cannot imagine my first day of not being able to think "I've seen your bottom"… He sounds like a really fun guy … I think you have to realise that there are certain things you can post.
>
> (Alumno, Darcy, Support Officer [p. 4 line 10–19])

In this context, the actor exercised discretion and the nude images did not affect their management judgement regarding recruitment. Yet we are in a more permissive society, use of social media has forced us to confront how it is all too easy to send or post unwarranted images. Interestingly, on viewing the online content of one HR actor, they regularly shared photos of themself in highly provocative or risqué poses, is this contradictory behaviour? Moreover, is it fair they are the moral arbiter in this case? Interestingly, this social actor had widely accepted requests to interconnect with work colleagues stating that:

> I initially wanted it to be for close friends, however I quickly realised that everybody was starting to friend request me.. people on floors who I have never spoken to before…and I just thought this right okay this is how it is… so I just accepted.
>
> (Fiona, HR Partner, Charta)

The reason this actor gave her decision to accept friend requests was because she did not want to be too selective and form in-groups or make other people uncomfortable because of her HR role if she failed to connect with them. Interestingly, the individual suggested they felt they were "more careful about what I put [on social media]getting drunk".

I explored with this further with the social actor/HR manager and asked whether they had any expectations around what images and content people should post on social media. They stated: "no there isn't" and I asked further if this was no holds barred they replied "it is". The actor infers she is fine with lewder images and content. This is surprising given their HR role. On one hand, this suggests the approach in this organisation is fair and relaxed. It can also be inferred that this is too lax, misleading, and confusing. The actuality was this actor was both pre-profiling and screening people out without their awareness and on an ad hoc basis.

Importantly, this is raised to suggest who is guiding HR actors in their decision-making, particularly where fellow peers in HRM roles would suggest:

> Perhaps you should not post that picture of yourself in a bikini.
>
> (Beth, Tiro, Recruitment Director)

This also highlights contradictions in corporate HR practices which may be misleading for the workforce.

**Discussion box 24**

**Discussion:**

Discuss the extent to which you edit your photos?

Do you ever vet your posts and take them down?

What are your views on images of body art on social media? Do you think HR practitioners are right to negatively judge applicants?

Do you think it is right to judge future workers or job applicants for their recreational habits without their awareness?

What are your views on people making angry comments about partners, friends, sportspeople, or celebrities? Do you think people should be reprimanded and disciplined or simply made to take these posts down?

Do you think it is unfair that HR practitioners and recruiters fail to tell you that they are using your posts to make subjective judgements about your online content or appearance?

**Pause for reflection:**

How can we make HR and management more accountable for making subjective judgements about our inline content?

**Act summary**

This section has focused on how we are more willing and readily judged by our social media content. A fundamental issue with such scrutiny is that this highlighted how HR and management practitioners seem to be on the lookout for nudity, sexuality, and laxed forms of behaviour. This was all viewed negatively, whilst this may or may not impact on our employment. The issue with nudity and sexuality in both on- and offline work contexts is that it forces management to accept employees are primal (Watson, 2006). This reminds management they have a role in addressing uncontrollable human urges. Culturally, we often seek to portray ourselves in an angelic, wholesome, and attractive way, which one actor termed the halo and horns effect.

My aim here is to suggest that sexualised content and intoxicated forms of (mis)behaviour are often more prevalent and, therefore, form a contradiction with our expected work identity. My findings suggest these types of images are not simply being posted by frontline workers who engage in this type of aestheticised behaviour. This sexualised online behaviour also includes HR and leaders. This is an often-overlooked area of work, where certain type of workers are perceived as being sexless or behaving to more wholesome norms (Ackroyd and Thompson, 2003).

Importantly, as Poster (1990, as cited in Dundon and Rollinson, 2011) suggests, this is becoming unnoticed due to a pervasiveness of these digital technologies. These perspectives are positioned to ground and embed ethical approaches to professional surveillance, monitoring behaviours, and seeing beneath forms of subjective stereotyping or manipulative behaviours, bringing to the foreground a growing need for greater critical reflection in HR practices in this context (Hørup, 2004; Yanow and Tsoukas, 2009).

I have tried to illustrate how this has led to shallower forms of recruitment practices. The empiricism illustrates how key social actors in work made spurious decisions over whether to hire someone based on their physical appearance and attributes such as body art (Nath et al, 2016; Timming, 2015). This is positioned to underpin the employment relationship and EB by showcasing normative and enthusiastic employees who go beyond their employment contract. Moreover, this is concerning and forms a part of wider discriminatory HR practices.

These signify new digital manifestations of aesthetic labour (Nath et al, 2016), digitised forms of emotional labour (Hochschild, 1983), and impression management (Richey et al, 2016) which are now more prevalent in work. Conceptually, Casey (1995) states such organisational practice and discourse evoke notions of designer employees and "corporatized selves". This suggests non-normative behaviours are somehow abnormal, thus, management and HR actors were shocked at alternative voice or social media displays of bitchiness, nudity, or hatred online by employees. Moreover, they rarely addressed these types of behaviour and simply asked employees to take materials down or, worst, dismissed them without clarification about why this had occurred. These conversations led to differing forms of social media misbehaviour, which are discussed in the next section.

# Section 5

# Act 4

## Conflict, resistance, and social media (mis)behaviours

This section focuses on how social media are used to shed light on issues of worker resistance, conflict, and emerging forms of social media workplace misbehaviours. The aim is to provide greater discussion on the growing possibilities for employees to use social media for differing forms of employee voice to air their concerns about issues at work or to be involved in forms of workplace decision-making. In this context, social media are increasingly used to democratise workplaces, allowing workers to have a say about their work and to challenge the ways of being in work.

The second scene focuses on how social media create a Petri dish for differing or emerging forms of misbehaviour. The aim is to provide greater discussion and debate about these novel misdemeanours and crimes emerging in this space, providing a space for greater reflection on the nature of discipline and punishment in work and how to address these actions.

DOI: 10.4324/9781003137269-12

# Act 4. Scene 1 Can you hear me?

## Stories of resistance, employee voice, and sousveillance in online contexts

***Scene summary:*** This section focuses on forms of employee resistance and how social media are incorporated by employees to both challenge and observe the hierarchies and cliques in organisations. The scene explores how social media is used for employee voice purposes, where employees may air concerns about the conditions of their work or intimate problems which management should reflect on and address these issues. This scene examines how this may give rise to emerging forms of in-work activism, and in doing so, critically reflects on how social media impacts on employee freedom of speech and expression of opinion about work. The narratives of the characters will highlight how social media widens capacity for vulnerability, particularly for those who come from diverse communities. This has ramifications for regulations, legislation, and examines how employers may address or view outward/external forms of expression. This scene allows for a full discussion on the growing possibilities for employees to use social media for differing forms of employee resistance. The scene introduces how employees use social media for sousveillance purposes. This is where employees may use social media to observe their management, acting as a reverse peephole or panoptic device. The aim is to broaden discussion from notions of surveillance to how social media empowers employees to challenge or resist employers in contemporary and evidenced ways. Thus, developing new conceptual notions of resistance and suggesting sousveillance is a new technology which influences power dynamics within contemporary employment relationships.

### Key learning points

- Social media allow workers to create greater capacity for employee voice and to create informal pressure groups from which to air their concerns regarding issues in the workplace.

DOI: 10.4324/9781003137269-13

- Using social media to interlink with leaders and managers allows workers a chance to observe those in power which to some degree levels the playing field of power in work.
- Sousveillance and the use of digitised media allow workers the capacity to capture evidence of management wrongdoings which tilt power dynamics in work.
- Social media allow us to fabricate evidence due to the textual nature of these devices. Therefore, we need to be more aware of the complex nature of purported misbehaviours in this context.

## Using social media to engage with the workforce

In most organisations, there is discussion about how engaged their workforce is, and how they can enable greater staff engagement. This is believed to a bundle of approaches and support for employees to:

> have a sense of personal attachment to their work and organisation; they are motivated and able to give of their best to help it succeed – and from that flows a series of tangible benefits for organisation and individual alike.
>
> (McLeod and Clarke, 2009: 7)

Having a positive work environment, therefore, will recognise the value of their people and involve them more readily in the labour production process to drive better performance. There is no simple route forward with engagement; however, four key enablers have been determined which are supposed to drive employee engagement (McLeod and Clarke, 2009). These are as follows:

1. Strong leader who are able to create a transparent and positive culture and can clearly articulate a strong vision and strategic narrative.
2. Engaging management who are clear about workforce goals and expectations, fully appreciate individual employees' effort, recognise employee contribution and value; and ensure that the workforce is supported and resourced to fulfil their job.
3. The creation of a corporate culture where there are clear values which enable trust and integrity to thrive.
4. The final facet of employee engagement, as discussed in the opening section, is an enduring employee relations concept which centres on employee voice this is where the workforce is listened to and are able to speak up about how they are feeling, voice their ideas and concerns about their job and in decision-making, and may work with management to jointly resolve problems and challenges. Social media cut across these factors as a way to drive and improve both engagement and worker cooperation, production, and participation in work.

Employee voice encompasses a range of actions which offer employees a means to discuss and influence work situations. This usually rests on the interests of managers to create employee voice mechanisms (Cullinane et al, 2012; Martin et al, 2015). Formal arrangements include regularly calendared meetings with trade union partners or committees. Over time, this has included social media, again dependent on how leaders incorporate this form of communication to listen and work with the workforce via more digital means, given that in the first few sections many of these HR and management practitioners viewed social media as highly risky and needed tight control. Therefore, there is a need to be more pragmatic regarding how HR works with employees who have an issue with management or workplace concerns. This highlights workers are more unlikely to simply acquiesce with management, and there needs to be greater emphasis on workplace channels to discuss issues.

Therefore, we need to accept social media is a huge part of employee voice and resistance, capturing issues and addressing wider injustices of work, as many great case examples highlight, such as the Partygate Scandal and #Me Too campaigns have illustrated both in the UK and worldwide.

One HR director incorporated social media to complement the suite of employee voice mechanisms in the workplace. The purpose was to specifically help with the process of engaging with workers in the workplace in ways that felt comfortable for employees:

> to provide more effective inter communication, engage with people about particular topics, 'cause that's where people are chatting and talking about it, in the same way they would do in the staff room. So you've got that element of you know a good effective communication tool. Not in replacement of face to face [meetings] and other things that you would do, but in addition to. There's one sort of aspect there, but the other one was about the democratisation of hierarchy really.
>
> (HR Director, Vita Health, Devlin)

**Discussion box 25**

**Discussion:**

Discuss the extent to which you are allowed to contribute to decision-making at work?

Discuss how often management engage with you in work through formal meetings or other workplace worker forums?

Are you aware of whether there are any trade unions who represent different workers in your place of work or study?

Do these mechanisms help you feel more engaged, supported, and help you to perform in work?

Do you have a social media or platforms, internally or externally, where you can contribute views about work? Are there any problems with the dialogue in these platforms?

How important do you think it is that HR and management listen to work concerns and issues in work?

**Pause for reflection:**

How important do you think it is that HR and management listen to work concerns and issues in work?

How can management and HR be more accountable for improving employee engagement and voice at work?

This emphasises how some leaders and directors are more keen to deploy progressive approaches for employee voice. This was an additional mechanism to hear worker issues and was not to replace the idea of formally meeting around the table to discuss workplace issues in face-to-face terms. These two approaches must work in tandem.

An interesting facet of the discussion was how the HR director discussed the notion of workplace democratisation. This links with pluralist notions of managing workplace conflict and resistance. A key enabler to this approach was to create more successful employment engagement and to harmonise the workforce which was perceived to be more advantageous in enhancing workplace practices. The discussion centred on how social media devices are incorporated to create real-time dialogue with their workforce as the following quote illustrates:

> so you've got a range of sort of views that are coming on that are assimilating information going on and helping to provide that feedback in a very sort of useful way about what's going on and what people are thinking about it.
>
> (HR Director, Vita Health, Devlin)

The immediacy of social media provides a platform to sense-check the immediate views and feedback of employees in the workforce. However, whilst this is a progressive use of digital media, the HR director in this scenario had to provide guidance to the workforce on how to appropriately work with social media so that it became:

> Less social networking and more about work.
>
> (HR Director, Vita Health, Devlin)

The real driver for employee engagement is to harness employees in positive ways to drive effective performance. In doing so, this should create a happy and more content workforce, as a number of studies have been reported to show.

One of the key levers for utilising social media to enhance employee voice in this study was HR directors recognised workers are using these devices anyway. Therefore, incorporating social media in work was a recognition of the major cultural changes in using these devices to aid wider worker engagement (Martin et al, 2015; Taylor, 2018).

Getting worker concerns and opinion in the current UK context is vital. There are many issues which corporations need to aware of regarding employee experiences in work over concerns they have over pay and conditions. This was found to be particularly useful for one HR director due to the volatility in the UK health sector:

> You get a sense of the way things are going …you get a sense of the mood around, what it's doing in a way that I could never had done if I was not on X (formerly Twitter).
>
> (HR Director, Vita Health, Devlin)

The director was not simply using social media to engage with workers; they were also using other platforms to understand perceptions of trade union leaders and other key stakeholders to more deeply understand the full experience of the workforce and, more broadly, consumers who are impacted by issues with the services. More broadly, the director would use their newly developed understanding to table and inform wider employee voice mechanisms and agendas, using these to develop strategic questions about issues. The participant quote below shows this will elicit a minimal range of worker views. To further develop broader workplace debate, the director would then pose questions on wider social media platforms. This enabled a wider participation with workers to discuss their issues and capture a greater number of perspectives. These views were used to rudimentarily determine the frequency of issues and determine some preference of workers on certain key workplace concerns and issues. This was interpreted to suggest organisations can capture richer data which could quantify worker likes or dislikes. This rudimentary form of analysis codified worker language to determine and measure the feelings as shown:

> But those views will then dictate in a way those first few things that are said, the mood or the sense of what other people say. So some people disagree and disengage, other people will be all for it and, so you can come out of the room

> with 2 or 3 people having spoken, most people being quiet. And a sense, the thing that we get through using [internal platform] is you put something out there, you know somebody will say something in the same way they would do in a meeting but then people start liking it or not liking it, or commenting on it 'cause it's a much safer environment. And then you find those views from the people that have always said that sort of thing, have got 50 dislikes. So you get … that democratisation of allowing views to come forward where people … they can sort of say it on there and see the reactions and see that people like it and it generates other comments and thoughts. So the richness of the information, the written information that you get far outweighs the meeting… .

This illustrates how social media content is used to change how HR and management understand workplace concerns and issues comfortably and constructively. This is not easy for management. The discussion illustrates how workers may be brutally honest about their work experiences, more so since the advent of social media.

However, there are benefits to such honesty and resistance. Using social media provides a richness of material for management to consider and to use captured evidence to jointly resolve these concerns with their workforce. The issue with this last element is that not all management appropriately engage with their workforce. This requires management to increasingly view and treat employees as sentient human beings with feelings, rights, and wider responsibilities. This includes development of more flexible working patterns and to develop standard which counteract the symptoms of stress and well-being in work (McLeod and Clarke, 2009). As shown in the previous sections, we have a long way to go on how man management view social media commentary, and how this may inform wider development and decision-making in this area of work.

The approaches shown in this and previous sections highlight that management in some large UK corporations may still inhibit both employee engagement and voice. This is because there is still a wide disconnect between the strategic narratives for social media and the people management approaches which underpin use of these. Further, there was little clarity around the rules and regulatory process. On the use of social media, the rules and practices were inconsistent. And whilst some corporations sought workers to use social media for voice purposes, some HR practitioners and management did not share this view or the belief that these are a facet of contemporary work and employment. This is probably due to the risks they felt were omnipresent with social media and how this would affect employee productivity which led to worker disengagement.

Furthermore, corporations were shown to not offer training or development to enhance behaviours and communication skills on social media, which affect the variability and commitment to incorporating social media to enhance voice and engagement.

Given such scepticism about social media, I wondered if management and HR tracked those individuals who were perceived to be more conflictual, militant, challenging on these platforms, and whether the corporation may try to address those types of behaviours. In this scenario, the actor was open to the idea of a healthy debate and was accepting regarding forms of worker resistance, particularly when addressing issues of pay, working time, or issues which link to potential legal public disclosures:

> I have to say that although you've got the occasional abuse that sort of comes through… what we also find on social media is it starts to sort of self-moderate really.
>
> So someone will come and say well you know it's all very well for you and your fat salary… ..but you get other people coming in and saying actually I think the way that he's presented it is you know you might not agree with him but he's always been genuine about it. And you get that sort of debate coming out.

**Discussion box 26**

**Discussion:**

Do you think social media enhances the richness of data and information you can gather about workplace issues?

How do you think management should respond to these online dialogues and narratives?

Discuss the extent to which you witnessed aggressive employee comments in either a meeting or social media workplace discussion?

Why do you think workers feel they can be more emotive in these forums? Or do you think they do this in face-to-face meetings?

Have you ever raised any issues regarding forms of aggression and conflict with management?

How do you think management and HR should address these issues?

**Pause for reflection:**

How important do you think it is that HR and management offer guidance about human emotion and anger in the workplace? Or do you feel we should allow all emotions to be more present in work?

This highlights how workplace commentary may be both abusive and challenging for management to handle. The director continually alluded to the fact that individuals feel braver on social media than they would in the presence of a leader or co-worker. The distance between the parties acts as a metaphor for a safety barrier. The director further elaborated on the more antagonistic aggressive forms of employee voice:

> So you know around all that sort of controversial stuff comes on and you get the occasional troll that you get that you can sort of filter out. But I find that it's either very constructive debate, if somewhat challenging at times, but also that there's, people who see that there's other views. You know its recognising people who have got complex stuff to navigate and trying to do it in an open, honest and transparent way.

This illustrates how influential HR practitioners who truly understand the power of employee voice mechanisms will use these online dialogues to help them address complex workplace problems. The social actor felt that rather than minimising employee voice online these allowed them to fully see the depth of workplace problems to try and make sense of what workers are saying. Whilst there is recognition this is more challenging, they felt this gave them a more balanced and realistic perspective on issues at work, and therefore acted as a barometer and sense-check.

Management and leadership clearly need to remain composed in these real-time dialogues so their responses do not fan the flames of conflict. This requires timely action on management behaviours. My point here is that workers who take to social media to air concerns must not feel ignored, and when they raise their issues, they should be meaningfully consulted and addressed. This is vital in the current context, where situations across the UK in a variety of sectors have become more antagonistic. We are witnessing a recent wave of industrial action. Social media are used to articulate a number of issues. This has led how such forms of freedom of expression may be legally challenged under the auspices of the wider legislation. Thus, the right to protest is becoming harder to achieve.

### *Enhancing employee voice through informal WhatsApp pressure groups*

A new avenue for employee voice is through more informal means. In organisations where social media sites like Yammer are integrated, these are controlled by management. Thus, many employees may be more fearful about airing concerns or how they respond to workplace discussions which are directed by management. This was shown in the previous section where formalised meetings and online chats with management did not always gain worker discussion and response. This highlights there is a variability in when and how workers choose to engage and work with management.

Formal approaches may or may not be meaningful to some workers. Often workers suggest they feel unheard by management but feel supported and listened to by their co-workers. Social media therefore offers capacity for a more open space for greater worker interconnections to manifest. Indeed, the empiricism shows how workers are likely to create WhatsApp groups or used closed groups in other platforms to discuss their workplace issues or concerns.

Interestingly, this shows how social media allow new forms of solidarity and collectivism to emerge. This may also pose a challenge for more formal worker participation and activism through trade unions. The empirical findings highlight how workers creatively used internal sites and WhatsApp as a platform to create informal channels. The online dialogue allowed them to freely discuss and comment on issues. These were used to garner worker solidarity and gather information or evidence which they felt may enhance facilitation of organisational work practices, processes, or design.

These devices, therefore, give employees empowerment to informally mobilise collectively using their discussion in digital platforms for participatory means, leveraging greater employee voice and action. The following quote highlights how prevalent this is becoming:

> … employees were setting up weird groups like the carpark appreciation society…quite funny stuff. So it was kind of by people's choice that they started using it.
>
> (Senes, Elizabeth, CSR Manager [p. 6 line 28–32])

This highlights how social media open up new avenues to discuss workplace issues. The case highlights how social media inverts more formal dynamics and mechanisms we associate with employee voice. We may now readily use WhatsApp, messenger, and Snapchat to set up discussion groups. In work these can be akin to sub-pressure groups. In this case, the workforce created a pressure group to address a health and safety issue in their workplace carpark which they ironically termed "The Carpark Appreciation Society".

The HR director found that staff who used the carpark were using discussion groups to air their concern about how this facility was waterlogged and unsafe. This is a genuine risk under health and safety legislation. The discussion raised concerns about if workers did fall or were hurt. Management were therefore more culpable; if they left the carpark issue unresolved, there could be a penalty on the organisation.

The solidarity of these workers meant they eventually used the group discussion to articulate their worries. They used content to evidence and capture the issues. The strength of the dialogue on these platforms ensured they got the carpark issue addressed.

These forms of dialogue are created by entrepreneurial workers who wish to challenge their employer. These groups are informally coordinated and tend to allow a freer flow of conversation as they are seemingly not policed or controlled by management. These allow both participation and mobilisation to take action in the workplace (Martin et al, 2015). This illustrates how leaders understand how tense these issues are through the visible sharing of content in these sub-pressure groups.

This creates an evident competing tension where informal organising via social media may potentially collide with formal arrangements for employee voice in the organisation. As stated, this may also impact on trade union mobilisation and action. The solidarity of the workers using these platforms ensured they got the issue addressed. Trade union leaders may also wish to think about how this impact on strategies to capitalise on memberships with non-trade union employees or indeed work with non-union members in tandem to garner a better workplace experience and outcome.

Further, it would be germane to mention this may have repercussions if online dialogues are misinterpreted by management (Kaufman, 2015). Thus, both trade union representatives, management, and HR practitioners need to carefully position how social media are integrated as a facet of both engagement and voice. This includes guidance on how to interact in volatile situations so that more antagonistic dialogues do not impact negatively on the mechanisms or approaches to express and address workplace issues, employee voice, or hinder problem-solving moving forward.

**Discussion box 27**

**Discussion:**

What is your view about workers creating smaller independent, informal sub-pressure groups through social media platforms?

Discuss what you foresee maybe the key issues and problems for these types of groups?

Discuss how management could use these to improve employee engagement and voice, if they are provided with any issues or evidence from these informal groups?

**Pause for reflection:**

How may informal WhatsApp groups affect the position of key stakeholders such as trade unions? Discuss how this may be a potential benefit to trade unions?

Discuss how it may be a potential conflict of interest for trade unions?

## Employee sousveillance, levelling the field of observation

In terms of resistance and challenge to management behaviours, sousveillance can be used by employees to capture management misdemeanours or discuss management misbehaviour and hegemonic practices via social media. As discussed, sousveillance merged as an alternative construct in the dialogue of all actors in this study who all acknowledged that they were fearful of being observed by their peers and management. This may have greater implications if they are management themselves.

In this case, Darcy, a supervisor, expressed a fear regarding how her posts caused tensions to arise when she was observed by her peers during a period when they thought she should be in work.

> People were emailing me back going oh Darcy you are on Facebook during work time.
>
> (Alumno, Darcy, Support Officer [p. 6 line 30–32])

Darcy was, in fact, using social media when she was on a later start time. However, this case illustrates how co-workers use social media to monitor those in positions of power to level the field of observation on management behaviours. Darcey discussed how her posts and profiles were scrutinised by her subordinates who were using these platforms to make judgements regarding absence, timekeeping, their whereabouts, and application to work tasks.

This shows how sousveillance adds to conflict in work. This further demonstrates the changing nature in online veillance practices in organisations (Mann et al, 2003; Taylor, 2018). Sousveillance is an inverted form of surveillance or bottom-up observation (Fernback, 2013; Ganascia, 2010). The discourse on sousveillance establishes how digital devices, such as phones, are used by workers to gather intelligence evidence which tracked management movements and employees alike. I have incorporated social media into this mix as we can use these to film, record, or capture images, content, and dialogue.

This aim here is to also suggest how online materials are increasingly used primarily for disciplinary purposes and indeed one-upmanship between co-workers. Emerging forms of sousveillance further contribute to sources of conflict between co-workers and management. This is perceived to act as a further breach in contemporary employment relationships (Edwards, 2003; McDonald et al, 2016; Spooner and Haidar, 2006).

## I want roses! Irresponsible autonomy

Ackroyd and Thompson (2003) made a great contribution to discussion on irresponsible autonomy. This is perceived as contradictory and unique forms of workplace activity and behaviour which they suggest is where supposedly rational people act in atypical ways. Social media is now used to capture the way we may breach expected behaviours in work, furthermore, how this now includes how workers use sousveillance to capture how management may misbehave.

In this case, a director made a throwaway, less thoughtful comment on X (formerly Twitter). The comment was observed by their co-workers and caused great offence as they explained this issue:

> on Valentine's Day last year I'm tweeting like: "Some employees better start bringing me some roses or I'm gonna start firing people". You know, am I actually going to fire people? No; but there were some people who really didn't think it was a joke.
>
> (HR Director, Erica)

This comment, made by an HR director, intended their tweet to be witty and ironic on St Valentine's day. This highlights how we need to be more circumspect with the types of comments we make online. These crossover and link with negative work experiences and relationships. In this case, comments are also akin to more comedic forms of communication which occur at work such as office banter, sarcasm, mimicry, and gossip, which are ubiquitous in life and work (Ackroyd and Thompson, 2003). These types of dialogue are even more prevalent because of the advent of social media. Our comments are now viewed by the many, as this case highlights. This is perceived to impact on micro-politics at work where work groups self-organise to create informal hierarchies. In this case, the group sousveilled the HR director and reacted badly to their seemingly innocuous comments. These comments were observed, screen-captured, and raised with a further director to challenge their power. This had a practical effectiveness. The HR director realised you have to be careful what you say and to think about your comments when you are a leader with an audience who will judge you:

> Yeah at your peril… you know you do have to be sensible about what you tweet.
>
> (Erica, HR Director, Senes)

This shows that elite actors also struggle with their impulsivity and being inconsistent with their professional sense of responsibility and self-moderating when on social media. Therefore, we all need to be more aware that as humans we are reactionary and that our other fellow users may interpret humour differently.

There are a great many case law precedents in the UK where social media has been discussed in connection with capturing examples of banter and horseplay, including within the outgoing previous UK Conservative Government. It is again shrewd to note that material evidence of this can be hard to prove as there has been a furore in this case regarding how we can set timers to delete messages, and moreover, how messages can seemingly disappear. The same can be said of work groups where they too can record messages that will set to delete. The aim of this discussion is to enforce that leaders and management who may be in these groups to think someone in your ranks at some point may find your narrative abhorrent. Those messages may form the bedrock of a case against management. Further questions from within your workforce may centre on management transparency. Particularly if the banter and perceptions show a distasteful view of key individuals or group of employees in your workforce, and how much more damaging this is for employee engagement and cooperation. Therefore, we must more greatly understand that regardless of our status, we cannot say what we want on social media, even in closed groups, without this being sousveilled watched, potentially misinterpreted, or used to gain some form of justice.

Throughout this text I have tried to emphasise social media use is reliant and pursuant on responsible autonomy. This is where we behave acceptably online and are less impulsive. This case illustrates how social media are used to turn the gaze on irresponsible autonomy by a manager/director. This shows how these devices are used to capture evidence of distinct and unique forms of management misbehaviour. This contribution is important. Uncharacteristic management behaviour or subversion is rarely discussed. In extant literature, management usually devise and categorise all forms of behaviour in organisations. Yet in this case, workers use sousveillance to challenge distinctive misbehaviour.

## Whistleblowing

The observation of management helps to emancipate workers in hegemonic employment relationships (Taylor and Dobbins, 2021). These cases require greater reflection on human resource management (HRM) strategies and policies to enable adaptation in both voice, social media, and veillance practices. Yet conversely, some HR actors perceived employees who took to social media as a form of public disclosure on working conditions were breaching their procedures and employment contracts:

> Social media in a way is like whistleblowing gone mad. You are not using the proper whistle blowing channels…they are now firing off a FB comment or an article and press send.
>
> (Alumno, Debbie, Policy Development Team [p. 7 line 33 39])

This perception drew attention to an HR perspective on whistleblowing which suggested that social media comments constitute a contemporary form of sabotage and resistance by individuals, rather than a duty to inform society of a corporate wrongdoing (Ackroyd and Thompson, 2003; Noon et al, 2013; van den Broek and Dundon, 2012). In this case, an academic had made comments about the institution.

Another HR director took a different view to social media commentary and used these to investigate issues where users appear to make derogatory comments about work or colleagues:

> They are talking about you, they are talking about their services.. this may draw heat and a bit of fire…… .if someone tells you they are bad mouthing an employee or something…I can investigate it… .if they are saying something inappropriate then I will drop them an email saying, sorry to hear about this… .we will look into this… you might just want to delete that.
>
> (HR Director, Vita, Devlin)

The HR director took a very responsible approach where they felt it was more forgiving to try and understand why this person had gone online and made these comments. The director felt prior to the emergence of social media they would have endeavoured to understand and discuss the substantive issues in a face-to-face investigatory meeting. They felt the fact social media was used should not change this and sought a more human-centric approach. This shows a level of empathy and realisation that we are imperfect and get angry about work issues. Social media simply puts these under a microscope and is just another medium to view these imperfections. The problem is the size and scale of these issues are now publicly broadcast to potentially vast audiences which may attract greater attention. The effects these types of posts may impact on corporate reputation was discussed more broadly. One actor stated:

> It's just in a more public space, but I find it quite forgiving… .I think you can manage them.
>
> (HR Director, Vita, Devlin)

This type of activity may stimulate debate over what is typified as misbehaviour and what is viewed as a legitimate reason for employee resistance. Simply put, social media are used as a means to air these issues in order to survive work (van den Broek and Dundon, 2012; Thompson, 2016). How these issues are investigated and the potential outcomes are again down to management to decide. What this type of online activity and content does is more deeply focus management and HR attention on the need to use social media commentary to address issues with working conditions and to take appropriate action, if possible.

The reality is many organisations would also perceive such activity to bring the organisation into disrepute. This has indeed formed the bedrock of formal disciplinary action and case law taken by employers (Biro, 2011; Broughton et al, 2010). This demonstrates how employees need to more deeply understand both wider discipline and grievance procedures or the Public Interest Disclosure Act (1998). The act usefully enables employees to take action in respect of victimisation and acts of hegemony at work. The narratives drew attention to the dexterity of the manager to approach work situations with care, particularly if they are the root cause of such emotions or to address management behaviours:

> ..we are not just recommending that individual is subject to disciplinary but recommending that managers actually need to be more responsive.
>
> (Alumno, Davina, HR Policy Development [p. 8 line 13–14])

This indicates organisations are more widely using social media commentary to understand and to be more receptive to hearing alternative worker experiences, using these alerts to address conditions in work. This can only improve employee voice and engagement. This requires management to more holistically and actively hear worker concerns as one actor suggested:

> it is not just closing your eyes to the stuff that's happening. At least if you're on it you're aware of what's being said and you have at least got an opportunity to try and correct sort of misconceptions.
>
> (Vita, HR Director, Devlin)

This infers that HRM best practice uses social media to encourage reflection upon management behaviours, working conditions, and practices which negatively affect employees. This was not conclusive across the case analysis. Further, even though these comments are observed, this did not suggest managers actually made any changes or as a consequence would be disciplined for any unethical management approaches.

In the empiricism, only one organisation conducted wider investigations into management approaches which impacted on workers as follows:

> "...where they have breached the disciplinary process... if they themselves have stepped out of process.
>
> (Pala, Charlotte, HR Consultant [p. 11 line 34–37])

This suggested procedural justice was far from clear. It does highlight that management were more leniently dealt with if they were caught breaching the disciplinary process. Yet as discussion has shown, many workers may not understand these. So it may be too fearful to challenge management.

Resolving problems which occur on social media are on the increase and cause greater issue for HR and management to address:

> We're spending too much time on dealing with the breaches that will happen because of some of those reputational things. And in the meantime the reputation I think for you as an organisation engaging with your employees has been lost.
>
> (Vita, HR Director, Devlin)

This suggests social media contexts leave all workers in precarious and unprotected situations. The dialogue illustrates how HRM and management practices fail to truly unpick all sides of the issues and we now spend inordinately more time on the procedures rather than addressing the workplace concerns.

**Discussion box 28**

**Discussion:**

Discuss whether you were aware of the term *sousveillance* and how social media can be used to observe co-workers and management?

Do you think this levels the playing field of power?

What is your view about using social media platforms to capture evidence of wrongdoing by management or a co-worker?

Discuss what you foresee maybe the key issues and problems for type of activity in formal investigations?

**Pause for reflection:**

Discuss how management may react if they were observed and their actions commented on by their subordinates?

## Targeting and aggressive behaviour content

It is increasingly apparent some workers used social media to observe, challenge, resist, and capture evidence of more aggressive forms of (mis)behaviour (Taylor, 2018). Sousveillance in this genre of behaviour also included use of mobile devices and text messages. One HR director noted the rise in this activity:

> We get stuff … where you know, people on Facebook have been abusive to other members.

This case comment highlights how tensions between group members in both online and offline contexts can spill over. In all cases individuals had witnessed how this can spiral out of control; often angry members took to social media to make bitch or malevolent comments about one another.

I have witnessed this in my own social media feed where friends disagree over political or major pandemic issues. It is also more prevalent within my university role, particularly where students are assigned to live together or work together in groups to complete assessment tasks. I have been involved in resolving issues where students use WhatsApp to coordinate assessment tasks. This becomes heightened when one student is perceived to be underperforming and led to some griping and bitching.

In some social settings, students witnessed and experienced more aggressive behaviours. Often students begin to storm and agitate each other because the group begins to gang up on their own members due to friendships or romances going awry. These issues may also spill out into online forums. This relates to wider forms of irresponsible autonomy where we fail to regulate what we are saying online, in subgroups, or via text messages (Ackroyd and Thompson, 2003). In these type of cases, employees, co-workers, and fellow students tend to use sousveillance of online and digital content of either media to observe and capture abhorrent behaviours.

The visibility of the online dialogue can be used to capture comments for the purpose of disciplinary action. In this case, a group of students discussed how in-group membership deteriorated and had spilled into text and WhatsApp messages:

> Yeah, that's the picture that me and my friend sent… she told the university I am always nasty…but then she did not show the pictures her and her friends sent.
>
> (Beau, Student)

This case highlights how animosity in any social situation will heighten conflict. This may lead to more vitriol and vile comments online. The sousveillance process in this scenario was used as a means to capture forms of misbehaviour between a student groups and instigate a corporate response to investigate both sides of the issue. This case highlights how types of evidence need to be carefully investigated to protect both parties. Primarily because the materials produced as evidence were purportedly fabricated. Essentially, this case highlights how individuals can be made targets, so all is not as it may seem with sousveillance technologies. Because we may rely on the written text it is natural that some individuals may tilt and distort situations in their favour and, as the last case suggests, fabricate evidence due to the textual nature of these devices. In this scenario, a female student claimed a male student, a former boyfriend, had been abusive toward her. Their groups of friends took sides and played this out online. The female student states this included both friendship groups using social media to send physically threatening messages, including death threats. The young male was very upset and shocked at the allegations as they felt the relationship had simply terminated and couldn't understand how this had escalated after the split stating:

> They blocked me and then put on Facebook if you have anything nasty to say about me, say it to my face.
>
> (Beau, Student)

In this case, the member dialogue seemingly grew to be more direct, targeted, and chilling with one group member being singled out:

> I will control Maisie [the singled out student] with my fist… don't take me anywhere near her or she is dead.

This text was used in a university case of harassment. The text and online evidence appeared to be compelling and led to an investigation looking into the social media accounts of a range of over 20 students. The sousveillance evidence was put forward. The male student had also brought their own device to the investigatory meeting to prove and show they had not sent or created any of the pictures or texts. Therefore, this case was not upheld by the university or the police.

In this discussion, I asked whether students had been made aware of social media or harassment policies or wider student codes of conduct. The students were not aware and simply were told:

> just to behave well and be nice to other people.
>
> (Ellie, Student)

Knowing most universities have a range of policies for social media, harassment, and codes of behaviours, it was apparent these regulations are often obscured to students in their induction processes and beyond. These young students, like workers, are often bombarded with information that is quickly forgotten. My point here is to suggest it is unlikely that sousveillance as a form of observation will be picked up in these processes.

In most interviews the actors had not heard of sousveillance practices. This suggests these policies focus on surveillance and not the other alternative veillance practices. Thus, it is unlikely they may not cover issues of different forms of observation and the impact this may have on workplace conflict and resistance. Further, HR do not overtly explain how evidence will be thoroughly checked to verify and ensure these are both factual and are not being used to target individuals. This illustrates how some workers or students may try to manipulate the process to divert attention away from their own misbehaviour. These dialogues led to me discussing how misbehaviour is more prevalent, and there are emerging forms which may include sousveillance and fabrication of evidence due to the textual nature of these devices.

Further, little discussion is given on how management may retaliate and manipulate the annals of power if they were caught on maybe a minor aspect of their work approach through sousveillance. Indeed in the empirical findings, I have highlighted how management are often more softly reprimanded than those workers in lower positions. This highlights how worker dissent and resistance overlap with forms of management (mis)behaviour as workers seek to fight back over work and working practices in order to gain justice (van den Broek and Dundon, 2012; Thompson, 2016; Taylor and Dobbins, 2021) My point here is to say sousveillance is both complex and problematical. This suggests leaders and management have to accept and recognise their imperfections, inadequacies, and fragilities. Importantly, they must also be disciplined should they breach their own regulations and codes of behaviour. The escalation of the latter case is discussed in Act 4 Scene 2, where I begin to elaborate on wider emerging forms of misbehaviour in this context to further build on previous literature.

# Act 4. Scene 2 People do dumb stuff on social media

## Novel crimes and contradictory social media (mis)behaviours

In the last section, my focus centred on how the front stage display of behaviours by social actors and their use of social media lean towards workplace conflict, resistance, and the emergence of misbehaviour to become more visible. This demonstrates navigating work is not all about perfect employees. In fact, organisational life now centres on how people management processes which address more contradictory behaviours.

Few texts have focused on organisational misbehaviours to highlight some of the main issues (Ackroyd and Thompson, 2003). This section aims to build on this body of work to explore emerging cases of digital misbehaviours which were found to exist in this study. The aim is to contribute to wider discussion on how some employees may act counterproductively on social media and how corporations may react to such forms of behaviour.

Weitz et al (2012) suggest there are various antecedents which contribute to forms of misbehaviour. These include feelings of injustice, exploitation, immorality, opportunism, dissatisfaction, pay inequality, and general frustrations. Thompson (2016) suggests workers use these to resist and destabilise power relations. The cases in this section were observed in this study. These are not an exhaustive list of misbehaviours which occur on social media; there will be more. The aim is to simply highlight some common ones and to reflect upon HR and management strategies which seek to address these.

**Scene summary:** The scene uses differing case study examples on emergent forms of misbehaviour by both workers and management, which are becoming ever-present in this digitised context. Focus is chiefly given to management misbehaviours which are rarely focussed on, examining how social media is used for more subversive behaviours and alternate or ulterior portrayal of the self. The central discussions focus on how such activity poses a challenge for human resource management (HRM). The scene will explore emerging forms of online misbehaviours such as profiteering, theft, absenteeism, online harassment, predatory behaviours, duplicity, countercultures, and radicalism. Misbehaviour

DOI: 10.4324/9781003137269-14

is rarely discussed and stuns workplaces, thus affecting relationships in work. This final scene discusses the ineptitude of traditional management and seeks to explore new horizons for radical management approaches.

## Catalysts for online misbehaviour and conflict in the employment relationship

This section focuses on categorising key issues that may occur within employment relationships at work and how use of social media brings these into sharper focus. Each case vignette highlights the complexity of managing cases of misbehaviour in the corporate contexts. The first case focuses on how we tend to vent our feelings on social media, which is perceived to bring the organisation into disrepute:

### I hate you… .A bad day in the office

One of the main areas of confusion for employees is the perception they can say whatever they want about work on their seemingly *private* social media profiles. This is a myth which needs dispelling. We cannot put what we want and become more tenuous if employees also state where they work on their profile details.

All the HR actors in this study discussed how there had been a plethora of cases where employees had made the following types of comment about the corporation or making derogatory comment about their superiors:

> I've had a crap day and hate working here…I hate this place.
>
> (Beatty, HR Manager, Tiro Recruitment)

> I've had a rubbish day at work and my boss is an X?YZ?
>
> (France, Credit Control, Charta)

On the face of it, these comments may seem fairly ambiguous or mild. Yet it was apparent from the discourse that this is a common reoccurring issue. The HR actors all discussed how many employees perceive they can vent their upset and anger about work or their colleagues to their online friends. The main point to emphasise is that organisations and their HR departments took these comments seriously. These comments have the likelihood to be copied, sent on, and, therefore, have the potential to be seen by wider audiences and end-users or consumers of their services. This has formed some case law (shown in the introductory literature section). I explored with management and HR actors what action they took to address these type of issues. In all instances, informal disciplinary processes were invoked to ascertain how injurious this may be to the organisation or the individuals involved.

The effect was all organisations in this study asked the individuals to first remove all the comments and explained these are viewed as detrimental to their corporate reputations. In the more formal disciplinary issues, the individuals posting their concerns were invited to wider investigations. Outcomes were dependent on a number of factors. This may be because the individual may have a huge amount of followers or they placed a continuous run of similar messages which had been repeatedly viewed or regularly sent on to other co-workers, creating a catalyst which required management to take greater action. This often led to the individual being dismissed.

This misbehaviour is common. Many workers will discuss how they are feeling about peers, life, politics, work, or colleagues and not all will be in glowing terms or fit with the corporate notion of professionalism. All too readily they will put this on their feeds. I asked the HR actors what advise they gave to their employees who had made these comments and what warnings they gave regarding any similar future action. They suggested that they asked the individuals to not put where they worked to mitigate against any further reputational damage.

They also felt that dismissing employees sent out a signal to others and may act as a deterrent. This does not feel as though this will fully address the underlying issue of any perceived poor working relations or work cultures. Thus, in all likelihood, it will never fully address the issue of someone else repeating this type of posts. Employees therefore need to understand what they can post and be encouraged to act responsibly when they discuss issues about work to protect their own interests. Ideally, staff should discuss issues about work with management or with trade union representatives. This is not particularly easy if management are the issue. This feeds into the next case which highlights the impact of derogatory comments about management.

## You B@$tard: A case of bad mouthing management

As discussed, a common reoccurring issue affecting employers and employees is when co-workers post derogatory or defamatory comments about their fellow co-workers. This vignette illustrates the reaction of a manager who observed a group of employees commenting on their management style on Facebook. Using the reverse peephole of social media the manager can critically gaze on their sense of self through the eyes of their team. This highlights how online behaviours stimulate a shock to the very core of ourselves as we can see how others view us. This may be potentially psychologically harmful for the individual concerned:

> The manager actually came to me himself and broke down and it affected him in a bad way.
>
> (Aedis, Alan, Property Services Manager [p. 4 line 22])

This demonstrates the psychological effect and depth of emotion experienced when online activity exposes allegations of direct bullying. In order to resist such management practices, employees may misconceive their right to exercise their freedom of speech and express their discontent through opinion online:

> I can say what I want.
>
> (Aedis, Alan, Property Services Manager [p. 5 line 9])

Organisations need to make it fundamentally clear to employees they cannot necessarily say what they want online. Management and HR will review the social media feeds to ascertain what is being said and will investigate issues which impact the perception of the individual or the corporation. Further to this, management will also review the timescale, the level of activity, and number of posts. This will ascertain whether the individual is making these comments when they should be working. If the level of posts is significant, management will view this as a huge distraction from work, as well as the posts being detrimental to reputation.

Further, HRM may use the reverse peephole of content to view management practices as this may offer insight into individual approaches which need addressing. This is a process which would deliver greater procedural justice to protect wider employees from psychologically harmful aspects of work.

These cases highlight how social media is used to voice concerns over and resist working practices (van den Broek and Dundon, 2012; Thompson, 2016). Employees in this case were given verbal warnings and told not to make online comments again. This presents a potential issue in how allegations of online discourse are dealt with in the long term. These may have implications for these devices as an employee voice mechanism as employees may choose to air their concerns to wider audiences in order to "whistleblow" on important issues if they believe they are seemingly misheard. This has implications for regulating social media use as a mechanism for employee voice. In this case, workers are viewed by management to simply vent dissatisfaction (Holland et al, 2016). This suggests workers use social media to influence or control their working environments and that this activity is simply viewed by management as misbehaviour (Thompson, 2016).

Whilst each case has to be treated on its own merit, there are legal implications which state consistency must be applied to social media cases. This poses an interesting challenge for investigation and conflict resolution. This presents a need to reintegrate teams using facilitation or group mediation to ensure that teams can begin to regain some sense of cohesion through a more controlled means.

The next case focuses on opportunism and financial gain.

**LinkedIn ownership and contacts**

LinkedIn is widely used in business and contributes to new forms of labour production. The ownership of LinkedIn contacts is a contested topic in employment tribunals. It is argued that the corporation owns these contacts through intellectual property as it is perceived that contacts are built up through being employed in the company and therefore may argue the organisation legally owns these and thus is considered confidential information. Yet, employees may argue that they own these contacts through their own personal networking and work endeavours.

Emerging case law centres on how these contacts cause a potential threat to corporations through loss of revenue. This vignette highlights the contentious issues in how the appropriation and ownership of LinkedIn contacts constitute growing conflict in work. Legally, who owns LinkedIn information may be covered within the employment contract. Therefore, employees must consult these documents before they consider appropriating online contacts for their own use. If this is stipulated and employees use them for opportunistic gain, this is considered a misuse of confidential information and a breach of an implied duty of good faith expressed within the employment contract. Furthermore, the protection of clients is often covered within restrictive covenants, which are also mostly detailed in employment contracts. Both of these principally serve to legally protect the employer.

This case scenario focuses on how an employee who worked for a recruitment agency, Jason, used a corporate database to contact his personal LinkedIn contacts. This was for the purposes of recruiting himself as a permanent internal recruiter for these targeted client contact organisations. This is considered a breach of their employment contract.

A recruitment agency sales director, Beth, detailed the moment she was informed by a commercial client who was one of the recipients of this action:

> he [the client] sent me an email from his personal email address…it comes up as Jason Smith, speccing himself in as an internal resourcer, speccing himself in as an internal recruitment person.
>
> This email categorically said staff are more likely to stay with you if you recruit them directly than through an agency, companies waste £3 billion a year in the UK on agency fees, companies waste time and effort simply using agencies.
>
> Liiterally.., he sent that to everybody on his LinkedIn…he emailed that list from work to his home address one night, at 7.30pm, rang in sick the next day and then emailed 700 people, my contacts, my 12 years of building up that database, slagging off recruitment agencies and suggesting that he could do a better job if he looked internally for that company.
>
> (Tiro, Beth, Sales Director [p. 3 line 2–16])

There are two issues at play in this scenario:

1. The employee is using a corporate database of contacts to tout for employment. These are owned by the recruitment organisation, not the individual.
2. They used their personal LinkedIn contacts, which is a grey area in law. However, this action is perceived to bring the current recruitment agency employer into disrepute.

The commercial contact felt strongly that this was an employment breach by the employee Jason, who has sent an email to them as a recruitment agency client suggesting he could be their internal recruiter. This is clearly at odds with the commercial angle of their role as Jason suggests that using a recruitment agency is a considerable waste of money. This is a ballsy position given Jason is employed by the recruitment agency. Clearly, this is a direct threat to the recruitment agency business and would affect both the revenue earnings of the recruitment agency and furthermore brings their brand reputation into disrepute.

This is considered to be an opportunistic route for the employee. This demonstrates how we may seek wider opportunities to advantageously use social media contacts for our own self gain. Many employees may confuse who owns LinkedIn contacts. These may be covered within corporate policy. This highlights how employees may be in direct conflict with their employer who is seeking both loyalty to the brand and a degree of self-discipline in their role (van den Broek and Dundon, 2012).

Organisations, therefore, must consider mechanisms which determine how to address these emerging forms of employee misbehaviour (Weitz et al, 2012). In this case, the recruitment agency director discussed how this act of defiance was approached. This led to a formal disciplinary investigation into actions:

> The very first thing that they do [The corporation] ... our MD, legal, HR is they make him print off everybody, all his connections, they write a letter saying this is what you have to do. It's our intellectual property...you only have these connections potentially because you've worked for Tiro Recruitment.
>
> Categorically we have covenants coming out of our ears in our contract, so categorically soliciting our clients in any way, shape or form including LinkedIn, Facebook and Twitter is absolutely unacceptable and a serious offence which we pursued.
>
> (Tiro, Beth, Sales Director [p. 3 line 30–36])

This illustrates a prevailing unitary approach and a cumulative display of power used to discipline the employee (Cradden, 2011; Edwards, 2003). In terms of current advice, it is suggested corporations should articulate who has the ownership and use of online contacts within the initial employment deal. This needs stipulating in the terms and conditions of the employment contract and wider social media policies. The corporation in this case had outlined these stipulations in the employment contract and further to this included use of wider restrictive covenants on elements of intellectual property. This is traditionally highlighted to all employees during induction processes so they are clear that they should not solicit clients for other purposes than recruitment agency business.

Restrictive covenant clauses are now commonplace in employment contracts, particularly in sales environments. There are debates whether such clauses are enforceable. It is pertinent to add, some restrictive covenants last for a significant period of time, even after the employee has left the organisation. It is worth considering this when you start a new role.

When employees act in contradictory ways, this has an emotional aspect on management. This was explored with the director:

> It was shock … I know it's really mean to call somebody stupid, he's not stupid at all but that lack of common sense... it's emotional awareness isn't it … He thought he was better than me … I was shaking when I sacked him, literally the most angry I have ever been with anybody … because I felt it was a personal insult on me… which is obviously a ridiculous thing to feel, but that is how it made me feel ..it's frightening how one little thing like that could literally make or break you in theory ... It does make you realise how fragile the whole thing is I think.
>
> (Tiro, Beth, Sales Director [p. 5 line 9–16])

The director in this situation discusses how they perceived the employee to lack emotional intelligence and common sense. The case illustrates the frustration and anger at the actions of an employee who until that point had been a good worker. The narrative portrays how the psychological contract between the employee and employer had been broken to the extent that the employee is now perceived as calculating and speculative. There was a clear breakdown in relations between the director and the individual which demonstrates how trust is violated and quickly erodes within the employment relationship (Edwards, 2003; McDonald et al, 2016). This shows how schisms in work relationships develop when attitudes and perceptions differ over the purpose of work. This occurs over time as employee commitment to the corporation decreases (Kuo et al, 2015).

There is a strong correlation between worker dissatisfaction and sabotage in the workplace (Ackroyd and Thompson, 2003; Thompson, 2016; Weitz et al, 2012). The noticeable changes in behaviour in the employee were further explored with the sales director. The director reflected on noticeable signs that the employee had changed over time from when they were first recruited:

> sometimes you'll come across somebody like Jason that you have a feeling about them and that you think "He's a bit weird, would I have bought from him"...Then you think well actually he is a complement to the rest of us. He's steady, he's married, he's got two young kids, he needs to earn good money.
>
> (Tiro, Beth, Sales Director [p. 6 line 16–21])

This discourse provides some perceptual insights into the mind of those who are recruiting employees. The quote illustrates how the director observed was unsure at the start of the implied employment relationship. The director recalls they perceived the individual to be quirkier than their usual recruitment sales applicants from the onset. Yet they recruited the individual on the basis that they found the future employee to be more wholesome and stable because they had a family. This is positioned to relate to further subjective, traditional corporate codes which are used to judge and favour supposed normality in workers. The codes in this instance relate to the fact that the individual is married and has a family to support, therefore will naturally need to be productive to earn bonuses. Further, this relates to how sales environments operate and tend to rely on younger workers.

What makes someone self-sabotage a career? This subjective bias may have been felt by the worker. This could have had an effect on how they may have felt out of sorts in work and what they experienced in terms of treatment. Did they or were they made to have felt different? Did this unwittingly make them feel like an outsider from the onset. Further, this suggests, in work, we subliminally create in-groups where certain archetypes are favoured due to their identity and behaviours and others know they are considered different. This may undoubtedly trigger forms of resentment if employees feel management actions are unfair (Weitz et al, 2012). If workers know they are considered less normal or weirder than their work colleagues, this could trigger dissatisfaction and lead to their overall disengagement. This suggests we need to address how some employees may experience work cultures. Reflecting on this point, if employees are unhappy and dissatisfied in their job roles, are they likely to use their LinkedIn to seek employment elsewhere? The answer is yes, probably. This case highlights it is all too easy to use social media for economic self-gain, causing harm to organisational reputation and productivity (McDonald et al, 2016; Moussa, 2015). The slight snag in this case was they did not simply suggest they were open to new work on their LinkedIn profile, which is somewhat more legitimate. They actively breached their contract by downloading the platform contacts and used wider email technologies to tout for work. This clearly is a form of misbehaviour and gives corporate legitimacy to discipline the labour effort of employees.

This is a difficult area of the employment relationship to navigate. The ownership of social media contacts as stated is a particularly grey area of legislation, particularly if LinkedIn contacts are in the public domain and have been built up over time. This, it can be argued, may not constitute confidential corporate information as LinkedIn is defined as being personal to the account holder under LinkedIn's own terms and conditions.

Some employers in the sample range actively used LinkedIn as part of customer relationship marketing tools which further blurs these boundaries. Advice given to employers is to stipulate which platforms are the sole properties of the organisation. Some organisations advise employees to create new accounts so they can control and monitor online activity. This form of conflict is now inevitable and expected to grow and present wider issues for case law.

The next case focuses on humour and banter on social media.

**Discussion box 29**

**Discussion:**

Discuss whether your place of work has a policy or stipulation about who owns social media contacts if you are expected to use platforms such as LinkedIn, X [formerly Twitter], or Facebook for work purposes?

Discuss whether you think it is fair that organisations can claim ownership of your personal social media contacts?

**Pause for reflection:**

Reflect on how HR and management could approach the issue of ownership of social media contacts more effectively.

### Just Bantz: Posting materials which breach client confidentiality

Social media posts are much more visible, and the content we post does not always neatly fit with corporate expectations. The boundaries between work and privacy are much more blurred. We tend to post things about work which are now more often cited in case law as affecting corporate reputation. Some of these are done in jest and not intended to be malicious. In this case vignette, an actor, Brittany, who worked in a recruitment role, discussed how they breached data protection, employment law, and social media policy by posting a photo of a potential recruitment candidate on Facebook. The case highlights Brittany simply did not think. It was a case where the individual clearly did not fully understand the rules of her job role in relation to her private use of social media:

> So I took a picture of them [picture of the applicant] and sent it to him [a work colleague] on Facebook. It was just the picture … . no personal details

> … and I said, "You've got a doppelganger." The HR Generalist reported me to the HR Manager and they were going to take me through disciplinary.
>
> (Tiro, Brittany, Recruitment Sales [p. 2 line 4–52])

Posting images and details of applicants on Facebook is considered a major breach of client confidentiality under the General Data Protection Regulations in the UK. I wanted to understand why Brittany had even thought posting an image of a prospective applicant was a good idea. Brittany explained this was because she thought the applicant looked uncannily like one of her current work colleagues. Brittany explained she wanted to share this with her peers for the purpose of office banter. This shows how common sense does not prevail in the age of social media. We seem trigger happy to post materials. This case highlights how this may affect client confidentiality and shows how employee conduct on social media requires a greater understanding of the law in this domain and in their role. There is clearly an issue here with both self-discipline and responsible autonomy (van den Broek and Dundon, 2012; Thompson, 2016). Autonomy and impulsivity are, therefore, considered to be a predictor for the rate of misbehaviour (Ackroyd and Thompson, 2003; Weitz et al, 2012). More broadly, if there are loose parameters of control or any vague understanding of rules, this is considered to create an environment for forms of misbehaviour to become more prevalent.

What makes this case truly unique is that the individual in this case, Brittany, was employed as a recruitment specialist. Brittany had been trained on the greater need for her to understand the "rules" of client confidentiality set out in the Data Protection Act (1998) and in wider aspects of legal practices associated with the recruitment sector. In the discussion, Brittany clearly assumes because she posted just an image of an applicant on social media and did not disclose any further personal details, this would be alright. The irony of the discourse is paramount. Brittany had failed to reflect that a picture of a person is enough to be recognised.

Weitz et al (2012) suggest that personality traits are a strong predictor of workplace delinquency. This includes conscientiousness and experience as forecast for ethical worker behaviour. In this case, conscientiousness was explored with Brittany, particularly how this applied to the knowledge and awareness of how to use social media:

> They have that many different policies and there was that much red tape, it was like really, you never knew what you could and couldn't do. In terms of the severity of what I did, I didn't think there was anything wrong with it, to the point where the whole of the HR team was laughing. Everybody knew what I had done and everybody was laughing about it… it was one of the HR team that then reported me … and it escalated from there but I wasn't aware of doing anything wrong.
>
> (Tiro, Brittany, Recruitment Sales [p. 3 line 44–49])

The clarity regarding social media and general data protection policy is key to the employee interpretation and sense-making regarding how they understand and interpret what appropriate behaviour should look like.

In this case, Brittany had lost all perspective of these expectations. Brittany's perception was that the regulation in this domain was overly bureaucratic; this correlates to findings demonstrated in Act 1 of this text, where I highlighted that employees find it very difficult to locate and understand social media policy. Brittany intimates this was deemed too difficult. Brittany is clearly not thinking about the ramifications of punitive action and has focused on banter and humour. The interesting element is she states her peers were laughing about this in the first instance. Her mission is complete. However, this is an HR department and inevitably a work colleague reported her for this post. Brittany was outraged.

This case further shows that even within HR and people management departments, who develop and embed rules, there is confusion about an interpretation of regulatory practices. So these need to be watertight for all levels of understanding. This demonstrates the importance of being adequately trained on legal elements associated with our roles and the expectation of social media use. This development will constantly need to be refreshed, so that employees are reminded of their duty which may have made Brittany more aware of both confidentiality, General Data Protection Regulation (GDPR), and punitive disciplinary measures should you breach behaviours (Biro, 2011; Broughton et al, 2010; Moussa, 2015).

Brittany was lulled into a false sense of security because her work colleagues found her action funny. She was clearly shocked her actions and behaviour had been exposed by her fellow HR colleagues. I explored how being caught by a "*friend*" made her feel:

> I'm quite a trusting character, you see. I'm a real people person and I'm quite a trusting character, so when you befriend people, you don't expect them to use it against you. I would have expected if they were a friend, to turn around and say, "[Brittany], you know, you need to take that off", whereas they didn't; they went and totally blew it... they had discussed it between them and together escalated it. So it was like the two of them against me... kind of thing, without my knowledge, it just came out of the blue. So it kind of made me very sceptical of new people.
>
> (Tiro, Brittany, Recruitment Sales [p. 7 line 49–56])

Brittany articulates how she felt a strong sense of betrayal by her so-called friends. This draws attention to the wider implications of employee social media sousveillance, where colleagues use online content as evidence to report and highlight misdemeanours and misbehaviour to management. This demonstrates how actions such as this have a huge ramifications for wider inter-team relations (Mann et al, 2003).

This case lends itself to a dramaturgical sense of revenge being played out in our employment through employment relationships as the investigation process unfurled.

Brittany further disclosed how she felt about this process:

> I was made an example of … I was kind of like really screwed over.
>
> (Tiro, Brittany, Recruitment sales [p. 7 line 26–27])

Brittany intimated she still did not fully understand why she was being disciplined. She explained that she knew this could lead to her being dismissed. Yet she deemed the punitive measures to be far too harsh. Brittany discussed how she felt the situation could have been informally resolved. What was poignant was Brittany's belief she had not posted this picture maliciously and highlights a naivety regarding her actions.

A key issue for management and HR is to sufficiently articulate and outline to employees what the details regarding the initial disciplinary issue are under the discipline and grievance procedures (ACAS, 2015). The employer must determine whether in this case there is some form of misconduct or a capability issue. Further, they must try to resolve the issue informally where possible. This may involve some form of discussion to ascertain the employee's knowledge and understanding of the situation. This also can involve assessing whether the employee has breached the organisation's rules in this instance. This can also include actions which take place outside of work, including breaches in social media misuse. The employer must ensure they fairly follow the stipulated discipline and grievance procedures (2015). In investigating the issues, they must notify the employee and outline what the potential issue and consequences are should the case be upheld. In this case, the employer followed the correct protocols.

What was more telling is, sadly, Brittany left the organisation before she was summarily dismissed. This was due to her perception this would keep her record of employment clean. This hygiene factor means Brittany is still unaware of the consequences of her actions. This raises concerns over how HR in practice addresses forms of misbehaviour, so regardless of whether the employee leaves the organisation, they are fully conversant with the issue and why they are being disciplined. This would better clarify issues and lead to improved intended outcomes for the future (Biro, 2011; Blackwell, 2004; Moussa, 2015).

The case demonstrates the precarious nature and confusion over how social media are incorporated for both work and more social contexts. This does need further development, as the case highlights how a trickle-down approach to embedding any form of policy affects employee interpretations of this type of activity and the regulation which should protect others.

The next case focuses on the growing serious issue of posting nude images on social media.

## Peep show: A case of cyberflashing and posting nude images

A growing issue with social media is the more permissive nature of their use. There is a growing number of cases where social media users send inappropriate images to fellow users without their consent. This is now observed as a legislative issue. This was a reoccurring construct in the dialogue of HR practitioners where they articulated how much they were aware these platforms are being used by co-workers to portray an uninhibited sense of self, drunkenness, and nudity. They also felt that when scrutinising workers on their social media sites, they found content which increasingly may contain more gendered, misogynistic, or sexualised images.

One of the main issues in addressing this type of behaviour is that we have favoured and continually perpetuated a myth that we don't cultivate personal or sexual relations through work (Collins, 1983; Ackroyd and Thompson, 2003). There have been seminal studies which develops the notion we are sexual beings in work and beyond. These link to emotional and aesthetic labour and the commodification of predominantly females to display and project a more sexualised version of their identity (Hochschild, 1983).

At this intersection, social media has allowed us to create new ways to develop a sexualised, desirable version of ourselves, and additionally throws in a way to visibally capture sexual antics. Therefore, we need to educate workers to ensure this conflictual use of social media is more fully understood. Moreover, to ensure both management and HR practitioners are able to address sexual issues at work in a more sensitive way. We must not demonise workers for who they seek to be out of work, so long as what they do is not breaking any relevant legislation. My aim here is to suggest such attempts at lurking or voyeurism and surveillance is a further way to subjectivise workers.

Moreover, we need to be more aware of sousveillance which will be increasingly used to capture evidence of dick picks, upskirting, and other forms of sexual harassment which are all inappropriate forms of misconduct which will jar with employer expectations. These types of issues have grown in proportion societally and encompass a range of misbehaviours which we must take more seriously (Ringrose et al, 2021; McGlynn and Johnson, 2020/ 2017).

Image-based sexual harassment is more prevalent and worryingly starts in school. Research suggests group norms dictate sexualised behaviour in online contexts. It shows an increase in adolescents sending and receiving nude images online (Baumgartner et al, 2010). This is rarely discussed or reported by adolescents. This suggests that if we do not address these behaviours and leave them unresolved, this somehow normalises, forgets, and reifies such behaviour. Moreover, such behaviour is likely to continue and, therefore, is likely to follow individuals into work environments.

Image-based sexual harassment includes two types of digital sexual violence:

(a) unwanted sexual images (e.g. cyberflashing or unsolicited dick pics) and,
(b) unwanted solicitation for sexual images. Images encompass all forms of visual content. Including: photographs, videos, live videos, chats.

(McGlynn and Johnson, 2020: 7)

Sending individual images of nudity online causes a huge impact on victims but is all too often dismissed in peer groups as a form of banter. This type of individual or employee behaviour contradicts notions of professional identity, posing an issue for employee codes of conduct in employability. This suggests employee awareness is required to understand that deeper scrutiny of their social media accounts is more widely practised by employers. More importantly, this case highlights a growing need for managers to set strict guidelines for personal conduct on social media, both in and beyond work. This includes sending of images which others may deem offensive and thus detrimental to their employment relationships. Actively being involved in a group which shares these images is a form of agency, which can lead to convictions.

Ackroyd and Thompson (2003) suggest sexuality like power is everywhere. On social media we are more prone to notice or even post more sexualised images of our self and our identity. Limiting access to your profile may diminish the chance of anonymous people scrutinising online materials. This case draws attention to the fact employees have little awareness on the containment of such images or how these are used to judge our potential behaviour in work.

But this is something more than a growing presence of a less inhibited sense of self. This is relating to misconduct and an acknowledgement we are increasingly exposed to emerging forms of sexual misbehaviours and crimes. To highlight the growing nature of these types of issues, three organisations in this study stated sexual and nude online content may be classified as gross misconduct. They stated this was an ever-present issue.

Interestingly, one HR actor took a philosophical view to sexual misconduct on social media:

> I once had an employee …He took a close-up picture of his erect penis and sent this to a lot of his work colleagues. So, that's just life. People will do dumb stuff on social media. Get over it. … you'll never get the benefits.
>
> (Senes, Erica, HR Director [p. 10 line 38–41])

The discussion occurred prior to such offences becoming enshrined in UK law. In 2024, cyberflashing became a criminal offence. This shows how there was a lag in addressing this issue legally. This statement suggested how sexualised behaviour online is a fundamental aspect of our humanity and is worryingly normalised. This highlighted differing approaches in how HRM and management may choose to tackle this form of misbehaviour. This contributes to new knowledge on the significance of nudity and employability (Ackroyd and

Thompson, 2003) and further how to control such activity (Moussa, 2015; Taylor, 2018).

This is a key issue. Corporations need to create better understanding and development to address issues of portraying sexuality, sexual misconduct, and crimes such as cyberflashing in work. As Ringrose et al (2021) suggest, with each new emergent digital technology, this creates a new space for different manifestations of sexual violence to increase and be normalised. Corporations must take these issues into account and take greater responsibility for disciplinary measures rather than brushing these off as horseplay and humour. The next case focuses on when lurking and observation moves towards more insidious forms of cyberstalking.

## I'm always watching you: A case of cyberstalking

Given the nature of social media, we do more closely scrutinise each other. But this can lead to something more than just lurking and random observation. This can become overbearing and lead to intolerable levels of being observed, perhaps when a friendship or romantic relationship breaks down. This can lead to a form of stalking which is defined in the UK as

> a pattern of fixated and obsessive behaviour which is repeated, persistent, intrusive and causes fear of violence or engenders alarm and distress in the victim

Stalking and harassment offences are outlined within the Protection from Harassment Act 1997 UK (PHA, 1997), Section 42A (1) Criminal Justice and Police Act 2001, and further within Section 32 Crime and Disorder Act 1998 which focuses on religious or racist aggravated forms of harassment. The latter currently gain higher maximum sentences than basic PHA offences (Crown Prosecution Service, 2024). The Equality Act (2010) also covers offences of sexual harassment. Stalking and harassment are actions which make one feel threatened, scared of distressed, and can include text messages, cyberstalking, and forms of unwarranted attention to name a few. Social media can therefore be used a medium for this type of crime.

The Suzy Lamplugh Trust suggests 45% of people who contacted their website for support experience forms of stalking from someone who is known to them or who was an ex intimate partner. This case highlights how a young male student felt when he could not escape the attention of his ex-partner. The student discussed how they:

> could not get away from my ex altogether, even Twitter was a problem… I worked out she kept stalking me…I found this more annoying as I had broken up with her ten months ago and she still feels the need to follow my life.

The student was asked what they tried to do to combat this intrusion. They had tried to unfriend or block the constant gaze of the ex-partner. The response shows how they found this more difficult to do.

> I can block her but there are ways round this, she can create a second account which I don't know about.

This illustrated how blocking and unfriending is perhaps only a short-term answer to a more pervasive problem, which is becoming more prevalent in these scenarios. This is where individuals can create ulterior accounts to still follow and stalk ex-partners. This highlights how we accept friendships from almost anyone without reflection on who they are. Further, social media allows us to facilitate a greater anonymity. This poses a conundrum for social media corporations in how to force users to be more honest about their identity. Exacerbating this issue is the fact that not all of these organisations require us to prove who we are. This creates a broader issue with accountability and an organisational capability to confront users.

Using an ulterior identity is an inconsistency and a fracture in our perceived identity. In this case, we may become more predatory. Thus social media is culpable in facilitating wider forms of bullying, cyberbullying, and trolling. This case did take a nasty turn when the student was accused of violence and harassment towards the ex-partner:

> She told them I was abusive towards her and apparently I had isolated her out of our friend group … and sending her death threats.

These allegations of violence and abuse were made to the university where they were both studying. This was obviously a very traumatic period for the young persons involved. In order to verify their innocence, they were called in to discuss the nature of the issue and to provide evidence with an ethics committee. This shows how these more social issues may spill over into our place of work or study. Bennett et al (2021) suggest issues involving more violent or domestic forms of abuse are not simply private matters any more. They suggest there is a much greater need for corporations to be more aware of the issues, to offer support for individuals, and to work with wider key stakeholders to ensure the safety of all. This should include appropriate support for victims and perpetrators. I say this as cases of harassment and bullying are often complex and intertwined.

In this scenario, the university had trouble resolving who was the true victim. The case became more complex due to the evolution of digitalisation and realistic fake information, making it harder to determine who was at fault or disprove any guilt. The supposed victim had manufactured a number of false texts and emails, which they had to further investigate. In this case, the young person who was originally perceived as being the perpetrator was able to give clear evidence using their devices to disprove the claims made and show a different version of reality in this case. Further, this was used with the police to ensure that no further action was taken. Whilst this case was resolved, this left the young person sad. They felt they were never fully explained why the ex-partner had made these allegations up or tried to smear their reputation. This highlights the victims may need to be given access to wider psychological support after the case has closed.

The next case focuses on how sousveillance is used to capture evidence of feigned illness which is compared with activity and whereabouts on social media.

**Discussion box 30**

**Discussion:**

Discuss whether your place of work or study has a policy regarding stalking, harassment, and issues such as cyberflashing?

Have you been offered any information in your organisation about what to do if you were getting unwanted attention from someone?

Were you aware the legislation in the UK had changed about sending nude images?

Discuss whether you think your organisation should offer any support or development insights into cyberflashing or online sexualised misconduct?

Discuss whether your place of work or study works with wider stakeholders on any issues associated with sexual harassment or abuse?

**Pause for reflection:**

How could HR and management focus on women's experiences of sexualised misbehaviour and should they approach men's experiences differently? Reflect on how HR and management could approach these issues more effectively.

## Feeling mighty sick: A case of absenteeism

The following vignette draws attention to how social media profiles are used to track employee whereabouts, both by colleagues and management alike. The content is used to make distinctions between illness and availability for work. Ackroyd and Thompson (2003) define absenteeism as an unexcused and habitual withdrawal from work. This case narrative focuses on a supervisor who observed a feigned illness due to the online content posted by an employee. The colleague, who phoned in sick, then posted that they were in the local public house drinking with other friends. This contributes to new forms of absence, misbehaviour, and different forms of veillance practices by co-workers:

> I said I hope you're all right, she had a really craggy voice…I looked at her sickness record and I got this really weird feeling to have a look on Facebook, …I saw this picture of her … "getting pissed with [friend]" … during work, when she was supposedly sick.
>
> (Alumno, Darcy, Support Officer [p. 6/7 line 58–2])

Tribunal cases have cited Facebook activity to prove employees are *swinging the lead.* This illustrates the perception of employees who arouse suspicion and growing mistrust in the employment relationship (McDonald et al, 2016; McDonald et al, 2016). The Facebook feed in this case alerted the manager to the fact the individual was in the pub. The idea that workers are malingering was often captured in the empiricism of this study.

Absence is a conception of the organisation, regimes of control, and recording of problematical behaviours (Ackroyd and Thompson, 2003). Absence management is an attempt to control employees and also to manage wider perceptions of injustice by fellow workers. In this case, employees also saw the social media feed as they were all interconnected.

European data protection authorities did call for employers to abandon use of in-employment screening of employee social media profiles. Suggesting that this should not take place on regular basis and that content which make distinctions on employees could lead to discrimination and unfair dismissal claims. (www.telegraph.co.uk/technology/2017/07/13/bosses-told-stop-snooping-employees-facebook-profiles/)

Darcy illuminated on how she raised the matter of fake illness with the individual in the return to work interview:

> She said well you shouldn't have checked my Facebook anyway. I said I didn't, you're my friend on Facebook… you were as bold as brass, so what does that say to your other team members that know you're off on sick.
>
> (Alumno, Darcy, Support Officer [p. 7 line 4–6])

The growing visibility of employee movements is not only tracked by management. There is a pressure for formal management practice, routine surveillance, and policing attendance. Employers use Facebook content to defend disciplinary actions, particularly where employees utilise the exact number of sickness days stipulated in policy. In the upheld case, Metroline V Ajaj UKEAT/0185/15/RN, the employee stated they were unfit for work; however, it transpired this was not the case. The employer took great steps to disprove this using covert surveillance using occupational health to do a comparison with Ajaj symptoms.

(http://hrmagazine.co.uk/article-details/how- pulling-a-sickie-could-lead-to-grounds-of-gross-misconduct). This again shows how corporations will use all their might to protect their interests. This case is unique and legal advice should be sought before any veillance practices are used.

Further, online pictures are used by colleagues to highlight disparities in work behaviour and to telltales on co-workers. This is a complex area of HR practice, as some employees who post on Facebook during an absence are legally protected by being declared unfit for work on the grounds of mental ill health and therefore may be fit to so some activities. This case adds to knowledge on employee surveillance and absenteeism and highlights a growing need for employers to articulate when and what forms of surveillance are practised (Moussa, 2015).

**Act summary**

Ackroyd and Thompson (2003) suggested that there needs to be a greater articulation of the typologies of organisational misbehaviour and required behaviours. I have used this premise in this text to further highlight a range of ulterior employee performance and behaviours. I wanted to illustrate how these forms of misbehaviour have emerged and may stem from the opportunities social media present. This centres on the economic climate, the pressure on employees such as high targets, a distinct lack of adequate social media development and policy, use of hard management techniques, or differing emerging veillance practices.

The six illustrative cases highlight that employees may capitalise on unclear rules regarding engagement with social media. Furthermore, there is a lack of unawareness regarding monitoring and observation which may be used to counteract any forms of misbehaviour in this context. These add new perspectives on misbehaviour and regulation of labour production in this context.

The main issues, as Watson (2006) suggests, are HR and management fail to view employees as flesh and blood. They all too readily assumed workers will simply acquiesce and behave appropriately. The case narratives highlight HR and management actors have a tendency to describe employees as inert properties, rather than acknowledging workers as human sentient beings who are capable of misbehaving and were often perplexed by the latter. The case vignettes show emerging ways employees choose to misbehave and expose their self and their identity in counterproductive, emotive, and permissive ways on social media.

We need greater exploration on why workers choose to take to social media and behave in contradictory ways. Moreover, we need to reimagine HRM practices to reflect the challenges such behaviours present (Islam, 2012). The growing conflict between the private/public spaces, which social media straddles, must now marry with a growing corporate need to improve policy, regulation, practices, and development in this context. New practices which simultaneously must not demonise employees or their freedom to express themselves. Therefore, the way forward must be carefully balanced to mitigate against any significant impact this may have on the employment relationship.

This is not just about increasing the scrutiny or observation of employees online which is becoming a distinct routine practice. Indeed, the regulations suggest employers need to be more careful and less invasive in this activity. In these latter two scenes, I have sought to show this as a form of HR/management (mis)behaviour as they did not disclose where or when observation was taking place and is therefore more discrete and covert. This seems a tad divisive. Moreover, employees seemed dumbfounded that any form of surveillance activity took place.

Further, I wanted to highlight how surveillance and subjective methods of monitoring or measuring online performance is now a key factor of contemporary work (Ball, 2005; Islam, 2012). This is problematical. I have shown in the earlier scenes that corporations have not articulated what they want in terms of calculable outcomes or outputs from employee social media use as part of the labour process. This is likely to affect the disciplinary process and fails to protect both parties. This provides a lens on the forgetfulness of HRM to remember a duty of care to develop fair systems in complex digital contexts. This contributes to understanding regarding the formless social media management arrangements and HR practices which wrap around digital working contexts.

I was keen to illustrate how HR and management approaches still concentrate on how they seek employees to display positive emotions online and are keen to replicate an aesthete of a happy corporate culture and identity (Ackroyd and Thompson, 2003; Nath et al, 2016; Strati, 1999). These visible manifestations highlight a unitarist focus of organisations (Cradden, 2011; Edwards, 2003; Fox, 1966). The discourse demonstrates a utopian ideal of harmony to support corporate monocultures (Bullingham and Vasconcelos, 2013).

These conceptually force a front stage dramaturgical performance which controls and conceals how workers truly feel in work and through their online interactions (Goffman, 1959). The constant portrayal of a positive self online leads to emotional labour which adds further tension in employment relationships and working conditions (Hochschild, 1983; Spooner and Haidar, 2006). Primarily, these create aesthetic labour processes which further commodify and label workers (Nath et al, 2016; Strati, 1999; Townley, 1994; Taylor, 2018). This has serious repercussions if candidates challenge prejudicial judgements of criteria under the Equality Act (2010) (McDonald et al, 2016). This finding is used to prick the conscience of HRM practitioners and management to draw attention to approaches which must now incorporate ethical HRM practices. As Islam (2012: 43) states:

> reification is tantamount to a forgetfulness of the recognitive bases of human relations, striving for a normatively sound HRM approach is less a question

> of finding correct values than of "remembering" or attending to the values implicit in our social system, i.e., the unquestioned notions of civility that social actors expect from each other but are often left unexplicit in contractual terms or day-today work relations.

Thus, there is a need to improve the basic human principles which augur positive employment relations and civility in both online and offline environments. Civility in work is an interesting notion of this text. I sought to illustrate how this is compromised through work environments where management coercively control workers to direct their effort and minimise distractedness of social media and mobile device use in work. Throughout I have illustrated how hard HRM approaches are used by management to manipulate workers into productivity, such as standing over employees and shouting at them. These approaches lack finesse and competence. Such regimes are therefore likely to be the cause of worker dissent and resistance (Thompson, 2016; van den Broek and Dundon, 2012) and are perceived to contribute and yield the various manifestations of misbehaviours witnessed in online contexts in this text.

I have sought to show how digitisation is juxtaposed with either highly traditional or lax managerial regimes of control (McDonald et al, 2016; McDonald et al, 2016). Further, HRM approaches and aesthetic codes are used to commodify and coerce employees to aesthetically look pleasing and are seduced into using emotional labour to survive work (Hochschild, 1983). Such practices may create the premise for an anti-identity to emerge.

Anti-identity is perceived as a wider form of misbehaviour, where individuals do not conform to our original proscribed identity. The case vignettes demonstrably show how practices and weak regulations simply encourage employees to circumvent rules and resist managerial practices by taking to social media to either vent about work experiences or to use other approaches to dig themselves a way out of oppressive work regimes.

Furthermore, HR and management actor narratives also suggested how they also struggle with appropriately behaving online and struggle to conceal their own emotions regarding social media use and misbehaviour. They described losing control when employees misbehaved or ostracised them online. They discussed their own impulsivity making "funny" comments. This reveals how these actors must navigate their humour and emotions more carefully, such as anger and upset, at the loss of affiliation or being defriended by colleagues. This adds to new insights regarding management misbehaviour and worker resistance in this context (McDonald et al, 2016). This illustrates how HR and management require dexterity, emotional resilience, and intelligence to survive work online and offline. This draws attention to how social media altercations may affect employee well-being in management roles.

The cases highlight how all actors misunderstood the ephemerality of social media and how this is juxtaposed with their own daily practices. A phrase from the narrative beautifully encapsulates employee misbehaviour in this context: "*people do dumb stuff on social media*" *(Erica)*. The case studies illustrate how employees behave in unique ways and capture how we use these to improvise, perform, and act in your own inimitable way.

In some cases, the naïve performances represent a comedic attempts by employees who are trying to survive work through a collective sense of humour or bawdy, sexual conduct. Joking and online banter is ubiquitous and correlates to notions of misbehaviour in literature (Ackroyd and Thompson, 2003; Watson, 2006). Such behaviour is now more synonymous with an authentic freer self and was done with very little thought on the consequences. This highlights how employees are hugely unclear and, therefore, ill-advised on what constitutes appropriate online behaviours. This intimates that there is a greater need for suitable HR approaches to support and guide employees on their social media use and requires an ability to reflect in action (Yanow and Tsoukas, 2009). These altercations collide with a panoptic view of online performance and builds on notions of our growing digital corporeality (Mann et al, 2003; McDonald et al, 2016).

Importantly, some employees experienced negative online behaviours (Freya, Beth). This demonstrates a variety of gaps in the appropriation of appropriate social media behaviours, particularly where nudity and sexuality are concerned. This is a growing area of concern as highlighted by issues of sexually motivated harassment or sexual image based contents (Ringrose et al, 2021). The cases further highlight a lack of self-regulation and a growing misunderstanding regarding the boundaries which now exist between work and our private lives, which are increasingly diminishing. Employees simply cannot comment on organisations and colleagues as they may have done in the pub, without serious repercussions.

Nudity and sexuality online was a key construct in the discourse regarding emerging social media misbehaviours by employees or future recruits. The narratives of management and HR actors suggested employees and candidates exposed themselves online regularly or presented themselves in inappropriate ways (McDonald et al, 2016; McDonald et al, 2016). There was a full gamut of reasons why people did this. Some cases demonstrate we may post more provocative sexualised images to increase self-confidence, be adored, and to construct an adult identity (Freya), some for the purposes of humour or office japes. Watson (2006) argues sexuality, nudity, and humour are expressions of the human spirit. Yet these dramaturgical displays of a freer self may not be deemed appropriate and are at the mercy of management style and whether they deem such acts punishable through regulation.

The significance of this portrayal of self is this is now observed contemporaneously with the offline sense of self. This "staged" online version of the self contradicts perceptions of professionalism, brand reputation, and misbehaviour (Moussa, 2015; McDonald et al, 2016). Furthermore, some employees will take this type of behaviour further and send unwarranted sexual images to other users. Worryingly, we have normalised such sexual activity and may be seen as a construct of affiliation with peers. Significantly, we must acknowledge that the law has changed in this domain where cyberstalking and cyberflashing are now punishable crimes (CPS, 2024). Therefore, HR management practices must adapt to reflect the severity of this.

A noteworthy issue in tackling any form of social media misbehaviours, nudity, sexual deviancy, or derogatory comments is the lack of consistency in how management and HR actors address these issues. Some managers allowed employees to get away with online misdemeanours because of their social capital and the financial worth they brought to the organisation. This is observed to suggest power can be subverted by employees and used to shape infinite fields of possibility (Lukes, 2005; Thompson, 2016; van den Broek and Dundon, 2012).

Core to misbehaving is the panoptic effect of social media and the appeal for differing veillance practice to emerge. This includes both surveillance and sousveillance techniques (Mann et al, 2003; McDonald et al, 2016). Social media present a viable and cheap option for management to track employee movements and compare whether employees are fit for work or swinging the lead. Absenteeism has always been rife. However, social media are now used increasingly by management and co-workers to evidence fellow employee misbehaviour and misuse of time (Moussa, 2015). I am careful to make a distinction between absence and illness, as these are broad terms and involve differing approaches to individual recovery, particularly mental health issues, where we may post our activities whilst absent from work and which may form part of our personal aims to improve health and which should be treated on a case by case basis.

In terms of sousveillance, I have further highlighted how evidence in some cases is not always clear-cut. Ascertaining who the victim is maybe crucial, particularly as some victims may use fake evidence to gain one-upmanship on ex-partners, co-workers, or peers.

In conclusion, the case studies demonstrate how employees are thrown into a digital world and may use a plethora of stages for the experimentation with more subversive identities and behaviours. This highlights the growing overlap between misbehaviour and forms of worker resistance (McDonald et al, 2016; Thompson, 2016). A lack of clarity in how to use social media enables organisational misbehaviour to flourish in digital contexts, not because employees are inherently bad but because they operate within confusing environments with little understanding of policy or training approaches which aid their positive development. This heighten the precarious nature of social media use for employees.

*Table 5.1* Social media misbehaviours captured in this study

| *Misbehaviours* | *Management approach* | *Action taken* |
|---|---|---|
| Bad mouthing colleagues or organisation | Investigation of evidence | Informal dispute discussions. In one case, some employees were disciplined and in the other they were not |
| Timewasting | Observation, investigation of social media evidence | Email, discussion |
| Appropriation of LinkedIn contacts for personal gain | Observation, investigation of social media evidence, use of legal teams, and in-house solicitors and gardening leave. | Formal termination and summarily dismissed |
| Images posted of applicants | Investigation of evidence, disciplinary meetings | Resignation tendered before summary dismissal |
| Images and contents of social media used in recruitment | Observation and surveillance of SNS into individuals' background with no formal training. | None. Clear area of reification in HR practices |
| Images of nudity posted | Observation and pre-recruitment surveillance | None. Position was offered |
| Feigning illness and posting images whilst ill | Investigation of evidence, assessment of previous levels of absence in line with sickness and absence policy, return-to-work interviews, fit-notes, and disciplinary meetings | Formal discussion on absence levels and new targets set with individual performance appraisal objectives or discussions with teams to outline social media posts are legitimate without breaching confidentiality |
| Legitimacy of posts (peers infighting and misconceptions of posts) | Observations/sousveillance by peers of SNS posts brought to attention of management. Used to snitch on fellow colleagues | Investigations, informal discussions with individuals |

SNS, social networking sites.

A specific issue to address is the misconception regarding the boundary-less nature of digitalised work. This has led to the emergence of a more pervasive employment relationship which extends beyond the office. This threatens our right to retain a private and segregated identity (McDonald et al, 2016) and highlights a major issue where the varietal use of social media platforms is prone to leak between the sites (Kerrigan and Hart, 2016).

Employees are, therefore, more susceptible to having to create perfect profiles, aesthetically using images and content to support a positive and mono-identikit (Nath et al, 2016; Webb, 2006). This is a contradiction of work itself, particularly as some working conditions are more oppressive and may induce quite the opposite. Therefore, do we need to create work which induces these feel-good factors?

This concludes the empirical findings and cross-case analyses of novel crimes and differing forms of misbehaviours found to exist in this study (see Table 5.1).

# Finale Illusory social butterflies

## Conclusions, future research, and reading

This section aims to summarise the book and the main key themes which have been developed to offer an insight into some of the issues which face corporations, their leadership, management, and their employees when they endeavour to integrate social media use into their work regimes. The focus of the research, which culminated in the development of this book, centred on a growing sense of urgency that there was a need to review and reflect on the many issues which shape or compound the appropriate use of these devices.

The main premise for this programme of work was and is because of the growing raft of social media case law in the UK. These highlight that over the years the use of these devices is misunderstood. Within work environments we have witnessed a rising number of problems which impact on co-workers and management alike. From a management perspective, this includes how these devices have impacted on worker productivity and made us more distracted at work. A great focus was on how workers seem to post and say inappropriate things about the business or colleagues. These comments are problematical for corporate reputations as they are more visible to consumers and service users, thus are perceived to affecting brand reputation. Further, the higher degree of infighting and backbiting which was occurring online. Against this backdrop, there were growing concerns by academics about the nature of surveillance in this domain. The focus still remains on how management use social media to access rich data into prospective and current employees on a very regular basis without thinking through the ethical ramifications of such actions. These give rise to issues such as unconscious bias in recruitment and selection practices and are used as a mechanism for aesthetic and emotional labour. This is only part of the narrative about an emerging range of *veillance* practices in this domain and fails to account for how workers may use social media to observe management through sousveillance.

Therefore, it seemed to me this required greater exploration regarding the impact these veillance practices have on our employment relationships and the growing conflict this may cause in inter-team relations and power dynamics.

DOI: 10.4324/9781003137269-15

The book has sought to build on extant literature, combining a number of themes which affect how we stage corporations and individual identity online, and how these may lead to different forms of conflict, resistance, and misbehaviour in and beyond work.

Extant literature was useful in the development of this text. There are a number of wider discussions around greater understanding of the corporate and human resource management (HRM) approaches both of which embed the strategies for corporate social media use and the thornier issues of creating a regulatory framework for their use in differing work contexts that aim to govern how workers use these devices both in work and more socially. This includes how social media are used as tools which extend the field of vision to more closely observe and monitor workers through their social media activity. I also recognised there were gaps in knowledge, primarily how workers use these devices to observe and monitor management. Literature has failed to capture how we can interconnect more broadly with those in positions of power and can see what they are doing through their use of social media.

Therefore, I wanted to more deeply explore the contradictions these devices pose for HR and management in the current context. Primarily because their use is fascinating and straddles the boundaries which previously existed between work and privacy. This creates both an ethical conundrum on issues of employee privacy and our authentic identity creations on a number of platforms. I wanted to show how these are multidimensional and much more liminal. Whilst we may be trying true to our sense of self online on differing platforms, we must understand and consider how these may jar with corporate expectations. This creates a seepage from our private use of these platforms with our professional use. This is now more complex to manage and has impacted on the disciplinary and regulatory nature of social media use.

The approaches used to control social media use have become more draconian and have impacted on our notion of employment relations, which now extends beyond work into other spheres of life. Therefore, I wanted to take into account a greater connection between the impact and effect this may have on the way we integrate them, the way they intertwine with the dualities of use, and importantly, how corporations and management within them seek to govern their use. The aim was to more deeply understand and explore the impact these devices have on those workers who hold critical roles which underpin the basis of our employment relationships in work. The roles of management, HR, and frontline employees were perceived to collectively underpin all contemporary employment relationships.

Through the management and leadership roles, we embed, develop, and create strategies to use and control social media in a number of growing workplace practices. Through HR roles, we develop an understanding of the policy, rules, and disciplinary approaches to govern social media, and in the frontline operational roles, we either adhere to or breach the corporate ways of using social media. I therefore sought to more deeply understand the differing perceptions and approaches these individuals develop to create a finer insight into the issues associated with the use of social media and how this may differ contextually and from their own personal use of these devices.

Primarily, this study began because of the growing plethora of case law in the UK and my own work experiences which suggested workers using social media in these growing digital contexts were confused about the appropriate use of these devices. Further, extant literature and case law suggested workers failed to understand not only the rules of use but also how they should engage with each other beyond work. Alongside this, there was a subtext which highlights a growing societal concern about the misuse of social media. In the UK, a raft of emerging legislation, which now wraps around the use of social media, adds to these issues.

Further, I wanted to develop a book which collectively pulled together the nature and nuances of social media use. The purpose, therefore, was to create both a study and texts, which explored the social media context in greater depth, to gain a deeper understanding of the impact its use had on identity and the employment relationship, using an interpretative, multi-perspective design from an in-depth, sociological, and qualitative perspective. The main emphasis was there seemed to be little by way of understanding why employees lack awareness and ability to understand corporate regulations associated with social media use. Moreover, there was little on how management operationalise and control social media use and the effect this has on employees from a number of angles which impact on censorship, expression, and privacy. These issues are still relevant as their use continues to impact on corporate and individual reputations.

It has been suggested that we need research to understand context-specific and sensitive issues in work (Edwards, 2003); Watson, 2008). I used this premise to explore how several corporations integrate social media, the rules governing their use, the regulatory and disciplinary approaches developed and used to control employees in this domain, and the growing number of unique issues which affect work. This involved exploring the novel ways management create mechanisms to control use, the way we portray our identity online, and the way we voice workplace concerns or resist management online. The text has distilled the findings into the four key thematic areas observed in the four different acts presented as empirical chapters. The acts focused on how the differing social media platforms are adopted and used as stages to present corporate and individual identity, the power and control mechanisms used to create identity compliance, and the variety of dramaturgical identity performances which are presented in the final case vignettes which articulate and present and build on novel forms of social media misbehaviour. The key points raised from the analysis were used to develop the thesis for this text to add to wider research contributions on HR and employment relations practices. I felt it was important to understand more deeply why workers may take to social media with their problems. This gave rise to further workplace issues such as the conflictual nature between who work want us to be and how we portray our identity online. Further, this gave rise to a number of emerging forms of online misbehaviour.

For employment relations, both employee voice and freedom of expression have collided and which are now exercised through these channels. These create a context for workplace conflict to perpetuate and grow more visibly, which Edwards (1986) termed a *structured antagonism* of work. The visibility of our content clearly shows how employer brands are more deeply impacted by the differences of workplace interests and our telling of truths in this domain.

To analyse the issues, I have sought to use the key employment relations frames of reference: *Unitary, Pluralist and Radical HRM.* These are differing approaches which impacted on the corporate ideologies. They underpin corporate cultures and, in turn, the development of gaining workplace coordination and cooperation. These were used to depict how the rules which govern the phenomenon of social media are perceived and embedded in each context.

In trying to ascertain the way social media are used and governed, I wanted to explore whether over time corporations had developed more inclusive, objective, and adaptive approaches for social media use which allowed all employees greater access, and which may contribute to these technologies being used to enhance employee voice mechanisms in work. This was not the case as many organisations in the empiricism operated in a way which both minimised worker capacity to engage in social media. This highlighted how many management and HR actors view social media with scepticism.

The text, therefore, highlights how the digital terrain still requires a growing and clear need for much greater critical thinking, particularly on social media regulations and policy for management. This needs to more clearly articulate appropriate use of social media surveillance and pre-profiling of employees. My aim here is to suggest that HRM practitioners must stand back from deeply ingrained encultured belief systems regarding social media use, identity, and online aesthetic labour and behaviours for more ethical reasons. Islam (2012) stated HRM practices are traditional, cost-oriented, and rarely focus on workers in this context. This text has sought to build on this notion to highlight that there was little critical appraisal or evaluation of HR or management practices or techniques associated with controlling or developing effective digital device use.

From the onset, there was little reflection on how digital, information and communication technology (ICT), or social media policy and regulation was difficult to navigate and did not neatly filtrate across the organisations. This makes it impossible for employees to understand regimes of control. Particular ethical emphasis was also paid to the individual approaches used by individuals on activities such as pre-screening, surveillance, and hard HRM management techniques which are all observed in the text. Some of these were hugely subjective and biased about our looks and rarely centred on job criteria and competence. These accounts illustrate how HR practitioners have allowed such activities to develop and become reified. These are inculcated in wider corporate tactics which are perceived to cast forgetfulness on the rights of employees.

This is expected to grow with the integration of artificial intelligence (AI) and other technologies which cause fear societally and in work. As digital technologies grow, HRM is called upon to critically evaluate such traditionally held beliefs and to innovate on more ethically appropriate practices which adopt a more permeable human-centric approach to the presentation of identity and the self. Embedding use of critical reflective practice would challenge, evaluate, and adapt presuppositions regarding social media and wider technologies. The text highlights that there were a number of subjective opinions about the use of these devices which perhaps need addressing in management and HR circle. Moreover, there were a number of biases about workers and the way they look and stage themselves online. This suggests that HR, in general, needs to adapt and critically reflect on how to innovate in this area of work in organisations.

Critical thinking is a principal requirement of the UK CIPD professional standards and needs to be carefully aligned to the code of conduct and ethical HR practices (CIPD, 2023). This places a greater emphasis on HR professionals to possess a good moral character and to develop fair and inclusive practices which champions equitable treatment for all. This includes striving to create more inclusive working practices and enabling workers the capacity to speak up using employee voice mechanisms, to name but a few areas of concentration. Further, they suggest practices which allow development, role modelling, and mentorship are used to address issues. This text critically highlights some flaws in the management and HR practices on these elements to demonstrate that there is a way to go before this is realised.

This text highlights how in each case organisation there was little development or training to support social media use. More importantly, most corporations sought to govern social media by giving little access to use these devices in the first instance. This highlights how social media were not really viewed as necessary tools for promoting and marketing the corporation, brands, and services. The findings fly in the face of HR professional guidance and illustrate confused opinions regarding corporate strategy to innovate and integrate social media and digital device use more fully.

Instead, most corporations opt to create a variety of mechanisms and rules which seek to create boundaries to stop workers from using and accessing social media or digitalisation. In this text, this includes Firewalls and management approaches to more deeply scrutinise worker activity on these platforms, including quantifying and calculating data usage. These boundaries were found to be weak measures of control as many workers simply circumnavigated rules using their own devices. This revealing finding highlighted that management breach their own rules. Further, management bastardised corporate governance and created their own rules to stop workers being distracted from both their mobile devices and social media use by taking phones away from workers. Again the findings in this text highlight this does not necessarily contribute or greater control of employee use of social media. Therefore, I suggest there is more work to be done on how we embed these as tools which may enhance workplace practices and worker voice.

These approaches can be viewed as catalysts for wider employee voice capacity and forms of workplace resistance and misconduct to unfurl. The text has by no means captured the full range or extent of these. As suggested, there will be more creative ways in which employees get their concerns raised, and this will lead to differing forms of misbehaviour to emerge as new platforms become apparent.

What I hope to illustrate throughout the text is how misbehaviour is not just the sole domain of frontline employees in the digital contexts which run parallel with work. The text has shown how HR and management are equally capable of misbehaving on social media, including the development of ulterior and anti-identities where they developed parody accounts to question corporations. The text highlights how employees may increasingly, therefore, use social media for sousveillance purposes to capture evidence of how management and HR misbehave. This is positioned to suggest a need for greater scrutiny of management and HR practitioners is increasingly required but is rarely discussed in literature. Critical reflection, therefore, would allow a greater adaptation within professional roles beyond a basic appraisal of social media issues. This suggests a paradigm shift is needed to move towards a deeper critical appraisal of elite social actors and their actions and behaviours in this domain. This requires HR practitioners to examine and challenge their own deeply held assumptions about workers who use social media to ensure that reasoning is aligned to programmes of transformative change, both across the organisation and within their own personal perspective and practices.

Table 6.1 captures a multi-perspectival comparison of the themes captured in the text.

## Implications for future research

There are many research limitations to this text. It would be pertinent and purposeful to use this text and previous extant literature to scope and conduct further research programmes which more greatly understand the differing perspectives and issues presented in the book.

There are a number of gaps which would build on the key themes. Here are a few suggestions.

Further study into the aesthetic nature of labour relations would be interesting. I suggest a focus on how HR practitioners make sense of evolving identity

*Table 6.1* A multi-perspectival comparison of the themes of social media use between actors in key roles

| *Theme* | *HR* | *Management* | *Employee* |
|---|---|---|---|
| **Participation and use** | Stratified and top-level interconnectivity; SM used for CPD and strategic purposes | Selectiveness of interconnectivity; upwards/sideways level; used for CPD and strategic purposes | Socialising and interconnectivity with similar strata of peers |
| | Unitary and managerial agendas; silo working on policy development | Unitary and managerial agendas; adaptation of policy to suit own agendas | Trickle down regulation means policy is diluted, unclear, and lacks procedural fairness across organisations |
| **SM skills** | Social media skill deficits; HR elite are likely to need a full range of digital skills for blogging, etc. | Social media skill deficits | Skilled in social use of SM; lacking in professional staging of SM identity and content |
| **Power and control** | Scripting and staging, scenes of power, aesthetic manipulation of content | Performance of power through traditional management styles | Performance as antagonists |
| **Surveillance** | Surveillance and lurking of others; little reflective/ reflexive practice | Surveillance and use of panoptic HRM management techniques | Observed both formally and informally; used sousveillance to balance the power and to render management in a field of vision |
| **Employee voice** | Staging and controlling of employee voice | Minimal stakeholder role in employee voice | Lack of collective power and employee voice |
| | Lead role in the development of legal regulatory and procedural aspects of SM use | Lead role in embedding and shaping regulatory and procedural aspects of SM use | Subjected to regulatory and procedural use of power to shape compliance in SM use |

(*Continued*)

*Table 6.1* (Continued)

| *Theme* | *HR* | *Management* | *Employee* |
|---|---|---|---|
| **Identity and dramaturgical performance** | Moral and liminal individual identity; creative use of subversive anti-identity and avatar | Evaluative and liminal individual identity | Liminal social identity; *birds of a feather* collective sense of being on SM |
| | Attribute and appearance informed | Attribute and appearance informed | Attribute and appearance shaped |
| **Resistance, misbehaviour, and conflict** | Dialogues of discipline and misbehaviour | Dialogue of positive emotions and presentation of self. | *People do dumb stuff* |
| | Attitude informed | Attitude informed | Esteem informed |

CPD, Continuing Professional Development; HRM, human resource management; SM, social media.

and the unconscious bias they bring into work activities such as pre-profiling would be of interest to address the growing level of unethical practices. Focus could centre on implications of competing discourses on the perpetuation of a wholesome and idealised image of an employee. This could involve eye tracking to observe how practitioners operate when pre-profiling.

As hate and vitriol are more present in social media, much work is needed to understand forms of hate speech and the impact this has on individuals in different contexts, work countries, and in professional roles. This can be achieved through the aim of qualitative research to explore the effect of such activity on our well-being, psychology or identity templates to ascertain the implications this has on employees from diverse backgrounds. Particular emphasis would centre on exploring these conceptions in relation to equality legislation.

Future research would be useful to examine dominant cultural views and how this influences use of technology, particularly those emerging from HR practitioners. A key issue that struck me whilst doing this text was the dissonance between HRM and its role in championing new technologies. The traditional, paternal, and unitary views exposed in this study created a differing approach to sense-making of both the integration of new technologies and the rules which govern emerging uses. These often seemed out of kilter with a contemporising of our employment relationships and the integration of these technological innovations, particularly where there is no obvious development for use. Qualitative research may contribute to deeper understanding of these emerging phenomena and contribute to the development of inclusive regulatory practices.

As identity is evolving on social media, further research is perhaps required on greater understanding about the use of face-altering technologies, fake identities, and anti- and ulterior-identities to understand the issues these present both in and beyond work and for our psychological well-being. Qualitative studies are much needed to more deeply explore how individuals may use technology to mask their authentic self. This would then give insight into emerging forms of misbehaviour in the digital age.

Further research on how employees use social media for informal collective challenges to management would also be good to explore and understand the impact on both shaping employee resistance, voice, and conflict at work, including how these may challenge formal trade union activism, or how these work simultaneously to address worker concerns and issues.

Lastly, this text overwhelmingly found HR and management actors reify practices associated with the regulation and their role in controlling social media use. This is used as a premise to suggest that more quantitative studies are needed to examine HRM practices of surveillance and, more importantly, to explore the growing use and practices of sousveillance. Quantitative research could be used to objectify and statistically analyse these emerging veillance practices in this area and the impact these have on labour and disciplinary processes.

## Suggested further reading

There are a number of great texts which have influenced my thinking. These are captured in the reference list. My suggestions below are a great starting point for readers who wish to adapt the digital ways of working or are beginning to think differently about their own workplace behaviour, role identity, technology, freedom of speech and expression, and human-centric working practices. Chief amongst these are:

- *Organisational Misbehaviour* (Ackroyd and Thompson, 2003).
- *Organisations, Identities, and the Self* (Webb, 2006).
- *The New Digital Workplace: How Technologies Revolutionise Work* (Briken et al, 2017).
- *The Routledge Companion to Freedom of Expression and Censorship* (Steel and Petley, 2024).
- *Reframing Human Resource Management: Power, Ethics and the Subject at Work* (Townley, 1994).
- *Sociology, Work and Industry* (Sixth Edition) (Tony Watson).
- *The Human-Centric Workplace* (Fenton-Jarvis, 2022).

# References


Abercrombie, N. and Longhurst, B. (1983). Interpreting Mannheim. *Theory, Culture & Society*, 2(1), 5–15.

Abes, E. S., Jones, S. R., and McEwen, M. K. (2007). Reconceptualizing the model of multiple dimensions of identity: The role of meaning-making capacity in the construction of multiple identities. *Journal of College Student Development*, 48(1), 1–22.

ACAS (2010). Workplaces and social networking: The implications for employment relations. In Andrea Broughton, Tom Higgins, Ben Hicks, and Annette Cox (eds.). The Institute for Employment Studies. http://www.acas.org.uk/2016 www.acas.org.uk/index.aspx?articleid=3378. Last accessed 04/06/2017.

Ackland, R. and J. Zhu (2015). Social network analysis. In P. Halfpenny and R. Procter (eds.), *Innovations in Digital Research Methods* (pp. 221–244). London: Sage Publications.

Ackroyd, S. and Thompson, P. (1999/2003). *Organizational Misbehaviour*. London: Sage Publications.

Adams, H., Scheuing, S., and Feeley, S. (2000). E-Mail monitoring in the workplace: The good, the bad and the ugly. *Defense Counsel Journal*, 1, 32–46.

Adams, S. and Purtova, N. (2017). Introducing the special issue "Rethinking surveillance: Theories, discourses, structures, and practices". *Philosophy & Technology*, 30(1), 5–7.

Advisory, Conciliation and Arbitration Service (ACAS) (2015). Code of Practice for Discipline and Grievance Procedures. www.acas.org.uk/acas-code-of-practice-on-disciplinary-and-grievance-procedures. Last accessed 23/08/2024.

Ahern, K. J. (1999). Pearls, pith, and provocation: Ten tips for reflexive bracketing. *Qualitative Health Research*, 9(3), 407–411.

Aguado, D. et al. (2016). Applicant reactions to social network web use in personnel selection and assessment. *Revista de psicología del trabajo y de las organizaciones*, 32(3), 183–190.

Albert, S. and Whetten, D. A. (1985). Organizational identity. *Research in Organizational Behavior*, 7, 263–295. Retrieved from http://lcproxy.shu.ac.uk/login?url=https://search-proquest- com.lcproxy.shu.ac.uk/docview/617106976?accountid=13827

Allen, B. (2011). The role of professional identity commitment in understanding the relationship between casual employment and perceptions of career success. *Career Development International*, 16(2), 196–216. doi: 10.1108/13620431111115631.

Alvesson, M., Ashcraft, K., and Thomas, R. (2008). Identity matters: Reflections on the construction of identity scholarship in organization studies. *Organization*, 15(1), 5–28.

Alvesson, M. and Karreman, D. (2000). Varieties of discourse: On the study of organizations through discourse analysis. *Human Relations*, 53(9), 1125–1149. Google Scholar Link.

Alvesson, M. and Robertson, M. (2006). The best and the brightest: The construction, significance and effects of elite identities in consulting firms. *Organization*, 13(2), 195–224.

Alvesson, M. and Sköldberg, K. (2009). *Reflexive Methodology: New Vistas for Qualitative Research* (2nd ed.). Los Angeles: Sage.

Alvesson, M. and Willmott, H. (2002). Identity regulation as organizational control: Producing the appropriate individual. *Journal of Management Studies*, 39(5), 619–642.

Andersson, T. (2010). Struggles of managerial being and becoming: Experiences of managers' personal development training. *Journal of Management Development*, 29(2), 161–176.

Andrews, T. (2012). What is social constructionisim? *Theory Review Journal*, 11(1), http://groundedtheoryreview.com/2012/06/01/what-is-social-constructionism/ Grounded

Archer-Brown, C., Marder, B., Calvard, T., and Kowalski, T. (2018). Hybrid social media: Employees' use of a boundary-spanning technology. *New Technology, Work and Employment,* 33(1), 74–79.

Archibald, M. Clark, A., and Alexander, M. (2014). Twitter and nursing research: How diffusion of innovation theory can help uptake. *Social Media Journal of Advanced Nursing*, 70(3), e3–e5 [Peer Reviewed Journal].

Arendt, H. and Kohn, J. (1994). *Essays in Understanding: 1930–1955* (1st ed.). New York: Harcourt Brace.

Argyris, C. (1960). *Understanding Organisational Behaviour*. Homewood: Dorsey Press.

Arnold J., Silvester, J., Patterson, F., Robertson, I., Cooper, C., Burnes, B. (2005). *Work Psychology Understanding Human Behaviour in the workplace FT Prentice Hall* (4th ed.). Prentice Hall.

Ashforth, B. E. (2001). *Role Transitions in Organizational Life: An Identity-Based Perspective*. Mahwah, NJ: Erlbaum.

Ashforth, B. E. and Humphrey, R. H. (1993). Emotional labor in service roles: The influence of identity. *Academy of Management Review*, 18(1), 88–115.

Ashforth, B. E., Kreiner, G. E., and Fugate, M. (2000). All in a day's work: Boundaries and micro role transitions. *Academy of Management Review*, 25(3), 472–491.

Ashforth, B. E. and Mael, F. (1989). Social identity theory and the organisation, academy of management. *The Academy of Management Review*, 14(1), 20–39.

Ashworth, P. (2003). The phenomenology of the lifeworld and social psychology. *Social Psychological Review*, 5(1), 18–34 [Google Scholar].

Babbie, E. (1995). *The Practice of Social Research* (7th ed.). Belmont: Wadsworth. www.bailii.org/uk/cases/UKEAT/2015/0004_15_0308.html. Last accessed 04/08/2017.

Backhaus, K. and Tikoo, S. (2004). Conceptualizing and researching employer branding. Career Development International, 9(5), 501–517. https://doi.org/10.1108/13620430410550754

Bain, G. S. and Clegg, H. A. (1974). A strategy for industrial relations research in Great Britain. *British Journal of Industrial Relations*, 12, 91–113. doi: 10.1111/j.1467-8543.1974.tb00006.x

Bain, P. and Taylor, P. (2000). Entrapped by the "electronic panopticon"? Worker resistance in the call centre. *New Technology, Work and Employment,* 15(1), 2–18.

Ball, K. (2005). Organization, surveillance and the body: Towards a politics of resistance. *Organization*, 12(1), 89–108.

Ball, T. (1976) as cited in: Lukes, S., Power: A radical view and Nagel 1975, *Political Theory*, 4, 246–249.

Bandura, A. (1997). *Self-efficacy: The Exercise of Control.* New York: Freeman.

Bandura, A. (1999). Moral disengagement in the perpetration of inhumanities. *Personality and Social Psychology Review* [Special Issue on Evil and Violence], 3, 193–209.

Bandura, A. (2002). Selective moral disengagement in the exercise of moral agency. *Journal of Moral Education*, 31(2), 101–119. doi: 10.1080/0305724022014322

Bandura, A., Barbaranelli, C., Caprara, G. V., and Pastorelli, C. (1996). Mechanisms of moral disengagement in the exercise of moral agency. *Journal of Personality and Social Psychology*, 71, 364–374.

Barratt, E. (2002). Foucault, Foucauldianism and human resource management. *Personnel Review*, 31(2), 189–204. https://doi.org/10.1108/00483480210416865

Barry, M. and Wilkinson, A. (2016). Pro-social or pro-management? A critique of the conception of employee voice as a pro-social behaviour within organizational behaviour. *British Journal of Industrial Relations*, 54(2), 261–284.

Bar-Tal, D., Nets-Zehngut, R., and Sharvit, K. (Eds.). (2017). *Self-Censorship in Contexts of Conflict: Theory and Research.* Springer International Publishing/Springer Nature. https://doi.org/10.1007/978-3-319-63378-7

Bartosik-Purgat, M. and Jankowska, B. (2017). The use of social networking sites in job related activities: Cross-cultural comparison. *Entrepreneurial Business and Economics Review*, 5(2), 177–193.

Baumgartner, S. E., Valkenburg, P. M., Peter J. (2010). Assessing causality in the relationship between adolescents' risky sexual online behavior and their perceptions of this behavior. *Journal of Youth and Adolescence*. 39(10), 1226–1239.

Baxter, M. (1999). Constructing adult identities. *Journal of College Student Development*, 40(6), 629–644.

Baxter-Magolda, M. B. (2003). Identity and learning: Student affairs' role in transforming higher education. *Journal of College Student Development* , 44(2), 231–247. The Johns Hopkins University Press. Retrieved November 13, 2017, from Project MUSE database.

BBC (2016). Cyber crimes. www.bbc.co.uk/news/business-36854285/

BBC (2017). Instagram "Worst for young mental health". www.bbc.co.uk/news/health-39955295

BBC Care homes abuse report (2012). www.bbc.co.uk/news/av/uk-17810136

Beautiful people.com (2013). BeautifulPeople.com Launches Recruitment Service for Employers Seeking Good-looking Staff. www.prnewswire.co.uk/news-releases/beautifulpeoplecom-launches-recruitment-service-for-employers-seeking-good-looking-staff-209885451.html

Beech, N. (2008). On the nature of dialogic identity work organization. *Organization (London, England)*, 15(1), 51–74.

Beer, M., Spector, B., Lawrence, P., Mills, D. Q., and Walton, R. (1984a). *Human Resource Management: A General Manager's Perspective*. Glen Coe, IL: Free Press.

Beer, M., Spector, B., Lawrence, P., Mills, D. Q., and Walton, R. (1984b). *Managing Human Assets*. Glen Coe, IL: Free Press.

Beersma, B. and Van Kleef, G. A. (2011). How the grapevine keeps you in line: Gossip increases contributions to the group. *Social Psychological and Personality Sciecnce*, 2, 642–649. doi: 10.1177/1948550611405073

Belcourt, M., Bohlander, G., Snell, S. (2008). *Managing Human Resources* (5th ed.). Toronto: Nelson.

Bell, J (2005). *Doing | Your Research Project* (4th ed.) Maiden Head: Open University Press.

Benford, D. R. and Hunt, A. S. (1992). Dramaturgy and social movements: The social construction and communication of power. *Sociology Inquiry*, 62(1), 36–55.

Bennett, A., Wibberley, G., and Paterson, A. (2021). It's not just a private matter: Developing effective policy and procedure for addressing the impact of domestic abuse in the workplace. In: CIPD Applied Research Conference, Manchester.

Bennett, J., Owers, M., Pitt, M., and Tucker, M. (2010). Workplace impact of social Networking. *Property Management*, 28(3), 138–148.

Bennett, T. (2010). Employee voice initiatives in the public sector: Views from the workplace. *International Journal of Public Sector Management*, 23(5), 444–455.

Berger, P. and Pullberg, S. (1966). Reification and the sociological critique of consciousness. *New Left Review*, 35, 56–71.

Berger, P. L. and Luckmann, T. (1966). *The Social Construction of Reality: A Treatise in the Sociology of Knowledge*. Garden City: Doubleday.

Bernstein, R. (1983). *Beyond Objectivism and Relativism: Science, Hermeneutics, and Praxis*. Blackwell.

Berthon, P. et al. (2005). Captivating company: Dimensions of attractiveness in employer branding. *International Journal of Advertising*, 24(2), 151–172.

Beyer, J. and Hannah, D. (2002). Building on the past: Enacting established personal identities in a new work setting. *Organization Science*, 13(6), 636–652.

Jones, S. (2010). *Beautiful People expels 5,000 members after festive weight gain* Reported in The Guardian, UK. www.theguardian.com/lifeandstyle/2010/jan/04/beautiful-people-rid-dating-slobs. Last accessed 02/09/2024.

Fuller, G (2006). *Driver and Vehicle Licensing Agency charges 65 more staff with gross misconduct for computer misuse* Reported in Personnel Today 31 October, 2006. www.personneltoday.com/hr/driver-and-vehicle-licensing-agency-charges-65-more-staff-with-gross-misconduct-for-computer-misuse/. Last accessed 02/09/2024.

Billington, M. G. and Billington, P. J. (2012). Social media tools for leaders and managers. *Journal of Leadership, Accountability and Ethics*, 9(6), 11–19.

Bingham, C. (2016). *Employment Relations: Fairness and Trust in the Workplace*. London: Sage.

Biro, P. L. (2011). Social media and the employment relationship: Balancing the employer's right to regulate and the employee's privacy interest. www.weirfoulds.com/files/7610_Articles_2011-02-24_ACC%20Toronto_PLB_Social%20Media.pdf. Last accessed 28/12/2016.

Bishop, J. (2007b). Increasing participation in online communities: A framework for human–computer interaction. *Computers in Human Behavior*, 23(4), 1881–1893. doi:10.1016/j.chb.2005.11.004

Blackwell, C. W. (2004). Current employee privacy issues. *The Journal of Applied Management and Entrepreneurship*, 9, 113–118. Google Scholar.
Blaikie, N. (2000). *Designing Social Research: The Logic of Anticipation.* Cambridge: Polity Press.
Blaikie, N. (2007). *Approaches to Social Enquiry* (2nd ed.). Cambridge: Polity Press.
Blaikie, N. (2010). *Designing Social Research: The Logic of Anticipation* (2nd ed.). Cambridge: Polity Press.
Blasi, A. (1995). Moral understanding and the moral personality: The process of moral integration. In W. M. Kurtines and J. L. Gewirtz (eds.), *Moral Development: An Introduction* (pp. 229–253). Boston: Allyn & Bacon.
Blumer, H. (1969). *Symbolic Interactionism: Perspective and Method.* Prentice Hall: Englewood Cliffs.
Blyton, P. and Turnbull, P. (2004). *The Dynamics of Employee Relations* (3rd ed.). Palgrave Macmillan.
Blyton, P. et al. (2012). *The SAGE Handbook of Industrial Relations.* Sage Publications.
Bondarouk, T. and Brewster, C. (2016). Conceptualising the future of HRM and technology research. *The International Journal of Human Resource Management,* 27(21), 2652–2671.
Botan, C. H. (1996). Communication work and electronic surveillance: A model for predicting panoptic effects. *Communication Monographs*, 63, 1–21.
Boulianne, S. (2015). Social media use and participation: A meta-analysis of current research. *Information, Communication & Society*, 18(5), 524–538.
Boxall, P. (1996). The strategic HRM debate and the resource-based view of the firm. *Human Resource Management Journal*, 6(3), 59–75.
Boxall, P. (2013). Mutuality in the management of human resources: Assessing the quality of alignment in employment relationships. *Human Resource Management Journal*, 23(1), 3–17. Google Scholar CrossRef.
Boxall, P., Alexander, M., Baird, M., and Pocock, B. (2014). The future of employment relations from the perspective of human resource management. *Journal of Industrial Relations*, 56(4), 578–593.
Boxall, P. and Purcell, J. (2011). *Strategy and Human Resource Management*. New York and Basingstoke: Palgrave Macmillan. Google Scholar.
Boxall, P. F. and Purcell, J. (2022). *Strategy and Human Resource Management* (5th ed.). London: Bloomsbury Academic.
Boxall, P., Purcell, J., Wright, P. (2007). Human resource management: Scope, analysis, and significance. In Boxall P., Purcell J., Wright P. (eds.), *The Oxford Handbook of Human Resource Management* (pp. 1–16). Oxford: Oxford University Press. Google Scholar.
boyd, D. (2008). Why youth (heart) social network sites: The role of networked publics in teenage social life. In D. Buckingham (ed.), *Youth, Identity, and Digital Media* (pp. 119–142). Cambridge: MIT Press.
boyd, D. M. and Crawford, K. (2012). Critical questions for big data. *Information, Communication & Society*, 15(5), 662–679. doi: 10.1080/1369118X.2012.678878
boyd, D. M. and Ellison, N. B. (2007). Social network sites: Definition, history, and scholarship. *Journal of Computer Mediated Communication* , 13(1), 210–230.

Bradley A. J. and McDonald M. P. (2011). *The Social Organization: How to Use Social Media to Tap the Collective Genius of Your Customers and Employees*. Boston: Harvard Business Review Press. Google Scholar.

Braverman, H. (1974/1998). *Labor and Monopoly Capital: The Degradation of Work in the Twentieth Century*. New York: Monthly Review Press.

Brewer, M. B. (1991). The social Self on being the same and different at the same time. *Personality and Social Psychology Bulletin*, 17, 475–482.

Briken, K., Chillas, S., Kryzwdzinski, M., and Marks, A. (2017). *The New Digital Workplace: How New Technologies Revolutionise Work*. London: Palgrave Macmillan.

Brimelow (2005). 'Blog' dismissal should prompt policy on usage. *Personnel Today* 1st February. www.ptod.com/27490.article. Last accessed 02/09/2024.

Brocki, J. M. and Wearden, A. J. (2006). A critical evaluation of the use of interpretative phenomenological analysis (IPA) in health psychology. *Psychology & Health*, 21(1), 87–108. doi: 10.1080/14768320500230185

Bromley, D. B. (1986). The Case-Study Method in Psychology and Related Disciplines. Chichester: John Wiley & Sons.

Bruns, A. (2006). Towards produsage: Futures for user-led content production. In Sudweeks, Fay, Hrachovec, Herbert, and Ess, Charles (eds.), *Proceedings Cultural Attitudes towards Communication and Technology* (pp. 275–284). Tartu: Estonia.

Bryman, A. (2013). *Social Research Methods*. Oxford: Oxford University Press.

Bryman, A. and Burgess, R. G. (1994). *Analyzing Qualitative Data*. Routledge.

Bryson, A., Gomez, R., and Willman, P. (2010). Online social networking and trade union membership: What the Facebook phenomenon truly means for labor organizers. *Labor History*, 51(1), 41–53.

Budd, J. (2014). The future of employee voice. In A. Wilksinson, J. Donaghey, T. Dundon and R. Freeman (eds.), *The Handbook of Research on Employee Voice* (pp. 477–488). Cheltenham: Edward Elgar.

Bull, M. and Taylor, C. (2014). Teaching reflective practice: Can human resource management (HRM) learn from research in other disciplines. Paper presented at the 25th SPACE Network in Barcelona, 23–25 April 2014.

Bullingham, L. and Vasconcelos, A. (2013). 'The presentation of self in the online world': Goffman and the study of online identities. *Journal of Information Science*, 39(1), 101–112.

Burr, V. (1995). *An Introduction to Social Constructionism*. London: Routledge.

Burrell, G. and G. Morgan (1979). *Sociological Paradigms and Organizational Analysis*. London: Heinemann.

Butler, J. (1990). *Gender Trouble*. New York: Routledge.

Butler, J. (1993). *Bodies that Matter: On the Discursive Limits of "Sex"*. New York: Routledge.

Cadell, L. (2013). Socially practical or practically unsociable? A study into social media policy experiences in Queensland Cultural Heritage Institutions. *Australian Academic & Research Libraries*, 44(1), 3–13.

Cairney, P., Heikkila, T. and Wood, M. (2019). *Making Policy in a Complex World*. (1st ed.). Cambridge: Cambridge University Press.

Callero, P. (1994). From role playing to role using: Understanding roles as a resource. *Social Psychology Quarterly* , 57(3), 228–2543.

Callon, M. (1999). Actor network theory – the market test. *Sociological Review*. 47(1_ suppl), 181–195. doi: 11.111/j.1467-954X.1999tb03488.x
Cammaerts, B. (2015). Neoliberalism and the post-hegemonic war of position: The dialectic between invisibility and visibilities. *European Journal of Communication (London)*, 30(5), 522–538. https://doi.org/10.1177/0267323115597847
Cappelli, P. (2001). Making the most of on-line recruiting. *Harvard Business Review*, March.
Cappelli, P. and Neumark, D. (2001). Do high-performance work practices improve establishment-level outcomes? *Industrial and Labor Relations Review*. 54(4), 737–775.
Carbado, D. and Gulati, M. (2000). Discrimination and inequality emerging issues working identity. *Cornell Law Review*, 85, 1259–1742.
Carroll, B. and Levy, L. (2008). Defaulting to management: Leadership defined by what it is not. *Organization*, 15, 75–96. Google Scholar Link.
Carter, S. M. and Little, M. (2007). Justifying knowledge, justifying method, taking action: Epistemologies, methodologies, and methods in qualitative research. *Qualitative Health Research*, 17(10), 1316–1328. doi: 10.1177/1049732307306927
Casey, C. (1995). *Work, Self and Society*. London and New York: Routledge.
Casey, C. and Schellenberg, K. (1997). Work, self and society: After industrialism. *Canadian Journal of Sociology*, 22(2), 264. Retrieved from http://lcproxy.shu.ac.uk/login?url=https://search-proquest-com.lcproxy.shu.ac.uk/docview/220525284?accountid=13827
Cassar, V. and Buttigieg, S. (2015). Psychological contract breach, organizational justice and emotional well-being. *Personnel Review*, 44(2), 217–235.
Castells, M. (2000a). *The Rise of the Network Society* (2nd ed.). Oxford: Blackwell.
Castells, M. (2000b). Toward a sociology of the network society. *Contemporary Sociology*, 29(5), 693–699.
Castells, M. (2011). A network theory of power. *International Journal of Communication*, 5(1), 773–787.
Caza, B. B. and Bagozzi, R. (2009).*Testing a Professional Identity Based Theory of Resilience at Work*. Champaign: University of Illinois.
Cerulo, K. A. (1997). Identity construction: New issues, new directions. *Annual Review of Sociology*, 23(1), 385–409. http://changingminds.org/explanations/emotions/basic%20emotions.htm. Last accessed 03/11/2016.
Chan, J., and Pun, N. (2010), Suicide as protest for the new generation of Chinese migrant workers: Foxconn, global capital, and the state. *The Asia-Pacific Journal*, 8(37), 2–10.
Chartered Institute of Personnel and Development (CIPD) (2009). *Employee Voice [Online]*. Factsheet. London: Chartered Institute of Personnel and Development. Available at: www.cipd.co.uk/hrresources/factsheets/employee-voice.aspx [Accessed March 14, 2013].
Chartered Institute of Personnel and Development (CIPD) (2012a). *A Collection of Thought Pieces: Harnessing Social Media for Organisational Effectiveness [Online]*. London: Chartered Institute of Personnel and Development. Available at:www.cipd.co.uk/hr-resources/research/harnessing-social-media.aspx[Accessed March 14, 2013].
Chartered Institute of Personnel and Development (CIPD) (2012b). *Learning and Talent Development [Online]: Annual Survey Report*. London: Chartered Institute of

Personnel and Development. Available at: www.cipd.co.uk/hr-resources/survey-reports/learning-talentdevelopment-2012.aspx [Accessed March 14, 2013].

Chartered Institute of Personnel and Development (CIPD) (2013a). *Deterioration in Employee Voice and Employee Engagement at Record Low*. London: Chartered Institute of Personnel and Development.

Charted Institute of Personnel and Development (CIPD) (2013b). *Social Technology, Social Business Survey Report*. www.cipd.org/globalassets/media/zzz-misc---to-check/112social-technology-social-business_2013_tcm18-10323.pdf. Last accessed 02/09/2024.

Charted Institute of Personnel and Development (CIPD) (2013c). *Pre-Employment Checks: An Employers Guide*. Published by Chartered Institute of Personnel and Development. www.cipd.org/uk/knowledge/guides/pre-employment-checks-guidance-for-organisations/

Charted Institute of Personnel and Development (CIPD) *Guide to Reflective Practice*. www.cipd.co.uk/Images/reflective-practice-guide_tcm18-12524.pdf [Accessed June 6, 2017].

Chartered Institute of Personnel and Development (CIPD) (2023). Code of Conduct and Ethics Published Online January 2023. www.cipd.org/globalassets/media/comms/code-of-conduct/2023-cipd-code-of-conduct-and-ethics.pdf

Chartered Institute of Personnel and Development (CIPD) (2024). Digital technology. www.cipd.org/uk/the-people-profession/the-profession-map/explore-the-profession-map/core-knowledge/technology-people

Christakis, N. A. and Fowler, J. H. (2009). *Connected: The Surprising Power of Our Social Networks and How They Shape Our Lives*. Harper Press.

Cingel, D. P., Carter, M. C., Krause, H. V. (2022). Social media and self-esteem. *Curr Opin Psychol*. 45, 101304. doi: 10.1016/j.copsyc.2022.101304

Clare, L. (2002). We'll fight it as long as we can: Coping with the onset of Alzheimer's disease. *Aging and Mental Health*, 6, 139–148.

Clare, L. (2003). Managing threats to self: Awareness in early-stage Alzheimer's disease. *Social Science and Medicine*, 57, 1017–1029.

Clark, C. L and Roberts, S. J. (2010). Employers use of social networking sites: A socially irresponsible practice. *Journal of Business Ethics*, 95, 507–525.

Clark, D. (2012). *Social Media Is Making You a Smarter Leader*. Harvard Business Review Blog Network.

Coe (2022). The draft online safety bill and the regulation of hate speech: Have we opened Pandora's box? *The Journal of Media Law*, 14(1), 50–75. https://doi.org/10.1080/17577632.2022.2083870

Coleman, J. (1988). Social capital in the creation of human capital. *American Journal of Sociology*, 94, s92–s120.

Collins, E. G. C. (1983). Managers and lovers. *Harvard Business Review*, 61, 142–153.

Communications Act (2003). UK Public General Acts 2003 c. 21 published online. www.legislation.gov.uk/ukpga/2003/21/contents. Last accessed 21/08/2024.

Cooper, A. and Inglehearn, A. (2015). Perspectives: Managing professional boundaries and staying safe in digital spaces. *Journal for Research in Nursing*, 20(7), 625–633. doi: 10.1177/1744987115604066

Cornelius, C. and Radlund, A. (2011). Building global collaboration with a new social network at Ericsson. *Strategic Communication Management*, 15(9), 20–23.

Cornelius, D. (2010). *Social Media Policies: Crafting a Uniform Policy Across your Organization and Enforcing It.* Originally presented at the Virtual Corporate Counsel Forum on September 30, 2010. www.compliancebuilding.com/files/ALM-social-medi apolicy.pptx. Last accessed 20/12/2016.

Coule, T. (2013). Theories of knowledge and focus groups in organization and management research. *Qualitative Research in Organizations and Management: An International Journal*, 8(2), 148–162. https://doi.org/10.1108/QROM-09-2011-1006

Cover, R. (2012). Performing and undoing identity online: Social Networking, identity theories and the incompatibility of online profiles and friendship regimes. *The International Journal of Research into New Media Technologies*, 18(2), 177–193.

Coyle-Shapiro, J. A. M. and Kessler, I. (2003). The employment relationship in the UK public sector: A psychological contract perspective. *Journal of Public Administration Research and Theory*, 13, 213–230.

Coyle-Shapiro, J. A. M. and Neuman, J. H. (2004). The psychological contract and individual differences: The role of exchange and creditor ideologies. *Journal of Organizational Behavior*, 64, 150–164.

Cradden, C. (2011). *Unitarism, Pluralism, Radicalism…and the Rest? Sociograph – Working Paper No 7*. Geneva: University of Geneva.

Creed, D, W. E. and Scully M. A. (2005). Songs of ourselves. *Journal of Management Inquiry*, 9(4), 391–412.

Creswell, J. W. (1994). *Research Design: Qualitative and Quantitative Approaches.* Thousand Oaks: Sage.

Creswell, J. W. (1998). *Qualitative Inquiry and Research Design: Choosing among Five Traditions*. Thousand Oaks: Sage.

Crotty, Michael and Crotty, M. (1998). *The Foundations of Social Research: Meaning and Perspective in the Research Process*. London, Thousand Oaks: Sage Publications.

Crown Prosecution Service (CPS) (2016). Violence Against Women and Girls Crime Report 2016–17. www.cps.gov.uk/publication/cps-violence-against-women-and-girls-crime-report-2016-2017. Last accessed 20/08/2024.

Crown Prosecution Service (CPS) (2017). Guidance on Prosecuting Social Media and Other Electronic Communications Offences. www.cps.gov.uk/legal-guidance/social-media-and-other-electronic-communications

Crown Prosecution Service (CPS) (2018). Violence Against Women and Girls Report 2018–19. www.cps.gov.uk/sites/default/files/documents/publications/cps-vawg-rep ort-2019.pdf. Last accessed 02/09/24.

Crown Prosecution Service (CPS) (2024). Cybercrimes Prosecution Guidance. www.cps.gov.uk/legal-guidance/cybercrime-prosecution-guidance. Last accessed 02/09/2024.

Cullinane, N., Donaghey, J., Dundon, T., and Dobbins, T. (2012). Different rooms, different voices: Double-breasting, multi-channel representation and the managerial agenda. *The International Journal of Human Resource Management*, 23(2), 368–384.

Culnan, J. M., McHugh, P., and Zubillaga, J. I. (2010). How large U.S. companies can use Twitter and other social media to gain business value. *MIS Quarterly Executive*, 9, 243–259.

Cunliffe, A. L. (2016). Republication of "on becoming a critically reflexive practitioner". *Journal of Management Education*, 40(6), 747–768. https://doi.org/10.1177/1052562916674465

Curtis, S., Gesler, W., Smith, G., and Washburn, S. (2000). Approaches to sampling and case selection in qualitative research: Examples in the geography of health. *Social Science and Medicine*, 50, 1001–1014.

Cyberflashing (2024). epilepsy-trolling and fake news to put online abusers behind bars from today – GOV.UK (www.gov.uk)

D'Abate, C. P. and Eddy, E. R. (2007). Engaging in personal business on the job: Extending the presenteeism construct. *Human Resource Development Quarterly*, 18(3), 361–383.

Dambrin, C. (2004), How does telework influence the manager-employee relationship? *International Journal of Human Resource Development & Management*, 4, 358–374.

Deloitte. (2009). Social networking and reputational risk in the workplace: Deloitte LLP 2009 Ethics & Workplace Survey results. Retrieved July 16, 2009 from www.deloitte.com/dtt/cda/doc/content/us_2009_ethics_workplace_survey_220509.pdf

Denyer, D. and Neely, A. (2004). Introduction to special issue: Innovation and productivity performance in the UK. *International Journal of Management Reviews*, 5/6 (3 and 4), 131–135.

Denzin, N. K. and Lincoln, Y. S. (eds.) (2000). *Handbook of Qualitative Research* (2nd ed.). Thousand Oaks: Sage.

Dessler, G. (2015). *Human Resource Management* (14th ed.). Pearson Education Ltd.

Devers, K. J. and Frankel, R. M. (2000). Study design in qualitative research—2: Sampling and data collection strategies. *Education for Health*, 13, 263–271.

Dietz, G. (2004). Partnership and the development of trust in British workplaces. *Human Resource Management Journal*, 14(1), 5–24.

Dillon, T. W. and Thomas, D. S. (2006). Knowledge of privacy, personal use, and administrative oversight of office computers and e-mail in the workplace. *Information Technology, Learning, and Performance Journal*, 24(2), 23–34.

Dobbins, A. and Gunnigle, P. (2009). Can voluntary workplace partnership deliver sustainable mutual gains? *British Journal of Industrial Relations*, 546–570. doi: 10.1111/j.1467-8543.2009.00715.x 47:3

Docherty, T. (2024). *Academic Freedom and Constrained Expression Chapter 22—The Routledge Companion to Freedom of Expression and Censorship*. Routledge. https://doi.org/10.4324/9780429262067

Donnelly et al. (2013). The integration of occupational therapy into primary care: A multiple case study design. *BMC Family Practice*, 14, 60.

Dores Cruz, T. D., Balliet, D., Sleebos, E., Beersma, B., Van Kleef, G. A., and Gallucci, M. (2019). Getting a grip on the grapevine: Extension and factor structure of the motives to gossip questionnaire. *Frontiers in Psychology*, 10, 1190. doi: 10.3389/fpsyg.2019.0119

Dufty, N. F. and Fells, R. E. (1989). *Dynamics of Industrial Relations in Australia*. Sydney: Prentice Hall.

Duggan, M., Ellison, N. B., Lampe, C., Lenhart, A., and Madden, M. (2015). Social media update 2014. Pew Research Center. Retrieved from www.pewinternet.org/2015/01/09/socialmedia-update-2014/

Dundon, T. and Rollinson, D. (2011). *Understanding Employment Relations* (2nd ed.). London: McGraw-Hill Higher Education.

Dutton, J. E., Morgan Roberts, L., and Bednar, J. (2010). Pathways for positive identity construction at work: Four types of positive identity and the building of social resource. *Academy of Management Review*, 35(2), 265–293.

Dyne, L. Ang, S., and Botero, I. (2003). Conceptualizing employee silence and employee voice as multidimensional constructs. *Journal of Management Studies*, 40(6), 1359–1392.

Eatough, V. and Smith, J. A. (2008). Interpretative phenomenological analysis. In C. Willig and W. StaintonRogers (eds.), *The Sage Handbook of Qualitative Research in Psychology* (pp. 179–194). London: Sage.

Eberle, C. (2011). Organizing around social media. *Workforce Management*, 20–22.

Edwards, M. R. (2010). An integrative review of employer branding and OB theory. *Personnel Review*, 39(1), 5–23.

Edwards, P. and Wright, M. (2001). High-involvement work systems and performance outcomes: The strength of variable, contingent and context-bound relationships. *The International Journal of Human Resource Management*, 12(4), 568–585.

Edwards, P. (1986). *Conflict at Work: A Materialist Analysis of Workplace Relations*. Oxford and New York: Basil Blackwell.

Edwards, P. K. (2003). *Industrial Relations: Theory and Practice* (2nd ed.). Malden, MA: Blackwell Publishing.

Edwards, R. (1979). *Contested Terrain*. London: Heinemann.

Eger, L. et al. (2018). Employer branding on social media and recruitment websites: Symbolic traits of an ideal employer. *E+Mekonomie a Management*. 21(1), 224–237.

Ehrenreich, R. (2000–2001). Privacy and power. *Georgetown Law Journal*, 89, 2047.

Ehret, Michael, Vishal, K., and Jochen, W. (2013), Business models: Impact on business markets and opportunities for marketing research. *Industrial Marketing Management*, 42(5), 649–655.

Ekman, P., Davidson, R. J., and Friesen, W. V. (1990). The Duchenne smile: Emotional expression and brain physiology II. *Journal of Personality and Social Psychology*, 58(2), 342–353.

Elias, S.R., Chiles, T.H., Duncan, C.M., and Vultee, D.M. (2018). The aesthetics of entrepreneurship: How arts entrepreneurs and their customers co-create aesthetic value. *Organization Studies*, 39(2–3), 345–372.

Elliot, M. J. (2011). '*Privacy, identity and disclosure*', Keynote talk at The International Conference on Communication, Computing and Security. Rourkela. As Cited in Halfpenny, P. & Procter, R. (2015) *Innovations in Digital Research Methods: hbk*. SAGE.

Ellison, N. B., Steinfield, C., and Lampe, C. (2007). The benefits of Facebook friends: Social capital and college students' use of online social network sites. *Journal of Computer-Mediated Communication*, 12, 1143–1168.

Embree, L. and Mohanty, J. N. (1997). Introduction. In L. Embree et al (eds.), *Encyclopedia of Phenomenology* (pp. 1–10). Dordrecht: Kluwer Academic Publishers.

Emmott, M. (2015). *Employment relations over the last 50 years: Confrontation, consensus or neglect? Employee Relations*, 37(6), 658–669.

Employment Rights Act (1996). www.legislation.gov.uk/ukpga/1996/18/contents. Last accessed 21/08/2024.

ENEI.org.uk (2012) – The nature of bias and discrimination. www.enei.org.uk/pages/the-nature-of-bias-and-discrimination-.html. Last accessed 27/06/2013.

Equality Act (2010). www.legislation.gov.uk/ukpga/2010/15/contents. Last accessed 21/08/2024.

Erikson, E. H. (1964). *Insight and Responsibility*. New York: Norton.

Erikson, E. H. (1968). *Identity: Youth and Crisis*. New York: Norton.

Etzioni, A. (1964). *Modern Organizations*. Englewood Cliffs: Prentice-Hall.

Everett A. M., Wong Y. Y., and Paynter J. (2006). Balancing employee and employer rights: An international comparison of e-mail privacy in the workplace. *Individual Employment Rights*, 11, 291–310. Google Scholar.

Ezzamel, M., Willmott, H., and Worthington, F. (2001). Power, control and resistance in 'the factory that time forgot'. *Journal of Management Studies*, 38(8), 1053–1079.

Fang, R., Landis, B., Zhang, Z., Anderson, M. H., Shaw, J. D., and Kilduff, M. (2015). Integrating personality and social networks: A meta-analysis of personality, network position, and work outcomes in organizations. *Organization Science*, 26(4), 1243–1260. https://doi.org/10.1287/orsc.2015.0972

Fenton-Jarvis, S. (2022). *The Human-Centric Workplace: Enabling Communities and our Planet to Thrive*. Lid Publishing.

Fernback, J. (2013). Sousveillance: Communities of resistance to the surveillance environment. *Telematics and Informatics,* 30(1), 11–21.

Fineman, S. (2006). On being positive: Concerns and counterpoints. *Academy of Management Review*, 31, 270–291.

Finlay, L. (2009). Debating phenomenological research methods. *Phenomenology & Practice*, 3(1), 6–25.

Flexman v BG Group plc ET/2701998/11 as cited in Exten-Wright, J. (2013). The shifting sands of social media. *Employers' Law*, 14–15.

Folkman, S. and Moskowitz, J. T. (2000), Positive affect and the other side of coping. *American Psychologist*, 55, 647–654.

Fong, J. and Burton, S. (2008). A cross-cultural comparison of electronic word-of-mouth and country-of-origin effects. *Journal of Business Research*, 61(3), 233–242.

Foucault, M. (1970). *The Order of Things.* London: Tavistock.

Foucault, M. (1975/77). *Discipline and Punish; The Birth of the Prison*. Reprint (1991). London: Penguin.

Foucault, M. (1983). The subject and power. In Dreyfus, H. and Rabinow, P. (eds.), *Michel Foucault: Beyond Structuralism and Hermeneutics* (1st ed., pp. 208–226). Taylor & Francis Group. https://doi.org/10.4324/9781315835259

Foucault, M. (1991). The ethic of care for the self as practice of freedom in Rasmussen, D.M., Bernauer, J., 1988. *The final Foucault*. Cambridge, MA: MIT Press.

Foucault, M. and Gordon, C. (1980). *Power-Knowledge: Selected Interviews and Other Writings, 1972–1977*. Harvester Press.

Fournier, V. and Grey, C. (2000). At the critical moment: Conditions and prospects for critical management studies. *Human Relations*, 53(1), 7–32.

Fox, A. (1966). Industrial sociology and industrial relations; Royal Commission on Trade Unions and Employers' Associations, Research Papers, 3, London: HMSO.

Francis, H, Parkes, C., and Reddington, M. (2014). EHR and international HRM: A critical perspective on the discursive framing of e-HR. *The International Journal of Human Resource Management*, 25(10), 1327–1350. doi: 10.1080/09585192.2013.870309
French, J. and Raven, B. H. (1959). The bases of social power. In D. Cartwright (ed.), *Studies in Social Power* (pp. 150–167). Ann Arbor: Institute for Social Research.
Friedman, A. (1977). *Industry and Labour:Class Struggle at Work and Monopoly Capitalism*. London: Macmillan.
Frowe, I. (2001). Language and educational research. *Journal of Philosophy and Education*, 35(2), 175–186. http://dx.doi.org/10.1111/1467-9752.00219
www.ft.com/content/d91dddea-3d7d-11e3-9928-00144feab7de accessed 16/09/2017.
Fukuyama, F. (ed.) (1995). *Trust: The Social Virtues and the Creation of Prosperity*. New York Free Press.
Gagliardi, P. (1996). Exploring the aesthetic side of organizational life. In S. R. Glegg, C. Hardy, and W. R. Nord (eds.), *Handbook of Organization Studies* (pp. 565–580). Sage. Google Scholar.
Ganascia, J. (2010). The generalized sousveillance society. *Social Science Information*, 49(3), 489–507.
Geanellos, R. (1998). Hermeneutic philosophy. Part I: Implications of its use as methodology in interpretive nursing research. *Nursing Inquiry*, 5(3), 154–163.
Geelan, T. (2015). Danish trade unions and young people: Using media in the battle for hearts and minds. Cited in Hodder and Kretsos (2015) *Young Workers and Trade Unions A Global View*. Palgrave Macmillan.
Geertz, C. (1973). *The Interpretation of Cultures*. New York: Basic Books. Google Scholar.
Gergen, K. J. (2001). Psychological science in a post modern context. *American Psychologist*, 56, 803–813.
Gergen, K. J. (2009). *Relational Being: Beyond Self and Community*. New York: Oxford University Press.
Gergen, K. J. (2011). The self as social construction. *Psychological Studies*, 56(1), 108–116.
Giacalone, R. and Rosenfeld, P. (1990). *Impression Management in the Organization*. Psychology Press, Routledge.
Giddens, A. (1991). *Modernity and Self-Identity: Self and Society in the Late Modern Age*. Polity.
Gill, J. and Johnson, P. (2010). *Research Methods for Managers* (4th ed.). Los Angeles, London: Sage.
Gill, M. J. (2013). Elite identity and status anxiety: An interpretative phenomenological analysis of management consultants. *Organization*, 22(3), 306–325.
Gill, M. J. (2014). The possibilities of phenomenology for organizational research methods. *Organizational Research Methods*, 17(2), 118–137.
Gioia, D. A., Schultz, M., and Corley, K. G. (2000). Organizational identity, image, and adaptive instability. *The Academy of Management Review*, 25(1), 63–81.
Giorgi, A. and Giorgi, B. (2003). The descriptive phenomenological psychological method. In P. M. Camic, J. E. Rhodes, and L. Yardley (eds.), *Qualitative Research in Psychology: Expanding Perspectives in Methodology and Design* (pp. 243–273). Washington, DC: American Psychological Association.

Glenn, J. C. (2009). *Collective Intelligence – One of the Next Big Things, Futura*. Helsinki: Finnish Society for Futures Studies.

Godard, J. (2014). The psychologisation of employment relations? *Human Resource Management Journal*, 24, 1–18. doi:10.1111/1748-8583.12030

Goffman, E. (1959). *The Presentation of Self in Everyday Life*. New York: Doubleday.

Goffman, E. (1971). *Relations in Public: Microstudies of the Public Order*. London: Penguin. doi:10.1093/sf/51.4.504 www.gov.uk/government/uploads/system/uploads/attachment_data/file/616966/trade-union-membership-statistical-bulletin-2016-rev.pdf

Gov.UK (2024). Monitoring. www.gov.uk/monitoring-work-workers-rights/email-cctv-and-other-monitoring

Granovetter, M. (1973). The strength of weak ties. *American Journal of Sociology*, 78, 1360–1380.

Gray, D. E. (2014). *Doing Research in the Real World*. London: Sage.

Greig, A. and Taylor, J. (1999). *Doing Research with Children*. London: Sage.

Grey, C. (2009/2013). *A Very Short, Fairly Interesting and Reasonably Cheap Book about Studying Organizations*. London: Sage Publications Ltd.

Griffiths, M. (2005). A "components" model of addiction with in a biopsychosocial framework." *Journal of Substantial Use*, 10 (4), 191–197. doi: 10.1080/14659890500114359

Grix, J. (2004). *The Foundations of Research*. London: Palgrave Macmillan.

Groenewald, T. (2003). *The Contribution of Co-operative Education in the Growing of Talent*. Unpublished doctoral dissertation, Rand Afrikaans University, Johannesburg, South Africa.

Groenewald, T. (2004). A phenomenological research design illustrated. *International Journal of Qualitative Methods*, 3(1), 42–55. https://doi.org/10.1177/160940690400300104

Guba, E. G. and Lincoln, Y. S. (1994). Competing paradigms in qualitative research. In N. K. Denzin and Y. S. Lincoln (eds.), *Handbook of Qualitative Research* (pp. 105–117). London: Sage.

Guest, D. (1990). Human resource management and the American dream. *Journal of Management Studies*, 27(4), 377–397.

Guest, D. (1991). Personnel management: the end of orthodoxy?. *British Journal of Industrial Relations*, 29(2), 149–175.

Guest, D. (1992). Right enough to be dangerously wrong: An analysis of the "In Search of Excellence" phenomenon. In G. Salaman (Ed.), *Human Resource Strategies* (pp. 56–74). London: Sage.

Guest, D. and Conway, N. (2001). *Employer Perceptions of the Psychological Contract*. CIPD Publishing.

Guest, D. and Conway, N. (2002). *Pressure at Work and the Psychological Contract (Research Report)*. CIPD.

Guest, D., Michie, J., Sheehan, M., and Conway, N. (2003). A UK study of the relationship between human resource management and corporate performance. *British Journal of Industrial Relations*, 41(2), 291–314.

Guignon, C. (2012). Becoming a person: Hermeneutic phenomenology's contribution. *New Ides in Psychology*, 30, 97–106.

Guynn, J. (12 May 2015). Google's "bias busting" workshops target hidden prejudices. USA Today. Retrieved from www.usatoday.com/story/tech/2015/05/12/google-unconsciousbias-diversity/27055485

Hackman, J. R. (2009). The perils of positivity. *Journal of Organizational Behavior*, 30, 309–319.

Halfpenny, P. and Proctor, R. (2015). *Innovations in Digital Research Methods*. Sage Publications.

Hall, R. (2010). Renewing and revising the engagement between labour process theory and technology. In P. Thompson and C. Smith (eds.), *Working Life: Renewing Labour Process Analysis*. London: Palgrave MacMillan.

Hammersly, M. (1989). *The Dilemma of Qualitative Method: Herbert Blumer and the Chicago Tradition*. London: Routledge.

Hammersley, M. (1992). *What's Wrong with Ethnography?* London: Routledge.

Hancock, P. (2005). Uncovering the semiotic in organizational aesthetics: The interdisciplinary journal of organization, theory and society. *Organization*, 12(1), 29–50.

Harrington, J. (2009). July 24 Facebook Ads with your photos – steps to stop. http://phtobusinessforumblogspot.com/2009/07/facebook-ads-with-your-photos. Last accessed 2010. Photo Business New & forum.

Hart, D. (1992). Self-understanding and its role in social and moral development. In M. Bornstein and M. E. Lamb (eds.), *Developmental Psychology: An Advanced Textbook* (3rd ed., pp. 421–464). Hillsdale: Erlbaum.

Hart, D., Atkins, R., and Ford, D. (1998). Urban America as a context for the development of moral identity in adolescence. *Journal of Social Issues*, 54(3), 513–530.

Hatch, M. J. and Cunliffe, A. L. (2013). *Organization Theory: Modern, Symbolic, and Postmodern Perspectives* (3rd ed.). New York: Oxford University Press.

Hawi, N. S. and Samaha, M. (2017). Relationships among smartphone addiction, anxiety, and family relations. *Behaviour & Information Technology*, 36(10), 1046–1052. https://doi.org.10.1080/0144929X.2017.1336254

Hay, C. (2002). *Political Analysis*. Basingstoke: Palgrave Macmillan.

Hay, C. (2011). Interpreting interpretivism interpreting interpretations: The new hermeneutics of public administration. *Public Administration*, 89(1), 167–182.

Headworth, A. (2015). *Social Media Recruitment: How to Successfully Integrate Social Media Into Recruitment Strategy*. London: Kogan Page.

Heckscher, C. and Carré, F. (2006). Strength in networks: Employment rights organizations and the problem of coordination. *British Journal of Industrial Relations*, 44(4), 605–628. Available at SSRN: https://ssrn.com/abstract=945221 or http://dx.doi.org/10.1111/j.1467-8543.2006.00516.x

Heidegger, M. (1926/2010). *Being and Time*. Translated by Joan Stamburgh. State University of New York Press.

Hochschild, A. (1983/2003). *The Managed Heart: Commercialization of Human Feeling*. Berkeley: University of California Press.

Hodder, A. (2015). 'Old Dusty Men'? Young people and trade unions in the UK. In: Hodder A. and Kretsos L. (eds.), *Young Workers and Trade Unions*. London: Palgrave Macmillan.

Hodder, A. (2020). New technology, work and employment in the era of COVID-19: Reflecting on legacies of research. *New Technology, Work and Employment*, 35(3), 262–275. doi: 10.1111/ntwe

Hodder, A. and Houghton, D. (2020). Unions, social media and young workers – Evidence from the UK. *New Technology, Work and Employment*, 35(1), 40–59.

Hodder, A. and Kretsos, L. (eds.) (2015). Young workers and trade unions: A global view. *Journal of Industrial Relations*, 58(4), 564–566.

Hoffman, D. L. and Fodor, M. (2010). Can you measure the ROI of your social media marketing? (return on investment). *MIT Sloan Management Review*, 52(1), 41.

Hogg, M. and Terry, D. (2000). Social identity and self-categorization processes in organizational contexts. *The Academy of Management Review*, 25(1), 121–140.

Hogg, M. A. and Terry. D. J. (2001). *Social Identity Theory and Organisational Processes*. Philadelphia Psychology Press.

Holland, P. and Bardoel, A. (2016). The impact of technology on work in the twenty-first century: Exploring the smart and dark side. *The International Journal of Human Resource Management,* 26(11), 1520–1521. https://doi.org/10.1080/09585192.2015.1021155.

Holland, P., Cooper, B., and Hecker, R. (2015). Electronic monitoring and surveillance in the workplace. *Personnel Review*, 44(1), 161–175.

Holland, P., Cooper, B. K., and Hecker, R. (2016). Use of social media at work: A new form of employee voice. *The International Journal of Human Resource Management*, 27(21), 2621–2634. doi: 10.1080/09585192.2016.1227867.

Holroyd, A. E. M. (2007). Interpretive hermeneutic phenomenology: Clarifying understanding. *Indo-Pacific Journal of Phenomenology*, 7(2), 2–12.

Honneth, A. (2008a). Reification and recognition: A new look at an old idea. In M. Jay (ed.), *Reification: A New Look at an Old Idea* (pp. 17–96). Oxford: Oxford University Press. Google Scholar.

Hoque, K., Wass, V., Bacon, N., and Jones, M. (2018). Are high-performance work practices (HPWPs) enabling or disabling? Exploring the relationship between selected HPWPs and work-related disability disadvantage. *Human Resource Management*, 57(2), 499–513.

Høyrup, S. (2004). Reflection as a core process in organizational learning. *The Journal of Workplace Learning*, 16(8), 442–454.

Hughes, C. (1994). From field notes to dissertation: Analysing the stepfamily. In Bryman, Burgess, Bryman, Alan, and Burgess, Robert G. (eds.), *Analyzing Qualitative Data* (1st ed., pp. 35–46). Oxford: Routledge. https://doi.org/10.4324/9780203413081-3

Human Rights Act (1998). www.legislation.gov.uk/ukpga/1998/42/contents. Last accessed 02/09/2024.

Hume, D., Norton, D. F., and Norton, M. J. (2000). *A Treatise of Human Nature*. Oxford: Oxford University Press.

Humphreys, M. and Brown, A. (2002). Narratives of organizational identity and identification: A case study of hegemony and resistance. *Organization Studies*, 23(3), 421–447.

Hunter-McDonnell, M. and King, B. (2013). Keeping up appearances; reputational threat and impression management after social movement boycotts. *Administrative Science Quarterly*, 58(3), 387–419.

Huselid, M. (1995). The impact of human resource management practices on turnover, productivity, and corporate financial performance. *Academy of Management Journal*, 38(3), 635–672.

Husserl, E. (1931). *Ideas: General introduction to Pure Phenomenology*. Translated by Gilson W. R. B. New York: Humanities Press. Original work published in 1913.

Hyman, J. and Mason, B. (1995). *Managing Employee Involvement and Participation*. London: Sage Publications.

Ibarra, H. (1999). Provisional selves: Experimenting with image and identity in professional adaptation. *Administrative Science Quarterly*, 44(4), 764–791.

IDS Employment Law Brief (September 2012). *Social Media in Work* 1, 957, 13–19 available through Westlaw Edge UK, Thompson Reuters. Last accessed 02/09/2024.

IDS Employment Law Brief (October 2012). *Social Media in Work* 2, 958, 19–23 available through Westlaw Edge UK, Thompson Reuters. Last accessed 02/09/2024.

Introna, L. D. (1997). Privacy and the computer: Why we need privacy in the information society. *Metaphilosophy*, 28(3), 259–275.

Inwood, M. (2000). *Heidegger: A Very Short Introduction*. Oxford: Oxford University Press.

Inyang, B. J., Awa, H. O., and Enuoh, R. O. (2011). CSR-HRM nexus: Defining the role engagement of the human resources professional. *International Journal of Business and Social Sciences*, 2(5), 118–126.

Islam, G. (2012). Recognition, reification, and practices of forgetting: Ethical implications of human resource management. *Journal of Business Ethics*, 111(1), 37–48.

Jacobson, W. S. and Howle-Tufts, S. (2012). To post or not to post. *Review of Public Personnel Administration*, 33(1), 84–107.

Jansen, S. C. (2024). Freedom of expression in the twentieth century. In S. John and P. Julian (eds.), *The Routledge Companion to Freedom of Expression and Censorship* (pp. 85–95). New York: Routledge.

Jeffery, M. (2002a). Information technology and workers privacy. *Comparative Labour Law and Policy Journal*, 23(4), 251–280.

Jenkins, H., et al. (2006). Confronting the Challenges of Participatory Culture: Media Education for the 21st Century, [online] Available at: White paper, MacArthur Foundation, http://digitallearning.macfound.org/atf/cf/%7B7E45C7E0-A3E0-4B89-AC9C-E807E1B0AE4E%7D/JENKINS_WHITE_PAPER.PDF

Jenkins, R. (1996). *Social Identity*. London: Routledge.

Jeske, D. and Schultz, K. S. (2015). Using social media content for screening in recruitment and selection: Pros and cons. Work Employment and Society, 30(3), 535–546. doi: 10.1177/0950017015613746.

Johnson, G. and Scholes, K. (1999). *Exploring Corporate Strategy* (5th ed.). Essex: Prentice Hall.

Johnson, P. and Duberley, J. (2000). *Understanding Management Research: An Introduction to Epistemology*. London: Sage.

Josselson, R. (1996). *Revising Herself: The Story of Women's Identity from College to Midlife*. Oxford: Oxford University press.

Kahn, W. (1990). Psychological conditions of personal engagement and disengagement at work. *Academy of Management Journal*, 33(4), 692–724.

Kahn-Freund, O., 1900–1979. (1972). *Labour and the Law*. London: Stevens [for] the Hamlyn Trust.

Kalleberg, A. L. and Moody, J. W. (1994). Human resource management and organizational performance. *American Behavioral Scientist*, 37(7), 948–962. doi: 10.1177/0002764294037007007

Kaplan, A. M. and Haenlein, M. (2010). Users of the world, unite! The challenges and opportunities of Social Media. *Business Horizons*, 53(1), 59–68. https://doi.org/10.1016/j.bushor.2009.09.003. www.sciencedirect.com/science/article/pii/S0007681309001232

Kärreman, D. and Alvesson, M. (2004). Cages in tandem: Management control, social identity, and identification in a knowledge-intensive firm. *Organization*, 11(1), 149–175.

Kaufman, B. (2015). Theorising determinants of employee voice: An integrative model across disciplines and levels of analysis. *Human Resource Management Journal*, 25(1), 19–40.

Keenoy, T. and Kelly, D. (1998). *The Employment Relationship in Australia.* Sydney: Harcourt Brace.

Kelly, C. and Kelly, J. (1994). Who gets involved in collective action? Social psychological determinants of individual participation in trade unions. *Human Relations*, 47, 63–68.

Kerrigan, F. and Hart, A. (2016). Theorising digital personhood: A dramaturgical approach. *Journal of Marketing Management*, 32(17–18), 1701.

King, B. and Whetten, D. A. (2008). Rethinking the relationship between reputation and legitimacy: A Social actor conceptualization. *Corporate Reputation Review*, 11(3), 192–207. https://doi.org/10.1057/crr.2008.16

Kitzinger, J. (2005). Focus group research: Using group dynamics. *Qualitative Research in Health Care*, 1, 56–70.

Kizza, J. M. and Ssanyu, J. (2005). Workplace surveillance. In J. Weckert (ed.), *Electronic Monitoring in the Workplace: Controversies and Solutions* (pp. 1–18). Hershey: Idea Group.

Kluemper, D. and Rosen, P. (2009). Future of employment selection methods: Evaluating social networking websites. *Journal of Managerial Psychology*, 24(6), 567–580.

Knudsen, H., Ole, B., and Jens, L. (2011). Work environment quality: The role of workplace participation and democracy. *Work, Employment & Society* , 25(3), 379–396.

Koch, T. (1995). Interpretive approaches in nursing research: The influence of Husserl and Heidegger. *Journal of Advanced Nursing*, 21, 827–836.

Kochan, T. A. (2004). Restoring trust in the human resource management profession. *Asia Pacific Journal of Human Resources*, 42, 132–146. doi: 10.1177/1038411104045352

Kreiner, G., Ashforth, B., and Sluss, D. (2006). Identity dynamics in occupational dirty work: Integrating social identity and system justification perspectives. *Organization Science,* 17(5), 619–636.

Kroll, E., Veit, S., and Ziegler, M. (2021). The discriminatory potential of modern recruitment trends—A mixed-method study from Germany. *Frontiers in Psychology*, 12, 634376. 10.3389/fpsyg.2021.634376.

Kruger, D. (1988). *An Introduction to Phenomenological Psychology* (2nd ed.). Cape Town: Juta.

Kumar, A., Bezawada, R., Rishika, R., Janakiraman, R., and Kannan, P. K. (2016). From social to sale: The effects of firm-generated content in social media on consumer behavior. *Journal of Marketing*, 80(1), 7–25.

Kunze, F., Boehm, S.A., and Bruch, H. (2011). Age diversity, age discrimination climate and performance consequences—a cross organizational study. *Journal of Organizational Behavior*, 32(2), 264–290.

Kuo, C. C., Chang, K., Quinton, S., Lu, C. Y., and Lee, I. (2015). Gossip in the workplace and the implications for HR management: A study of gossip and its relationship to employee cynicism. *The International Journal of HRM*, 26(18), 228–2307. doi: 10:1080/09585192.2014,985329.

Kvale, S. (1996). *Interviews – An Introduction to Qualitative Research Interviewing*. Thousand Oaks: Sage.

Kvale, S. (2006). Dominance through interviews and dialogues. *Qualitative Inquiry*, 12, 480. http://qix.sagepub.com.12/3/480

Lam, H. (2016). Social media dilemmas in the employment context. *Employee Relations*, 38(3), 420–437.

Langdridge, D. (2007). *Phenomenological Psychology: Theory, Research and Method*. London: Pearson Education.

Larkin, M., Watts, S., and Clifton, E. (2006). Giving voice and making sense in interpretative phenomenological analysis. *Qualitative Research in Psychology*, 3, 102–120.

Lee, J, Arnason, A., Nightingale, A., and Shucksmith, M. (2005). Networking: Social capital and identities. *European Rural Development*, 45(4), 270–283.

Legge, K. (1995a). Human resource management: Are the promises fulfilled? *Asia Pacific Journal of Human Resources*, 30, 1–15.

Legge, K. (1995b). HRM: Rhetoric, reality and hidden agendas. In J. Storey (ed.), *Human Resource Management: A Critical Text* (pp. 33–61). London: Routledge.

Legge, K. (1995c). *Human Resource Management: Rhetorics and Realities*. London: Macmillan.

Lenhart, A. (2009). *Teens and Sexting: How and Why Minor Teens Are Sending Sexually Suggestive Nude or Nearly Nude Images via Text Messaging*. Washington, DC: Pew Internet & American Life Project.

Leonardi, P. M., Huysman, M., and Steinfield, C. (2013). Enterprise social media: Definition, history, and prospects for the study of social technologies in organizations. *Journal of Computer-Mediated Communication*, 19(1), 1–19. 10.1111/jcc4.12029.

Leonardi, P. M. and Treem, J. W. (2012). Knowledge management technology as a stage for strategic self-presentations: Implications for knowledge sharing in organizations. *Information and Organization*, 22(1), 37–59.

LeVasseur, J. J. (2003). The problem of bracketing in phenomenology. *Qualitative Health Research*, 13(3), 408–420.

Lewis, P., Thornhill, A., and Saunders, M. (2003). *Employee Relations: Understanding the Employment Relationship* (1st ed.). Harlow: Pearson Education.

Linstead, A. and Thomas, R. (2002). "What do you want from me?" A poststructuralist feminist reading of middle managers' identities. *Culture and Organization*, 8(1), 1–20.

Lopez, K. A. and Willis, D. G. (2004). Descriptive versus interpretive phenomenology: Their contributions to nursing knowledge. *Qualitative Health Research*, 14(5), 726–735.

Lucero, M. A., Allen, R. E., and Elzweig, B. (2013). Managing employee social networking: Evolving views from the National Labor Relations Board. *Employee Responsibilities and Rights Journal*, 25(3), 143–158.

Lukacs, G. (1971). *History and Class Consciousness*. Translated by R. Livingstone. Cambridge: MIT Press.

Lukes, S. and British Sociological Association. (2005). *Power: A Radical View* (2nd ed.). Basingstoke: Palgrave Macmillan.

Lundgren, H. and Poell, R. F. (2016). On critical reflection: A review of Mezirow's theory and its operationalization. *Human Resource Development Review*, 15(1), 3–28. https://doi.org/10.1177/1534484315622735

Luyckx, K., Goossens, L., and Soenens, B. (2006). A developmental contextual perspective on identity construction in emerging adulthood: Change dynamics in commitment formation and commitment evaluation. *Developmental Psychology*, 42, 366–380.

Macky, K. and Boxall, P. (2008). High-involvement work processes, work intensification and employee well-being: A study of New Zealand worker experiences. *Asia Pacific Journal of Human Resources*, 46(1), 38.

MacLeod, D. and Clarke, N. (2009). Enagaging for success; enhancing performance through employee engagement Report. Available through https://engageforsuccess.org/wp-content/uploads/2020/12/engaging-for-success.pdf. Last accessed 02/09/2024.

Malaterre, A. M., Rothbard, N. P., and Berg, J. M. (2013). When worlds collide in cyberspace: How Boundary work in online social networks impacts professional relationships. *Academy of Management Review*. 38(4), 645–669.

Manaf, M., Mursyiddin, A., Ghani, Erlane K., and Jais, Ismie Roha Mohamed. (2013). Gossip has it! An in-depth investigation of Malaysian employees on gossip activities at workplace. *Canadian Social Science*, 9(4), 34–44.

Manders, C. (2013, June). Moving surveillance techniques to sousveillance: Towards equiveillance using wearable computing. *2013 IEEE International Symposium* on *Technology and Society (ISTAS)* (pp. 19). IEEE.

Mangham, I. (1996). Beyond Goffman: Some notes on life and theatre as art. *Studies in Cultures, Organizations and Societies*, 2(1), 31–41. Google Scholar.

Mann, S. and Ferenbok, J. (2013). New media and the power politics of sousveillance in a surveillance-dominated world. *Surveillance & Society*, 11(1/2), 18–34.

Mann, S., Nolan, J., and Wellman, B. (2003). Sousveillance: Inventing and using wearable computing devices for data collection in surveillance environments. *Surveillance & Society*, 1(3), 331–355.

Mannheim, K. (1960a). *Ideology and Utopia*. London: RKP.

Mannheim, K. (1960b). *The Problem of the sociology of Knowledge in Ideology and Utopia*. London: RKP.

Marchington, M. and Wilkinson, A. (2008). *Human Resource Management at Work: People Management and Development* (4th ed.). CIPD: London.

Marler, J. H. and Parry, E. (2015). Human resource management, strategic involvement and e-HRM technology. *The International Journal of Human Resource Management*, 27, 2233–2253. doi: 10.1080/09585192.2015.1091980

Marsden, R. (1993). Marx, realism and Foucault : An enquiry into the problem of industrial relations theory. Unpublished PhD thesis, University of Warwick.

Martey, R. and Consalvo, M. (2011). Performing the looking-glass self: Avatar appearance and group identity in second life. *Popular Communication*, 9(3), 165–180.

Martin, G., Parry, E., and Flowers, P. (2015). Do social media enhance constructive employee voice all of the time or just some of the time? *Human Resource Management Journal*, 25(4), 541–562.

Martin, G., Reddington, M., Kneafsey, M. B., and Sloman, M. (2009). Scenarios and strategies for Web 2.0. *Education + Training*, 51(5/6), 370–380. Permanent link to this document: http://dx.doi.org/10.1108/00400910910987183

Martin, G. R. R. (1996). *A Game of Thrones*. New York: Bantam Books.

Martin, K. and Freeman, R. (2003). Some problems with employee monitoring. *Journal of Business Ethics*, 4, 353–361.

Mason, J. (1996). *Qualitative Researching*. London: Sage.

Mason, J. (2002). *Qualitative Researching* (2nd ed.). London: Sage.

Matisse, H. (1953). *Looking at Life through the Eyes of a Child Liquiritia Word Press.com*. Last accessed 24/08/2012.

McAuley, J., Duberley, J., and Johnson, P. (2007). *Organization Theory: Challenges and Perspectives*. Harlow: Prentice Hall.

McDonald, P., Thompson, P., and O'Connor, P. (2016). Profiling employees online: Shifting public–private boundaries in organisational life. *Human Resource Management Journal*, 26(4), 541–556.

McDonald, S., Damarin, A. K., McQueen, H., and Grether, S. T. (2022). The hunt for red flags: Cybervetting as morally performative practice. *Socio-Economic Review*, 20(3), 915–936. 10.1093/ser/mwab002.

McGlynn, C. and Johnson, K. (2020). Criminalising cyberflashing: Options for law reform. *The Journal of Criminal Law*, 0022018320972306. https://doi.org/10.1177/0022018320972306

McGlynn, C., Rackley, E., and Houghton, R. (2017). Beyond "Revenge Porn": The continuum of image-based sexual abuse. *Feminist Legal Studies*, 25(1), 25–46. https://doi.org/10.1007/s10691-017-9343-2

McGregor, D. (2006). *The Human Side of Enterprise*. McGraw-Hill, 1960; annotated ed., McGraw-Hill, 2006.

Mead, G. H. (1934). *Mind, Self and Society*. Chicago: University of Chicago Press.

Mergel, I. (2010). Government 2.0 revisited: Social media strategies in the public sector. *PA Times, American Society for Public Administration*, 33(3), 7 and 10.

Mergel, I. (2013). Social media adoption and resulting tactics in the U.S. federal government. *Government Information Quarterly*, 30(2), 123–130.

Miles, M. B. and Huberman, A. M. (1984). Qualitative Data Analysis: A Sourcebook of New Methods. Newbury Park: Sage.

Milgram, S. (1974). *Obedience to Authority: An Experimental View*. Tavistock.

Milkman, R. (1997). *Farewell to the Factory: Auto Workers in the Late Twentieth Century*. Berkeley: University of California Press.

Miller, S. and Weckert, J. (2000). Privacy, the workplace and the internet. *Journal of Business Ethics*, 28(3), 255–265.

Mills, C. P. (1982). The contract of employment: Control is economic reality. *Australian Business Law Review*, 10(4), 270–278.

Mintel/Kantar Social Media (2023). *Sharing and Socialising Report (UK)*. Last accessed 27/04/2024.

Miškolci, J., Kováčová, L., and Rigová, E. (2020). Countering hate speech on Facebook: The case of the Roma minority in Slovakia. *Social Science Computer Review*, 38(2), 128–146.

Moon, J. (1999). *Learning Journals: A Handbook for Academics, Students and Professional Development*. London: Kogan Page.

Moqbel, M., Nevo, S., and Kock, N. (2013). Organizational members' use of social networking sites and job performance: An exploratory study. *Information Technology & People*, 26(3), 240–264. doi: 10.1108/ITP-10-2012-0110

Moran, D. (2000). *Introduction to Phenomenology*. London: Routledge.

Morrison, E. W. and Robinson, S. L. (1997). When employees feel betrayed: A model of how psychological contract violation develops. *Academy of Management Review*, 22(1), 226–256.

Morriss, P. (2002). *Power: A Philosophical Analysis* (2nd ed.). Manchester: Manchester University Press; 1st edn 1987. As cited in Lukes, Steven. *Power : A Radical View*, Bloomsbury Publishing Plc, 2004.

Mostaghimi, A. and Crotty, B. (2011). Professionalism in the digital age published. *Annals of Internal Medicine*, 154(8), 560–562. doi: 10.7326/0003-4819-154-8-201104190-00008

Moussa, M. (2015). Monitoring employee behavior through the use of technology and issues of employee privacy in America. *SAGE Open*, 5(2), 2158244015580168. https://doi.org/10.1177/2158244015580168.

Mowbray, P. K., Wilkinson, A., and Tse, H. H. (2015). An integrative review of employee voice: Identifying a common conceptualization and research agenda. *International Journal of Management Reviews*, 17(3), 382–400. https://doi.org/10.1111/ijmr12 326.12045

Mumby, D. (2005). Theorizing resistance in organization studies. *Management Communication Quarterly*, 19(1), 19–44.

Nardi, B., Whittaker, S., and Schwarz, H. (2002). Networkers and their activity in intentional networks. *The Journal of Computer-supported Cooperative Work*, 11(1–2), 205–242.

Nath, V., 2011. Aesthetic and emotional labour through stigma: National identity management and racial abuse in offshored Indian call centres. *Work, Employment and Society*, 25(4), 709–725.

Nath, V., Bach, S., and Lockwood, G. (2016). ACAS Research Paper: Dress Codes and Appearance Norms at Work: Body Supplements, Body Modifications and Aesthetic Labour. King's College London: School of Management and Business.

Newton, T., Deetz, S., and Reed, M. (2011). Responses to social constructionism and critical realism in organization studies. *Organization Studies*, 32, 7–26.

Nichols, T. (1986). The British Worker Question: A New Look at Workers and Productivity in Manufacturing. Routledge and Kegan Paul.

Nickson, D., Warhurst, C., Witz, A., and Cullen, A. M. (2001). The importance of being aesthetic: Work, employment and service organization. In A. Sturdy et al. (eds.), *Customer Service* (pp. 170–190). Basingstoke: Palgrave.

Noon, M. (2018). Pointless diversity training: Unconscious bias, new racism and agency. *Work, Employment and Society*, 32(1), 198–209.

Noon, M. (1992). HRM: A map model or theory?. In P. Blyton. and P. Turnbull (eds.), *Reassessing Human Resource Management* (pp. 16–31). London: Sage.

Noon, P., Blyton, M., and Blyton, P. (2013). *The Realities of Work* (14th ed.). Basingstoke: Palgrave Macmillan.

Nyhan, B. (2003). *Facing up to the Learning Organization Challenge. Vol.1, Key Issues from a European Perspective* (Cedefop reference series; 41–I). Luxembourg: Office for Official Publications of the European Communities.

Nyhan, B. Tomassini, M., Kelleher, M., and Poell, R. (2003). *Facing up to the Learning Organization Challenge.* Vol.1, Key issues from a European erspective (Cedefop reference series; 41-I). Luxembourg: Office for Official Publications of the European Communities.

Oakes, P. J. (1987). The salience of social categories. In J. C. Turner, M. A. Hogg, P. J. Oakes, S. D. Reicher, and M. S. Wetherell (eds.), *Rediscovering the Social Group: A Self-Categorization Theory* (pp. 117–141). Oxford and New York: Basil Blackwell.

OFCOM (The Office of Communication) (2023). *Adult Media Use and Attitude Report.* www.ofcom.org.uk/siteassets/resources/documents/research-and-data/media-literacy-research/adults/adults-media-use-and-attitudes-2023/adults-media-use-and-attitudes-report-2023.pdf?v=329409. Last accessed 02/09/2024.

Olivier, R. and Verity, J. (2008). Rehearsing tomorrow's leaders: The potential of mythodrama. *Business Strategy Series*, 9(3), 138–143. doi: 10.1108/17515630810873375. Permanent link to this document: http://dx.doi.org/10.1108/17515630810873375

Online Safety Act (2023) c 50. www.legislation.gov.uk/ukpga/2000/23/contents. Last accessed 20/08/2024.

Onwuegbuzie, A. J. and Collins, K. M. (2007). A typology of mixed methods sampling designs in social science research. *The Qualitative Report*, 12(2), 281–316. Retrieved from http://nsuworks.nova.edu/tqr/vol12/iss2/9

Ouchi, William G. (1981). *Theory Z.* New York: Avon Books.

Outhwaite, W. (1975). *Understanding Social Life: The Method Called Verstehen.* London: George Allen & Unwin.

*Oxford Dictionary* (1914). www.oed.com/dictionary/shirk_v?tab=meaning_and_use#22933962, Oxford University Press.

Oxford Internet Institute, Gallacher, J. D., Kaminska, M., Kollanyi, B., and Howard, P. N. (2017). Junk news and bots during the 2017 UK General Election: What are UK voters sharing over Twitter? *Data Memo 2017.5.* Oxford: Project on Computational Propaganda. comprop.oii.ox.ac.uk.

Palfrey, J. and Gasser, U. (2008). *Born Digital.* Basic Books, Perseus Books Group.

Park, N. and Peterson, C. (2003). Virtues and organizations. In K. S. Cameron, J. E. Dutton, and R. E. Quinn (eds.), *Positive Organizational Scholarship: Foundations of a New Discipline* (pp. 33–47). San Francisco: Berrett-Koehler.

Park, N. and Peterson, C. (2009). Character strengths: Research and practice. *Journal of College and Character*, 10(4).

Paterson, M. (2002). Monitoring of employee emails and other electronic communications. *University of Tasmania Law Review*, 21(1), 1–19.

*People Management Magazine* November 2012.

Peterson, C. and Seligman, M. (2004). *Character Strengths and Virtues: A Handbook and Classification.* Washington, DC: American Psychological Association.

Pettinger, L., 2005. Gendered work meets gendered goods: Selling and service in clothing retail. *Gender, Work & Organization*, 12(5), 460–478.

Pietkiewicz, I. and Smith, J. A. (2012). A practical guide to using interpretative phenomenological analysis in qualitative research psychology. *Czasopismo Psychologiczne*, 18(2), 361–369.

Porter, M. E. (1997). Competitive strategy. *Measuring Business Excellence*, 1(2), 12–17.

Prasad, A. and Prasad, P. (2002). The coming of age of interpretive organizational research. *Organizational Research Methods*, 5(1), 4–11.

Prasad, P. (2005). *Crafting Qualitative Research: Working in the Post Positivist Traditions*. New York, London: ME Sharpe Armonk.

Prowse, P. and Prowse, J. (2007). Is there still a public sector model of employment relations in the United Kingdom? *International Journal of Public Sector Management*, 20(1), 48–62.

Public Interest Disclosure Act (1998) www.legislation.gov.uk/ukpga/1998/23/contents. Last accessed 20/08/2024.

Purcell, J. and Ahlstrand, B. (1993). *Strategy and Style in Employee Relations*. Oxford: Oxford University Press.

Purcell, J. and Sisson, K. (1983). Strategies and practice in the management of industrial relations. In G. Bain (ed.), *Industrial Relations in Britain*. Oxford: Blackwell.

Putnam, R. (1993). *Making Democracy Work*. Princeton: Princeton University Press.

Raghuram, S. (2013). Identities on call: Impact of impression management on Indian call centre agents. *Human Relations*, 66(11), 1471–1496.

Reagle, J. M. (2015). *Reading the Comments: Likers Haters and Manipulators at the Bottom of the Web*. London: The MIT Press.

Regulation of Investigatory Powers Act (2000). www.legislation.gov.uk/ukpga/2000/23/contents. Last accessed 20/08/2024.

Reid, D. and Reid, F. (2004). 'Insights into the social and psychological effects of text messaging text messaging', January 15, 2012, Available at: http://educ.ubc.ca/courses/etec540/May08/suz/assests/SocialEffectsOfTextMessaging.pdf

Reid, K., Flowers, P., and Larkin, M. (2005). Exploring the lived experience. *The Psychologist*, 18, 20–23.

Reinharz, S. (1993). *On Becoming a Social Scientist: From Survey Research and Participant Observation to Experiential Analysis* (4th ed.). New Brunswick, NJ: Transaction Books.

Reissner, S. C. (2010). Change, meaning and identity at the workplace. *Journal of Organizational Change Management*, 23(3), 287–299.

Remenyi, D., Williams, B., Money, A., and Swartz, E. (1998). *Doing Research in Business and Management*. London: Sage Publications.

Richardson, K. and Hessey, S. (2009). Archiving the self? Facebook as biography and relational memory. *Journal of Information, Communication and Ethics in Society*, 7(1), 25–38.

Richey, M., Ravishankar, M. N., and Coupland, C. (2016). Exploring situationally inappropriate social media posts: An impression management perspective. *Information Technology & People*, 29(3), 597–617.

Riedy, M. and Wen, J. (2010). Electronic surveillance of Internet access in the American workplace: Implications for management. *Information & Communications Technology Law*, 19(1), 87–99.

Rifkin, G. (1994). Information technology: Privacy matters. *Harvard Business Review*, 72(4), 8.

Ringrose, J., Regehr, K., and Milne, B. (2021). *Understanding and Combatting Youth Experiences of Image-Based Sexual Harassment and Abuse*. London: Department of Education, Practice and Society, UCL Institute of Education.

Ripken, S. K. (2009). Corporations are people too: A multi-dimensional approach to the corporate personhood puzzle. *Fordham Journal of Corporate & Financial Law*, 15(1), 97–177.

Ritchie, J., Lewis, J., and Elam, G. (2003). Designing and selecting samples. In J. Ritchie and J. Lewis (eds.), *Qualitative Research Practice* (pp. 77–108). Thousand Oaks: Sage.

Robinson, D., Perryman, S., Hayday, S. (2004). *The Drivers of Employee Engagement Report 408, Institute for Employment Studies* . www.employment-studies.co.uk/pubs/summary.php?id=408. Last accessed 05/07/2013.

Robinson, O. C. (2014). Sampling in interview-based qualitative research: A theoretical and practical guide. *Qualitative Research in Psychology*, 11(1), 25–41. doi: 10.1080/14780887.2013.801543

Rogers, A. (2012). Emotional geographies of method acting in Asian American theater. *Annals of the Association of American Geographers*, 102(2), 423–442.

Rogers, A., Bhowmik, D. (1970). Homophily-heterophily: Relational concepts for communication research. *Public Opinion Quarterly*, 34(4), 523–538 [Peer Reviewed Journal].

Rogers, E. (1962/2003). *Diffusion of Innovations*, (5th ed.). New York: Free Press.

Rollinson, D., Handley, J., Hook, C., and Foot, M. (1997). The disciplinary experience and its effects on behaviour. *Work, Employment and Society*, 11(2), 281–311.

Rolls, L. and Relf, M. (2006). Bracketing interviews: Addressing methodological challenges in qualitative interviewing in bereavement and palliative care. *Mortality*, 11(3), 286–305.

Rooney, D., Paulsen, N., Callan, V., Brabant, M., Gallois, C., and Jones, E. (2010). A new role for place identity in managing organizational change. *Management Communication Quarterly*, 24(1), 44–73.

Rose, E. (2008). *Employment Relations* (3rd ed.). Harlow: Financial Times Prentice Hall.

Rosen, L., Carrier, L. M., and Cheever, N. A. (2010). *Rewired: Understanding the iGeneration and the Way They Learn*. New York: Palgrave Macmillan.

Rothbard, N. P. and Ramarajan, L. (2009). Checking your identities at the door: Positive relationships between nonwork and work identities. In L. M. Roberts and J. E. Dutton (eds.), *Exploring Positive Identities and Organizations: Building a Theoretical and Research Foundation* (pp. 125–148). New York: Routledge.

Rousseau, D. M. (1989). Psychological and implied contracts in organizations. *Employee Responsibility and Rights Journal*, 2, 121–139.

Rousseau, D. M. (1995). *Psychological Contracts in Organizations*. Thousand Oaks: Sage Publications.

Rousseau, D. M. and Tijoriwala, S. A. (1998). Assessing psychological contracts: Issues, alternatives and measures. (Special Issue: The Psychological Contract at Work). *Journal of Organizational Behavior*, 19, 679.

Royal Society for Public Health (2017). #NewFilters to manage the impact of social media on young people's mental health and wellbeing. www.rsph.org.uk/static/uploaded/23180e2a-e6b8-4e8d-9e3da2a300525c98.pdf. Last accessed 21/08/2024.

Rudesill, D. S, Caverlee, J., and Sui, D. (2015). *The Deep Web and the Darknet: A Look Inside the Internet's Techniques to Identify Themes*. https://doi.org/10.1177/1525822X02239569 massive black box. STIP: Woodrow Wilson International Center for Scholars.

Ryan, G. W. and Bernard, R. (2003). Techniques to identify themes. *Field Methods*, 15(1), 85–109. https://doi.org/10.1177/1525822X02239569

Sabatier, P. (1986). Top-down and bottom-up approaches to implementation research: A critical analysis and suggested synthesis. *Journal of Public Policy*, 6(1), 21–48. www.jstor.org/stable/3998354. Last accessed 27/05/2016.

Salih, S. (2002). *Judith Butler (Routledge Critical Thinkers: Essential Guides For Literary Studies)*. London: Routledge.

Sallis, A., Birkin, R. (2014). Experiences of work and sickness absence in employees with depression: An interpretative phenomenological analysis. *J Occup Rehabil*, 24, 469–483. Retrieved from: http//:weirfoulds.com/showpublication.aspx?show=2175

Sarti, A. (1999). *Organization and Aesthetics*. Sage Publications.

Saunders, M. N. K., Lewis, P., and Thornhill, A. (2012). *Research Methods for Business Students* (6th ed.). Harlow: Pearson Education.

Saundry, R., Antcliff, V., and Jones, C. (2011). Discipline, representation and dispute resolution—Exploring the role of trade unions and employee companions. *Workplace Discipline Industrial Relations Journal*, 42(2), 195–211.

Schlenker, B. R. and Wowra, S. A. (2003). Carryover effects of feeling socially transparent or impenetrable on strategic self-presentation. *Journal of Personality and Social Psychology*, 85(5), 871–880.

Schultz, D. E. and Peltier, J. (2013). Social media's slippery slope: Challenges, opportunities and future research directions. *Journal of Research in Interactive Marketing*, 7(2), 86–99.

Schwalbe, M. L. and Gecas, V. (1988). Social psychological consequences of job-related disabilities. In J. T. Mortimer and K. M. Borman (eds.), *Work Experience and Psychological Development Through the Life Span* (pp. 233–272). Boulder: Westview.

Schwandt, T. A. (1997). *Qualitative Inquiry: A Dictionary of Terms*. Thousand Oaks: Sage.

Schwandt, D. (2005). When managers become philosophers: Integrating learning with sensemaking. *Academy of Management Learning & Education*, 4(2), 176–192.

Schwandt, T. A. (2001). Dictionary of qualitative inquiry. In *Dictionary of Qualitative Inquiry* (pp. xxxiv–281). Thousand Oaks: Sage.

Scott, L. (2015). *The Four Dimensional Human, Ways of Being in the Digital World*. London: William Heinemann.

Seaman, J. (2024). P2P speech regulation gossip, reputation and norm policing on social media. The Routledge Companion to Freedom of Expression and Censorship. Routledge. https://doi.org/10.4324/9780429262067

Sewell, G. and Wilkinson, B. (1992). Someone to watch over me: Surveillance, discipline and just-in-time labour processes. *Sociology*, 26(2), 271–291.

Shaver, Phillip, Schwartz, Judith, Kirson, Donald, O'Connor, Cary Sherman, and Steven J. (eds.) (1987). Emotion knowledge: Further exploration of a prototype approach. *Journal of Personality and Social Psychology*, 52(6), 1061–1086.

Shea, K. and Wesley, J. (2006). How social networking sites affect students, career services and employers. *National Association of Colleges and Employers Journal*, 66(3), 26–32. https://hpu.edu/CareerServices/Documents/socialnetworking.pdf

Siegert, S. and Löwstedt, J. (2019). Online boundary work tactics: An affordance perspective. *New Technology, Work and Employment,* 34(1), 18–36.

Simpson, C. and Carroll, B. (2008). Re-viewing 'Role'. *Processes of Identity Construction Organization*, 15(1), 29–50. https://doi.org/10.1177/1350508407084484

Sims, D. (2003). Between the millstones: A narrative account of the vulnerability of middle managers' storying. *Human Relations*, 56(10), 1195–1211.

Sims, D. (2005). You bastard: A narrative exploration of the experience of indignation within organizations. *Organization Studies*, 26(11), 1625–1640. https://doi.org/10.1177/0170840605054625

Sivertzen, A., Nilsen, E., and Olafsen, A. (2013). Employer branding: Employer attractiveness and the use of social media. *Journal of Product & Brand Management*, 22(7), 473–483.

Smith, H. J. (1993). Privacy policies and practices: Inside the organizational maze. *Communications of the ACM*, 36(12), 105–122.

Smith, J. A. (1996). Beyond the divide between cognition and discourse: Using interpretative phenomenological analysis in health psychology. *Psychology & Health*, 11(2), 261–271.

Smith, J. A. (2011). Evaluating the contribution of interpretative phenomenological analysis: A reply to the commentaries and further development of criteria. *Health Psychology Review*, 5(1), 55–61.

Smith, J. A., Flowers, P., and Larkin, M. (2009). *Interpretative Phenomenological Analysis: Theory, Method and Research*. London: Sage.

Smith, J. A., Jarman, M., and Osborn, M. (1999). Doing interpretative phenomenological analysis . In M. Murray and K. Chamberlain (eds.), *Qualitative Health Psychology: Theories and Methods* (pp. 218–240). London: Sage.

Smith, J. A. and Osborn, M. (2003). Interpretative phenomenological analysis. In J. A. Smith (ed.), *Qualitative Psychology: A Practical Guide to Methods* (pp. 51–80). London: Sage.

Snelson, C. L. (2016). Qualitative and mixed methods social media research. *International Journal of Qualitative Methods*, 15(1), 1609406915624574. https://doi.org/10.1177/1609406915624574

Snyder, M. (1974). The self-monitoring of expressive behavior. *J. Personality Soc. Psych.* 30, 526–537.

Sommer, K. L. and Baumeister, R. F. (1998). The construction of meaning from life events: Empirical studies of personal narratives. In Wong, P. T. P. and Fry, P. S. (eds), *The Human Quest for Meaning* (pp. 143–161). London: Lawrence Erlbaum Associates.

Sonnenberg, M., Koene, B., and Paauwe, J. (2011). Balancing HRM: The psychological contract of employees. *Personnel Review*, 40(6), 664–683.

Sørensen B. M. (2010). St Paul's conversion: The aesthetic organization of labour. *Organization Studies*, 31, 307–326.

Spiess, L. and Waring, P. (2005). Aesthetic labour, cost minimisation and the labour process in the Asia Pacific airline industry. *Employee Relations*, 27(2), 193–207.

Spooner, K. and Haidar, A. (2006). Defining the employment relationship. *International Journal of Employment Studies*, 14(2), 63–82.

Starks, H. and Trinidad, S. B. (2007). Choose your method: A comparison of phenomenology, discourse analysis, and grounded theory. *Qualitative Health Research*, 17(10), 1372–1380.

Stead, G. B. (2004). Culture and career psychology: A social constructionist perspective. *Journal of Vocational Behavior*, 64, 389–406.
Steel, J. (2012). *Journalism and Free Speech*. Oxon, UK, and New York: Routledge.
Steel, J. and Petley, J. (2024). *The Routledge Companion to Freedom of Expression and Censorship*. Routledge. https://doi.org/10.4324/9780429262067
Steimer, T. (2002). The biology of fear- and anxiety-related behaviors. *Dialogues in Clinical Neuroscience*, 4(3), 231–249.
Stets, J. and Burke, P. (2000). Identity theory and social identity theory. *Social Psychology Quarterly*, 63(3), 224–237.
Stewart, J. and Rigg, C. (2011). *Learning and Talent Development*. London: Kogan Page Publishers.
Storey, J. (1992). *Developments in the Management of Human Resources*. Oxford: Basil Blackwell.
Strasberg, L. (1966). (As cited in Rogers 2012) Strasberg at the Actor's Studio: Tape recorded sessions, R. Hethmon (ed.). London: Jonathan Cape. n.d. Definition of acting. Los Angeles: The Lee Strasberg Creative Center, by arrangement with Encyclopaedia Britannica, Inc.
Strati, A. (1999). *Organization and Aesthetics*. London and Thousand Oaks: Sage Publications.
Strauss, G. and Feuille, P. (1978). Industrial relations research: A critical analysis. *Industrial Relations: A Journal of Economy and Society*, 17(3), 259–277.
Stride, C., Wall, T. D., and Catley, N. (2007). *Measures of Job Satisfaction, Organizational Commitment, Mental Health and Job-Related Well-Being: A Benchmarking Manual* (2nd ed.). New York: John Wiley & Sons Ltd.
Stukas, M. and Sicker, D. C. (2004). An evaluation of VoIP traversal of Firewalls and NATs within an enterprise environment. *Information Systems Frontiers*, 6(3), 219–228.
Sveningsson, S. and Alvesson, M. (2003). Managing managerial identities: Organizational fragmentation, discourse and identity struggle. *Human Relations*, 56(10), 1163–1193. Google Scholar Link.
Swanson, R. A. and Holton, E. F. (eds.). (1997). *Human Resource Development Research Handbook*. San Francisco: Berrett-Koehler.
Tajfel, H. and Turner, J. C. (1979). An integrative theory of intergroup conflict. *The Social Psychology of Intergroup Relations*, 33, 47.
Tapscott, D. (2011). *View of the Age of Networked Intelligence: Unleashing the Power of Social Networking for the Enterprise*. Moxie Software. Retrieved from www.e2conf.com/innovate/exhibitor-whitepapers/Don_Tapscott--Social_Networking_for_the_Enterprise.pdf as cited in http://digitalcommons.www.na-businesspress.com/JLAE/BillingtonMG_Web9_6_.pdf
Taylor, C. (2018). *Evolving Identities, Social Media and the Employment Relationship: An Interpretative Phenomenological Analysis*. Unpublished Doctoral thesis. Sheffield: Sheffield Hallam University.
Taylor, C. (2024). Vitriol and voice, battlegrounds to control employee expression on social media in work. In S. John and P. Julian (eds.), *International Companion on Freedom of Speech*. London: Routledge.
Taylor, C. and Dobbins, T. (2021). Social Media: A (new) contested terrain between sousveillance and surveillance in the digital workplace. *New Technology, Work and Employment*. https://doi.org/10.1111/ntwe.12206

Taylor, J. (2011). www.psychologytoday.com/blog/the-power-prime/201107/common-sense-is-neither-common-nor-sense. Last accessed 17/09/2017.

Taylor, S. S. and Hansen, H. (2005). Finding form: Looking at the field of organizational aesthetics. *Journal of Management studies*, 42(6), 1211–1231.

The Guardian (2005). Barham, P.: *Blogger sacked for sounding off.* www.theguardian.com/technology/2005/jan/12/books.newmedia/. Last accessed 20/08/2024.

The Guardian (2017). Marsh, S. and Elgot, J.: *Ministers vow to end employment tribunal fees after court defeat.* www.theguardian.com/money/2017/jul/26/union-supreme-court-fees-unfair-dismissal-claims. Last accessed 17/09/2017.

The Guardian (2024a). Fazakerley A.: *Universities deplore 'McCarthyism' as MP demands list of tutors lecturing on Brexit.* www.theguardian.com/education/2017/oct/24/universities-mccarthyism-mp-demands-list-brexit-chris-heaton-harris

The Guardian (2024b). Croft, J.: *Tribunal cases to rise as UK firms push back on remote working, experts say.* www.theguardian.com/business/article/2024/jun/04/employment-tribunal-cases-remote-working-from-home-office. Last accessed 20/08/2024.

The Guardian (2024b). Haidt, J.: *Generation Anxiety: smartphones have created a gen Z mental health crisis – but there are ways to fix it.* www.theguardian.com/books/2024/mar/24/the-anxious-generation-jonathan-haidt-book-extract-instagram-tiktok-smartphones-social-media-screens. Last accessed 21/08/2024.

Thistle, B. M. and Molinaro, V. (2016). Driving organizational transformation through strong leadership accountability: It's time for HR leaders to step up. *People and Strategy*, 39(3), 28–31.

Thomas, R. and Davies, A. (2005). Theorizing the micro-politics of resistance: New public management and managerial identities in the UK public services. *Organization Studies*, 26(5), 683–706.

Thompson, E. (1991). Democracy undermined: Reforms to the Australian Public Service from Whitlam to Hawke. *The Australian Quarterly*, 63(2), 127–142.

Thompson, P. (2003). Fantasy Island: A Labour Process critique of the 'age of surveillance'. *Surveillance & Society*, 1(2), 138–151.

Thompson, P. (2011). The trouble with HRM. *Human Resource Management Journal*, 21(4), 355–367.

Thompson, P. (2016). Dissent at work and the resistance debate: Departures, directions, and dead ends. *Studies in Political Economy,* 97(2), 106–123.

Thompson, P. and McHugh, D. (1990). Work organizations: A critical introduction. *Organization Studies*, 15(1), 125.

Thompson, P., McDonald, P., and O'Connor, P. (2020). Employee dissent on social media and organizational discipline. *Human Relations*, 73(5), 631–652.

Tietze, S. (2005). Discourse as strategic coping resource: Managing the interface between "home" and "work". *Journal of Organizational Change Management*, 18(1), 48–62.

Tietze, S. and Musson, G. (2005). Recasting the home-work relationship: A case of mutual adjustment? *Organization Studies*, 26(9), 1331–1352. www.timeshighereducation.com/news/bullied-blogger-can-you-find-it-find-it/404992.article

Timming, A. R. (2015). Visible tattoos in the service sector: A new challenge to recruitment and selection. *Work, Employment and Society*, 29(1), 60–78. doi: 10.1177/0950017014528402

Touroni, E. and Coyle, A. (2002). Decision-making in planned lesbian parenting: An interpretative phenomenological analysis. *J. Community. Appl. Soc. Psychol.*, 12, 194–209. doi: 10.1002/casp.672

Townley, B. (1994). *Reframing Human Resource Management: Power, Ethics and the Subject at Work*. Sage Publications.

Towns, D. and Cobb, L. (2012). Notes on GPS technology: Employee monitoring enters a new era. *Labor Law Journal*, 63(3), 203–208.

Tranfield, D., Denyer, D., and Smart, P. (2003). Towards a methodology for developing evidence-informed management knowledge by means of systematic review. *British Journal of Management*, 14(3), 207–222.

Tripathy, M. and Kaur, T. (2012). Perceptions of employees on information checks by employers using social networking sites in IT sector. *Management and Labour Studies*, 37(4), 345–358.

Tuckett, A. G. (2004). Qualitative research sampling: The very real complexities. *Nurse Researcher*, 12(1), 47–61 http://dx.doi.org/10.7748/nr2004.07.12.1.47.c5930

Tufford, L. and Newman, P. (2012). Bracketing in qualitative research. *Qualitative Social Work*, 11(1), 80–96.

Turkle, S. (2003). Technology and human vulnerability. *Harvard Business Review*, 81(9), 43–131. Harvard Business School Publishing Corporation.

Turkle, S. (2015). *Reclaiming Conversation: The Power of Talk in a Digital Age*. Penguin Press.

Turner, J. C., Hogg, M., Oakes, P., Reicher, S., and Wetherall, M. (1987). *Re-Discovering the Social Group: A Self-Categorisation Theory*. Oxford Blackwell.

Turner, V. W. (1960). *Rites of Passage*. London: Routledge.

Tymieniecka, M. T. (2003). Introduction: Phenomenology as the inspirational force of our times. In M. T. Tymieniecka (ed.), *Phenomenology World-Wide: Foundations – Expanding Dynamics – Life-Engagements: A Guide for Research and Study* (pp. 1–10). London: Kluwer Academic. Google Scholar.

Uldam, H. (2017). Corporate responses to stakeholder activism: Partnerships and surveillance. *Critical Perspectives on International Business*, 13(2), 151–165.

Ulrich, D. (1997). HR of the future: Conclusions and observations. *Human Resource Management*, 36, 175–179.

Ulrich, D. (2010). *Are We There Yet? What's Next for HR*. Michigan Ross Business School Executive White Paper Series.

UN Human Rights Committee (2011). *General Comment No. 34, Article 19, Freedoms of Opinion and Expression*. UN Doc. CCPR/C/GC/34. www2.ohchr.org/english/bodies/hrc/docs/gc34.pdf

Van Buren, H. J., Greenwood, M., and Sheehan, C. (2009). Strategic human resource management and the decline of employee focus. *Human Resource Management Review*, 21(3), 209–219.

Van den Broek, D. and Dundon, T. (2012). (Still) up to no good: Reconfiguring the boundaries of worker resistance and misbehaviour in an increasingly unorganised world. *Relations Industrielles/ Industrial Relations*, 67(1), 97–121.

Van den Hoonaard, W. C. (1997). Working with sensitizing concepts: Analytical field research. *Qualitative Research Methods*, 41. Thousand Oaks, London: Sage Publications.

Van Gramberg, B., Teicher, J., and O'Rourke, A. H. (2014). Managing electronic communications: A new challenge for human resource managers. *International Journal of Human Resource Management*, 25(16), 2234–2252. https://doi.org/10.1080/09585192.2013.872166

Van Knippenberg, D. (2000). Work motivation and performance: A social identity perspective. *Applied Psychology*, 49(3), 357–371.

Van Laer, K. and Janssens, M. (2011). Ethnic minority professionals' experiences with subtle discrimination in the workplace. *Human Relations*, 64(9), 1203–1227.

Van Manen, M. (1984). Practising phenomenological writing. *Phenomenology and Pedagogy*, 2(1), 36–69.

Van Manen, M. (1990). *Researching Lived Experience*. London: University of Western Ontario.

van Woerkom, M. (2003). *Critical Reflection at Work: Bridging Individual and Organizational Learning*. Unpublished doctoral dissertation. Enschede: University of Twente.

Wallace, M. and Wray, A. (2011). *Critical Reading and Writing for Postgraduates*. London: Sage Publications.

Walsh, D. and Downe, S. (2006). Appraising the quality of qualitative research. *Midwifery*, 22, 108–119. Elsevier.

Walsham, G. (1993). *Interpreting Information Systems in Organizations*. Chichester: Wiley.

Walton, R. (1985). From control to commitment in the workplace. *Harvard Business Review*, 64(5), 12–16.

Warhurst, C. and Nickson, D. (2001). *Looking Good, Sounding Right*. London: Industrial Society.

Warhurst, C. and Nickson, D. (2007). Employee experience of aesthetic labour in retail and hospitality. *Work, Employment and Society*, 21(1), 103–120. https://doi-org.ntu.idm.oclc.org/10.1177/0950017007073622

Warhurst, C., Nickson, D., Witz, A., and Marie Cullen, A. (2000). Aesthetic labour in interactive service work: Some case study evidence from the 'new' Glasgow. *The Service Industries Journal*, 20(3), 1–18.

Warhurst, C., Van den Broek, D., Hall, R., and Nickson, D. (2009). Lookism: The new frontier of employment discrimination?. *Journal of Industrial Relations*, 51(1), 131–136.

Warhurst, R. (2011). Managers' practice and managers' learning as identity formation: Reassessing the MBA contribution. *Management Learning*, 42(3), 261–278.

Warren, S. D. and Brandeis, L. D. (1890). The right to privacy. *Harvard Law Review*, 4, 193–220. As cited in Steel (2012).

Watson, T. (2002). Organisations and management. In Watson, Tony J. (ed.), *Organising and Managing Work: Organisational, Managerial and Strategic Behaviour in Theory and Practice* (pp. 33–56). Harlow: FT/Prentice Hall.

Watson, T. (2008). *Sociology, Work and Industry* (5th ed.). London and New York: Routledge.

Watson, T. J. (2006). *Organising and Managing Work: Organisational, Managerial and Strategic Behaviour in Theory and Practice*. Harlow: Pearson Prentice Hall.

Webb, J. (2006). *Organisations Identities and the Self*. London: Palgrave Macmillan.

Weber, M. (1949 [1917]). *The Methodology of the Social Sciences*. Translated by Edward A. Shils and Henry A. Finch. New York: Free Press.

Weick, K. E. (1995). *Sensemaking in Organizations*. Thousand Oaks, CA: Sage.

Weil, M. and Rosen, L. (1997). *Technostress: Coping with Technology @work @home@ play*. John Wiley and Sons Inc.

Weitz, E., Vardi, Y., and Setter, O. (2012). Spirituality and organizational misbehavior. *Journal of Management, Spirituality & Religion*, 9(3), 255–281. doi: 10.1080/14766086.2012.730782

Welman, J. C. and Kruger, S. J. (1999). Research Methodology for the Business and Administrative Sciences. Johannesburg: International Thompson.

Wesch, M. (2009). YouTube and you: Experiences of self-awareness in the context of the collapse of the recording webcam. *Explorations in Media Ecology*, 8(2), 19–34. http://krex.k-state.edu/dspace/handle/2097/6302

Westaby, J., Pfaff, D., Redding, N., and Anderson, N. B. (2014). Psychology and social networks. *American Psychologist*, 69(3), 269–284.

Westekamp, P. and Esmi, R. (2011). Arbitrating social media grievances. *New Jersey Lawyer Magazine* (April 2011/No. 269).

Whitmar Publications Ltd v Gamage & Ors (2013) EWHC 1881 (Ch) Published online July 2013 available through Employment Cases Update https://employmentcasesupdate.co.uk/content/whitmar-publications-ltd-v-gamage-ors-2013-ewhc-1881-ch.aad89df3747746c493e262c4a7b9cb6e.htm. Last accessed 03/09/2024.

Whitty, M. and Carr, A. (2006). New rules in the workplace: Applying object-relations theory to explain problem internet and email behaviour in the workplace. *Computers in Human Behaviour*, 22, 235–250.

Wilkinson, A., Barry, M., and Morrison, E.W. (2020). Toward an integration of research on employee voice. *Human Resource Management Review*, 30(1), 1–6. https://doi.org/10.1016/j.hrmr.2018.12.001

Williams, R. (2000). *Making Identity Matter: Identity, Society and Social Interaction*. Durham: Sociology Press.

Willig, C. (2001). *Introducing Qualitative Research in Psychology: Adventures in Theory and Method*. Buckingham: Open University Press.

Will-Zocholl, M. (2016). New topologies of work: Informatisation, virtualisation and globalisation. *Automotive Engineering*, 31–51. doi: 10.1057/978-1-137-48087-3_3

Witz, A., Warhurst, C., and Nickson, D. (2003). The labour of aesthetics and the aesthetics of organization. *Organization* 10(1), 33–54.

Wojnar, D. M. and Swanson, K. M. (2007). Phenomenology: An exploration. *Journal of Holistic Nursing*, 25(3), 172–180. doi: 10.1177/0898010106295172

Woods, A. (2014). *The Rise of the Network Labour Movement: The Case of Our Wallmart, Conference Presentation, Crisis and Social Change: Towards Alternative Horizons*. Department of Sociology, University of Cambridge.

Woods, A. (2017) *The gig economy requires unions to embrace the internet.* https://speri-blog.sites.sheffield.ac.uk/blog/2017/the-gig-economy-requires-unions-to-embrace-the-internet. Last accessed 02/09/2024.

Yadav, M. and Pavlou, P. (2014). Marketing in computer-mediated environments: Research synthesis and new directions. *Journal of Marketing*, 78(1), 20.

Yanow, D. and Tsoukas, H. (2009). What is reflection-in-action? A phenomenological account. *Journal of Management Studies*, 46(8), 1339–1364.

Yardley, L. (2000). Dilemmas in qualitative health psychology. *Psychology and Health*, 15, 215–228.

Young, R. and Collin, A. (2004). Introduction: Constructivism and social constructionism in the career field. *Journal of Vocational Behaviour* , 64(3), 373–388.

Zeidner, R. (2007). How deep can you probe? *HR Magazine*, 52(10), 57–62.
Zerubavel, E. (1991). *The Fine Line: Making Distinctions in Everyday Life*. New York: Free Press.
Zuboff, S. (2019). The Age of Surveillance Capitalism: The Fight for a Human Future at the New Frontier of Power. New York: Public Affairs.

# Index

FSC
www.fsc.org
MIX
Papier | Fördert gute Waldnutzung
FSC® C083411

Kolibri 360 GmbH
Ferdinand-Jühlke-Straße 7
99095 Erfurt, Deutschland
produktsicherheit@kolibri360.de